Kathleen Sears
from
Virginia Taylor
1938

HOME BOOK OF THE OPERA

Enrico Caruso as Radames in "Aida"

HOME BOOK
of the
OPERA

INCLUDING THE STANDARD OPERA GLASS

Detailed Plots of the Celebrated Operas

With Critical and Biographical Remarks and Dates

By CHARLES ANNESLEY

With an Introduction by
OLIN DOWNES

WITH A DOUBLE INDEX AND 16 ILLUSTRATIONS

THE DIAL PRESS, INC.
NEW YORK
1938

PRINTED IN THE UNITED STATES OF AMERICA
BY VAN REES PRESS, NEW YORK

THE DIAL PRESS, INC., WISHES TO EXPRESS ITS APPRECIATION FOR THE USE OF NUMEROUS PHOTOGRAPHS TO MISS EVELYN MILKMAN AND TO
Musical America

LIST OF ILLUSTRATIONS

HOME BOOK OF THE OPERA

INTRODUCTION

By OLIN DOWNES

A book of opera plots is introduction to the rich and varied repertory of the music-drama. In this repertory there is something for every taste and every degree of musical knowledge. Technical matters of music need not enter into the question at all. The composer's intention is to drive home, by means of his special art, the emotional essence of the drama. Understand that drama, and if you have the average person's susceptibility to the average tune, the rest will take care of itself with repeated hearings.

Thus a collection of opera plots serves a two-fold purpose. It acquaints you in rough outline with the dramatic motives of the opera you are to hear, and it apprises you of the very large and interesting list of operas available for your personal delectation.

If you are in the habit of opera, the plots of the familiar works are coals carried to Newcastle. But assuming that you are not, or that the opera you are going to hear tonight is unknown to you, a word of advice which may run counter to orthodoxy: if you listen for an hour, and are still bored, get up and get out. This is advice of the highest value. Don't pretend to like anything you really don't like. Don't feel obliged to like something merely because that particular thing happens to be generally respected. Don't think it is your duty to like anything. You have duties enough in the world, God wot, and art isn't a thing of duty;

it is a thing which is presumed to bring you beauty and delight, or to move you deeply by its intense representation of human feeling. If music doesn't do that for you, something else will, whether it be painting, literature or cabbages. Life is short, full of wonder and of things to enjoy. Don't waste your sacred capacity for enjoyment on something that happens to be foreign to your temperament.

Carry this principle through all that you do. If music itself doesn't appeal to you, leave it alone. Better a thousand enthusiastic golfers and one real lover of music than 999 professed music lovers who are liars and ought to be sincerely and enthusiastically playing golf. Or you may like music, but dislike opera. Act accordingly. Remember that tastes differ; you are consulting your tastes—not some one else's. If as great a composer as Tschaikowsky couldn't appreciate Brahms, and as great a conductor as Arturo Toscanini can't appreciate Tschaikowsky, then don't worry if you fail to be thrilled by Verdi's "Falstaff." Also remember this: he who listens and runs away may return to listen another day. Either walk out on an opera you don't like till you are in a different mood, or pick up your book of plots and try another one that sounds interesting.

For it is much the same with music as it is with books, except that music is the more universal and immediately intelligible and emotional language. Here is a library, with all sorts of literature in it—fiction from Conan Doyle and Bret Harte to Conrad and Robert Louis Stevenson; tales that unfold themselves like vast frescoes, from "Rienzi" to Tolstoi's "War and Peace"; histories and biographies without number; poetry all the way from jingles by Edgar Guest to the magnificent imaginings of Coleridge and the thunder of Homer. If you are a reading person you are only confronted with an embarrassment of riches. If you are not, or never had time to know the fascination of books, pick up something at random. Throw away "Lord Jim" because at first sight you cannot stand the psychologizing and the circumlocutions, and try "The Cloister and the Hearth"—great story-telling, of the finest. The chances are that one day you'll go back to Conrad, and in the course of years find yourself reading men as far apart as George Meredith and Dostoievski, and liking it. There is no limit to adventure along these lines, and the same thing that is true of books is true of music.

You are going to find out then, what kind of opera you prefer. There are masterpieces in all styles. Is it the sort of opera in which the composer cares little about his orchestra, and almost everything for broad, tuneful melodies and bravura airs for the singers? Try "Trovatore." Or, a work just as melodious, but in a more modern spirit, "Rigoletto." Or go farther back than Verdi of the middle period. There is Donizetti's "Lucia di Lammermoor." It has some fine tenor airs, duets, the noble sextet, the thrice familiar and coruscating "Mad Scene" of the unfortunate Lucia. And don't let any one tell you that it is an unworthy opera. Or listen to Bellini of "Sonnambula" or "Puritani" or the great "Norma"—if and when they have singers accomplished enough to perform it. As for Rossini, he wrote much in the old florid style, but the work we now acclaim as his greatest is the incomparable comedy, "The Barber of Seville."

After Verdi's operas of the middle period, if you want to go along with the Italian school, comes the superb "Aida," the greatest living example of the classic grand opera. But if you have the enterprise to follow Verdi farther than that, the day will come when you feel that one of the finest of all existing music dramas is his setting of Shakespeare's "Othello," or his final masterpiece, "Falstaff."

But all is not Italian opera, by any means. Gounod's "Faust" contains perhaps more melodies to the square inch than any other modern lyric drama, and it has scenes of true feeling and incontestable mastery. The third act, including the Garden Scene, is unique in inspiration and workmanship. And, talking of French opera, what of "Carmen"—that vivid and intense work of genius, with its exotic rhythms and color and swift tragedy which Nietzsche well called "Mediterranean"—an opera for everybody, for the most learned musical savant and for the person whose knowledge of music-drama has hitherto been confined to selections from "Traviata."

Do you know the "Manon" of Massenet, adorable equally in the decorative 18th century manner of the music as for its ardent and youthful sentiment? Offenbach's "Tales of Hofmann" is something else again—the introduction, in which Hofmann, melancholy and distraught, begins the story of his loves—"the first was Olympia"; the narrative developed in the next three acts by characters which are rather the personifications of a poet's dream than humans; and the poignant epilogue in the cellar, when the muse of art bespeaks the poet's devotion, which she will reward as no mortal woman ever may. Talk of fantasy! Here is Weber's opera of glorious youth, "Der Freischütz," with its delicious aroma of the forest and its mysteries, and the naïve tale of Max and his faithful maiden. And Beethoven's "Fidelio," for some reason one of the very few dramas which celebrate the triumph of virtue and wifely love, with the unforgettable scene of the rescue in the prison—the opera which would be famous if it had only begotten the immortal Third "Leonore" Overture—supreme example of the German genius for dramatic expression in instrumental music.

We come to the fabulous domain of Wagner and the music-dramas that have changed music history, works once scornfully referred to as "music of the future," now the admiration and the inspiration of the man in the street—the early ones, "Tannhäuser," "Lohengrin" and the occasionally performed "Dutchman"; the supreme elegy of mortal love, "Tristan und Isolde"; the immortal comedy, "Meistersinger"; the grandures of the Ring, the singular blend of mysticism and theatricality which is "Parsifal." These works alone suffice many opera goers for a life-time. Then look at the post-Wagnerian repertory: at the volcanic passion of that astonishing little explosion of genius, "Cavalleria Rusticana," and its companion piece "Pagliacci," for Italian realism in music; at the masterly stage technic and the long curving melodies of Puccini in his finest work "La Bohème," in his grim melodrama, "Tosca," in the very popular "Madame Butterfly" and the youthful but vigorous and prophetic "Manon Lescaut"—the same subject which Massenet treated with better taste, less sheer realism and more native sympathy for the theme. And here is Richard Strauss' "Salome," so strangely evocative of the Oriental night, so terse, sinister and glamorous. "Electra" is a more terrible and modern score; "Rosenkavalier," with its Viennese flavor, its grace and broad humor, and wonderful drawing of character, and Viennese waltzes, has pages that approach Mozart. What variety in the operas of this our age! Listen to Montemezzi's "Love of Three Kings," with its medieval beauty, its melody, at once racial and aristocratic, its love-scene in which the Italian inevitably remembered the method of Wagner in "Tristan!" Each opera worthy of the name is engrossing in its special manner; each one is different.

In general it will be noticed that composers before the 19th century relied principally upon the voice and the singer to convey their message, giving the orchestra a subsidiary rôle; whereas the composers after 1800 increasingly avail themselves of the evocative power of the instruments.

These are things for the reader to seek out for himself by listening. There is no more fascinating voyage of discovery. Remember: The plot is the general index to the emotional situation—no more. Some operas move swiftly from the standpoint of action. In most of them the action is deliberately slow, so that the composer may have full opportunity for musical expression. Let this be understood and expected. Listen to the drama *in* the music. Then comes the full thrill of Manrico's savage war-cry, "Di quella pira," or the pathos of the remembrance of the kiss in the poignant final scene of "Othello." Listen when Wotan and Brünnhilde, father and daughter, look at each other, once more, and yet again, for the eternal farewell; when he places her in the care of Loki the Fire-god, on the rock, and irresistible sleep steals like a drug through her veins, and dimly she is aware of the retreating form of the All-father, lost in a strange vision of glimmering flames. All this is hymned in Wagner's orchestra.

Of such are the devices of opera, and such the gifts of the music-drama.

ABU HASSAN

Comic Opera in one act by WEBER

Text by HEIMER

This little opera, composed by Weber in his early youth and first represented at Dresden under the composer's own direction, for a time fell into utter oblivion, but has lately been reproduced.

Though short and unpretending, it really deserves to be heard, the music is so full of sweetness, so fresh and pretty.

The text is taken from a tale of the Arabian Thousand and One Nights, and though full of nonsense, it amuses by its lightheartedness and gaiety of spirit.

Abu Hassan, favorite of the Calif of Bagdad, has lived above his means, and is now regaled with bread and water by his wife Fatima, whose only fault is that she sings better than she cooks. In order to better his fortunes, Abu Hassan hits upon a strange plan. He sends his wife to the Calif's wife, Zobeïde, to announce his (Hassan's) death, for which she will obtain 50 gold pieces and a piece of brocade. Fatima departs, and in the meantime enter Abu Hassan's creditors with the appeal for money. Unable to satisfy them, the debtor approaches the eldest and richest among them, and so pacifies him with sweet words, which he is given to understand Fatima has sent him, that old Omar consents to pay all the creditors.

When they are gone, Fatima returns with Zobeïde's presents, and Abu Hassan prepares to go in his turn to the Calif, in order to repeat a similar death-story about his wife and get a like sum. While he is away Omar reappears. He has bought all Hassan's accounts from his numerous creditors and offers them to Fatima for a kiss. At this moment the husband returns. Omar is shut into the adjoining cabinet, and the wife secretly points out the caged bird to her spouse, who begins to storm at finding the door of the next room closed, greatly to the anguish of the old sinner Omar,—anguish which is enjoyed by his tormentors to the full. In the midst of this scene Mesrur, messenger of the Calif, appears, to find out whether Fatima is really dead. The Calif and his wife having each received news of the death of the other's favorite, want to know who it was that died, and, if both are dead, who died first. The Calif affirms that it is Fatima—his wife, that it is Abu Hassan. They have made a bet, and Mesrur, seeing Fatima lying motionless on the divan, covered with the brocade, and her husband in evident distress beside her, runs away to convey the tidings to the Calif. He is hardly gone when Zobeïde's nurse, Zemrud, comes on a similar errand from her mistress. Fatima, who has just covered her husband with the brocade, receives her with tears and laments, and the nurse departs triumphantly.

Hassan presently comes to life again, but he and Fatima are not long permitted to congratulate one another on the success of their scheme, for the arrival of the Calif with his wife is pompously announced. Both throw themselves on the divans, covering themselves, and so the august couple finds them dead. The Calif, much afflicted by the sight, offers 1000 gold pieces to any one who can tell him which of the two died first. No sooner does Hassan hear this than, tearing aside his cover, he throws himself at the Calif's feet, crying out:

"It was I who died first!" at the same time craving the Calif's pardon together with the gold pieces. Fatima is also speedily resuscitated and the Calif pardons his favorites, Hassan meanwhile asserting that he only died badly in order to live better. Omar, who has paid their bills in the hope of winning Fatima's love, is driven away in disgrace.

L'AFRICAINE

Opera in five acts by MEYERBEER

Text by E. SCRIBE

L'Africaine, one of the Maestro's last operas (1865), unites in itself all the strength and at the same time all the weakness of Meyerbeer's composition.

The music is easy-flowing and enthralls us with its delicious melodies; but it only appeals to our senses, and nobler thoughts are altogether wanting. Nevertheless the opera finds favor by reason of these advantages, which are supplemented by an interesting though rather improbable libretto.

The famous Portuguese navigator Vasco da Gama (born in 1469) is the hero, though he does not appear in the best possible light, and is by no means strictly historical.

The first scene is laid in Lisbon. Donna Inez, Admiral Diego's daughter, is to give her hand to Don Pedro, a counsellor of King Emmanuel of Portugal. But she has pledged her faith to Vasco da Gama, who has been sent with Diaz, the navigator, to double the Cape, in order to seek for a new land, containing treasures similar to those discovered by Columbus. Reports have reached Lisbon that the whole fleet has been destroyed, when suddenly Vasco da Gama appears before the assembled council of state.

He eloquently describes the dangers of the unknown seas near the Cape and gives an account of the shipwreck, from which he alone has escaped. He then places his maps before the council, endeavoring to prove that beyond Africa there is another country, yet to be explored and conquered.

Vasco has on his way home picked up a man and a woman of an unknown race. These slaves however stubbornly refuse to betray the name of their country, and a lively debate ensues between the Grand Inquisitor and the younger, more enlightened members of the council as to the course which should be adopted with Vasco. At last, owing to the irritation caused by his violent reproaches, fanaticism is victorious, and instead of being furnished with a ship to explore those unknown lands, he is thrown into prison, on the plea of his being a heretic, for having maintained the existence of countries which were not mentioned in the Holy Scriptures.

The second act takes place in a cell of the Inquisition, in which Vasco has been languishing for a month past, in the company of the strange slaves Nelusko and Selika. The latter has lost her heart to the proud Portuguese, who saved her and her companion from a slave-ship. But Vasco is only thinking of Inez and Nelusko, who honors in Selika not only his Queen, but the woman of his love, tries to stab Vasco, the Christian, whom he hates with a deadly hatred. Selika hinders him and rouses the sleeping Vasco, who has been dreaming of and planning his voyage to the unknown country.

Selika now shows him on the map the way to her native isle, and he vows her eternal gratitude. His liberty is indeed near at hand, for hardly has he given his vow, than Inez steps in to announce that Vasco is free. She has paid dearly for her lover's deliverance, however, for she has given her hand to Vasco's rival, Don Pedro, who, having got all Vasco's plans and maps, is commissioned by government to set out on the voyage of discovery.

Inez has been told that Vasco has forgotten her for Selika the slave. In order to prove his fidelity, our ungrateful hero immediately presents her with the two slaves, and Don Pedro resolves to make use of them for the exploration.

In the third act we are on board of Don Pedro's ship in the Indian seas. Donna Inez is with her husband and Nelusko has been appointed pilot. Don Alvar, a member of the council and Don Pedro's friend, warns the latter that Nelusko is meditating treason, for they have already lost two ships; but Pedro disregards the warning. A typhoon arises, and Nelusko turns the ship again northward. But Vasco has found means to follow them on a small sailing vessel; he overtakes them, and knowing the spot well where Diaz was shipwrecked, he entreats them to change their course, his only thought being Donna Inez's safety. But Pedro, delighted to have his rival in his power, orders him to be bound and shot. Inez, hearing his voice, invokes her husband's mercy. Just then the tempest breaks out, the vessel strikes upon a rock, and the cannibals inhabiting the neighboring country leap on board to liberate their Queen Selika and to massacre the whole crew, in the fulfilment of which intention they are, however, arrested by Selika.

In the following acts Selika resides as Queen on the Isle of Madagascar. The people render her homage, but the priests demand the strangers' lives as a sacrifice to their gods, while the women are condemned to inhale the poisoned perfume of the manzanilla-tree.—In order to save Vasco, Selika proclaims him her husband, and takes Nelusko as witness, swearing to him that if Vasco is sacrificed she will die with him. Nelusko, whose love for his Queen is greater even than his hatred for Vasco, vouches for their being man and wife, and the people now proceed to celebrate the solemn rites of marriage.

Vasco, at last recognizing Selika's great love, and believing Inez dead, once more vows eternal fidelity to her; but, alas! hearing the voice of Inez, who is about to be led to death, he turns pale, and Selika but too truly divines the reason.

In the fifth act Selika is resolved to put her rival to death. She sends for her, but perceiving Inez's love, her wrath vanishes, her magnanimity soars above her hatred of the Christians, and she orders Nelusko to bring Inez and Vasco on board of a ship about to sail for Portugal.

Selika herself, unable to endure life without her beloved one, proceeds to the Cape, where the manzanilla-tree spreads its poisonous shade. Her eyes fastened on the vast ocean and on the white sail of the retiring vessel, she inhales the sweet but deadly perfume of the blossoms, and the returning Nelusko finds her dying, while an unseen chorus consoles her with the thought that in Love's eternal domain all are equal.

AÏDA

Grand romantic Opera in four acts by GIUSEPPI VERDI

Text by ANTONIO GHISLANZONI. Translated into German by S. SCHANZ. English version by KENNEY

This opera owes its great popularity not only to its brilliant music and skilful instrumentation, but also to its really magnificent outfit and decorations. Aïda ranks among the best operas of Verdi. The plot is taken from old Egypt; and the music, with its Eastern and somewhat sensuous coloring, is exquisitely adapted to the scenery.

The scene of action is alternately Memphis and Thebes, and the story belongs to the period when the Pharaohs sat on the throne.

In the first act we see the King's palace at Memphis. Ramphis, the High Priest of Pharaoh, announces to the Egyptian General Radamès that the Ethiopians are in revolt and that the goddess Isis has decided who shall be leader of the army sent out against them. Radamès secretly hopes to be the elected, in order to win the Ethiopian slave Aïda, whom he loves, not knowing that she is a King's daughter.

Enter Amneris, daughter of Pharaoh. She loves Radamès, without his knowledge, and so does Aïda. Amneris, suspecting this, swears to avenge herself should her suspicion prove correct.

The King's messenger announces that Amonasro, the Ethiopian King (Aïda's father) is marching to the capital, and that Radamès is chosen to conquer the foe.

Radamès goes to the temple to invoke the benediction of the goddess and to receive the sacred arms.

In the second act Amneris, in order to test Aïda's feelings, tells her that Radamès fell in battle, and finds her doubts confirmed by Aïda's terror. Amneris openly threatens her rival, and both hasten to receive the soldiers, who return victorious. In Radamès' suite walks King Amonasro, who has been taken prisoner, disguised as a simple officer. Aïda recognizes her father, and Amonasro, telling his conqueror that the Ethiopian King has fallen, implores his clemency. Radamès, seeing Aïda in tears, adds his entreaties to those of the Ethiopian; and Pharaoh decides to set the prisoners free, with the exception of Aïda's father, who is to stay with his daughter. Pharaoh then gives Amneris to Radamès as a recompense for his services.

In the third act Amonasro has discovered the mutual love of his daughter and Radamès and resolves to make use of it. While Amneris prays in the temple that her bridegroom may give his whole heart to her, Amonasro bids his daughter discover the secret of the Egyptian war plans from her lover. Amonasro hides himself, and Aïda has an interview with Radamès, in which he reveals all to her. She persuades him to fly with her, when Amonasro shows himself, telling him that he has heard all and confessing that he is the Ethiopian King. While they are speaking, Amneris overtakes and denounces them. Amonasro escapes with his daughter, Radamès remains in the hands of Ramphis the High Priest.

In the fourth act Radamès is visited in his cell by Amneris, who promises to save him from the awful death of being buried alive, if he renounces Aïda. But Radamès refuses, though she tells him that Aïda has fled into her country, her father being slain on their flight.

Amneris at length regrets her jealousy and repents, but too late! Nothing can save Radamès; and she is obliged to see him led into his living tomb. Amneris curses the priests, who close the subterranean vaults with a rock. Radamès, preparing himself for death, discovers Aïda by his side. She has found means to penetrate into his tomb, resolved to die with her lover.

While she sinks into his arms, Amneris prays outside for Radamès peace and eternal happiness.

ALESSANDRO STRADELLA

Romantic Opera in three acts by FLOTOW

Text after the French by W. FRIEDRICH

Flotow, who composed this little opera when at Paris in the year 1844, that is long before his Martha, had the satisfaction of scoring a great success on the evening of its first representation in Hamburg. The pleasant impression then made by its agreeable and lovely melodies has not faded the less that, after hearing many of our stormy and exciting modern operas, one often and ardently longs for the restful charm and guileless pleasure of a piece like this.

The libretto is interesting and touching, without being over-sensational.

Stradella, the celebrated Venetian singer, has fallen in love with Leonore, ward of a rich Venetian citizen named Bassi. She returns his love, but is strictly guarded by her uncle, who wants to marry her himself. Stradella succeeds in deceiving Bassi and, aided by his friend, carries her off during the Carnival. In the second act we find the lovers in a little village near Rome, where a priest unites them for ever and gives them his benediction.

But Malvolio, a bandit, has sought them by Bassi's orders, and discovers their refuge. Entering the villa, where he finds open doors but no people, he meets with another bandit, in whom he recognizes his friend Barbarino, also sent, as it turns out, on the same errand.

They decide to do the business together, that is to say,

to kill Stradella, and to carry his wife back to her guardian. Under the mask of pilgrims going to a sacred festival they find a kindly shelter in Stradella's house and are won by the latter's fine voice, as well as by the charm of his noble behavior, so that they wholly abandon their evil purpose.

But in the third act Bassi appears, and, not finding his order executed, offers such a large sum of gold to the banditti that they at length promise to stab Stradella during his next singing performance. While they lie in wait for him, Stradella sings the hymn of the Holy Virgin's clemency towards sinners so touchingly that his pursuers cast their swords away and sink on their knees, joining in the refrain. Full of astonishment, Stradella learns of the danger in which he had been, but in the end he willingly pardons not only the banditti but also his wife's uncle, who, won over, like the ruffians, by the power of Stradella's song, humbly asks for the singer's friendship, which is granted to him.

The people lead their favorite in triumph to the festival, which he helps to glorify with his wondrous voice.

L'AMICO FRITZ

A lyric Comedy in three acts by PIETRO MASCAGNI

Text after ERCKMANN-CHATRIAN'S novel of the same name

After the immense success of Cavalleria Rusticana, the first representation of Amico Fritz was awaited with feverish impatience by the whole musical world.

But the high-strung expectations were not fulfilled. Though many pretended that the music was nobler and more artistic than that of the author's first work, the success was by no means as great as Mascagni's friends anticipated. In Vienna and Berlin it was even received with partial coolness. But, lo! the first representation in Dresden on June 2, 1892, took place with a marked and decided success.

The artistically trained orchestra brought out to perfection all the finesses, all the delightful shades of the music, and since that day the opera has not failed to bring a full house.

The subject in itself is too simple for Mascagni's strong dramatic talent, hence the lack of interest, hence the disillusion of so many.

Granting this, we cannot but admire the genius which can compose an opera so full of refined and noble sentiment, based on such a simple plot.

No music more charming than the march, taken as well as the Pastorale from a national Alsatian song, none more sweet and melodious than the Intermezzo and the Cherry duet. The finely depicted details in the orchestra are a delight for musical ears.

The simple text follows strictly the French original.

Fritz Kobus, a well-to-do landowner, receives the felicitations of his friends on his fortieth birthday. At the same time his old friend Rabbi David, as consummate a match-maker as Fritz is an inveterate bachelor, receives from the latter a loan of 1200 francs, which is to enable a poor girl to marry her lover. Fritz gives it very graciously, congratulating himself that he is free from hymen's bonds.

He treats his friends to a hearty dinner, in which Susel, his tenant's daughter, who comes to present her landlord with a nosegay of violets, joins. Fritz makes her sit beside him, and for the first time remarks the growing loveliness of the young maiden. While they are feasting, a gipsy Seppel plays a serenade in honor of the birthday, which makes a deep impression on fair Susel. When the latter has departed, the joviality of the company increases. Hanczo and Friedrich, two friends, laughingly prophesy to the indignant Fritz that he will soon be married, and David even makes a bet, which, should he prove right, will make him owner of one of his friend's vineyards. At the end of the first act a procession of orphans hail the landlord as their benefactor.

In the second act we find our friend Fritz as guest in the house of his tenant. Susel is sedulously engaged in selecting flowers and cherries for her landlord, who, coming down into the garden, is presented by her with flowers. Soon she mounts a ladder, and, plucking cherries, throws them to Fritz, who is uncertain which are the sweeter, the maiden's red lips, or the ripe cherries which she offers him. In the midst of their enjoyment the sound of bells and crackling of whips is heard; Fritz's friends enter. He soon takes them off for a

Beniamino Gigli as Vasco da Gama in "L'Africaine"

walk; only old David stays behind with Susel, pleading fatigue. Taking occasion of her presenting him with a drink of fresh water, he makes her tell him the old story of Isaac and Rebecca, and is quite satisfied to guess at the state of her feelings by the manner in which she relates the simple story. On Fritz's return he archly communicates to him that he has found a suitable husband for Susel, and that he has her father's consent. The disgust and fright which Fritz experiences at this news reveals to him something of his own feelings for the charming maiden. He decides to return home at once, and does not even take farewell of Susel, who weeps in bitter disappointment.

In the third act Fritz, at home again, can find no peace anywhere. When David tells him that Susel's marriage is a decided fact he breaks out, and in his passion downright forbids the marriage. At this moment Susel appears, bringing her landlord a basket of fruit. She looks pale and sad; and when Fritz sarcastically asks her whether she comes to invite him to her wedding, she bursts into tears. Then the real state of her heart is revealed to him, and with passionate avowal of his own love, Amico Fritz takes her to his heart. So David wins his wager, which, however, he settles on Susel as a dowry, promising at the same time to procure wives before long for the two friends standing by.

L'AMORE DEI TRE RE

Tragic Grand Opera in Italian. Three acts. By

ITALO MONTE MEZZI

Text by SEM BENELLI

The first production occurred in Milan, 1913. The scene is the remote mountain country of Italy, and the action is supposed to happen about the tenth century. In the mythical country of Altura the rule of King Archibaldo, one of the northern barbarian conquerors, has been established. Forty years have elapsed since then, and the King is now blind. His beloved son Manfredo, carefully nurtured, is absent in war. Two of the conquered royal line, Fiora, now spouse of Manfredo, and Avito, are remaining with the hoary King Archibaldo, within the castle.

During Act I the old King, sleepless and a prey to unrest, visits the impregnable battlements of the castle, being accompanied by his trusty attendant Flaminio. On the walls of the fastness a torch is kept flaring as a sign for Manfredo's return. The aged ruler, harassed by strange forebodings, talks to Flaminio about his son, speculating on the latter's homecoming. Fiora, whose union with Manfredo was an enforced one, suddenly makes her appearance with Avito, the man to whom she was formerly betrothed, just after Archibaldo has gone back to his chamber for rest. The two converse, but at dawn Avito goes away. Archibaldo now shows himself once more, and although Fiora attempts to conceal her presence the old king becomes aware of her proximity, and when she avoids replying to him, he suspects her of having met a lover secretly. However, he keeps his suspicions to himself. Manfredo now is seen returning. Longing for his beautiful wife has hastened his coming. But to his impassioned avowals of his feelings Fiora turns an indifferent ear. Both retire to their nuptial chamber, and the blind old father, more than ever troubled, thanks a kind fate that he cannot see approaching disaster.

The second act touchingly portrays Manfredo's dignified but earnest wooing of his young and charming spouse. Upon the ramparts of the stately stronghold he takes leave of her, asking her for some farewell token of her wifely love. She rather coldly agrees. Standing upon the terrace in front of the castle she waves her scarf at the departing hero and his band of followers, in sign of good wishes. The departing Manfredo and his men remain for a long time within vision. But as they draw out of sight, Avito again may be noticed climbing up the stairs. He is disguised in the garb of Flaminio. She recognizes him, however, and meaning to be faithful to her lord she pleads with him to leave her. Avito, blinded by passion, refuses to listen to her. Fiora once more resorts to her scarf, waving it at the departing husband as a pledge of her affection. While Avito stormily continues to plead his cause with her, kneeling and uttering endearments, Fiora's resistance droops more and more. Avito seizes the hem of her robe which he kisses rapturously. Fiora yields to him. But while this takes place the old king steals upon them. Avito, though, swiftly evades pursuit, and is not recognized, while the blind man has clearly made out the voice of Fiora. To his insistent inquiries she acknowledges having a lover, but will not betray his name. Archibaldo thereupon becomes angered beyond all self-control, seizes Fiora by the throat, and when she still declines to confess the name of the guilty one, he throttles her. The dead body of Fiora is stretched out upon the ground, and the aged ruler is standing before it in an effort to conceal it, when Manfredo enters. Manfredo has hastened home when he no longer noticed his wife signaling to him, as agreed, with her scarf. Then he becomes aware of the lifeless body, and his father, torn by pity and remorse, tells Manfredo the sad facts, but is unable to give the culprit's name. Manfredo is broken-hearted, being at a loss, besides, to account for the fact that his wife, when he had such a wealth of love to bestow on her, should have been unresponsive. He conceives a hatred for his father, whom he shrinks from as a murderer, and the old king bears the corpse away.

In the last act Fiora lies dead in the mausoleum of the castle, being lamented over by old and young in the castle. They are whispering that she was wickedly murdered out of revenge. Avito enters, approaches the bier on which the body lies in state, and after driving the curious away, kneels down in utter woe and prays that he may die with her. Imprinting wild kisses on the still lips, he imbibes a virulent poison which the old king, hoping thereby to trap the unknown guilty, has spread over them. Avito falls down lifeless. Manfredo also enters, approaches the bier, and perceives Avito, already breathing his last. The truth that Avito must be the lover of his dead wife, then dawns on him, and in his wrath he comes near stabbing the moribund Avito. The latter taunts him and forbids his touching the lips of the dead. But Manfredo does, and dying in his turn, is surprised by his blind father who has not recognized the voice of his own son and deems him to be the illegitimate lover for whom he had spread the deadly snare. Manfredo, however, with the broken accents of the dying, reveals to him the fact that he himself, the blind king, has caused not alone the death of the guilty couple but also that of his innocent son.

L'AMORE MEDICO

An opera bouffe in two acts by E. WOLF-FERRARI

Book founded on Molière's comedy "L'Amour Medico,"

by E. GOLISCHIANI

This opera, "L'Amore Medico" (Dr. Cupid), saw its first presentation at the royal opera house in Dresden, 1913. The scene is in France, and the time is the 17th century.

The first act occurs at the villa of a wealthy landowner. Arnolfo, a very selfish father, cannot explain to himself his daughter's curious illness. She is wasting away, and the doctor is unable to fathom the reason. To prevent her from leaving home and marrying, he is treating her as a child. She must dress in infantile fashion, and he addresses her in the same way, presenting dolls and toys, and even using baby talk to her. The daughter is listless in his presence, until he puts to her the question whether some young gaby has found approval in her eyes. She instantly replies, "Yes, papa!" The father grows angry at this, and still more when the pert maid, Lisetta, joins the conversation by saying that what Lucinda, the daughter, really requires to cure her is a husband. Later Clitandro, the young gallant who has made an impression on Lucinda's heart, is serenading her and after a song in which he ardently confesses his love, he throws a rose through the window. Lucinda is so overwhelmed by her feelings that she faints. Arnolfo returns and there is a monologue in which he expresses longing for the time when his daughter will be too old and unattractive to marry, and may thus devote all her time to the nursing of her father, as all daughters ought to do. He falls asleep, but is awakened by outcries from his child, and loud demands by Lisetta for a doctor. He sends her forth to get doctors, and they come in a mass.

The second act exhibits the doctors in conclave. At first they behave with courtesy toward one another, and each listens to the theory of the other as to the causes of the young girl's illness. But soon they disagree, and almost come to blows. Arnolfo enters, and the four physicians deluge him with Latin nonsense, and all demand a fat fee. These are paid before Arnolfo remembers that with all their noise they have not told him what was really the matter with his child and what treatment should be given her. But just at that moment Lisetta comes in, having Clitandro with her, who is disguised in the long wig and formal costume of a physician. The new doctor proclaims as his specialty the healing of sick hearts. Arnolfo watches the doctor, who seems unnecessarily long about the person of the patient. The final diagnosis is that Lucinda's trouble is mental. As she merely imagines that she wants a husband, the best way would be to humor her and pretend to give her one. For that purpose even he, the doctor, will offer himself as the subject of an experiment. Arnolfo consents to enter into the plan and promises, always in jest only, to give the two half his property. A notary is called and draws up the settlements, and a ceremony is performed, and then a group of merrymakers stream in. The father becomes too late aware that he has been the victim of a successful practical joke.

ANDRÉ CHÉNIER

Tragic Opera in four acts by UMBERTO GIORDANO
Text by VICTORIEN DECAZES

This opera was first produced at Milan, 1896. The book is based on historical facts interwoven with events during the great French Revolution.

The first act takes place during the early part of the Revolution. The scene is a ballroom, being prepared for a festivity. Gérard, a servant secretly devoted to the revolutionary cause, is anxiously awaiting the end of his term of service, avowing his principles in the course of a conversation. The Countess de Coigny, the hostess, comes in accompanied by Madeleine, a young girl, and by Bersi, her attendant. Madeleine speaks reprovingly of the great extravagance shown in the preparations for the ball, contrasting them with the general misery under which the people are groaning. André Chénier, the rising young poet, and Fleville, the author, arrive among the first guests. The good abbé deplores the lot of the poor, and tells the latest disquieting news. But Fleville laughingly tells everybody to enjoy themselves, for *après nous le déluge.* The festivity proceeds, and during its continuance Madeleine begs Chénier, the poet, to compose on the spot a poem glorifying Love. Chénier does so, but in the course of it draws a bitter parallel between wealth and poverty. The countess animates her guests to dance and forget what to-morrow may have in store for them. There is gay dancing and merry jesting, when Gérard breaks in upon the scene with a ragged crowd. The countess orders the intruders to leave, and the father of Gérard, an old and attached servant, vainly urges indulgence. The rabble are driven out, and the ball goes on.

The second act is at the Café Hottot, Paris. Bersi and a spy for the Jacobin Club are at one table, and André Chénier at another. A sansculotte, by name Mathieu, and a waiter are in attendance. A tumbril with the day's condemned rumbles heavily past on its way to the guillotine. A friend of André Chénier enters and implores the poet to take flight, having secured for him a passport signed by the committee of safety. The poet, however, being engrossed with a love affair, scorns to take advantage of the offer. His friend earnestly warns him to be careful. Robespierre, with a ragged throng of his followers behind him, passes by in the street. Gérard enters and inquires of the spy the whereabouts of Madeleine. Bersi asks Chénier to await the coming of an unknown lady whom she calls "Speranza." Chénier decides to wait. Darkness falls, and the spy watches in the shadows until Madeleine enters, meeting Chénier. Then he recognizes them and runs to inform Gérard. Madeleine asks André to save her, and both avow their love. When on the point of flight Gérard stops them, and tries to spirit away Madeleine. Roucher takes her home. There is a duel between André and Gérard, and when the latter is wounded he begs André to take care of Madeleine. The poet becomes a fugitive and a mob gathers about the wounded Gérard, demanding to know the name of his assailant, but he pretends ignorance.

In the third act the revolutionary tribunal is seen, and Mathieu greets the mob when Gérard is brought in. Gérard makes an appeal to the mob. An old woman,

Madelon, pushes her way to the front, and presents her young grandson to the country's service. The spy enters and tells Gérard that André has just been apprehended and that Madeleine is close by. Gérard, torn by a conflict of feelings, means to denounce André to the revolutionary tribunal, but finally refrains from doing so. Madeleine comes in, and Gérard declares affection for her. She tries to flee, but then offers her honor for André's life. Gérard is touched by her grief and unselfish love, and promises to assist her. The judges arrive, and André is brought in to face instant trial. He denies, however, the charge and offers proof of the contrary. Gérard also pleads for him, but the bloodthirsty rabble demand his head. He is led away to prison.

In the last act night has come, and André is seen in prison. He writes and composes a love song. Roucher is close by, and a touching farewell scene between the two takes place. Madeleine enters with Gérard, and she bribes the guards to let her take the place of another woman condemned to death and who is also on the list of that day's victims. She desires to perish together with André, her lover. Her wish is gratified, and jointly they ascend the scaffold.

APHRODITE

Tragic Opera in five acts by CAMILLE ERLANGER

Text after Pierre Louys' romance of the same name by

LOUIS DE GRAMONT

This opera was first performed in Paris, 1906, and has since been heard everywhere. The action occurs at Alexandria, Egypt, in B.C. 50. The scene shifts with every act, and the setting requires great pageantry and much gorgeous costume. The music shows originality and most of it is decidedly pleasing in character.

In the first act throngs are gathered upon the pier of Alexandria, among whom may be distinguished philosophers, courtiers, sailors, beggars, wandering traders, gay courtesans, and a rabble of the merely curious. There is talk of a splendid feast to be given by Bacchis, a wealthy woman of the town, who is to celebrate in that fashion the freeing of her pet slave girl, Corinna. A flute duet is being played by Myrto and Rhodis, and Theano dances publicly to its measure. Demetrius enters, the crowd opening a way for him. He is a famous sculptor whose latest work, an entrancing statue of Aphrodite, the goddess of love, has recently been placed in the temple devoted to her cult. Some of the courtesans present,—Musarion, Seso, Tryphera, and Philotis,—comment on the haughty ways of Demetrius, who is said to be the lover of the hour of Queen Berenice.

Then, after he has scorned all this gabble, the dreaded sorceress Chimairis comes on the scene and pronounces the doom of Demetrius, saying that his future will be one of crime and bloodshed. The death of two women will be on his hands, and thereafter his own. The sculptor scoffs at the prediction.

When the throng disperses, a noted wanton, Chrysis, passes near him. He is struck with her exquisite charms, and some bantering dialogue ensues. Chrysis refuses his gold for her favor, saying she craves but three things: a mirror, a necklace, and a comb, in exchange for which she vows to render the giver happy. Demetrius takes a solemn oath that he will procure the three gifts for her. But these three things, she goes on, are not easy to obtain. For the mirror is the famous silver one of Rhodope, the one that Sappho the fair once gazed upon; the comb is now in the tresses of the spouse of the High Priest; and the necklace is hung in seven rows of matchless pearls around the marble neck of his own Aphrodite in the inmost temple hall. But nothing daunts Demetrius. He swears he will obtain these fateful objects for her or die in the attempt. Chrysis smiles derisively, but pledges the delights of the gods in exchange if he makes his boasting come true.

In the next act the interior of the temple is seen. Demetrius has possessed himself of two of the desired objects, committing murder to do so. He now is on the point of robbing his own handiwork, the statue of Aphrodite, of the coveted necklace when temple servants enter and drive him to hiding. The High Priest makes his entrance at this juncture, with a body of courtesans in his train. The latter offer sacrifice, and while so employed Chrysis appears. There is question of admitting her, since she is only part Greek, part Jewess, but the High Priest himself takes her side, and she is welcomed. Chrysis, too, bears priceless offerings for the shrine of the goddess, among these being a necklace of emeralds. Demetrius unseen witnesses all this, and the sight of Chrysis inflames him with wild desire, and he renews his vow to despoil the goddess of the cherished bauble.

In the third act, the one replete with feverish action, revelry is in full swing at the house of Bacchis. Corinna is seated next to her mistress on a dais. Her six sisters, likewise slaves, are intensely jealous of the honors bestowed on their sister. Chrysis is one of the guests, with Timon beside her, but she is dispirited. Theano dances, and the feast waxes furious until the theft of the costly mirror is accidentally discovered. Chrysis rejoices. Bacchis suspects Corinna of having purloined the mirror, and Corinna's sisters amplify her charges. In a rage Bacchis orders Corinna to be crucified, and she herself helps the carrying out of the sentence. Chrysis has eyes and ears for nothing but the evidence that her lover, Demetrius, has risked much for her favor. The banquet is resumed, while Timon stands by the cross whereto is nailed the dying Corinna and solaces her last moments.

During the fourth act Demetrius is seen in his studio, when suddenly shouts of the multitude crying "sacrilege," pierce the distance. He is smitten with remorse at his crimes, when Chrysis comes forth from behind the screen, and all his thoughts turn to her. He puts the three coveted objects into her hands, she disrobes and adorns herself with his gifts, and the couple forget everything else in their passion. They exchange oaths of undying affection, and Chrysis offers to prove it by doing even more for him than he has for her. She swears it by the living God of Israel.

In the last act a maddened crowd, beside themselves with horror at the sacrilege committed upon the goddess Aphrodite, and dreading the wrath of the outraged deity, is swaying to and fro between the pier and Pharos. That the high priest's wife has been cruelly slain for the sake of her marvelous comb becomes known at this juncture. The throng, wrought to the highest pitch of excitement, are on their knees pleading for mercy from Aphrodite. Suddenly, in the midst of their despair, they perceive, on top of the first landing of the spiral stairs leading up to the tower of Pharos, a nude woman of ravishing beauty, wearing the mirror, comb and necklace which are attributes of the divine Aphrodite. The credulous mob leap at the conclusion that this is the goddess herself, and Chrysis (for she it is in reality) strengthens this belief by shouting down from her eminence that she is indeed the immortal goddess. But some have recognized her, and instantly there is a rush, and the woman is captured and borne by a furious, fanatical crowd to the prison, there to await the awful sentence for her sacrilegious deception. A touching jail scene shows Chrysis ready to die. The Queen sends her the fateful hemlock bowl to drink. Gradually her senses are benumbed, but she murmurs the words "Demetrius" and "love" till the last, while Demetrius himself is slain by outraged Love in a vision.

THE APOTHECARY

(LO SPEZIALE)

Comic Opera by JOSEF HAYDN (1768)

After a sleep of 125 years in the dust of Prince Esterhazy's archives at Eisenstadt, Dr. Hirschfeld received permission from Prince Paul Esterhazy of Galantha to copy the original manuscript.

It is Dr. Hirschfeld's merit to have revived and rearranged this charming specimen of the old master's genius. And again it was Ernst Schuch, the highly gifted director of the Dresden opera, who had it represented on this stage in 1895, and at the same time introduced it to the Viennese admirers of old Haydn by some of the best members of his company.

The music is truly Haydnish, simple, naïve, fresh and clear as crystal, and it forms an oasis of repose and pure enjoyment to modern ears, accustomed to and tired of the astonishing oddities of modern orchestration.

The plot is simple but amusing. A young man, Mengino, has entered the service of the apothecary Sempronio, though he does not possess the slightest knowledge of chemistry. His love for Sempronio's ward Grilletta has induced him to take this step, and in the first scene we see him mixing drugs, and making melancholy reflections on his lot, which has led him to a master who buries himself in his newspapers instead of attending to his business, and letting his apprentices go on as best they may.

Sempronio, entering, relates that the plague is raging

in Russia; and another piece of news, that an old cousin of his has married his young ward, is far more interesting to him than all his drugs and pills, as he intends to act likewise with Grilletta. This young lady has no fewer than three suitors, one of whom, a rich young coxcomb, enters to order a drug. His real intention is to see Grilletta. He is not slow to see that Mengino loves her too, so he sends him into the drug kitchen, in order to have Grilletta all to himself. But the pert young beauty only mocks him, and at Mengino's return Volpino is obliged to retire.

Alone with Mengino, Grilletta encourages her timid lover, whom she likes very much, but just when he is about to take her hand, Sempronio returns, furious to see them in such intimacy. He sends Mengino to his drugs and the young girl to her account books, while he buries himself once more in the study of his newspapers. Missing a map, he is obliged to leave the room. The young people improve the occasion by making love, and when Sempronio, having lost his spectacles, goes to fetch them, Mengino grows bolder and kisses Grilletta. Alas, the old man returns at the supreme moment and, full of rage, sends them to their rooms.

Mengino's effrontery ripens the resolution in the guardian's breast to marry Grilletta at once. He is, however, detained by Volpino, who comes to bribe him by an offer from the Sultan to go into Turkey as apothecary at court, war having broken out in that country. The wily young man insinuates that Sempronio will soon grow stone-rich, and offers to give him 10,000 ducats at once if he will give him Grilletta for his wife. Sempronio is quite willing to accept the Sultan's proposal, but not to cede Grilletta. So he sends Mengino away to fetch a notary, who is to marry him to his ward without delay. The maiden is quite sad, and vainly tortures her brain how to rouse her timid lover into action. Sempronio, hearing her sing so sadly, suggests that she wants a husband, and offers her his own worthy person. Grilletta accepts him, hoping to awaken Mengino's jealousy and to rouse him to action. The notary comes, in whom Grilletta at once recognizes Volpino in disguise. He has hardly sat down, when a second notary enters, saying that he has been sent by Mengino, and claiming his due. The latter is Mengino himself, and Sempronio, not recognizing the two, bids them sit down. He dictates the marriage contract, in which Grilletta is said to marry Sempronio by her own free will, besides making over her whole fortune to him. This scene, in which the two false notaries distort every word of old Sempronio's, and put each his own name instead of the guardian's, is overwhelmingly comical. When the contract is written, Sempronio takes one copy, Grilletta the other, and the whole fraud is discovered. Volpino vanishes, but Mengino promises Grilletta to do his best in order to win her.

In the last scene Sempronio receives a letter from Volpino, telling him that the Pasha is to come with a suite of Turks to buy all his medicines at a high price, and to appoint him solemnly as the Sultan's apothecary. Volpino indeed arrives, with his attendants, all disguised as Turks, but he is again recognized by Grilletta. He offers his gold, and seizes Grilletta's hand, to carry her off, but Sempronio interferes. Then the Turks begin to destroy all the pots and glasses and costly medicines, and when Sempronio resents this the false Pasha draws his dagger, but Mengino interferes and at last induces the frightened old man to promise Grilletta to him if he succeeds in saving him from the Turks. No sooner is the promise written and signed, than Grilletta tears off the Pasha's false beard and reveals Volpino, who retires baffled, while the false Turks drink the young couple's health at the cost of the two defeated suitors.

ARIANE ET BARBE BLEUE

Dramatic Opera in three acts by PAUL DUKAS

The libretto is by MAURICE MAETERLINCK, after the well-known tale about Bluebeard

The opera was first seen at Paris, 1907. The time is the Middle Ages, and the scene, a strong castle. Maeterlinck has here added a tinge of mysticism to the fairy tale, Ariane being, in a sense, a forerunner of the modern woman.

At the castle of Bluebeard a great uproar is going on. As the curtain rises the angry roar of the maddened crowd outside the strong walls is heard. This is because the news has spread that the evil knight has again succeeded in inveigling a new victim into his possession. It is known that he has murdered or tortured to death five previous wives, but Ariane, the latest addition, cannot believe these popular rumors, and insists on finding out the truth herself. She is particularly bound to learn the secret underlying it all, for secret there must be, she thinks. Ariane now enters with the attendant, carrying with her seven keys, silver all of them, save the last, which is of gold. And it is the last which opens the door behind which is hidden the mystery of mysteries, she has been told, the one which she is forbidden to use on pain of her life. One after the other these six less important keys are inserted in the locks, and as the threshold of each door is crossed a delightful surprise has been laid bare, and rarest gems have been found to ravish the eye. But the young wife is not gratified by all this display. She conceives it to be her duty and her woman's privilege to bare the mysterious attractions of the room from which alone she is to be excluded. The nurse in her wake begs and implores her to desist, but Ariane is stubborn. Curiosity piques her too strongly. So they turn the golden lock with the golden key, and as they do so they hear from afar the distant groans and tearful appeals of women. And before they can penetrate further or close and lock once more the portal they see Bluebeard coming in very coolly, saying: "Aha, you, too!" Then he tells Ariane in a lenient voice that he will exonerate her trespass if only she will abandon her project of further inspection. But Ariane is unable to do that. She is urged on by a power stronger even than life, and she bids Bluebeard defiance. The knight now becomes enraged, and tells her to follow in his steps. Her faithful attendant, however, once more hearing the bellowing throng outside the castle gates, rushes off and lets in the rabble. They advance upon him, but he draws his sword valiantly and prepares to sell his life dearly. At that point Ariane herself becomes the advocate of her husband, swearing that he is doing her no harm, and thus the crowd withdraws.

In the second act there is an underground chamber, and Ariane and her faithful nurse have been left in a secret vault close by the seventh room, the forbidden one, and still persist in their desire to investigate it. Ariane is convinced that those previous wives have not been murdered at all, but are merely kept prisoners. They have with them an ancient flickering lamp, and by its uncertain glare they see upon the floor of their dungeon, huddled in strange shapes, the shadowy forms of women. These, they discover, are really the previous five wives, not dead, but leading a wretched and cramped existence. So Ariane attempts to hearten them, and in trying to find some means of rescuing them, she sees at the far end of the gloomy room, the lamp having gone out, a faint glimmer of dawning light, and when they all turn thither, they become aware that it comes from a gate that has stood always open, by passing which they all of them are at large, and may issue into the wide realms of the world.

In the third act there is again the great hall of the castle. It turns out that the grounds surrounding the castle as well as the latter are enchanted, so that, after all, the wives cannot escape from its thrall. So they have turned back to the hall, where they find richest finery in great assortment, and they are all donning it by turns, simply to amuse themselves and while away time which is hanging heavily on their hands. Ariane is instructing the five wives how to win back their lost beauty, not only by dressing gaily, but by fresh air and exercise. The nurse comes to warn the women that Bluebeard is on his way back, and that the villagers are threatening to kill him. The fight takes place, and Bluebeard is defeated, together with his strong bodyguard, and is wounded grievously. The crowd are on the point of drowning him in the deep moat of the castle, having manacled him, but Ariane and the other wives interpose. Ariane in addressing the crowd dwells on the fact that it is she who is the most concerned in the whole business, and she induces them to carry Bluebeard into the hall of the castle, where she cuts his bonds, and next dresses his injuries. The throng leave her in undisputed possession of the field. Bluebeard, whose wounds are not very serious, now rises and gazes by turns at this and that one of the wives, but he has no more any desire to molest them. Ariane says farewell to him, and states that now her mission is over and that she must go away. Bluebeard regrets this, and in answer confesses his love and admiration for her. But Ariane smilingly does not respond to his pleading. The other five wives are told they may have their freedom if they so choose. But they, after consultation, declare their decision to stay with Bluebeard.

ARMIDA

Grand heroic Opera in five acts by GLUCK

Text by PHIL. QUINAULT

The poet Quinault wrote the libretto of this opera for another composer, Lully, but almost one hundred years later, Gluck, recognizing the genuine richness of this French production, availed himself of it for an opera the music of which is so sublime that it will for ever be considered classic.

The libretto is founded on an episode of Tasso's "Gerusalemme liberata."

The scene is laid in Damascus, where, during the Crusade of the year 1099, the Crusaders have arrived at the palace and gardens of Armida, the Queen and enchantress. Rinaldo, the greatest hero in Godfrey of Bouillon's army, is the only one who not only does not stoop to adore the beautiful Armida, but, on the contrary, pursues and hates her. He has been banished from Bouillon's presence, charged with the rash deed of another knight, who has not dared to confess his guilt, and he now wanders lonely in the forest.

Warned by a fellow-warrior, Artemidor, to avoid Armida's enchanting presence, he scorns the warning, saying that love for a woman is to him a thing unknown. In reality, however, Armida is already ensnaring him with her sorcery; he presently hears exquisitely sweet and dreamy melodies and, finding himself in a soft, green valley, he lies down and falls asleep.

Armida's opportunity has come, and she means to

stab him, but love conquers hatred, and the dagger falls from her hand. She vainly invokes the furies of hate; none can change her passion for the hero, and at last, ceasing to strive against her tender feelings, she surrenders herself entirely to him, and even succeeds by her charms and her devotion in enthralling him. Meanwhile Bouillon has sent two of his knights, Ubalt and a Danish warrior, to recall Rinaldo to his duty. They are detained by Armida's witchery; the Danish knight meets a demon, who has taken his bride's face, and tenderly calls him to her, but Ubalt destroys the charm and both succeed in approaching Rinaldo, who, his love-dream dissipated by the call of honor, resolves to return to the army with his companions. In vain Armida tries to change his resolution. In despair she curses him and her love, but, being unable to kill the man she loves, she suffers him to go away and turns her beautiful palace and gardens into a desert.

DER WAFFENSCHMIED

(THE ARMORER)

Comic Opera in three acts by ALBERT LORTZING

Text by himself

Though this opera does not equal in value Lortzing's "Czar and Zimmermann," it has nevertheless proved an admirable addition to the operatic repertory. It is attractive both on account of the freshness of its melodies and the popular character of its music and text.

The scene is located in Worms, in the 16th century. The Count of Liebenau has fallen in love with Mary, the daughter of a celebrated armorer, named Stadinger, and in order to win her, he woos her at first in his own rank as Count, then in the guise of a smith-journeyman, named Conrad. Mary, who cannot permit herself to think of love in connection with a person of such a position as a Count, nevertheless pities him and at last confesses, blushing, that she loves the poor smith Conrad. Inwardly triumphant, the Count pretends to be jealous. But father Stadinger, who more than once showed the door to the Count, will not accept either of the suitors, the Count standing too high above him, and his journeyman, Conrad, being too bad a laborer, though he has once saved Mary's life.

In order to withdraw her from the reach of her lovers, the armorer resolves to wed his daughter to his second journeyman, George, who is no other than the Count's valet. Stadinger is determined to present him as Mary's bridegroom on the occasion of a festival which is to take place in the course of the afternoon, and at which Stadinger's jubilee as master of armorers is to be celebrated. In vain George refuses his consent to this proposal. He is at length obliged to inform the Count, and the latter feigns to assault Stadinger's house. But it is of no avail; the old citizen, more firm than ever, denies him his child again, and as George decidedly refuses to marry his daughter, he gives her at last to Conrad. Great is Mary's surprise, and her father's wrath, when they discover that the Count and simple Conrad are one and the same person, but at last the old father yields, and the lovers receive his benediction.

L'ATTAQUE DU MOULIN

A four-act Opera, music by C. BRUNEAU

Text founded on a story by A. DAUDET

The first performance of this work took place in Paris, 1893. It is of a patriotic nature, and has enjoyed popularity in France.

The scene of the first act is laid in the mill of Father Merlier, shortly before the outbreak of the war of 1870-71. The housekeeper, Marcelline, is making great preparations in order to celebrate the formal engagement of Merlier's daughter, Franchette, to her young lover, Dominic. Old Merlier has become reconciled to the match, although at first he was strongly opposed to it. He indulges in pleasant speculation as to the prospective new management of the mill by the young couple. Swarms of guests are arriving, and all of them give joy to the lovers. Dancing is begun, and toasts to the happy couple are being proposed when a drum is heard. It is officially declared that war has commenced, whereupon the guests disperse in affright.

The second act happens but one month thereafter. It is the very day when the wedding of Franchette and Dominic was to be celebrated, but instead fighting is going on around the mill. A detachment of French soldiers have occupied the mill, and the Prussians are attacking it from without. Merlier, the miller, has been wounded while defending his homestead. Dominic, a skilled marksman, has scored many a hit. After a brave defense the French captain orders his men to retreat by way of the near-by forest. They go off in that direction. Franchette comes in with a knife in her hands. She explains that she carries it for self-protection. The Prussian troops now take possession of the mill. Their commander wants to know why Dominic has not gone with his company. Dominic in reply says he is not a Frenchman and did not belong to the company. He says he is Flemish, and only fought out of friendship for the family. Whereupon the Prussian captain, saying that he is a freebooter, declares his life forfeit and orders him shot for joining in the fight, but offers to pardon him if he will lead the Prussian troops through the woods. Dominic indignantly refuses. Alone in prison Dominic in a moving song bids farewell to life and home. Franchette, climbing to his window, points out to him a way of escape and gives him the details.

In the third act Dominic, after climbing out of his window, is discovered by the sentry, whom in the ensuing scuffle he stabs and mortally wounds. He has used Franchette's knife in doing so, and has dropped that before he escapes. Soldiers rush in and make Merlier and his daughter prisoners. Merlier is held responsible for the murder of the sentry. Although the miller knows the hiding place of Dominic, his future son-in-law, he resolves not to give up the latter to the enemy, as has been demanded, and rather to suffer the death penalty himself in order not to destroy Franchette's happiness. He informs the Prussian commanding officer that he is ready to undergo the full penalty. Franchette is unable to bear the strain and falls unconscious to the ground.

The fourth act opens again in the place before the mill. It is dawn. Marcelline, the housekeeper, looks about her and notes the Prussians wrapped in slumber.

Franchette appears, and a trumpet signal is heard telling of an approaching body of French soldiers. Dominic steals into the yard in disguise. He has wandered about the woods all night, unquiet regarding the fate of his friends. His sweetheart dares not tell him the truth. Just then Merlier and the Prussian captain enter, and Merlier, in an aside, implores his daughter not to reveal the facts, for fear that Dominic will spoil his plan. So they all purposely mislead Dominic. He thinks all is well. French bugles are heard again, and Merlier, in order to save at least his daughter and her betrothed, orders Dominic to run and advise the approaching French troops to come to the rescue. He bids farewell to his daughter, reminding her of happy days. Franchette thinks the Prussian captain has relented, and is calmed. The French soldiers appear at the same time as the Prussians, and just when the mill and its inhabitants seem safe at last, the Prussian commander gives orders to shoot Merlier, who falls riddled with bullets.

L'AUBE ROUGE

Tragic Opera in two acts by CAMILLE ERLANGER

Text by M. MARCON

This opera had its première at Rouen, in 1912.

Act. I. Olga is informed by her father, a Russian general named Lavaroff, that her lover Serge, a Nihilist, is dead in Siberia. Her father urges her to marry a famous French surgeon, M. Ruys. But Serge appears at the wedding supper, and Olga flees with him to the haunts of the Nihilists in the Quartier Latin, Paris. There Serge and she devote themselves with great enthusiasm to the "cause." Serge is chosen by his comrades to throw a bomb at a reactionary Russian diplomat visiting Paris. The struggle in his soul between his love for Olga and his devotion to his fellows is great, and he hesitates. His comrades, deeming him a traitor, sentence him to death. But the shot merely inflicts a severe wound, and he is taken to the hospital. When he wakes there from his narcotic slumber he finds he has been saved by the skill of his rival, the famous surgeon Ruys. Feeling conscious, however, of his duty to his mates he throws the bomb and is killed in the explosion. His sweetheart Olga becomes insane.

BALLO IN MASCHERA

or

GUSTAVUS THE THIRD

Opera in five acts by AUBER

Text by SCRIBE

This opera has had a curious fate, its historical background having excited resistance and given rise to scruples. The murder of a king was not thought a fit subject for an opera, and so the libretto was altered and spoilt.

The Italians simply changed the names and the scene of action; Verdi composed a new opera from the same matter and succeeded admirably the music being original and vivacious, as well as full of pleasant harmony and fine instrumentation.

The scene is laid in Stockholm in the year 1792. Gustavus the Third, King of Sweden, loves the wife of his friend and counsellor Ankarström, and is loved in return, both struggling vainly against this sinful passion. Ankarström has detected a plot against the King's life, and, warning him, asks that the traitor be punished, but Gustavus refuses to listen, trusting in his people and in his friend's fidelity. His minister Kaulbart desires him to condemn a sorceress named Arvedson, who is said to be able at will, by means of certain herbs and potions, to cause persons to love or hate each other. The King refuses to banish the woman unheard and decides to visit her. Ankarström tries to dissuade, but the King insists, and accordingly goes to Arvedson in disguise. During the witch's conjuration, Malwina, his lady-love, appears, who seeks help from the sorceress against her forbidden passion. The concealed King hears Arvedson tell her to go at midnight and gather a herb which grows on the graves of criminals, and, triumphant in his knowledge of Malwina's confessed love, Gustavus decides to follow her there.

When she has gone he mockingly orders the witch to tell him his fortune, and hears from her that he shall be killed by the man who first tenders him his hand. Just then Ankarström, who comes to protect the King against his enemy, enters, and they shake hands.

In the third act Malwina meets the King on the dismal spot to which she had been directed, but Ankarström, whose watchful fidelity never suffers him to be far from the King, and who is utterly ignorant of the deception being practised upon him, saves the lovers from further guilt. After a severe conflict with himself, Gustavus consents to fly in his friend's cloak, Ankarström having pledged his honor not to ask the veiled lady's secret, and to conduct her safely back to the city. This plan is frustrated by the conspirators, who rush in and are about to attack the Count. Malwina throws herself between him and the combatants, and the husband then recognizes in the King's companion his own wife. Full of indignation, he turns from her and joins the conspirators, promising to be one of them.

He swears to kill his unhappy wife, but not until another has first fallen.

In the fourth act the conspirators have a meeting in Ankarström's house, where they decide to murder the King. The lots being cast, the duty to strike the deathblow falls on Ankarström, and Malwina herself draws the fatal paper. At this moment an invitation to a masked ball is brought by the King's page Oscar, and the conspirators resolve to take advantage of this opportunity for the execution of their design.

In the last act the King, happy to know Malwina safe from discovery, resolves to sacrifice his love to honor and friendship. He is about to give Ankarström the proof of his friendship, by naming him Governor of Finland, and the minister is to depart with his wife on the morning after the ball. Meanwhile the King is warned, by a missive from an unknown hand, not to appear at the ball, but he disregards it. He meets Malwina at the ball. His page, thinking to do the King a service, has betrayed his mask to Ankarström. Malwina warns the prince, but in vain, for, while he presents her with the paper which is to send her and her husband to their own beloved country, Ankarström shoots him through the heart. Gustavus dies, pardoning his murderer.

BALLO IN MASCHERA

A Lyric Drama in five acts by VERDI

Text by F. M. PIAVE

Auber's success with the opera of the same name inspired Verdi to try his hand at it. He ordered his friend Piave to write the libretto for him, and in 1854 the opera was handed to the San Carlo Theatre in Naples, but was refused on the ground that the murder of a king must not be represented on the stage. Then Verdi laid the scene in Boston, and in this shape the opera was performed in Rome on Feb. 17, 1859, and met with great success.

From this time it conquered the stages of Europe, all but one, Auber's widow having stipulated that no opera rival to that of her husband's was to be given in Paris. The Ballo in Maschera was revived in Dresden in October, 1897, after having lain buried for over fifteen years; its success showed that it is still full of vitality. The music is exceedingly fresh and characteristic; indeed it surpasses both Trovatore and Rigoletto in beauty and originality. Verdi has scarcely ever written anything finer than the ensemble at the end of the second act, and the delightful quartetto "Is it a jest or madness, that comes now from her lips?"

The libretto may be explained shortly, as it is almost identical with Auber's Masked Ball.

Count Richard, Governor of Boston, is adored by the people, but hated by the noblemen, who resolve upon his death. He loves Amelia, the wife of his secretary and best friend René, who in vain tries to warn him of the plots of his enemies, but who faithfully watches over his safety.

An old sorceress of negro blood, Ulrica, is to be banished by the decree of the high judge, but Richard's page Oscar speaks in her favor, and the Count decides to see her himself and test her tricks. He invites his lords to accompany him to the sibyl's dwelling, and orders Osçar to bring him a fisherman's disguise. His enemies Samuel and Tom follow him.

The second act shows Ulrica in her cottage, seated at a table, conjuring Satan. A crowd of people are around her, amongst them Richard in disguise. A sailor, Sylvan, advances first to hear his fate, and while Ulrica is prophesying that better days await him, Richard slips a roll of gold with a scroll into Sylvan's pocket and so makes the witch's words true. Sylvan, searching in his pockets, finds the gold and reads the inscription on the roll: "Richard to his dear officer Sylvan," and all break out into loud praises of the clever sibyl.

A short while after a servant announces Amelia, and the sorceress, driving the crowd away, ushers her in, while Richard conceals himself. He listens with delight to the confession of her sinful love for himself, against which she asks for a draught which might enable her to banish it from her heart. Ulrica advises her to pluck at midnight a magic herb which grows in the field where the criminals are executed. Amelia shudders, but promises to do as she is bidden, while Richard secretly vows to follow and protect her. Amelia departs, and the people flock in again. Richard is the first to ask what is his fate. The sibyl reluctantly tells him that his life is to be destroyed by the first person who shall touch his hand on this very day. Richard vainly offers his hand to the bystanders, they all recoil from him, when suddenly his friend René comes in, and heartily shakes Richard's outstretched hand. This seems to break the spell, for everybody knows René to be the Count's dearest friend, and now believes the oracle to be false. Nevertheless Ulrica, who only now recognizes the Count, warns him once more against his enemies, but he laughs at her, and shows the sorceress the verdict of her banishment, which, however, he has cancelled. Full of gratitude, Ulrica joins in the universal song of praise sung by the people to their faithful leader.

The third act opens on the ghostly field where Amelia is to look for the magic herb. She is frozen with horror, believing that she sees a ghost rise before her; Richard now turns up, and breaks out into passionate words, entreating her to acknowledge her love for him. She does so, but implores him at the same time not to approach her, and to remain true to his friend. While they speak René surprises them. He has followed Richard to save him from his enemies, who are waiting to kill him. Richard wraps himself in his friend's cloak, after having taken René's promise to lead the veiled lady to the gates of the town without trying to look at her. René swears, but fate wills it otherwise, for hardly has Richard departed when the conspirators throng in, and, enraged at finding only the friend, try to tear the veil off the lady's face. René guards her with his sword, but Amelia, springing between the assailers, lets fall her veil, and reveals her face to her husband and to the astonished men, thereby bringing shame and bitter mockery on them both. René, believing himself betrayed by wife and friend, asks the conspirators to meet him in his own house on the following morning, and swears to avenge the supposed treachery.

In the fourth act, in his own house, René bids his wife prepare herself for death. He disbelieves in her protests of innocence, but at last, touched by her misery, he allows her to take a last farewell of her son. When she is gone he resolves rather to kill the seducer than his poor weak wife. When the conspirators enter he astonishes them by his knowledge of their dark designs, but they wonder still more when he offers to join them in their evil purpose. As they do not agree who it shall be that is to kill Richard, René makes his wife draw the lot from a vase on the table. The chosen one is her own husband. At this moment Oscar enters with an invitation to a masked ball from the court. René accepts, and the conspirators decide to seize the opportunity to put their foe to death. They are to wear blue dominoes with red ribbons; their password is "death."

The next scene shows a richly decorated ballroom. René vainly tries to find out the Count's disguise, until it is betrayed to him by the page, who believes that René wants to have some fun with his master. Amelia, waylaying Richard, implores him to fly, and when he disbelieves her warnings shows him her face. When he recognizes her he tenderly takes her hand, and tells her that he too has resolved to conquer his passions, and that he is sending her away to England with her husband. They are taking a last farewell, but, alas, fate overtakes Richard in the shape of René, who runs his dagger through him. The crowd tries to arrest the murderer, but the dying Count waves them back and with his last breath tells his unhappy friend that his wife is innocent. Drawing forth a document and hanging it to René, the unfortunate man reads the Count's order to send them to their native country. Richard pardons his misguided friend and dies with a blessing on his beloved country.

THE BARBER OF BAGDAD

Comic Opera in two acts by PETER CORNELIUS

It was a long time before this charming little opera took its place amongst so many fellow operas much less entitled to notice. The composer had died 15 years previously, without having gained the success he so fully deserved as poet as well as composer.

Liszt, the great redeemer of many a tried genius, brought the opera upon the stage on the 15th of December, 1858, in Weimar.

But the Intendant Dingelstedt was against him; the opera proved an entire failure, though it was meant more as demonstration against Liszt than against the opera. Liszt, tired of these disgraceful intrigues, quitted Weimar, only to return there from time to time in private. With his abdication, Weimar's glorious time was past. In 1889 at last the Barber of Bagdad took its rightful place after many years of oblivion.

Munich, Mannheim and Vienna came first, and, the music having been enthusiastically applauded, Dresden followed the good example in October, 1890. The music is full of sweet melody, the composition masterfully set. Its comic parts are not quite natural, but the lyric is almost classical, and the text, written by the composer himself, though lacking in action, shows that Cornelius was a true poet as well as a true musician.

The scene takes place in Bagdad, in the house of a wealthy young Mussulman called Nurredin. He is lying on a couch, surrounded by his servants, who think him dying. But it is only the flame of love which devours his strength and deprives him of all energy. As soon as Bostana, an old relative and companion of his lady-love, appears, in order to tell him that Margiana, his adored, is willing to receive him, Nurredin forgets his illness and only longs for the promised interview. The ensuing duet between him and Bostana, wherein she gives instruction about time and hour of the rendezvous, is delightfully fresh and piquant.

As Nurredin has neglected his personal appearance during his malady his first wish is for a barber, who is speedily sent to him by Bostana. This old worthy, Abul Hassan Ali Ebe Bekar, the barber, makes him desperate by his vain prattle. Having solemnly saluted Nurredin, he warns him not to leave the house today, as his horoscope tells him that his life is in danger. The young man not heeding him, Abul Hassan begins to enumerate all his talents as astrologer, philologer, philosopher, etc.; in short, he is everything and knows everything. When Nurredin orders him to begin his shaving he relates the fate of his six brothers, who all died before him and always of love. At last Nurredin's patience giving way, he calls his servants in to throw the old dotard out of doors. But Abul drives them all back, and Nurredin tries to pacify him with flattery, and finally succeeds.

Now Abul is curious, as all barbers are, and having heard Nurredin's sighs he determines to find out all about the young man's love. This scene is most ludicrous, when Abul sings his air "Margiana," which name he has heard from Nurredin's lips, and the latter is in despair at being left with only one side of his head shaved. This great work done at last, Abul wants to accompany the young lover to the house of the Cadi

Baba Mustapha, Margiana's father. Nurredin again summons his servants, who begin to surround Abul, pretending to doctor him. Nurredin escapes, but Abul, after having shaken off the servants, runs after him.

The second act takes place in the Cadi's house.

Margiana is full of sweet anticipation, while her father, who has already chosen a husband for his daughter in the person of an old friend of his youth, shows her a large trunk full of gifts from the old bridegroom. Margiana admires them obediently. A musical scene of surpassing beauty follows, where we hear the call of the Muezzin summoning the faithful to prayer. It is also the sign for Nurredin to appear. The Cadi hurries to the Mosque, and Bostana introduces the lover. Here ensues a charming love-duet, accompanied, originally enough, by a song from the old barber, who watches before the house. Suddenly they are interrupted by cries of alarm, and with dismay they learn from Bostana that the Cadi has returned to punish a slave who has broken a precious vase.

Nurredin, unable to escape unobserved, is hidden in the big trunk. Meanwhile Abul, having heard the slave's cries, and mistaking them for Nurredin's, summons the latter's servants and breaks into the Cadi's house to avenge his young friend, whom he believes to be murdered. Bostana angrily bids him carry away the trunk, signifying to him whom she has hidden in it, but the Cadi intervenes, believing the servants to be thieves who want to rob his daughter's treasure. The rumor of the murder gradually penetrates the whole town; its inhabitants gather before the house, and the appointed wailing women mingle their doleful lamentations with the general uproar. At last the Calif himself appears in order to settle the quarrel.

The Cadi accuses the barber of theft, while Abul calls the Cadi a murderer. To throw light upon the matter the Calif orders the trunk to be opened, which is done with great hesitation by Margiana. When the lid gives way, Nurredin is lying in it in a deep swoon. All are terrified, believing him to be murdered, but Abul, caressing him, declares that his heart still throbs. The Calif bids the barber show his art, and Abul wakens Nurredin by the love-song to Margiana. The young man revives, and the truth dawns upon the deceived father's mind. The Calif, a very humane and clement prince, feels great sympathy with the beautiful young couple, and advises the Cadi to let his daughter have her treasure, because he had told them himself that it was Margiana's treasure, kept hidden in the trunk.

The Cadi consents, while the Calif bids the funny barber come to his palace to entertain him with his stories, and invites all present to the wedding of the betrothed pair, to the great satisfaction of the people, who sing their Salaam Alëikum in praise of their prince —a brilliant finale, full of energy and melody.

IL BARBIERE DI SEVIGLIA

Comic Opera in two acts by ROSSINI

This opera may be called a miracle of Rossini's creation, as it not only is his best work but was written by him in a fortnight, a performance nearly incredible, for the music is so finely worked out, and so elegant, that the opera has grown to be a favorite with all nations.

The subject, taken from Beaumarchais's witty trilogy of "Figaros," had ere this lent inspiration to more than one composer; Mozart's "Figaro," though done before the "Barbiere," is in a certain sense the continuation of Rossini's opera.

The Barbiere had the peculiar misfortune to experience an utter reverse on the occasion of its first representation. It was composed for the Duke Cesarini, proprietor of the Argentina Theatre in Rome, and the cabals and intrigues of Paësiello's partisans (who had composed the same subject) turned the balance in Rossini's disfavor. But on the second evening good taste prevailed, and since then the opera has been a universal favorite.

Beaumarchais's tale was worked out anew by the Roman poet Sterbini; in our opera it runs as follows:

Count Almaviva is enamored of Rosina, the ward of Doctor Bartolo. She is most jealously guarded by the old man, who wishes to make her his own wife. In vain the Count serenades her; she does not appear, and he must needs invent some other means of attaining his object. Making the acquaintance of the lighthearted and cunning barber Figaro, the latter advises him to get entrance into Bartolo's house in the guise of a soldier possessing a billet of quartering for his lodgings. Rosina herself has not failed to hear the sweet love-songs of the Count, known to her only under the simple name of Lindoro; and with southern passion, and the light-heartedness which characterizes all the persons who figure in this opera, but which is not to be mistaken for frivolity, Rosina loves her nice lover, and is willing to be his own. Figaro has told her of Almaviva's love, and in return she gives him a note, which she has written in secret. But the old Doctor is a sly fox, he has seen the inky little finger, and determines to keep his eyes open.

When the Count appears in the guise of a half-drunken dragoon the Doctor sends Rosina away, and tries to put the soldier out of the house, pretending to have a license against all billets. The Count resists and, while Bartolo seeks for his license, makes love to Rosina, but after the Doctor's return there arises such an uproar that all the neighbors and finally the guards appear, who counsel the Count to retire for a time.

In the second act the Count gains entrance to Bartolo's house as a singing-master who is deputed to give a lesson instead of the fever-stricken Basilio. Of course the music lesson is turned into a love lesson.

When all seems to be going well the real Maestro, Basilio, enters and all but frustrates their plans. With gold and promises Figaro bribes him to retreat, and the lovers agree to flee on the coming night.

Almost at the last moment the cunning of Bartolo hinders the projected elopement. He shows a letter, which Rosina has written, and makes Rosina believe that her lover, whom she only knows as Lindoro, in concert with Figaro is betraying her to the Count. Great is her joy when she detects that Lindoro and Count Almaviva are one and the same person, and that he loves her as truly as ever. They bribe the old notary who has been sent for by Bartolo to arrange his own (Bartolo's) wedding with Rosina. Bartolo signs the contract of marriage, with Figaro as witness, and detects too late that he has been duped, and that he has himself united the lovers. At last he submits with pretty good grace to the inevitable, and contents himself with Rosina's dower, which the Count generously transfers to him.

THE BARTERED BRIDE

Comic Opera in three acts by FR. SMETANA

Libretto by K. SABINA

Poor Smetana! Nature had put on his brow the stamp of genius, but he never lived to see his glory. After grief and sorrow and direst need he died in a mad house, and now posterity heaps laurels on his grave. "The Bartered Bride" has been represented in Prague over 300 times, and it begins to take possession of every noted stage in Europe.

The subject forms a simple village idyll, without any strong contrasts. Its ethical motive lies in its representation of quaint old customs and in the deep-rooted patriotic love; but the whole opera is literally steeped in euphony.

The overture has its equal only in "Figaro," and a perfect stream of national airs flows through the whole.

The first chorus, "See the buds open on the bush," is most original, the national dance in the second act is full of fire, and the rope-dancers' march is truly Slavonic in its quaintness.

The scene is laid in a village in Bohemia. It is Spring-Kirmess, and everybody is gay. Only Mary, the daughter of the rich peasant Kruschina, carries a heavy heart within her, for the day has come on which the unknown bridegroom, chosen by her parents, will claim her hand. She loves Hans, known to her as a poor servant, who has come to her village lately, and who is in reality her bridegroom's half-brother. He consoles her, beseeching her to cheer up and be faithful to him, and then tells her that he comes of wealthy people. Having lost his mother early, his father wedded a second wife, who estranged his heart from the poor boy so that he had to gain his daily bread abroad. She deeply sympathizes with him, without guessing his real name.

Meanwhile, Mary's parents approach with the matchmaker, Kezul, a personage common in Bohemia, who has already won Kruschina's consent to his daughter's marriage with Wenzel, son of the rich farmer Micha by a second marriage. Mary's mother insisting that her child's will is to be consulted before all, the father consents to let her see the bridegroom before she decides. Kezul, though angry at this unlooked for obstacle, excuses the bridegroom's absence volubly, and sings his praise loudly, at the same time touching upon the elder son's absence, and hinting that he may probably be dead. When Mary steps in, Kezul woos her in due form, but is at once repulsed by her. The young girl owns to having given her heart to the humble servant Hans, in whom nobody has yet recognized Micha's son. Father Kruschina angrily asserts his promise to Kezul, cursing Wenzel's timidity, which hindered him from making his proposal in person. Kezul, however, resolves to talk Hans over to reason.

We find him in the second act, singing and highly praising the god of love. Afterward the would-be bridegroom, Wenzel, finds himself face to face with Mary, whom he does not know. When he tells her of his purpose, timidly and stammeringly, she asks him if he is not ashamed to woo a girl who loves another man, and who does not love him in the least. She at last so frightens the lad that he promises to look out for another

Louis D'Angelo and Mario Chamlee in "The Bartered Bride"

bride, if his mother permits him. Mary flirts with him, until he swears never to claim Kruschina's daughter. Meanwhile Kezul does his best to convert Hans. He promises to provide for him another bride, much richer than Mary, but Hans refuses. He offers him money, first one, then two, then three hundred florins. Hans, looking incredulous, asks: "For whom are you wooing my bride?" "For Micha's son," the matchmaker replies. "Well," says Hans, "if you promise me that Micha's son shall have her, and no other, I will sign the contract, and I further stipulate that Micha's father shall have no right to reclaim the money later; he is the one to bear the whole costs of the bargain." Kezul gladly consents and departs to fetch the witnesses, before whom Hans once more renounces his bride in favor of Micha's son. He coolly takes the money, at which they turn from him in disgust, and signs his name Hans Ehrentraut at the foot of the document.

The third act opens with a performance by tight-rope dancers. Wenzel, who has been quite despondent about his promised bride, is enraptured by their skill. He especially admires the Spanish dancer Esmeralda, who bewitches him so entirely that he woos her. The director of the band, being in want of a dancing bear, is not loath to take advantage of the lad's foolishness. He engages him as a dancer, and easily overcomes Wenzel's scruples by promising him Esmeralda's hand. Just when they are putting him in bear's skin, his parents appear on the scene with the marriage contract. To their great dismay he refuses to sign it, and when pressed runs away. Meanwhile, Mary has heard of her lover's fickleness, which she would fain disbelieve, but, alas! Kezul shows her the document by which Hans renounces her. Nevertheless, she refuses to wed any other man than the one her heart has chosen. Wenzel, approaching again and recognizing in Mary the bride he had renounced, is now quite sorry to give her up, and very willing to take her if she will only yield. Mary, praying to be left alone for a little while, abandons herself to her grief and is thus found by Hans, whom she bitterly reproaches for his faithlessness. But he only smiles, and recalls the whole chorus, coolly saying that it is his wish that Mary should wed Micha's son. That is too much for poor Mary's feelings. She declares that she is ready to do as they wish, but before she signs the contract, Hans steps forth in full view of his parents, who at last recognize in him their long-lost eldest son. Though his stepmother, Agnes, is in a rage about his trick, he claims his rights as son and heir, and the bride, of course, is not loath to choose between the two brothers. Kezul, the matchmaker, retires shamefaced, and when Wenzel shows himself in the last scene as a dancing bear, and stammeringly assures the laughing public that they need not be afraid of him, as he is "not a bear but only Wenzel," the final blow is dealt whereby he loses all favor in the eyes of Kruschina, who is now quite reconciled to give his daughter to Micha's elder son.

BÉATRICE ET BENEDICT

Opera in two acts by HECTOR BERLIOZ

The libretto is based on Shakespeare's comedy, "Much Ado About Nothing"

The first production of this opera was given at Baden-Baden in 1862.

Don Pedro, after a victorious campaign against the Moors, returns in triumph to Messina. But he finds that warlike Moslems are easier to subdue than the brilliant and captious Beatrice, Leonato's niece, whom he wishes to marry to Benedict, one of his officers. Hero, Leonato's daughter, is betrothed to Claudio, another of Don Pedro's gallant captains.

The marriage of Hero and Claudio is being celebrated with magnificent ceremonies. While the musicians rehearse the wedding serenade, Benedict, weary of the piqued indifference of Beatrice, seeks peace in the gardens of the palace. Here his friends come to him and tell him that Beatrice really loves him devotedly. At the same time her friends are busy assuring Beatrice that she will be most unwise to disdain the gallant officer's wooing. While Hero's wedding feast is in progress within the governor's palace, Beatrice and Benedict chance to meet in the garden. After a spirited quarrel, the young lovers exchange vows of eternal fidelity.

BENVENUTO CELLINI

Opera in three acts by HECTOR BERLIOZ

Text by de WAILLY and BARBIER, translated into German by PETER CORNELIUS

This opera by the spirited French musician has had a singular fate. Composed more than forty years ago, it never had in France the success it merited; a "succès d'estime" was the only result. Liszt, who was the savior of many a talented struggler, was the first to recognize the genius of the French composer. He brought the opera out upon the stage at Weimar, but without much success. Berlioz was not understood by the public. Devrient, in Carlsruhe, tried a similar experiment and failed, and so the opera was almost forgotten, until Germany, remembering the duty owed to genius, of whatever nationality it may be, placed it upon the stage in Dresden, on the 4th of November, 1888, under the leadership of one of the ablest of modern interpreters of music, Director Schuch. Its representation was a triumph. Though Berlioz can in nowise be compared with Wagner, whose music is much more realistic and sensual, Wagner may nevertheless be said to have opened a path for Berlioz's style, which, though melodious, differs widely from that of the easy-flowing Italian school, being more serious, as well as more difficult for the musical novice to understand. This explains why Berlioz's compatriots esteemed but never liked him; he was too scientific. Today our ears and understanding are better prepared for striking intervals and complicated orchestration, which latter is the most brilliant feature in the opera.

Indeed the instrumentation is simply perfect, the choruses are masterpieces of originality, life and melody, and the rhythm, with its syncopes, is so remarkable that one is more than justified in calling the style unique; it is Berlioz and no other.

The text is far less good than the music, though the hero, whose life Goethe found worthy of description in the 24th and 25th volume of his works, might well interest. The libretto is by no means strictly historical, and suffers from improbabilities which can only be excused in an opera.

The tale is laid in Rome in the year 1532, under Pope Clement VII, and comprises the events of three days, Monday before Shrove-tide, Shrove-Tuesday and Ash-Wednesday. Benvenuto Cellini, the Tuscan goldsmith, has been called to Rome by the Pope, in order to embellish the city with his masterpieces. He loves Teresa, the daughter of the old papal treasurer Balducci, and the love is mutual. At the same time another suitor, Fieramosca, the Pope's sculptor, is favored by her father. Old Balducci grumbles in the first scene at the Pope's predilection for Cellini, declaring that such an excellent sculptor as Fieramosca ought to suffice. He goes for a walk, and Cellini finds Teresa alone. To save her from Fieramosca he plans an elopement, selecting the close of the Carnival as the time best suited for carrying out their design. The rendezvous is to be the Piazza di Colonna, where he will wait for her, disguised as a monk in white, accompanied by a Capuchin, his pupil Ascanio. Unhappily the rival Fieramosca has entered unseen, and overheard all. The ensuing terzetto is a masterpiece. While the lovers are bidding each other farewell Balducci returns; and Cellini has scarcely time to hide behind the window-curtain before he enters. The father is surprised to find his daughter still up, and Teresa, seeking for an excuse to send him away, feigns to be frightened by a thief in her chamber. There Balducci finds the hapless Fieramosca hidden, and Cellini meanwhile escapes. Balducci and his daughter calling for help, all the female servants and women of the neighborhood appear armed with brooms and wooden spoons. They fall upon the hapless lover, and finally force him to escape through the window.

In the second act we find Cellini in a tavern with his pupils and friends. They have no money left to pay for their wine, when Ascanio brings gold from the Pope, which, however, he only delivers after Cellini has given a solemn promise to finish at once the statue of Perseus he is engaged upon. Great is the general wrath when they find the money consists of but a paltry sum, and they resolve to avenge themselves on the avaricious treasurer, Balducci, by personating him in the theatre. Fieramosca, who has again been eavesdropping, turns for help to his friend Pompeo, a bravo. And they decide to outwit Cellini, by adopting the same costumes as he and his pupil.

The scene changes; we see the Piazza di Colonna, and the theatre in which the pantomime of King Midas is acted. Balducci, who is there with his daughter among the spectators, recognizes in the snoring king a portrait of himself, and furiously advances to grapple with him. Cellini profits by the ensuing tumult to approach Teresa, but at the same time Fieramosca comes up with Pompeo, and Teresa cannot discern which is the true lover, owing to the masks. A fight ensues, in which Cellini stabs Pompeo. He is arrested, and Teresa flies with the Capuchin Ascanio to Cellini's atelier.

The enraged people are about to lynch the murderer, when three cannon shots are fired announcing that it is Ash-Wednesday; the lights are extinguished, and Cellini escapes in the darkness.

The third act represents Cellini's atelier with the workmen in it. Teresa, not finding her lover, is in great distress. Ascanio consoles her, and when the Miserere of the Penitents is heard both join in the prayer to the Holy Virgin.

Suddenly Cellini rushes in, and, embracing Teresa, relates that he fled the night before into a house. A procession of penitent monks passing by in the morning he joined them, as their white cowls were similar to his own disguise. He decides to escape at once to Florence with Teresa, but is already pursued by Balducci, who appears with Fieramosca and insists on his daughter's returning and marrying the latter. At this moment the Cardinal Salviati steps in to look for the statue. He is highly indignant that Cellini, thoughtless like all artists, has not kept his promise. Hearing him, moreover, accused by Balducci, he threatens severe punishment, and finally declares that Perseus shall be cast by another. Cellini, in the pride of genius and full of rage, seizes a hammer, and, surrounded by his workmen, declares that he will rather destroy his work than see it finished by another.

The Cardinal, overcome by fear of the loss, changes his tactics, and, in compliance with Cellini's request, promises him full pardon and Teresa's hand if he finishes Perseus in an hour's time, as Cellini offers to do. Should he fail in his gigantic task, his life will be forfeit.

All set to work at once; even Fieramosca, at the Cardinal's request, assists. More and more metal is demanded; Cellini sacrifices all his masterpieces in gold and silver. At last the casting is completed. Cellini breaks the mould, and the statue of Perseus shines faultlessly forth, a wonder of art, a thing of glory, bringing immortality to its maker. All present bend before the greatness of genius, and Fieramosca, the rival in art and love, is the first to kiss and embrace Cellini, who obtains full pardon and the hand of Teresa, along with her father's blessing.

Scene from "La Boheme" as given by the San Francisco Opera Company. From left to right: Ezio Pinza, Alfredo Gandolfi, Dino Borgioli, Lucrezia Bori and Richard Bonelli

LA BOHÈME

Opera in four acts by GIACOMO PUCCINI

Text by G. GIACOSA and L. ILLIČA

This charming opera was first presented at the Regio Theatre, Turin, February 1, 1896, and has been widely popular ever since. The material was gathered from Mürger's novel "Ve de Bohème," and the music, which is thoroughly Italian in character, is full of life and vigor, interspersed here and there with rare touches of sweetness and grace.

The scene is laid in the Quartier Latin of Paris in the year 1830, and the first act opens in a bare attic studio where Marcel, an artist, and his friend Rudolph, a poet, are seen huddled over a small stove, endeavoring to keep themselves warm by burning the numerous manuscripts of the good-natured poet. They are shortly joined by their friends Colline, a philosopher, and Schaunard, a musician. These four Bohemians form an inseparable quartet, who live, love, and work together in perfect harmony. They live entirely by their wits, spending their money freely when they have it, and cheerfully submitting to misfortune when she sees fit to frown upon them. Greatly to the surprise of his friends, Schaunard produces a pocket full of gold, with which they immediately purchase the much needed fuel, and a sumptuous feast. Their appetites not yet being appeased they decide to visit a nearby café to continue their meal, but Rudolph who has an important manuscript to finish, remains behind, promising to join them presently. He is interrupted in his work by a knock at the door, and Mimi, a beautiful flower girl who rooms below, enters to beg the loan of a candle. Her refined features and graceful figure appeal to the artistic sense of Rudolph, who immediately falls in love with her and induces her to accompany him to the Café Momus, where his friends are dining. In the midst of their jolly meal, Mademoiselle Musetta, a pretty and coquettish damsel, enters in company with a pompous old gentleman named Alcindoro, and they seat themselves at an adjoining table. It so happens that Musetta is an old-time love of Marcel's, and on seeing him she declares that the shoes she has on are pinching, and begs her dignified escort to go out and purchase a larger pair. As soon as he disappears, Musetta joins the merry Bohemians, and leaving both bills for poor old Alcindoro to pay they take their departure.

After a time Mimi and Musetta become dissatisfied with their Bohemian lovers on account of their poverty, as their chief ambition in life is to wear fine clothes and ride in broughams. They therefore leave them to seek the luxuries offered elsewhere. Their hearts, however, still yearn for their old lovers and the delightful little suppers of the Quartier Latin.

Rudolph and Marcel lead lonely and dejected lives after the departure of their sweethearts, and secretly long for the return of the old happy days. Some months after, while in the studio discussing the virtues of their respective loves, Musetta suddenly rushes in upon them in a state of great agitation, exclaiming that the deserted Mimi is below, half starved and dying. Rudolph runs madly down the stairs, and bringing up the unconscious girl in his arms, lays her tenderly upon the couch, and pours forth the love of his heart in her willing ear, swearing that never shall they be parted again. Soothed by his words of love, Mimi falls into a deep and peaceful sleep. The others, in the meantime, have brought food and medicine for the patient, and Rudolph going softly to the bedside to awaken her, finds that she has passed away. With an agonizing cry he falls sobbing on her lifeless body, while his sorrowful friends, dazed at the suddenness of the catastrophe, gather in pitying silence around them.

THE BOHEMIAN GIRL

Opera in three acts. Music by M. W. BALFE

Text by ALFRED BUNN, founded on "The Gypsy," by ST. GEORGES and MARZILLIER

This English sentimental opera, one of the earliest successful ones, was originally produced in London, 1843. The romantic plot has its scene laid in Hungary, the time being the 18th century. This operatic work is one of the most tuneful, although florid in style.

Count Arnheim, the imperial governor of Pressburg, Hungary, in the first act has in his palace assembled a vast number of nobles, retainers and servants for the chase. Not far away, on the banks of the Danube, a statue of the emperor is being unveiled with impressive ceremonies, the Austrian flag being raised. Count Arnheim and his nephew, Florestan, enter, and Arline, his little daughter, is being affectionately greeted by him. They all leave together, and the place before the castle is empty, when Thaddeus, a Polish nobleman in exile, rushes forth, and perceiving the statue of the emperor, he becomes aware that he is still in danger of discovery and death, and looks about for means of disguising himself. A wandering band of gypsies opportunely puts in an appearance, and their leader, Devilshoof, is spoken to by Thaddeus, who implores his help. He promises Thaddeus immediate assistance, puts him in gypsy garb, and makes him join the band. The pursuing soldiery are thrown off the right track, and the Pole goes off with the gypsies. Meanwhile Arline and her attendant have been attacked by some wild beast that was being pursued by the Count's huntsmen, and a fear is entertained that she may have been killed. Florestan has fled from the onslaught of the quarry, and Thaddeus, coming upon him in the deep woods, and hearing the latter's tale, wrests the weapon from his grasp, and hastens to the defense of the child. While everybody is still searching for the Count's little daughter, Thaddeus returns with her in safety. In recognition of his services the father thanks him and invites him to a banquet at the castle. Thaddeus, being urged, finally accepts. During the meal a toast is being drunk to the emperor, but the Pole haughtily declines to do so, splashing the contents of his goblet at the statue of the monarch. Count Arnheim remembers that Thaddeus is the savior of little Arline, forgives him, throws him a purse of gold for his reward, and bids him begone. The nobles present are about to seize the hot-headed Pole, when Devilshoof comes on the scene, threatening those who wish to harm the man he has taken under his protection.

Devilshoof, thereupon, himself is over-powered and cast into a dungeon, while Thaddeus is permitted to leave unharmed. But a short while after the word comes that Arline, left for a few moments to herself in her room, has vanished, and on search being made it is seen that the gypsy chief has escaped from his cell. He is seen by his pursuers climbing a steep mountain path, holding the girl in his arms. He eludes the retainers of the Count, by fleeing into the woods across a fallen tree trunk, and casting it behind him down the chasm.

Twelve years are supposed to have elapsed, and Arline is next seen asleep in the tent of the gypsy queen, Thaddeus guarding them, while the band are off on a nocturnal venture. Florestan, nephew of the Count, is robbed by the gypsies when returning from a drinking bout, and is despoiled of all his valuables. Count Arnheim is still mourning his daughter for lost or dead, never having been able in all that time to trace her. The gypsy queen, however, has Florestan summoned before her, and returns all his stolen property to him, save a gem-encrusted locket, Devilshoof having secreted that without her knowledge. There follows a scene in which Thaddeus declares his love for Arline, the latter having now become a very lovely young woman. They exchange vows, and he tells her of the adventure years before, when he rescued her from death, but he does not disclose her real identity. Then, at fair time, in Pressburg, Count Arnheim and his nephew are accidentally observing a group of gypsies, and Florestan falls in love with Arline's beauty. Later on he makes advances to her, but the girl spurns him. The gypsy queen artfully praises her for her independence of spirit, and adorns her with the locket as a reward. Florestan, angered at his being repulsed, causes the arrest of both Arline and Thaddeus, who had vigorously interfered with Florestan's pretensions.

In the justice hall of his palace is the Count, indulging in sad reminiscences of his vanished child. Just then Arline is brought before him on the charge of theft. The girl only now sees through the perfidy of the gypsy queen who, out of revenge for the preference shown by Thaddeus for Arline, instead of herself, has resorted to the ruse of decking her rival in stolen jewels. Arline too late discovers that she had no defense to make against the accusation, and in despair tries to stab herself. The Count stops her hand, and in doing so sees the tell-tale scar upon his daughter's wrist. Thaddeus, having just recovered his liberty, impressively confirms the girl's own story, and he and Devilshoof disappear during a scene of general rejoicing.

The third and last act shows Arline in the great hall of her father's palace, awaiting the guests to whom her father wants to introduce her. Florestan and her father join her, and Florestan once more asks her hand in marriage. But Arline rejects him, treasuring in her heart Thaddeus as her lover, even refusing her father when the latter seconds his nephew's suit. Thaddeus and Devilshoof enter the castle surreptitiously, and urge her to follow them and again join the gypsy band. Arline regretfully recalls all the happiness she enjoyed while roving with the gypsies, but she delays her decision so long that guests are approaching. Devilshoof takes flight, and Thaddeus is forced to hide. Meanwhile the gypsy queen has clandestinely followed these two, being still animated with vengeful feelings because of being scorned by Thaddeus, and now enters the castle and announces to Count Arnheim that his daughter is concealing a lover in her chamber. The angry father charges his daughter with this when Thaddeus steps forth from hiding and boldly confesses his passion for Arline. The Count orders him to leave instantly, but Arline threatens to follow him; and when it is later proven that Thaddeus himself comes of noble family, and can show his patent of nobility, the father relents. The marriage takes place with great solemnity. The gypsy queen, however, thirsting for revenge and having been so far baffled in all her schemes, hires an assassin from amongst her band, to murder Thaddeus. Devilshoof, though, succeeds in turning aside the weapon, so that the queen herself becomes the victim of her own murderous plot.

BORIS GODOUNOV

A Russian Tragic Opera, in a prologue and four acts. Music by M. P. MOUSSORGSKY

Libretto founded on PUSHKIN'S and KARAMZIN'S historical drama of the same name, written by the composer

The first performance of this work was at Petrograd, in 1874. The scene is in Moscow, partly on the frontiers of Poland, between 1598 and 1605, the time of the usurper, Boris Godounov. The music is characteristically Slavic.

In the prologue a vast concourse of people is seen in the interior of a monastery near Moscow, where Boris Godounov, although voices are whispering against him, is proclaimed czar of Russia. Boris, being appointed guardian of the minor children of Czar Ivan the Terrible, has caused the young heir to the throne, Dmitri, to be foully murdered, in order to become ruler himself. His coronation at the Kremlin is celebrated with great rejoicing on the part of the people.

Act I is in a cell of the Monastery of the Miracle, where the pious monk, Pimen, is laboriously writing a history of Russia. This he does with the fervid desire to tell the unvarnished truth, so that "he may not be ashamed" when God Himself reads it. There is with him in the cell a youth named Gregory, his features, his age and his general appearance presenting a great resemblance to the murdered Dmitri. The monk Pimen comments on this and tells the youth the circumstances of Dmitri's death and also other facts in connection with it. Gregory is much struck with the tale. Later on Gregory, disguised, escapes over the Russian border, being in great danger of arrest by the guards of Boris Godounov, as he is pursued for having escaped from the monastery with the intention of personating the vanished heir to the throne, Dmitri. Warrants are out for Gregory's apprehension, but he escapes.

In the second act the apartments at the Kremlin are seen, with the son, Feodor, and the daughter, Xenia, of the usurper. The latter enters, caresses his children, and then sits down to brood over his cares and fears. A war with Poland is threatening, and a party of his own nobles are plotting a rebellion. Prince Shouisky enters, seeking audience with the czar, who grants it reluctantly. Shouisky then tells about the rising of a pretender against Boris, and the latter in his fears and doubts asks Shouisky whether he really carried out his order to put Dmitri out of the way. Prince Shouisky relates all the grewsome details of the death of Dmitri, and convinces the usurper that he speaks the truth. But at the same time he gives the czar facts about the danger threatening from the pretender (Gregory), who has obtained the support of the Poles and is on the point of enforcing his claims. Boris is harried by the torments of his conscience and fears.

The third act opens in the apartments of Marina Mnichek in Poland, where a Jesuit priest influences her to use all her charms to beguile Dmitri (Gregory), to help in the plot of unseating Boris, and to seize the supreme power for the Polish pretender to the Russian throne. Dmitri overhears the plans of the Polish nobles. Marina later inflames Gregory's ambition that he may become a pliant tool in the hands of the Polish plotters. It is resolved to march, with a Polish army, to Moscow, oust Boris, and crown Gregory (as the false Dmitri) instead.

The last act takes us to Krom, where there is a rebellion of the peasants against the usurping czar and his adherents. Gregory (Dmitri) comes on the scene with a body of troops supporting him, and they acclaim him ruler of Russia. Meanwhile in the Kremlin a council of the nobles is in deliberation as to how to defeat the pretender and crush the uprising of the people. Shouisky enters and brings dreary news about Boris, who is haunted by spectres. While still reporting this Boris comes in, under the complete spell of visions. Voices are whispering to him: "Thou art a murderer!" Boris recovers, but soon after an old monk begs for an audience, and the monk historian, Pimen, enters, and relates the story of a miracle in which Dmitri appeared to an old shepherd. At the end of the tale Boris loses his senses, but comes once more to himself, and gives tearful advice to his son and heir, when he expires.

LA CAMPANA SOMMERSA

Opera in four acts by OTTORINO RESPIGHI

Libretto by CLAUDIO GUASTALLA, founded on Gerhart Hauptmann's drama, "The Sunken Bell"

This opera was first sung in New York at the Metropolitan Opera House on November 24, 1928.

The bell cast for the village church by Heinrich has been tipped into the lake through the machinations of the Faun. Heinrich is broken-hearted and Rautendelein, a beautiful water-sprite, takes pity on Heinrich, and decides to save him, when she hears he is being brought to his home, sick to death. Magda, Heinrich's wife, is anxiously awaiting the first stroke of the bell, and when her husband is brought home, she learns the truth of its loss. Heinrich bemoans his masterpiece and declares he will have to draw renewed life from a mystical blossom. The Pastor enters with a girl who is supposedly dumb, and tells Magda that she will help her care for her sick husband. The girl is really Rautendelein, and through the power of her love she gives Heinrich strength to fight his fight.

Heinrich now abandons his wife and goes to live with Rautendelein in the mountains. Nickelmann, the gnomes, and the Faun are enslaved by him and made to seek for treasure. Heinrich tells the Pastor of his ambitions to raise a temple to a new cult which will regenerate the earth, and declares: "May the sunken bell toll again when I depart from my purpose!" The villagers approach to destroy the lovers, but Heinrich vanquishes them and returns to Rautendelein. From out the mountain mists rise the wraiths of Heinrich's children bearing an urn containing the tears of their mother, Magda, which she wept when she threw herself in despair into the lake. Then from the depths of the lake rises the tolling of the sunken bell. Heinrich, tortured by conscience, leaves Rautendelein. Rautendelein descends into the well and there weds Nickelmann. Heinrich, who feels now that he cannot live without Rautendelein goes to the Witch, who grants him his wish to see her once before he dies. Rautendelein appears and reproaches him for driving her away from him to Nickelmann, but as he dies she forgives him.

CARLO BROSCHI

or

THE DEVIL'S PART

Comic Opera in three acts by AUBER

Text by SCRIBE

This composition might rather be called a vaudeville, with musical accompaniment, than an opera. The music is not above mediocrity, though we find many pleasing and even exquisite melodies in it. That it has held its present place on the stage for the past forty years is due principally to its excellent libretto, which is full of comical and ingenious situations. The principal rôle is given to Carlo Broschi. He is no other than the famous singer Farinelli, who, as a matter of fact, did heal a Spanish King from madness, though it was not Ferdinand IV but his predecessor, Philip V, the husband of Elizabeth of Ferrara. Notwithstanding these anachronisms, the libretto ranks with the best.

Carlo Broschi has placed his only sister Casilda in a convent near Madrid, to save her from the persecutions of the clergy, who have been trying, for reasons of their own, to give the beautiful maiden to the King. Casilda confesses to her brother that she is in love with an unknown cavalier, who entertains a like passion for her, but Carlo, a poor minstrel, considers that his sister, a milliner, does not stand high enough in the social scale to permit a lawful union with a nobleman.

Carlo meets the King accidentally. He has fallen into deep melancholy, and Carlo succeeds in cheering him by singing an old romance, which he learnt from his mother. Both King and Queen are full of gratitude, and Carlo soon finds himself at court, and loaded with honors. In his new position he meets with Raphael d'Estuniga, Casilda's lover.

In despair at having lost his lady-love he is about to appeal to the Devil for help, when Carlo appears, presenting himself as Satan. He promises his help on condition that Raphael shall give him one-half of all his winnings. This is a condition easily accepted, and Raphael is made a court official through Carlo's influence.

Meanwhile the clergy vainly try to ensnare the King again; Carlo is like his better self; he disperses his sire's melancholy by singing to him, and rekindles his interest in government.

Raphael, feeling quite secure in his league with the Devil, begins to play; he is fortunate, but Carlo never fails to claim his share, which is willingly surrendered to him.

All at once Casilda appears on the scene to put herself under the protection of her brother, the priests having found out her refuge. She recognizes the King, and tells her brother that it was he to whom she was taken against her will. The King believes her to be a ghost, and his reason threatens to give way, but Carlo assures him that the girl is living. The Queen, who knows nothing of her husband's secret, here interrupts the conversation and bids Carlo follow her.

Meanwhile Raphael and Casilda have an interview, but the King comes suddenly upon them and at once orders Raphael to be put to death, the latter having failed in the reverence due to his sovereign. Raphael, however, trusting in the Devil's help, does not let his spirits sink, and Carlo actually saves him by telling the King that Casilda is Raphael's wife.

But the Grand Inquisitor succeeds in discovering this untruth and in exciting the King's anger against his favorite. Carlo, much embarrassed, obtains an interview with the King, and, confessing the whole truth, assures him that the Queen knows as yet nothing, and implores him to give his thoughts and his affections once more to her and to his country. The King, touched to generosity, gives his benediction to the lovers, together with a new title for Raphael, who is henceforth to be called Count of Puycerda. Now, at last Raphael learns that the so-called Devil is his bride's brother, who tells him that this time his share lies in making the two lovers happy, a share which gives him both pleasure and content.

CARMEN

Opera in four acts by GEORGE BIZET

This opera is essentially Spanish. The music throughout has a southern character, and is passionate and original to a high degree.

Carmen, the heroine, is a Spanish Gipsy, fickle and wayward, but endowed with all the wild graces of her nation. She is adored by her people, and so it is not to be wondered at that she has many of the stronger sex at her feet. She is betrothed to Don José, a brigadier of the Spanish army; of course he is one out of many; she soon grows tired of him, and awakens his jealousy by a thousand caprices and cruelties.

Don José has another bride, sweet and lovely, Micaëla, waiting for him at home, but she is forgotten as soon as he sees the proud gipsy.

Micaëla seeks him out, bringing to him the portrait and the benediction of his mother, ay, even her kiss, which she gives him with blushes. His tenderness is gone, however, so far as Micaëla is concerned, as soon as he casts one look into the lustrous eyes of Carmen. This passionate creature has involved herself in a quarrel, and wounded one of her companions, a laborer in a cigarette manufactory. She is to be taken to prison, but Don José lets her off, promising to meet her in the evening at an inn kept by a man named Lillas Pastia, where they are to dance the Seguedilla.

In the second act we find them there together, with the whole band of gipsies. Don José, more and more infatuated by Carmen's charms, is willing to join the vagabonds, who are the same time smugglers. He accompanies them in a dangerous enterprise of this kind, but no sooner has he submitted to sacrifice love and honor for the gipsy than she begins to tire of his attentions. José has pangs of conscience, he belongs to another sphere of society, and his feelings are of a softer kind than those of Nature's unruly child. She transfers her affections to a bull-fighter named Escamillo, another of her suitors, who returns her love more passionately. A quarrel ensues between the two rivals. Escamillo's knife breaks, and he is about to be killed by Don José, when Carmen intervenes, holding back his arm. Don José, seeing that she has duped him, now becomes her deadly foe, filled with undying hatred and longing for revenge.

Micaëla, the tender-hearted maiden, who follows him everywhere like a guardian angel, reminds him of his lonely mother. Everybody advises him to let the fickle Carmen alone—Carmen who never loved the same man for more than six weeks. But in vain, till Micaëla tells him of the dying mother, asking incessantly for her son; then at last he consents to go with her, but not without wild imprecations on his rival and his faithless love.

In the fourth act we find ourselves in Madrid. There is to be a bull-fight; Escamillo, its hero, has invited the whole company to be present in the circus.

Don José appears there too, trying, for the last time, to regain his bride. Carmen, though warned by a fellow gipsy, Frasquita, knows no fear. She meets her old lover outside the arena, where he tries hard to touch her heart. He kneels at her feet, vowing never to forsake her, and to be one of her own people, but Carmen, though wayward, is neither a coward nor a liar, and boldly declares that her affections are given to the bull-fighter, whose triumphs are borne to their ears on the shouts of the multitude. Almost beside himself with love and rage, José seizes her hand and attempts to drag her away, but she escapes from him, and, throwing the ring, José's gift, at his feet, rushes to the door of the arena. He overtakes her, however, and, just as the trumpets announce Escamillo's victory, in a perfect fury of despair he stabs her through the heart, and the victorious bull-fighter finds his beautiful bride a corpse.

THE CAVALIER OF THE ROSE

Comic Grand Opera in three acts by RICHARD STRAUSS

Book by HUGO VON HOFFMANNSTHAL

This work was first heard in Dresden, in 1911. The scene is laid in Vienna, in the time of Empress Maria Theresa.

The first act shows the drawing-rooms of the Princess von Werdenberg. Her husband is conveniently absent on a trip to Arabia, hunting wild beasts, and the inconsolable spouse meanwhile is trying to make up for her loss by splendidly entertaining a young cavalier, the Count Octaviano Rofrano. While he is paying her fulsome compliments and maintaining a love-lorn attitude, she is only too conscious of her own dwindling attractions. Loud and importunate ringing of the house bell frightens the princess, who suspects a too early return of her lord. The count finds a ready way out of the embarrassing situation. He hastily dons the garments of the coquettish chambermaid, and then opens the door himself. It is only a cousin of the princess from the provinces, Baron Ochs von Lerchenau, who comes to ask his relative for advice in an important venture. His aim is to wed Sophie, the daughter of a wealthy army contractor, or rather her fat dowry. This wooer, puffed up with self-importance, shallow and vain, confesses outright that the bride-to-be does not matter to him, but solely her money. To open his campaign as a suitor for the young lady's hand, he proposes to send to her a personal representative with a rose fashioned of silver, as a time-honored emblem of his earnest intentions. And he desires the princess to tell him whom to send as a trusty messenger. Luncheon is served, of which both he and the princess partake, waited on during the meal by Octaviano in his rôle as maid. The baron is condescending enough to be smitten with the fascinations of this supposed waitress, and makes an appointment to meet her, or rather him. This angers the princess' notions of decorum, and in a spirit of spite she suggests Octaviano for the part of cavalier of the rose. This suits the baron. He goes away, and the princess, left by herself, sees a number of persons, needy and otherwise. Incidentally she once more consults her mirror as to whether she has not made a mistake in recommending Octaviano for the bearer of the baron's message, for she fears thereby to lose control of him.

The army contractor's luxurious apartments are the scene of the second act. Octaviano appears, solemn as a high priest, with the silver rose for Sophie. Her father, Faninal by name, is intensely flattered at the prospect of intimate connections with the higher nobility. But Octaviano is greatly impressed with the girl herself, and resolves to outdo the foolish old baron. Sophie on her part also likes him very much and feels a strong aversion to the baron when she meets him a little later. The baron leaves, and Octaviano is left alone for a short while with Sophie. He makes good use of his opportunity, and the two spying servants in the pay of the baron report these facts to the latter. A lively discussion between Octaviano and the baron follows, in which that worthy is practically told that he is an idiot and unworthy of such a phenix as Sophie. At this they draw their swords, and fall to. The baron, as great a poltroon as he is an absurd wooer, is slightly

Emanuel List as Ochs and Eva Hadrabova as Octavian in the third act of "Der Rosenkavalier"

wounded and cries out in pain. There is an uproar and Sophie's father comes on the scene. He commands his daughter to accept the baron for a husband, or else to go to a nunnery for life. The baron at this awakes from his swoon, especially as he remembers his appointment with the fictitious maid.

In act three Octaviano is seen hurrying to a hotel in a secluded part of the city, wearing a maid's costume over his own clothes. He has bribed some of the baron's servants to aid him in duping their master. Everything has been provided by the baron to capture the coy maid, as he supposes. There is a table laden with delicacies, gay music, choice wines, and a cloud of menials to carry out every one of his desires. But the flirting with the "maid" lags. The baron is irritated. Besides, the apartment seems to be haunted. Furious at meeting with this cold reception, he is beside himself when suddenly there enters the official Guardian of Good Morals, and forthwith proceeds to demand the "maid's" name and business. The baron vouches for his guest as Sophie, his betrothed. But the latter, informed in advance of what is going on, here enters with her father, and a complete exposure ensues. The baron becomes the butt of all when the maid slips off her outer costume and stands revealed as Octaviano. Of course, Octaviano now becomes the accepted lover of Sophie with her father's consent.

CAVALLERIA RUSTICANA

(SICILIAN RUSTIC CHIVALRY)

Opera in one act by PIETRO MASCAGNI

Text after Verga's drama of the same name by
TARGIONI-TOZZETTI and MENASCI

Son of a baker in Livorno, Mascagni was destined for the bar. But his love for music made him enter clandestinely into the Instituto Luigi Cherubini, founded by Alfreddo Soffredini. When his father heard of this, he confined him in his chamber, until Pietro's uncle Steffano promised to care for him in future. Pietro now was enabled to study diligently. He composed at the age of 13 years a small opera "In filanda," which was put on the stage by Soffredini. Another composition, on Schiller's poem "An die Freude" (To Joy), brought him money and Count Larderell's favor, who allowed him to study at his expense at the Conservatory at Milan. But Mascagni's ambition suffered no restraint, so he suddenly disappeared from Milan and turned up as musical director of a wandering troupe. In Naples he grew ill, a young lady nursed him, both fell in love and she became his wife. Hearing that Sonzogno offered a prize for the best opera, he procured himself a libretto, and composed the Cavalleria Rusticana in little more than a week, and gained the prize.

Henceforward all, of course, were anxious to hear the music of the unknown artist, and lo! the opera was an immense success.

It cannot be called a masterpiece, yet it is certainly

the offspring of genius, as fresh and as absolutely original as it is highly dramatic.

The text, though retaining little of the exquisite beauty of the original drama, which ought to be read before hearing its fragments in the opera, assists the music a good deal. The wave of human passion sweeps over it, passion as it occurs in daily life, for the composition belongs to the realistic style, as far as it is based on truth and reality alone.

The true local color makes it doubly attractive.

The following are the very simple facts of the story, which takes place in a Sicilian village.

Turridu, a young peasant, has loved and wooed Lola before entering military service. At his return he finds the flighty damsel married to the wealthy carrier Alfio, who glories in his pretty wife and treats her very well. Turridu tries to console himself with another young peasant girl, Santuzza, who loves him ardently, and to whom he has promised marriage.

The opera only begins at this point.

Lola, the coquette, however, cannot bear to know that her former sweetheart should love another woman. She flirts with him, and before the curtain has been raised, after the overture, Turridu's love-song is heard for Lola, who grants him a rendezvous in her own house.

This excites Santuzza's wildest jealousy. She complains to Turridu's mother, who vainly tries to soothe her. Then she has a last interview with Turridu, who is just entering the church. She reproaches him first with his treachery, then implores him not to forsake her and leave her dishonored.

But Turridu remains deaf to all entreaty, and flings her from him. At last, half mad through her lover's stubbornness, Santuzza betrays him and Lola to Alfio, warning the latter that his wife has proved false. After church, Alfio and Turridu meet in mother Lucia's tavern. Alfio refusing to drink of Turridu's wine, the latter divines that the husband knows all. The men and women leave while the two adversaries, after Sicilian custom, embrace each other, Alfio biting Turridu in the ear, which indicates mortal challenge. Turridu, deeply repenting his folly, as well as his falseness, towards poor Santuzza, recommends her to his mother. He hurries into the garden, where Alfio expects him; a few minutes later his death is announced by the peasants, and Santuzza falls back in a dead swoon; with which the curtain closes over the tragedy.

LA CENA DEL BEFFE

Opera in four acts by UMBERTO GIORDANO

The text is based on Sam Benelli's play

The first performance was given at Milan in 1924. The scenes are laid in Renaissance Italy under Duke Lorenzo the Magnificent.

Duke Lorenzo has commanded Tornaquinci to prepare a banquet of peace—for the feigned purpose of reconciling Giannetto Malespini and the brothers Chiaramentesi. Giannetto, a painter and poet, has been the butt of cruel jokes played by the brothers, Gabriello and Neri. A climax was reached when, upon Neri's discovery of Giannetto's clandestine love for Genevra, the brothers tattooed the poet with their daggers, then cast him into the Arno. The real purpose of the banquet is to enable Giannetto to revenge himself on the Chiaramentesi for their culminating affront.

At the supper of the jesters, Giannetto taunts the drunken Neri until the swaggering captain challenges the assembled company to make a test of his courage. Giannetto dares him to appear at Ceccherino's wine shop, the rendezvous of all the hot-tempered young blades of Forence who fight upon the slightest of pretexts—or none at all. When Neri staggers out, Giannetto sends his servant Fazio in advance to tell Ceccherino that the captain has gone mad and has sworn to turn the wine shop into a slaughterhouse. As Neri leaves Tornaquinci's house, Giannetto steals his housekey and appropriates his cloak which the drunken captain has forgotten.

Act II. The following morning Genevra learns from her maid Cintia that Neri has gone mad and is lying bound in the wine shop he wrecked. Genevra is puzzled. She assures the maid that Neri spent the night with her and was never more sane. Just then Giannetto appears and the mystery is solved. His protestations of love melt Genevra's anger and he promises to save her from the monster, the insane Neri. When the enraged captain is heard approaching, Genevra bars her door and refuses to let him enter, for she believes him mad. Giannetto sends for the Medici soldiers who bind the infuriated Neri and hurry him to one of the underground cells of Lorenzo's palace.

Act III. Giannetto and the doctor visit Neri in gaol. The doctor advises confronting the patient with the persons responsible for his condition. This will either restore Neri's sanity or cause his total collapse. Giannetto, therefore, brings in Trinca and three women, all victims of Neri's heartlessness. Believing the captain helpless, Trinca, Lucrezia and Giametta abuse him wrathfully, but Lisabetta, who still loves her seducer, plans to save him. While the others are out of the cell, she determines that Neri is sane and tells him how they may gain his freedom. Giannetto returns and, in answer to Lisabetta's plea that she be allowed to take the helpless Neri under her care, releases the captain's bonds. He is not convinced, however, that Neri isn't shamming, and so, as Lisabetta and the captain depart, he calls after them that he will spend the night with Genevra.

Act IV. Genevra sits talking with her maid. As they are enjoying a serenade by one of Genevra's admirers, Neri vaults through the window and, threatening death if they betray his presence, commands Genevra to prepare as usual for her new lover's coming. A red-cloaked figure enters, glides to Genevra's room and closes the door. Neri, rapier in hand, follows. A moment later the girl rushes screaming from her chamber while Neri comes after, exulting in the death of the poet. But his triumph is cut short—for Giannetto stands smiling against the opposite wall! He had yielded his place beside Genevra this night to Gabriello who was secretly in love with his brother's mistress. When Giannetto explains how, as a climax to his jesting, he has thus planned for Neri to kill his own brother, the captain becomes insane while the poet suddenly overwhelmed with horror, prays for forgiveness.

CENDRILLON

(CINDERELLA)

Fairy Opera in four acts by J. MASSENET

Text based on a French collection of fairy tales

Initial performance in Paris, 1899.

Act I. Shows Cendrillon at the home of her stepmother, Mme. Haltière, who with her two daughters is treating Cendrillon abominably. While the three are making elaborate preparations to attend a splendid court ball, Cendrillon is told to stay at home and mind the household. She is sitting before the hearth dreaming of future happiness, when her godmother, a benevolent fairy, makes her appearance. She brings magnificent garments with her, together with a marvelously small pair of slippers, and these fit as only fairy slippers ever do. Poor Cendrillon rapidly dons all, and the fairy tells her she may go to the ball herself, but must leave there promptly at twelve, unless evil is to befall her. A splendid glass coach and six are waiting, and she drives off with attendants in full livery.

Act II. Meanwhile the stepmother is vainly plying all her arts to make the host, Prince Charming, fall in love with one of her own daughters, but the prince pays no attention to either of them. Cendrillon enters, quite unrecognizable in her magnificent attire, and creates an enormous sensation. The prince is instantly bewitched by her charms, and devotes his attentions to her exclusively. It is a case of love at first sight, both for him and her. Time flies, and before Cendrillon realizes it, midnight strikes. She swiftly runs to the fairy coach that is waiting for her, but in her haste she loses one of her slippers.

Act III. The next day things at the house of Mme. Haltière are rather uncomfortable. She herself is furious at the success of her stepdaughter, and she upbraids her husband. Cendrillon sheds tears because she never expects to see the prince again, and when her father comes to console her, thinking that she is unhappy because of her treatment by the stepmother, he promises her to go with her and seek refuge elsewhere. But Cendrillon will not accept such a sacrifice. She flees alone into the dark, stormy night. The scene changes to the fairies' great oak tree. The weather is mild and clear and fairies are skipping about. Cendrillon comes, imploring protection. But Prince Charming is also there, in search of his beautiful unknown. Each recognizes the other's voice.

Act IV. Cendrillon is at home again. She is recovering from a fever. Suddenly a messenger from the king is heard proclaiming in the streets that on that very day Prince Charming will receive the ladies of the kingdom at his palace, and that she whose foot fits the small crystal slipper left behind at the recent court ball shall be his wife. All the ladies try, but only Cendrillon can get the slipper on her tiny foot. The change of scene shows Cendrillon acknowledged as the promised spouse of the prince, and the whole court does homage to her.

LE CHEMINEAU

Opera in four acts by XAVIER H. N. LEROUX
Text based on a novel by LUCIEN FAVRE

In the first act Le Chemineau, the best farm-hand of Pierre, a well-to-do farmer in France, and one who is always cheerful and ready for a joke, is introduced. Toinette, who is also in Pierre's employ, is deeply in love with him, and he with her. But Le Chemineau is even more fond of a roving life, and hates to assume steady responsibilities. Hence he makes up his mind to resume his wanderings and tells Toinette. She attempts to restrain him, and François, likewise in love with Toinette, mingles in the conversation, belittles Le Chemineau, and pleads with her. Pierre, the farmer, encourages Toinette to stay, while she wishes to join her sweetheart in his roving life. Le Chemineau cuts short the discussion by striding off, and while Toinette falls in a swoon and confesses that she has been his mistress, Le Chemineau's song of departure is heard from a distant field.

Twenty years have gone, and François has really married Toinette. But François is now an invalid, and both he and his wife worry because their only son, Toinet, is always sad. Aline, old Pierre's daughter, is fond of Toinet, but her father is opposed to marriage with him. Pierre even says that sooner than see her the wife of Toinet he would have her dead. He finally drives Toinette and François from his farm, and threatens to betray the fact that Toinet is really an illegitimate son of Le Chemineau. François, enraged, rushes at Pierre, but feebly totters and falls prone to the floor, upbraiding his wife for hiding for so many years the fact from him that Toinet is not his own son at all.

In Act III two farm hands, former co-workers with Le Chemineau and François, are discussing Toinet's hard lot, when the latter, wearied from long walking, enters the wayside inn where the discussion takes place. Catherine, the hostess, sends Toinet to the barn for a rest, while Le Chemineau, still very much his old self, drops in, singing and jolly. He has been all this time moving about from place to place. The farm hands recognize him, but he does not know them. From their talk he learns what became of Toinette, his former sweetheart, and feels sorry for her. While he is still seated Toinette comes to look for her vanished son, and she is taken to his couch. Chemineau remains, realizing with difficulty that Toinet is his own son. He also goes to the barn and there he meets Toinette, who accuses him of being the author of all her present misfortunes. He begs her forgiveness, which she grants.

The last act shows Toinette's house on Christmas eve. Aline and Toinet are now married, and prepare to go to midnight mass. Le Chemineau is also there, and he offers to stay with the invalid François if Toinette will join the young couple in their walk to church. Toinette accedes and hopes that her former lover, Le Chemineau, will never leave them. Old Pierre comes in and tells Le Chemineau that if only he will marry Toinette after François has died, he will make him comfortable for the rest of his life. Le Chemineau declines. François has heard all and thanks Le Chemineau. The latter goes away, resuming his wandering existence, while the bells are heard announcing the end of the mass.

THE CHIMES OF NORMANDY

Light Opera in three acts by R. J. PLANQUETTE
Libretto by CLAIRVILLE and GABET

The first production took place at Paris, in 1877. The scene is laid in Normandy, among the inhabitants of a fishing village.

The first act presents an attractive picture of village life with the annual fair at Corneville. The old Marquis de Villeroi has returned after a long absence from his estates, and the village population is therefore celebrating this event. Everybody is at the fair, old gossips and rustic lovers in particular. Their tongues wag most about Serpolette, a pert village beauty, and Gaspard, an old miser, whom folks envy and curse because of his wealth for which he is said to have sold himself to the evil one. It is mainly because of old Gaspard's cruel treatment of his niece, Germaine, that he is hated and despised. He wants to force her to marry the sheriff, an elderly and unattractive person, whereas she herself inclines much more to Jean Grenicheux, a bold young fisherman, who once rescued her from drowning. As servants are hired at the fair, Germaine and Jean both engage themselves to the marquis, hoping in this way to escape the sordid plans of old Gaspard.

The marquis has resolved to restore thoroughly his château, fallen into decay during the many years of his absence, and popularly believed to be haunted, so that the villagers have held it in great fear. At the beginning of the second act the marquis has therefore given orders that the whole of the immense building be completely overhauled. In doing this Gaspard, the old miser, who had purposely fostered the notion of spooks in the cellars because he has there kept his bags of gold, is found gloating over his treasures. The sudden interruption, together with the grief of being found out and perhaps losing all his gold, weigh so much on his mind that he runs off into the cold night a shrieking maniac.

The last act is presented at the banquet hall of the château, which now has been entirely restored and embellished. The marquis is feasting the whole village, and joy runs high among his guests. Serpolette is most conspicuous, and Jean, who formerly scorned her, assiduously is wooing her, for after the flight of Gaspard documents were found among his papers which seem to prove that she is the heiress to the miser's wealth. Gaspard himself has all this time been strolling about bereft of reason. The marquis on his part has fallen in love with Germaine, although she fills but the place of a servant in his household. The day comes, however, when the miser recovers his senses, and then everything changes, for it is then shown that, after all, Germaine is his niece and rightful heiress, and so the marquis may wed her. Serpolette steps down from her height and contents herself with an ordinary husband.

LE CID

Opera in four acts by JULES MASSENET

Text by DENNERY, GALLET and BLAU

This is considered by some to be the composer's best work, and it has been immensely popular from the time of its production in Paris in 1885. The music is easy flowing and brilliant, and is beautifully adapted to the libretto.

The first scene is in the house of the Count de Gormas, where several noblemen are discussing the coming honor of knighthood, which the King of Spain is about to confer on the popular young hero Rodrigo, son of Don Diego, a renowned warrior. The King is also to appoint on that day a preceptor for his daughter, and it is the general opinion that Count de Gormas will be the one selected to fill this honorable position.

Ximene, the beautiful daughter of Count de Gormas, is deeply in love with Rodrigo, who returns her affection. She confides her love to the Infanta, who in her turn confesses a passion for Rodrigo, but realizing her position as heir to the throne of Castile, promises Ximene to conceal her own feelings, and to assist in uniting the lovers.

In the next scene the knighthood of Rodrigo takes place amid the great rejoicing of the people. After the ceremony, the King appoints Don Diego preceptor for his daughter, much to the chagrin of Count de Gormas, who intentionally picks a quarrel with the aged Don Diego, and easily disarms him. Don Diego, overcome with shame at this disgrace, calls on his son to avenge his honor. Rodrigo is overwhelmed with grief when he hears that it is Ximene's father that he must meet, but the family name is at stake, and he swears to defend it.

They meet in a moonlit street near the Count's palace, and the Count is slain by Rodrigo. Ximene, hearing the disturbance, comes forth, and finding her father's dead body, swears to be revenged on his murderer, and goes immediately to the King demanding justice. The King is about to regretfully condemn Rodrigo to death, when a messenger arrives with news that a great army of Moors is approaching, and Rodrigo obtains the grace of a day to lead the attack against the enemy, promising that, if he survives, he will return and give himself up to justice. Before leaving he seeks an interview with Ximene, and tells her that he intends to let himself be killed in battle. This so frightens her that she confesses her love, and begs him to protect himself and defeat the enemy, and thus atone for his crime. Rodrigo goes forth to war with a light heart and vanquishes the Moors, and is hailed by them the "Cid" or conqueror. On his return he gives himself up to the King according to his promise, who gladly pardons him on hearing that Ximene has confessed her love and renounced her vengeance, and the lovers are happily betrothed amid great rejoicing of the people.

CLEOPATRA

Tragic Opera in four acts by X. H. N. LEROUX

Text based on SARDOU'S drama of the same name

This opera was first performed in Paris, 1890, and in America first in Chicago, 1919. The libretto follows closely historical events.

Mark Antony, in camp at Tarsus, is proclaimed victorious general of Rome, in the first act. The delegates of the conquered nations withdraw, save alone Spakos, the favorite of Cleopatra. Preceded by Charmion, her trusted slave girl, Cleopatra enters. Anthony, at first haughty and suspicious, is completely fascinated by Egypt's queen. Envoys from Rome bring an order from the Senate for his return, but he refuses to leave Cleopatra.

In the second act preparations are being made for the marriage of Anthony with Octavia. Ennius, just back from the Nile, tells of Anthony's orgies there. Octavia, on her way to the nuptial chamber, enters with Anthony; the latter demands of Ennius news regarding Cleopatra. Learning that Spakos is for the moment high in her favor, Mark Anthony grows fiercely jealous. When Octavia returns he discloses to her his relations with Cleopatra, and Octavia falls fainting. The scene that follows takes us to Alexandria, Egypt. Spakos and Cleopatra, disguised as a boy, enter an inn together. There is a mob, and one of them, a public dancer named Adamos, attracts Cleopatra. Spakos becomes frantic with jealousy, while Cleopatra takes off her

Antonio Scotti as Lescaut in "Manon'

costly headdress and praises the crowd for having amused her. Suddenly the approach of Mark Anthony is announced to her, and despite the furious outbreaks of Spakos she hastens to meet him.

There is a garden scene in the third act, with Cleopatra and Mark Anthony loitering in the shady paths. She offers to kiss that man who will afterwards empty a chalice filled with deadly poison. He dashes the vessel to the ground. Octavia enters unannounced, begging her husband to return to Rome for important affairs. Anthony, however, scorns her and her advice and prepares to meet Octavius on the battlefield. Spakos assures Octavia that Cleopatra has been his and shall be his again. Anthony comes in his battle chariot to bid farewell to Cleopatra.

In the last act Cleopatra is waiting news of the fight at Actium, lolling on a terrace overlooking the sea. She has made preparations for suicide in case Anthony is dead. Charmion comes with a basket of flowers in which an asp is concealed, and Cleopatra says she prefers death from snakebite to being exhibited in Octavius' triumphal procession. Spakos enters, telling her that Anthony believes her dead and will never return to her. Then he protests his undying love for her. Cleopatra stabs him to the heart. Anthony, having fallen on his own sword on hearing of Cleopatra's death, enters mortally wounded. As he expires, Cleopatra lays the asp to her bosom and dies before the entrance of victorius Octavius.

CLEOPATRA'S NIGHT

Opera in two acts by HENRY HADLEY

Libretto by POLLOCK after GAUTIER'S "La Nuit de Cleopatre"

First produced in New York in 1920. The action takes place in the summer palace of Cleopatra on the Nile during the first century of the Christian era.

Act I. Mardion, Cleopatra's maid, loves Meiamoun, an Egyptian lad, and is telling her companion, Iras, of her own innocent and her mistress' scandalous love-life when the queen appears. Cleopatra is preparing to seek refreshment in the bath from the heat of the day when an arrow falls at her feet. Mardion examines the papyrus attached to its shaft and finds the words "I love you!" The queen brightens at the prospect of an adventure. As she is about to step into the perfumed basin, Meiamoun emerges from the water. Her anger at his audacity is disarmed by his confession that it was he who sent the arrow. She offers him a night of love if at the next dawn he will drain a cup of poison. The lad accepts. Mardion, unable to dissuade him from complying with the queen's desires, stabs herself and is flung to the crocodiles. Meiamoun rides away with Cleopatra in the royal barge.

Act II. While the queen lingers within the palace with her lover, her guests wait on the terrace. She finally appears with Meiamoun who sits beside her as they watch the dancing of Greek girls and a band of desert maidens. The orgy ends at sunrise when the poisoned draught is brought to Meiamoun. Cleopatra wishes to keep him as king for a month but his doom is sealed by the coming of a messenger who announces the arrival of Mark Antony. Meiamoun drains the goblet and falls dead at her feet as trumpets herald Antony's approach. The queen presses a kiss on the slain youth's lips, then rises to greet the newcomer with equal fervor.

CLEOPATRE

Opera in four acts by JULES MASSENET

The first performance was given at Monte Carlo in 1914. The scenes are laid in Egypt during the first century of the Christian era.

Act I. The rising curtain shows Antony receiving tribute from the conquered nations at his camp at Tarsus. Cleopatra comes and Antony succumbs at once to her charms, disregarding an order to return to Rome.

Act II. Six months later he is celebrating his marriage to Octavia when Ennius brings word from Egypt that Antony has been succeeded by Spakos in Cleopatra's affections. Antony is overwhelmed with jealousy and tells Octavia of his passion for the fair Egyptian. Meantime, Cleopatra tires of Spakos and one evening they go to a dive in Alexandria in search of a new sensation. The queen is charmed by a dancer who is attacked by the jealous Spakos. As they are about to be mobbed by the crowd, Cleopatra throws off her disguise and at that moment her maid, Charmian, enters with news of Antony's sudden arrival.

Act III. Antony lingers by Cleopatra's side instead of joining his army. She taunts him with cowardice and when Octavia comes in search of her straying lord, Cleopatra adds her entreaties to those of his wife to hasten his departure for the battle front.

Act IV. Cleopatra, awaiting news of the conflict, intends to kill herself should Antony be defeated. She has had word of her death spread abroad but does not know that Spakos has told Antony that she is dead. She is deaf to Spakos' protestations of love. When she learns that he has not delivered her message to Antony, she stabs him. Just then Antony arrives, dying, for he has stabbed himself upon receiving the false message from Spakos. He dies and Cleopatra holds the poisonous asp to her bosom as the victorious Octavia enters, too late to triumph over her rival.

THE FOLKUNGS

Grand Opera in five acts by EDMUND KRETSCHMER

Text by MOSENTHAL

The first act represents the convent Nydal on the snowy heights of the Kyöles. Sten, the confidant of Bengt, Duke of Schoonen, has allured Prince Magnus, second son of King Erick of Sweden, out of his convent. He announces to the Prince that he may choose between death and a nameless life in the convent, and Magnus, having no choice, swears that he will be forever dead to the world.

The Abbot first subjects Magnus to a trial of his constancy, by letting him hold the night vigil outside the gates. Lars, the son of the Prince's nurse, appears and relates to Magnus that King Erick is dead, as well as his eldest son, and that Prince Magnus is called to come and claim his throne and bride, who is already being wooed by Bengt, and now the listener understands the plot against himself.

The second act shows us Princess Maria in her castle. She is the King's niece and successor to the throne. She takes a last farewell from her people, and Bengt appears to lead her to the coronation.

The next scene begins with the act of coronation. The crowned Queen Maria is to announce her choice of a husband from the Mora-stone, when her words are arrested by a look from Magnus.

Magnus, mindful of his oath, still denies his identity, and the Duke demands the impostor's arrest. But the

Queen recognizes Magnus, who then remembers he has broken his oath to the monks, and throws himself into the sea. Bengt is about to kill Sten, the only accomplice in his deed, when Maria, who has heard all, arrests his arm, and accuses him of murder. Then she rushes to the balcony to call her people to vengeance. Bengt draws his sword to stab her, but the people throng in, seize and throw him into the sea. Maria hears that Magnus lives and has driven away the Danes. With him enter the monks, whose Abbot releases the Prince from his oath. Maria, lovingly embracing him, places her crown on her bridegroom's head and all cry hail! to their King Magnus Ericson.

COPPELIA

Grand Ballet in three acts by LEO DELIBES

Text by CHARLES NUITTER and A. SAINT-LÉON

The ballet of action, when well conducted, is always a pleasing form of entertainment, and Coppelia has been a decided success from the time of its first production in Paris in 1870. The plot, which is founded on Hoffman's story "Der Sandmann," is clever and amusing. The ballet throughout is arranged with considerable skill and taste, and the music is bright and sparkling.

The scene is laid in a small town near Galicia, and in the first act the public square is shown with the residence of Coppelius prominently in view. At one of the barred windows of the house sits Coppelia, the beautiful and mysterious daughter of old Coppelius. She is apparently a prisoner in her father's house, as no one has ever seen her outside or even heard the sound of her voice. Many young gallants have tried to gain admittance, but old Coppelius will admit no one, and Coppelia remains the mystery of the village.

Swanilda, a young maiden of the town, suspects her lover Frantz of being in love with Coppelia, and appears before the house trying every means in her power to attract the attention of her rival, but all in vain. Becoming impatient, she is in the act of knocking at the door to gain admittance, when Coppelius appears at one of the windows. She then conceals herself in the shadow of the house, and while hiding there, her lover Frantz appears on the scene, and, observing Coppelia at her window, bows and throws kisses to her. Swanilda becomes madly jealous, and, pretending not to see Frantz, runs gaily after a passing butterfly. Frantz follows her, and, catching the butterfly, pins it to her coat, for which he is severely reproached by Swanilda for his cruelty. She then tells him that she has discovered his treachery, and that she no longer cares for him, and while Frantz is endeavoring to defend himself, they are interrupted by the entrance of the Burgomaster, and many peasants, who are preparing for the grand fête which is to take place the next day. Observing Swanilda, the Burgomaster promises that on the morrow she shall be wedded to Frantz, but she declares that she no longer cares for her fiancé, and will not marry him.

The peasants gradually disperse, and when the street is deserted Coppelius comes forth from his house and disappears in the darkness. Swanilda and some girl friends, who are secretly watching Coppelius, notice that he drops a key from his pocket, and on discovering that it is the key to his house, their curiosity gets the better of them, and they enter. Meanwhile, Frantz, who has been lurking in the neighborhood, has also noticed the departure of Coppelius, and obtaining a ladder, is in the act of entering the window of Coppelia's chamber when he is discovered by the enraged Coppelius, who has returned to look for his key.

The second act discloses the studio of Coppelius, where the frightened maidens are seen examining the weird ornaments of the mysterious room. At length they discover that Coppelia and all the figures are in reality nothing but automatons, and losing their fear they press the springs, and set the numerous figures to dancing and playing. They soon are disturbed in their merriment by the entrance of the enraged Coppelius, but all succeed in making their escape with the exception of Swanilda, who conceals herself behind a curtain. The persistent Frantz in the meantime again makes use of the ladder and enters the studio window, only to be pounced upon by Coppelius, who, pretending friendliness, induces him to drink of a magic potion, which he hopes will have the effect of taking a few sparks of life from Frantz's body, which he then will infuse into the automaton Coppelia. Mistaking Swanilda for Coppelia, he becomes wild with joy when he sees that his experiment is evidently successful, and that Coppelia is actually turning into a living woman. After practicing the deception for a time, Swanilda restores Frantz to himself, and they rush from the house together, leaving poor old Coppelius in the belief that his reason has deserted him.

In the tableau which follows, Frantz and Swanilda are happily married, and the house of Coppelius is ransacked by the guards, and his pieces of workmanship are smashed to atoms. He is partly appeased, however, by the Lord of the Manor, who, at Swanilda's request, gives him a purse of money.

The third act, which is a pantomime, deals with the fête of the Bell.

LE COQ D'OR

Opera pantomime in three acts. Prologue and epilogue by
NICOLAI RIMSKY-KORSAKOFF
Book by BIELSKY after PUSHKIN

The initial production was at Moscow in 1910. The setting is Russia during legendary times.

Act I. King Dodón, lazy and gluttonous, is oppressed by the cares of state. When he was young he had liked nothing better than leading his armies into battle, but now he is old and the invasions of his warlike neighbors interfere with his sleep. He holds council in the gorgeous hall of his palace with his Boyards and his two sons. The conflicting opinions of the young princes lead to uproar and confusion when suddenly an ancient Astrologer appears. He offers the King a golden cockerel which has the power to foretell events and will, when placed on the highest weather vane, give warning to the citizens of invasions. Dodón is overjoyed and offers the Astrologer any reward he desires, but the ancient magician says that he will come back later for his reward. The King has his bed brought upon the stage and relieved of all responsibility, he is tucked in by the royal housekeeper. He is no sooner asleep than the golden cockerel gives a frantic warning of an invasion on the western borders of the empire. One after the other, King Dodón's sons with their armies set out for the enemy's country. When they do not return, the monarch follows with an even vaster army.

Act II. The King reaches a narrow mountain pass

where he finds the bodies of his sons and their soldiers. But no enemy has slain the princes—they slew each other. The griefstricken father sees a tent under the hillside and hastens toward it, believing that there dwells the leader of the invasion. To his astonishment, the lovely Queen Shemakhan emerges—and Dodón understands why his sons turned their swords upon each other. The beautiful Shemakhan lures on the aged monarch, delighting him with her songs and mocking his own singing. But Dodón, if he cannot sing, can dance for his enchantress who summons her musicians. The King dances; the music swirls faster and faster. Dodón cannot stop until, breathless and exhausted, he falls at the feet of Shemakhan. She consents to become his bride.

Act III. Dodón and Queen Shemakhan lead a colorful procession through the streets of the royal city, crowded with his rejoicing subjects. While the triumphal welcome is at its height, the ancient Astrologer appears before the King. He reminds Dodón that he has not received his reward for the golden cockerel. The monarch bids him name his desire and it shall be his. "Shemakhan!" answers the magician. Dodón is furious and kills the Astrologer with a blow from his sceptre. The golden cockerel hurls itself upon the aged King and pierces his skull with one blow of his beak. Sudden darkness falls and through the crash of thunder rings Shemakhan's silvery mocking laughter. When light returns both the Queen and the magic bird have disappeared. The stupid populace mourn the death of Dodón—"prudent, wise and peerless."

In the epilogue, the Astrologer steps before the curtain and announces that the story is only a fairy tale and that in Dodón's kingdom, only the Queen and he are mortals.

DER CORREGIDON

Opera in four acts by HUGO WOLF

Text by MAYREDER-OBERMEYER

The first performance was given at Mannheim in 1896. The setting is Spain of the Nineteenth century.

Act I. The miller, Tio Lucas, and his beautiful Frasquita would be completely happy were it not for the unwelcome attentions which Don Eugenio di Zuñiga, the magistrate, forces upon Frasquita. One day the wife upsets the bench occupied by the amorous Don Eugenio who falls into the dust while Lucas, hidden in the arbor, laughs at the official's discomfiture. Don Eugenio departs, vowing revenge.

Act II. Tonuelo, the magistrate's summoner, knocks at the miller's door one evening shortly afterward and bids Lucas appear at once before the alcalde who has lent himself to Don Eugenio's scheme for vengeance. Frasquita, left alone, is singing to calm her fears when she hears a cry for help. It is the magistrate who comes in, dripping wet from a fall in the brook. The angry wife orders him away but he swoons at the threshold from fatigue and fright. His servant appearing at this moment, Frasquita admits them both to the house and goes in search of Lucas. When Don Eugenio awakens from his swoon he sends the servant after her and, hanging his wet clothes before the fire, he climbs into the miller's bed and goes to sleep.

Act III. In the darkness of the night, Lucas and Frasquita pass each other unseeing. The miller reaches his home. Before his fire hang the magistrate's clothes and through the keyhole he distinguishes the figure of Don Eugenio asleep in his bed! All is clear to Lucas. He reaches for his rifle to shoot his wife's seducer when a thought halts him. The magistrate, too, has a beautiful wife. He slips into Don Eugenio's damp clothes and goes back to town. Meanwhile, the magistrate has awakened and wants to go home. But he cannot find his clothes. He puts on those of the miller—and thus it happens that the alcalde's men, come to arrest Lucas, mistakingly administer a sound beating to the magistrate.

Act IV. When the magistrate reaches his own home, he receives another trouncing from Lucas who has just been cudgled for trying to intrude on Doña Mercedes de Zuñiga. Honors, therefore, are equal and Don Eugenio decides to confine his love-making to his own fireside while Lucas and Frasquita, reconciled, return happily to the mill.

COSI FAN TUTTE

Comic Opera in two acts by MOZART

Text by DA PONTE, newly arranged by L. SCHNEIDER and ED. DEVRIENT

This opera, though lovely in its way, has never had the success which the preceding Figaro and Don Juan attained, and this is due for the most part to the libretto. In the original text it really shows female fickleness, and justifies its title. But the more Mozart's music was admired, the less could one be satisfied with such a libretto. Schneider and Devrient therefore altered it and in their version the two female lovers are put to the test, but midway in the plot it is revealed to them that they are being tried—with the result that they feign faithlessness, play the part out, and, at the close, declare their knowledge, turning the sting against the authors of the unworthy comedy. The contents may be told shortly.

Don Fernando and Don Alvar are betrothed to two Andalusian ladies, Rosaura and Isabella.

They loudly praise their ladies' fidelity, when an old bachelor, named Onofrio, pretends that their sweethearts are not better than other women, and accessible to temptation. The lovers agree to make the trial, and promise to do everything which Onofrio dictates. Thereupon they announce to the ladies that they are ordered to Havana with their regiment, and, after a tender leavetaking, they depart, to appear again, in another guise, as officers of a strange regiment. Onofrio has won the ladies' maid, Dolores, to aid in the furtherance of his schemes, and the officers enter, beginning at once to make love to Isabella and Rosaura, but each, as was before agreed, to the other's affianced.

Of course, the ladies reject them, and the lovers begin to triumph, when Onofrio prompts them to try another temptation. The strangers, mad with love, pretend to drink poison in the young ladies' presence. Of course, these tender-hearted maidens are much aggrieved; they call Dolores, who bids her mistresses hold the patients in their arms; then, coming disguised as a physician, she gives them an antidote. By this clumsy subterfuge they excite the ladies' pity, and are nearly successful in their foolish endeavors, when Dolores, pitying the cruelly tested women, reveals the whole plot to them.

Isabella and Rosaura now resolve to enter into the play. They accept the disguised suitors, and even consent to a marriage. Dolores appears in the shape of a notary, without being recognized by the men. The marriage contract is signed, and the lovers disappear, to return in their true characters, full of righteous contempt. Isabella and Rosaura make believe to be conscience stricken, and for a long while torment and deceive their angry bridegrooms. But at last they grow tired of teasing, they present the disguised Dolores, and they put their lovers to shame by showing that all was a farce. Of course, the gentlemen humbly ask their pardon, and old Onofrio is obliged to own himself beaten.

THE CRICKET ON THE HEARTH

Opera in three acts by CARL GOLDMARK

Text after Dickens's tale by M. WILLNER

With this opera Goldmark has entered a novel way in composing. He has renounced all sensational effects and has produced an opera which is full of charming melodies, but which lacks the high dramatic verve to which we are accustomed from this composer; there are, however, remarkably fine pieces in the whole, the best of them being Dot's dancing song in the second act, the quintetto at the end of it, and the prelude in the third act, into which Goldmark has interwoven the popular song, "Weisst Du, wie viel Sternlein stehen."

The story is soon told, as everybody is supposed to know its contents from Dickens's famous fairy-tale. That it is less pretty than the original is not Mr. Willner's fault, who did his best to endue it with dramatic strength, and to make it more effective, an elevation to which the tale never aspired, its poetic simplicity being its great charm.

The scene is laid in an English village.

The cricket, a little fairy, lives with a postilion, John, and his wife Dot. They are a happy couple, the only thing wanting to their complete happiness being children, and even this ardent wish Dot knows will be fulfilled before long.

A young doll-maker, May, visits Dot to unburden her heavy heart. The young girl is to marry her old and rich employer Tackleton, in order to save her foster-father from want, but she cannot forget her old sweetheart, a sailor named Edouard, who left her years ago, never to come back. Dot tries to console her, and gives her food for her old father. When May has taken leave, Dot's husband John enters, bringing a strange guest with him.

It is Edouard, who has, however, so disguised himself that nobody recognizes him. Dot receives him hospitably, and while he follows her in another room, a very lively scene ensues, all the village people flocking in to receive their letters and parcels at John's hands.

In the second act John rests from his labor in his garden, while Dot, who finds her husband, who is considerably older than herself, somewhat too self-confident and phlegmatic, tries to make him appreciate her more by arousing his jealousy. While they thus talk and jest, May enters, followed by her old suitor, who has already chosen the wedding-ring for her. Edouard listens to his wooing with ill-concealed anxiety, and Tackleton, not pleased to find a stranger in his friend's house, gruffly asks his name. The strange sailor tells him that he left his father and his sweetheart to seek his fortune elsewhere, and that he has come back, rich and independent, only to find his father dead and his sweetheart lost to him. His voice moves May strangely, but Tackleton wants to see his riches. Eduard shows them some fine jewels, which so delight Dot that she begins to adorn herself with them and to dance about the room. Edouard presents her with a beautiful cross, and seizes the opportunity to reveal to her his identity, entreating her not to betray him. Then he turns to May, begging her to choose one of the trinkets, but Tackleton interferes, saying that his promised bride does not need any jewels from strange people. Dot is greatly embarrassed, and

Tackleton, mistaking her agitation, believes that she has fallen in love with the sailor, and insinuates as much to her husband, whom he invites to have a glass of beer with him.

This unusual generosity on the part of the avaricious old man excites the clever little wife's suspicion. May having withdrawn, she greets the friend of her youth with great ostentation (knowing herself secretly watched by John and Tackleton), and promises to help him to regain his sweetheart. John and his friend, who suddenly return, see them together, and poor old John gets wildly jealous. But when he is alone he falls asleep, and the faithful cricket prophetically shows him his wife fast asleep in a dream, while a little boy in miniature postilion's dress plays merrily in the background.

In the third act Dot adorns May with the bridal wreath, but the girl is in a very sad mood. All at once she hears the sailor sing; Dot steals away, and May, vividly reminded of her old love by the song, decides to refuse old Tackleton at the last moment, and to remain true to Eduard until the end of her life. The sailor, hearing her resolve, rushes in, tearing off his false gray beard, and catches May, who at last recognizes him, in his arms. Meanwhile Tackleton arrives gorgeously attired; he brings a necklace of false pearls and invites May to drive with him to the wedding ceremony in the church at once. A whole chorus of people interrupt this scene, however; they greet him, saying they are his wedding guests, exciting the miser's wrath. At last May, who had retired to put on her bridal attire, reappears, but, instead of taking Tackleton's arm, she walks up to Eduard, who, courteously thanking the old lover for the carriage standing at the door, suddenly disappears with May. The chorus detains the furious old Tackleton until the lovers are well out of the way.

Meanwhile Dot has explained her behavior to John, and, whispering her sweet secret into his ear, makes him the happiest man on earth. The cricket, the good fairy of the house, chirps sweetly and the last scene shows once more a picture of faithfulness and love.

CRISPINO E LA COMARE

Fairy Opera in three acts by G. RICCI

Words by P. CAVALIERI and D. VESTRI

This tuneful opera was first given six years after the composer's death, in 1865, in Paris.

Act I. Crispino and Annetta, his wife, are a luckless, penniless couple with a large family. He is a cobbler and she a street ballad vendor, and their miserly landlord is about to put them on the pavement for non-paid rent. Crispino, in despair, wants to throw himself into an old deep well, when a fairy appears in a mist, and hinders this attempt at self-destruction, promising henceforth to take care of him. The bargain she makes with him is this: he is to become a famous physician, and to perfect a cure in every instance where she, the fairy, will not be visible to him at the patient's bed.

Act II. Happiness at last seems to have come to the couple, for marvelous cures are effected by Crispino. This arouses the jealousy of the doctors.

Act III. Crispino, spoiled by success, becomes cruel to his wife and even forgets the fairy's warning. For punishment the fairy makes the ground swallow him up. Crispino sees terrible visions. As a last request he begs his protectress to let him see his wife and children once more. This brings about his forgiveness, and he finds himself again at home.

CRISTOFORO COLOMBO

Opera in three acts and an epilogue by

ALBERTO FRANCHETTI

Book by ILLICA

This opera was first produced in Genoa in 1892. The setting is Spain and the island of San Salvador at the end of the fifteenth century.

Act I. In the courtyard of a Salamancan convent, Roldano incites the mob against Columbus while within, the Council of Castile rejects his proposal to find a water route to India. Columbus appears and is greeted with mockery by the crowd. Just then Queen Isabella enters and with an inspired gesture, hands him her golden crown, symbolizing the pledging of the royal jewels to finance his expedition.

Act II. Aboard the caravel Santa Maria, Roldano stirs the sailors to mutiny. At the critical moment the outlook's cry of "Land!" is heard and Columbus points to a distant shore.

Act III. In Xaragua, near Columbus' camp, Roldano has slain the Indian king whose queen, Anacona, feigns love for the murderer, hoping thus to gain an opportunity to avenge her husband's death. But Anacona is betrayed by her daughter, Iguamota, who loves the Spaniard, Guevra. Roldano's intrigues at the Spanish court succeed and he is made viceroy in Columbus' stead. Roldano stabs Anacona, Iguamota commits suicide and Columbus is sent home in chains.

Epilogue. In the royal tombs of Spain, Columbus

and Guevra meditate over their frustrated lives. Guevra leaves in search of Isabella. Young girls enter the crypt with wreaths of flowers. Columbus learns from them that the good queen lies buried where he stands. He is overcome with grief and after an apostrophe to Isabella, he kills himself upon her tomb.

CYRANO DE BERGERAC

Dramatic Opera in four acts by FRANK DAMROSCH
Text based on ROSTAND'S well-known drama

The opening performance of this work occurred in New York, 1913. The scene is laid in the year 1640.

Act I shows the Hôtel de Bourgogne where the play, "La Clorisse," is about to begin. Montfleury, the leading actor, is in disgrace, and has been forbidden to act for a whole month by Cyrano's whim, the unfortunate star having incurred his displeasure not alone for bad playing but for his presumption in glancing at Cyrano's cousin, Roxane. Cyrano, although madly in love with Roxane, does not trust himself to avow his state of feelings, merely because nature has endowed him with a monstrous nose, and he fears ridicule like death. Christian, Baron de Neuvillette, is also secretly in love with Roxane, but her relative Guiche favors none of these, but rather the Viscount de Valvert for her suitor. However, Guiche fails in this, and a friend of Christian's, Lignière, has even composed a song of derision at Guiche's expense. LeBret, Cyrano's friend, is impatiently expecting the latter. Christian is jealous of Valvert. Christian detects the hand of a pickpocket in his clothes, and to obtain pardon the thief reveals to him a plot to set upon Lignière at the Porte de Nesle. So Christian goes to warn Lignière. Meanwhile Cyrano and Valvert cross swords, and the latter is wounded. Cyrano confesses to LeBret his love for Roxane. Cyrano is informed that Roxane wishes to meet him next morning.

In the second act this meeting takes place. It is at a fashionable cookshop's, and Cyrano sits down at a table to write a note to Roxane confessing all. Roxane enters and thanks Cyrano for the service done her and Christian the night before. She asks Cyrano to shield Christian with his invincible sword, because she loves him. Cyrano becomes depressed because of Roxane's confidences, especially as she does not scruple to admit her partiality for Christian. Guiche comes in, and Cyrano purposely offends him. Guiche is afraid to pick a quarrel with him. Christian, not knowing that Roxane has pleaded with her cousin to protect him, and being tired of serving forever as the butt for his fellow-cadets in the regiment, taunts Cyrano with the size and shape of his nose. Cyrano, although angered greatly, controls his wrath for the sake of his beloved Roxane. Left alone with Christian, Cyrano tells the young lover that he is conversant with all the facts, and that Roxane expects a letter from him. Christian is crestfallen, admits that writing is not his strong point, and then Cyrano offers him the letter he had written, but never delivered, to Roxane, telling him that it will do very well under the circumstances.

In Act III Guiche bids adieu to Roxane, being commanded to go with his regiment in defense of the town of Arras. Since her own lover, as one of the cadets, forms part of that regiment, she fears that Guiche may mean harm to Christian. So she impresses him with the notion that it would be wise to leave Cyrano's company behind, thus frustrating the latter's ambitious plans. Guiche does so. Cyrano, out of regard for his pledged word, makes love for Christian, deftly plying his powers of vicarious seduction until Roxane kisses the youth in Cyrano's very presence. Guiche returns, but Cyrano delays his interference long enough to have a priest pronounce Christian and Roxane man and wife. Out of revenge Guiche at once orders the young husband off to active service, to aid in the siege of Arras.

The last act shows the cadets, with Christian among them, before Arras. Famine is weakening their ranks. Dawn breaks and the reveille is heard. Guiche, more hated than ever, rebukes his troops fiercely. Cyrano comments on the injustice of it. There is a conversation between Christian and Cyrano, in which the former, unaware hitherto of Cyrano's passion for Roxane, comes to realize it. Roxane appears. She has all along received from her young husband letters so affectionate and high-souled as to make her fall in love with him deeper and deeper, but letters, unknown to her, every one of which was written by Cyrano. She is now resolved to join Christian in the field at all hazards. Full of overflowing enthusiasm she tells her husband that she would love him if he were ugly. Christian at last sees clearly that it is not himself in reality whom his wife loves, but the author of those letters, Cyrano. He frankly tells Cyrano about this. Then an assault is made by the foe, and Christian is killed. Cyrano rushes off to take part in the fight. Then there is a change of scene. When the battle ends LeBret is seen carrying Cyrano, mortally wounded, to a convent close by, and Roxane likewise goes there to join him.

CZAR AND ZIMMERMANN

or

THE TWO PETERS

Comic Opera in three acts by LORTZING

This charming little opera had even more success than Lortzing's other compositions; it is a popular opera in the best sense of the word. Lortzing ought to have made his fortune by it, for it was soon claimed by every stage. He had composed it for Christmas, 1837, and in the year 1838 every street organ played its principal melodies. But the directors paid miserable sums to the lucky composer. (For example, a copy of the work cost him 25 thalers, while he did not get more than 30 to 50 thalers from the directors).

The libretto was composed by Lortzing himself; he took it out of an old comedy.

Peter, Emperor of Russia, has taken service on the wharfs of Saardam as simple ship-carpenter under the assumed name of Peter Michaelow. Among his companions is another Peter, named Ivanow, a Russian renegade, who has fallen in love with Mary, the niece of the burgomaster Van Bett.

The two Peters, being countrymen and fearing discovery, have become friendly, but Ivanow, instinctively feeling his friend's superiority, is jealous of him, and Mary, a little coquette, nourishes his passion.

Meanwhile the ambassadors of France and England, each of whom wishes for a special connection with the Czar of Russia, have discovered where he must be, and both bribe the conceited simpleton Van Bett, who tries to find out the real Peter.

He assembles the people, but there are many Peters amongst them, though only two strangers. He asks them whence they come, then takes aside Peter Ivanow, cross-questioning him in vain as to what he wishes to know.

At last, being aware of Peter's love for Mary, he gives him some hope of gaining her hand, and obtains in exchange a promise from the young man to confess his secret in presence of the foreign nobleman. The cunning French ambassador, the Marquis de Chateauneuf, has easily found out the Czar and gained his purpose, while the phlegmatic English Lord, falsely directed by the burgomaster, is still in transaction with Ivanow. All this takes place during a rural festivity, where the Marquis, notwithstanding the claims upon his attention, finds time to court pretty Mary, exciting Ivanow's hate and jealousy. Ivanow with difficulty plays the rôle of Czar, which personage he is supposed to be as well by Lord Syndham as by Van Bett. He well knows that he deserves punishment if he is found out on either side. The burgomaster, getting more and more confused, and fearing himself surrounded by spies and cheats, examines one of the strangers after the other, and is, of course, confounded to hear their high-flown names; at last he seizes the two Peters, but is deterred from his purpose by the two ambassadors. They are now joined by a third, the Russian General Lefort, who comes to call back his sovereign to his own country. In the third act Van Bett has prepared a solemn demonstration of fealty for the supposed Czar, whom he still mistakes for the real one, while the real Czar has found means to go on board of his ship with the Marquis and Lefort. Before taking farewell, he promises a passport to Ivanow, who is very dubious as to what will become of him. Meanwhile Van Bett approaches him with his procession to do homage, but during his long and confused speech cannon-shots are heard, and an usher announces that Peter Michaelow is about to sail away with a large crew. The background opens and shows the port with the Czar's ship. Everybody bursts into shouts "Long live the Czar!" and Ivanow, opening the paper which his high-born friend left to him, reads that the Czar grants him pardon for his desertion and bestows upon him a considerable sum of money.

LA DAME BLANCHE

Comic Opera in three acts by BOIELDIEU

Text by SCRIBE

Boieldieu is for the French almost what Mozart was for the German. This opera especially may be called classic, so deliberate and careful is its execution.

The "Lady in White" is the chef-d'œuvre of all comic operas in French, as Mozart's Figaro is in German. The success of this opera, whose composer and whose poet were equally liked and esteemed in Paris, was enormous, and since then it has never lost its attraction.

The scene is laid in Scotland, the subject being taken from Walter Scott's romance "The Monastery."

George Brown, the hero of the opera, a young lieutenant in English service, visits Scotland. He is hospitably received by a tenant of the late Count Avenel, who has been dead for some years. When he arrives the baptism of the tenant's youngest child is just being celebrated, and seeing that they lack a godfather he goodnaturedly consents to take the vacant place.

Seeing the old castle of the Avenels he asks for its history, and the young wife Jenny tells him that, according to the traditions of the place, it is haunted by a ghost, as is the case in almost every old castle. This apparition is called the "White Lady," but, unlike other ghosts, she is good, protecting her sex against fickle men. All the people around believe firmly in her and pretend to have seen her themselves. In the castle there exists a statue which bears the name of this benevolent genius, and in it the old Lord has hidden treasures. His steward Gaveston, a rogue, who has taken away the only son of the Count in the child's earliest days, brings the castle with all its acres to public sale, hoping to gain it for himself.

He has a charming ward, named Anna. It is she who sometimes plays the part of the White Lady. She has summoned the young tenant Dickson, who is sincerely devoted to her, into the castle, and the young man, though full of fear, yet dare not disobey the ghostly commands.

George Brown, thirsting for a good adventure, and disbelieving in the ghost-story, declares that he will go in Dickson's place.

In the second act George, who has found entrance into the castle, calls for the White Lady, who appears in the shape of Anna. She believes that Dickson is before her, and she reveals her secret to him, imploring his help against her false guardian Gaveston, who means to rob the true and only heir of his property. She knows that the missing son of the Avenels is living, and she has given a promise to the dying Countess to defend his rights against the rapacious Gaveston. George gives his hand to the pretended ghost in token of fidelity, and the warm and soft hand which clasps his awakes tender feelings in him. On the following morning Dickson and his wife Jenny are full of curiosity about George's visit, but he does not breathe a word of his secret.

The sale of the castle, as previously announced, is to begin, and Dickson has been empowered beforehand by all the neighboring farmers to bid the highest price, in order not to let it fall into the hands of the hateful Gaveston. They bid higher and higher, but at length Dickson stops, unable to go farther. Gaveston feels assured of his triumph, when George Brown, recalling his vow to the White Lady, advances boldly, bidding one thousand pounds more. Anna is beside him, in the shape of the spectre, and George obediently bids on, till the castle is his for the price of three hundred thousand pounds. Gaveston, in a perfect fury, swears to avenge himself on the adventurer, who is to pay the sum in the afternoon. Should he prove unable to do so, he shall be put into prison. George, who firmly believes in the help of his genius, is quietly confident, and meanwhile makes an inspection of the castle. Wandering through the vast rooms, dim recollections arise in him, and hearing the minstrel's song of the Avenels, he all at once remembers and finishes the romance, which he heard in his childhood.

The afternoon comes, and with it McIrton, the justice of peace. He wants the money, and George begs to await the White Lady, who promised her help. Anna appears, bringing the treasure of the Avenels hidden in the statue, and with them some documents which prove the just claims of Edwin Count Avenel. This long-lost Count she recognizes in George Brown, whose identity with the playmate of her youth she had found out the night before. Gaveston approaches full of wrath to tear aside the ghost's white veil, and sees his own ward, Anna.

The happy owner of castle and country holds firm to the promise which he gave the White Lady and offers hand and heart to the faithful Anna, who has loved him from her childhood.

DAMNATION OF FAUST

Dramatic Legend in four acts by HECTOR BERLIOZ

Text by BERLIOZ, GERARD and GANDONNIERE

This remarkable opera, while deviating from Goethe's poem, is well worthy of being placed beside the original drama. The orchestral composition is probably unsurpassed in its weirdness and passion, and the opera as a whole ranks among the noblest examples of dramatic music. It was first presented in Paris in 1846.

The scene opens with Faust wandering alone in the fields of Hungary, singing to the awakening spring. The sight of the merry soldiers and peasants sends him home sad and melancholy, where we find him in the second act preparing a dose of poison to end his sufferings. The sweet strains of religious music in the distance stays his hand, and while in meditation, Mephistopheles suddenly appears, and persuades him to accompany him to the Inn of Auerbach in Leipsic. Faust soon tires of the vulgar songs of the students, and Mephistopheles wafts him away to the beautiful banks of the River Elbe, where the enchanting voices of sylphs and fairies soothe him to sleep, only to dream and long for his love, Marguerite.

In the third act Mephistopheles takes Faust secretly to Marguerite's chamber, where Faust pours forth his love in a song of such deep passion that the mother and friends of Marguerite are awakened, and come knocking at the door. The demon drags Faust away unseen, and the unhappy girl is left alone and defenceless.

At the opening of the fourth act Marguerite is in her chamber weeping and yearning for Faust, who has meanwhile retreated to a cavern in the forest, where he is bemoaning his separation from his love. Mephistopheles again visits him, and, working on his sympathy, persuades him to sign an oath to enter his service on the morrow, promising as a reward to conduct him immediately to Marguerite. Mounting two black steeds, they rush wildly through space, and after passing among witches and hideous monsters arrive in hell, where Faust is received with shouts of satanic joy by the demons.

In the epilogue which follows, the unhappy and repentant Marguerite is pardoned by the Almighty and ascends with the virgins to the Kingdom of Heaven.

DÉJANIRE

Tragic Grand Opera by C. C. SAINT-SAËNS

Text by LOUIS GALLET and the composer

This opera saw its first production at Monte Carlo, in 1911. The book is based on early Greek mythology.

In the first act the scene is placed upon a colonnade in front of the palace of Hercules, with the Acropolis visible in the distance. The followers of Hercules are lauding the valiant deeds of their hero, who is a son of Zeus and of Alkmene. Among his achievements they speak of his conquering Eurytus, the tyrant, and of his bringing back with him the latter's daughter, Iole. Iole appears, weeping at her lot and that of her women, the Oechalians. Philoctetes and Hercules enter, Hercules speaking of the hatred borne for him by Juno, and of the criminal passion he has for Iole. He begs his friend Philoctetes to convey a message of love to Iole and to appease the wrath of his legitimate wife, Dejanira, who is awaiting his return to her in Calydon. Then Phenice, sent by Dejanira, tells him that his wife wishes to meet him at the foot of the Acropolis, but Hercules declines to do this, and bids Dejanira return to Calydon. Phenice, who is a seeress, prophesies great evil, has visions of horrible events and sees rising flames. Then she rushes away in terror. Philoctetes discharges his mission, confessing the love Hercules bears to Iole, who scorns it, and the two instead avow an undying affection for each other. Dejanira on being told by Phenice that her husband commands her to go back to Calydon, is seized by convulsive jealousy, and goes to the palace to demand justice from Hercules. She recounts to a circle of admiring Aetolian women all the wonderful exploits divine Hercules has performed to win her. She deplores the fact that now her husband is proving faithless, and relates how Hercules and Nessus, the Centaur, met and how the latter was wounded mortally. In a transport of rage she finally disappears within the palace.

When the curtain rises on Act II Dejanira meets Iole. The two women silently appraise each other, and Dejanira boasts that she will take the sweetheart of her husband to Calydon with her, chained to the spokes of her chariot. Hercules enters, furious at his wife's conduct. Dejanira flees. But Hercules follows her, exacting her promise that she will obey his order. A fierce conjugal quarrel ensues, the wife denouncing the husband's errant fancies. Hercules sends for Iole and tells her of his love. He is answered that she cannot command her feelings, and when Philoctetes comes in, he is watched closely by Hercules who suspects him. Philoctetes and Iole confess their mutual love to Hercules, and Hercules replies by casting his follower into prison.

In Act III Dejanira is recounting the incidents prior to the death of Nessus, and especially how the latter made her a gift of his robe with the injunction that if donned this robe would infallibly work a renewal of love in the wearer. Iole enters, casts herself at the feet of Dejanira, and implores her assistance in trying to effect a union of herself and Philoctetes. Dejanira softens and promises her aid. Hercules surprises Iole, and forces her to submit to him by threatening her with the shameful death of Philoctetes. She yields. Later

Dejanira gives the shirt of Nessus to Iole, instructing her to present it to Hercules as a token of love. Iole consents, unwitting of the true significance of the matter. Phenice predicts evil to come from it all.

In the fourth and last act the scene is enacted before a temple of Jove, and Hercules, preparing sacrifices in honor of his nuptials with Iole, plays the lyre and sings of the joys of love. Iole comes with her companion women and bears the fatal gift, the garment of Nessus. Dejanira, having understood the meaning of this gift to be a renewal of her husband's affection for herself, is unobserved among the crowd of sightseers. Hercules dons the garment, and then leads Iole to the epithalamian throne. He gives the signal for the commencement of the sacrifices, scattering incense in the tripod, and calling upon his father, Jove, to descend in the rays of the setting sun and thus light the altar fire. As he, however, is pouring out the libation, he drops the cup, and grasping his bosom, cries out in sudden, intolerable torture: "The fire burns my flesh!" The ill-omened shirt is torn off his body, but Hercules is dying. Dejanira, now repentant, deplores her own fate and that of her truant husband. Hercules in agony mounts the altar and begs Jove to deliver him from his misery. A thunderbolt flashes out of a clear sky, and the fuel on the altar flames. Thick smoke obscures the whole scene, and when it clears off Hercules is seen seated on high among the gods, his mortal part consumed by fire.

IL DEMONIO

Fantastic Opera in three acts by ANTON RUBINSTEIN

Text after the Russian of ALFRED OFFERMANN

This opera of the great Russian musician has an entirely national character. The great features of Rubinstein's work are most fertile imagination and an immense power of expression, which, however, sometimes almost passes the permitted bounds, although the forms are perfectly mastered, and the fanciful subject is well calculated to afford it room for play. It is taken from the celebrated poem of Lermontoff, and it treats of the devices by which Satan seeks to ensnare the immortal souls on earth.

The plot is laid in Grusia, in the Caucasus.

The first scene represents a wild and lonely country; in the raging storm voices are heard of good and bad spirits alternately. The Arch-Fiend appears, weary of everything, even of his power. He curses the world; in vain he is warned by the Angel of Light to cease his strife against Heaven; the Demon's only satisfaction lies in opposition to and battle with all that is living and good.

He sees Tamara, daughter of Prince Gudal, who expects her bridegroom, the Prince of Sinodal, and, full of admiration for her loveliness, he woos her. Tamara, frightened, calls her companions, and they all return to the castle, but the words of the stranger, whom she has recognized, by the halo of light surrounding him, as a being from a higher world, vibrate in her ears:

"Queen of my love, thou shalt be the Empress of Worlds."

The following scene shows Prince Sinodal, encamping for the night with his suite; the roughness of the way has delayed his coming to Tamara. Near the camp is a chapel, erected in memory of one of his ancestors, who was slain there by a ruffian, and the Prince's old servant admonishes him to pray for his soul. To his destruction, he postpones it till morning, for during his sleep the Demon brings up his enemies, the Tartars, and the Prince's caravan is robbed, and he himself killed.

In the second act Tamara stands ready to receive her bridegroom, whose coming has been announced to her by a messenger.

Tamara's thoughts are with the stranger, though against her will, when an escort brings the dead body of Sinodal. While the poor bride is giving vent to her sorrow, and her father seeks to comfort her by offering religious consolation, she again hears the voice of the Demon, whispering soft seductions to her. At last she feels that her strength is failing before a supernatural power, and so she begs her father to let her enter a monastery. After offering many objections, he finally consents, for in truth his thoughts are only of avenging his children.

In the third act the Demon, who really loves Tamara, and regrets his wickedness, seeks to see her. The Angel of Light denies him the entrance, which, however, he finally forces. Passionately he invokes Tamara's pity and her love, and she, rent by unutterable feelings, implores Heaven's aid, but her strength gives way, and the Demon embraces and kisses her. At this moment the Angel of Light appears, and Tamara is about to hasten to him, when, with a loud cry, she sinks down lifeless. Satan has lost; despairing and cursing all, he vanishes and a thunder-bolt destroys the cloister, from amid the ruins of which the Angels bear the poor love-tortured Tamara to Heaven.

DINORAH: OU LE PARDON DE PLOERMEL

Opera in a prologue and three acts by JACOB MEYERBEER

Libretto by BARBIER and CARRE

This opera was first produced in Paris in 1859. The setting is the Breton village of Ploermel in legendary times.

Act I. When Dinorah and Hoel are on their way to be married, lightning destroys Dinorah's cottage. Hoel, in order to rebuild it, goes into a region haunted by evil spirits in search of hidden treasure. Dinorah, believing herself deserted, loses her reason and with her goat wanders through the mountains in search of Hoel. She comes to the cottage of Corentino who tells her of the fear which overwhelms him in that lonely region. Dinorah induces him to dance with her until, hearing someone approach, she jumps out of the window. Hoel enters and offers Corentino a share in the magic gold if he will help lift it from the cave. This seeming generosity is a ruse to escape the penalty attached to the discovery of the treasure since the first person to touch it must die. Not knowing this, Corentino agrees and they set out, following the tinkle of the goat's bell which they expect to lead them to the hidden gold.

Act II. Dinorah, in a moonlight grove of birches, sings the famous "shadow Song." A storm arises. Through the night, Dinorah sings the legend of the treasure and is overheard by Corentino who now seeks to persuade her to help find the gold. A flash of lightning shows Dinorah's goat crossing a ravine by a fallen tree. She runs after her pet and is swept into the swirling waters. Hoel plunges after her.

Act III. Hoel has rescued Dinorah whose reason returns when she finds herself in her lover's arms. The villagers enter, chanting the "Hymn of the Pardon." A procession forms for the wedding which is to make everyone happy, including the faithful goat.

DJAMILEH

A romantic Opera in one act by GEORGES BIZET

Text by LOUIS GALLET

German translation by LUDWIG HARTMANN

Djamileh was composed before Carmen, and was given in Paris in 1872. But after the years of war and bloodshed its sweetness was out of place, and so it was forgotten, until it was revived again in Germany. Though the text is meagre, the opera had great success on the stages of Berlin, Leipsic, Vienna and Dresden, and so its publisher, Paul Choudens in Paris, was right when he remarked, years ago, to a German critic, "l'Allemagne un jour comprendra les beautés de Djamileh."

There is no more exquisite music than the romance of the boatmen on the Nile, sung with closed lips at the opening of the first scene, and the ravishing dance of the Almée, an invention of Arabic origin, is so original, so wild and melancholy, and yet so sweet, that it enchants every musical ear. The plot is very simple and meagre.

Harun, a rich young Turk, has enjoyed life to its very dregs. He gives dinners, plays at dice, he keeps women, but his heart remains cold and empty; he disbelieves in love, and only cares for absolute freedom in all his actions, but withal his life seems shallow and devoid of interest. Every month he engages a new female slave, with whom he idles away his days, but at the end of this time she is discarded. His antipathy to love partly arises from the knowledge of his father's unhappy married life.

At the opening of the scene Harun lies on a couch, smoking, too lazy to move a finger, and lulled into dreams by the boatmen's songs. At last he rouses himself from his lethargy, and tells his secretary and former tutor, Splendiano, of his visions. The latter is looking over his master's accounts, and now tells him dryly that if he continues his style of living he will be ruined before the end of the year. This scarcely moves the young man, to whom a year seems a long way off; he also takes it coolly when Splendiano remarks that the latest favorite's month is up, and that Djamileh is to leave towards evening, to make room for another beauty. Harun carelessly charges his servant to look out for another slave. When Splendiano sees that Djamileh's unusual beauty has failed to impress his master, he owns to a tender feeling for her himself, and asks permission to win the girl. Harun readily grants this request; but when he sees Djamileh enter with sad and dejected looks he tenderly inquires what ails her. She sings him a strange and melancholy "Ghasel" about a girl's love for a hero, and he easily guesses her secret. In order to console her, he presents her with a beautiful necklace, and grants her her freedom, at which she brightens visibly, but refuses it. Harun, however, has no idea of losing either heart or liberty, and when some friends visit him he turns from her, to join them in a game, leaving her unveiled, and exposed to their insolent stares and admiration. Djamileh, covered with confusion, begins to weep, at which Splendiano interposes, trying to console her by the offer of his hand. Scornfully repulsed by her, he reveals to her the cruel play of his master, and her approaching dismissal, and drives her almost to despair. But she resolves to show her love to her master before she leaves him, and for this purpose entreats Splendiano to let her disguise herself and personate the new slave; promising to be his if her plans should fail, but vowing to herself to choose death rather than leave her beloved master. The evening approaches, and with it the slave-dealer with a whole bevy of beautiful young girls. Harun turns from them indifferently, ordering Splendiano to choose for him, but the slave-dealer insists upon showing up the pearl of his flock, a young Almée, who dances the most weird and passionate figures until she sinks back exhausted. She is selected, but Splendiano gives 200 zechines to the dealer, who consents to let her change her clothes with Djamileh. When the latter re-enters Harun's room veiled, he is astonished to find her so shy and sad. In vain he tries to caress her, she escapes him, but, suddenly unveiling herself, he recognizes her. With wild and passionate entreaty, she begs him to let her be a slave again, as she prefers his presence to freedom and fortune. At first he hesitates, but true love conquers, and he takes her in his arms. He has found his heart at last, and owns that love is stronger and better than any other charm.

LA DOLORES

Grand Opera in three acts by JUAN BRETON
Text from a tale by SALARES

La Dolores was first sung in Madrid, in 1895.

The popular waitress at the tavern kept by Gaspara in the Spanish town of Catalayud, is named Dolores. She has a host of admirers. One of them is the wealthy Patrizio whom Celemino, another one, advises to forget her, since she for the moment loves Melchior, a barber. Soldiers enter the inn, and their commander, Sergeant Rojas, at once falls in love with her. Gaspara's son, the priest Lazaro, secretly is likewise infatuated with Dolores. Melchior comes in and tells Dolores that he is about to marry another girl. Dolores threatens him with revenge. Patrizio enters with a merry chorus, the Rondalla, in which every participant imitates a musical instrument. The Jota (a favorite dance of Aragon) is being performed, all the dancers improvising couplets to accompany the measure. Melchior's mocking song impugns the honor of Dolores, who curses him.

The second act takes place in the yard of the tavern. Lazaro sings of his hopless love for Dolores, when Patrizio enters with gifts for Dolores, and later bull-fighters come, and Rojas boasts of his skill. Melchior asserts he is the favored lover of Dolores; she denies his claim, but secretly she makes an appointment with him. Lazaro enters, avows to Dolores his passion, and clasps her in his arms. Celemino roughly jests, and the two men fight. People are hurrying off for the bull-fight. Rojas is almost killed by the enraged bull, when Lazaro, the priest, rushes in and stabs the raging beast to death. There is great applause and Dolores promises her love to Lazaro.

The third act takes place at a room at the inn. Lazaro, the priest, is chanting the litany and Gaspara, his mother, retires for the night. Dolores whispers to Lazaro not to come to her that night, and Celemino tells Lazaro about Melchior's boast. Dolores invites both Rojas and Patrizio to her room and speaks of her fear of Melchior. She tells Gaspara that her son is in love with her, and the mother is horrified and bids him leave the house. Melchior enters and insults Dolores grossly. Suddenly Lazaro rushes into the chamber and seizes Melchior. Both fall out of the window. Melchior is killed by the fall, but Lazaro is merely injured. Patrizio and others rush in, and Dolores accuses herself before them all of having caused Melchior's death, but Lazaro takes the guilt of it upon himself.

LE DOMINO NOIR

Comic Opera in three acts by AUBER

Text by SCRIBE

This is one of the most charming comic operas which were ever written by this master. Graceful archness and elegance of style are its characteristics, and these lose nothing from the presence of a gay and easy temper which makes itself felt throughout. The same may be said of the libretto.

The plot is well worked out and entertaining. The scene is laid in Madrid in our century.

The Queen of Spain gives a masked ball, at which our heroine Angela is present, accompanied by her companion Brigitta. There she is seen by Horatio di Massarena, a young nobleman, who had met her a year before at one of these balls and fell in love with her, without knowing her.

This time he detains her, but is again unable to discover her real name, and, confessing his love for her, he receives the answer that she can be no more than a friend to him. Massarena detains her so long that the clock strikes the midnight hour as Angela prepares to seek her companion. Massarena confesses to having removed Brigitta under some pretext, and Angela, in despair, cries out that she is lost. She is, in reality, member of a convent, and destined to be Lady Abbess, though she has not yet taken the vows. She is very highly connected, and has secretly helped Massarena to advance in his career as a diplomatist. Great is her

"Don Pasquale" with Lucrezia Bori as given at the Metropolitan Opera House. Setting by Jonel Jorgulesco

anxiety to return to her convent after midnight, but she declines all escort, and walking alone through the streets she comes by chance into the house of Count Juliano, a gentleman of somewhat uncertain character, and Massarena's friend. Juliano is just giving a supper to his gay friends, and Angela bribes his housekeeper, Claudia, to keep her for the night. She appears before the guests disguised as an Arragonian waiting-maid, and charms them all, and particularly Massarena, with her grace and coquetry. But as the young gentlemen begin to be insolent, she disappears, feeling herself in danger of being recognized. Massarena, discovering in her the charming black domino, is very unhappy to see her in such company. Meanwhile Angela succeeds in getting the keys of the convent from Gil-Perez, the porter, who had also left his post, seduced by his love of gormandizing, and had come to pay court to Claudia. Angela troubles his conscience, and frightens him with her black mask, and flies. When she has gone, the housekeeper confesses that her pretended Arragonian was a stranger, by all appearance a noble lady, who sought refuge in Juliano's house.

In the third act Angela reaches the convent, but not without having had some more adventures. Through Brigitta's cleverness her absence has not been discovered. At length the day has come when she is to be made Lady Abbess, and she is arrayed in the attire suited to her future high office, when Massarena is announced to her. He comes to ask to be relieved from a marriage with Ursula, Lord Elfort's daughter, who is destined for him, and who is also an inmate of the convent, but whom he cannot love. Notwithstanding her disguise, he recognizes his beloved domino, who, happily for both, is released by the Queen from her high mission and permitted to choose a husband. Of course, it is no other than the happy Massarena; while Ursula is consoled by being made Lady Abbess, a position which well suits her ambitious temper.

DON CARLOS

Opera in four acts by VERDI

Text by MERY and CAMILLA DU LOCLE

This opera is one of the first of Verdi's. It was half forgotten, when being suddenly recalled to the stage it met with considerable success. The music is fine and highly dramatic in many parts.

The scene of action lies in Spain. Don Carlos, Crown Prince of Spain, comes to the convent of St. Just, where his grandfather, the Emperor Charles the Fifth, has just been buried. Carlos bewails his separation from his stepmother, Elizabeth of Valois, whom he loves with a sinful passion. His friend, the Marquis Posa, reminds him of his duty, and induces him to leave Spain for Flanders, where an unhappy nation sighs under the cruel rule of King Philip's governors. Carlos has an interview with the Queen, but, beside himself with grief, he again declares his love, though having resolved only to ask for her intervention with the King on behalf of his mission to Flanders. Elizabeth asks him to think of duty and dismisses him. Just then her jealous husband enters, and finding her lady of honor, Countess Aremberg, absent, banishes the latter from Spain. King Philip favors Posa with his particular confidence, though the latter is secretly the friend of Carlos, who is ever at variance with his wicked father. Posa uses his influence with the King for the good of the people, and Philip, putting entire confidence in him, orders him to watch his wife.

The second act represents a fête in the royal gardens at Madrid, where Carlos mistakes the Princess Eboli for the Queen and betrays his unhappy love. The Princess, loving Carlos herself, and having nurtured hopes of her love being responded to, takes vengeance. She possesses herself of a casket in which the Queen keeps Carlos's portrait, a love-token from her maiden years, and surrenders it to Philip. The King, though conscious of his wife's innocence, is more than ever jealous of his son, and seeks for an occasion to put him out of the way. It is soon found, when Carlos defies him at an autodafé of heretics. Posa himself is obliged to deprive Carlos of his sword, and the latter is imprisoned. The King has an interview with the Grand Inquisitor, who demands the death of Don Carlos, asserting him to be a traitor to his country. As Philip demurs, the priest asks Posa's life as the more dangerous of the two. The King, who never loved a human being except Posa, the pure-hearted Knight, yields to the power of the Church.

In the following scene Elizabeth, searching for her casket, is accused of infidelity by her husband. The Princess Eboli, seeing the trouble her mischievous jealousy has brought upon her innocent mistress, penitently confesses her fault and is banished from court. In the last scene of the third act Carlos is visited by Posa, who explains to him that he has only imprisoned him in order to save him, and that he has announced to the King that it was himself, Posa, who excited rebellion in Flanders. While they speak, Posa is shot by an arquebusier of the royal guard; Philip enters the cell to present his sword to Carlos, but the son turns from his father with loathing, and explains his friend's pious fraud. While Philip bewails the loss of the best man in Spain, loud acclamations are heard from the people, who, hearing that their prince is in danger, desire to see him.

In the last act the Queen, who promised Posa to watch over Carlos, meets him once more in the convent of St. Just. They are surprised by the King, who approaches, accompanied by the Grand Inquisitor, and into his hands the unhappy Carlos is at last delivered.

DON GIOVANNI

Opera in two acts by MOZART

Text by DA PONTE

Don Giovanni is Mozart's most beautiful opera; we may even say that it is the greatest work of this kind which was ever written by a German musician. The text, too, written by Mozart's friend, is far above the level of ordinary opera texts.

The hero, Don Giovanni, or in English, Don Juan, spoilt by fortune and *blasé,* is ever growing more reckless. He even dares to attack the virtue of Donna Anna, one of the first ladies of a city in Spain, of which her father, an old Spanish grandee, also noble and as strict in virtue as Don Juan is oversatiated and frivolous, is governor. The old father, coming forward to help his beloved daughter, with drawn dagger attacks Don Juan, who, compelled to defend himself, has the misfortune to stab his assailant.

Donna Anna, a lady not only noble and virtuous but proud and high-spirited, vows to avenge her father's death. Though betrothed to a nobleman named Octavio, she will never know any peace until her father, of whose death she feels herself the innocent cause, is avenged. Her only hope is death, and in that she offers the liveliest contrast to her betrothed, who shows himself a gentleman of good temper and qualities, but of a mind too weak for his lady's high-flown courage and truly tragic character. Though Octavio wants to avenge Donna Anna's father, he would do it only to please her. His one aim is marriage with her. Her passionate feelings he does not understand.

Don Juan, pursued not only by Donna Anna but also by his own neglected bride, Donna Elvira, tries to forget himself in debauches and extravagances. His servant Leporello, in every manner the real counterpart of his master, is his aider and abettor. A more witty, a more amusing figure does not exist. His fine sarcasm brings Don Juan's character into bold relief; they complement and explain each other.

But Don Juan, passing from one extravagance to another, sinks deeper; everything he tries begins to fail him, and his doom approaches. He begins to amuse himself with Zerlina, the young bride of a peasant named Masetto, but each time when he seems all but successful in his aim of seducing the little coquette, his enemies, who have united themselves against him, interfere and present a new foe in the person of the bridegroom, the plump and rustic Masetto. At last Don Juan is obliged to take refuge from the hatred of his pursuers. His flight brings him to the grave of the dead governor, in whose memory a life-size statue has been erected in his own park. Excited to the highest pitch and almost beside himself, Don Juan even mocks the dead; he invites him to a supper. The statue moves its head in acceptance of the dreadful invitation of the murderer.

Towards evening Donna Elvira comes to see him, willing to pardon everything if only her lover will repent. She fears for him and for his fate, she does not ask for his love, but only for the repentance of his follies, but all is in vain. The half-drunken Don Juan laughs at her, and so she leaves him alone. Then the ghostly guest, the statue of the governor, enters. He too tries to move his host's conscience; he fain would save him in the last hour. Don Juan remains deaf to those warnings of a better self, and so he incurs his doom. The statue vanishes, the earth opens, and the demons of hell devour Don Juan and his splendid palace.

DON PASQUALE

Comic Opera in three acts by DONIZETTI
Text done after SER MARCANTONIO by
SALVATORE GAMMERANO

This opera, one of Donizetti's last compositions, is a little jewel of the modern Italian kind. Its music is sparkling with wit and grace, and may rank among the best comic operas, of which we have not too many. The reason why it does not occupy the place on the German stage which is due to its undoubted merit is the somewhat deficient German translation of the text book, and the very small frame in which it plays, without any of the dramatic pomp and decoration the people are wont to see in our times, and finally it does not occupy a whole evening, and must needs have a ballet to fill it up. The four persons acting in the play have excellent parts for good singers, as Donizetti thoroughly knew how to treat the human voice.

The wealthy old bachelor Don Pasquale desires to marry his only nephew to a rich and noble lady, but, finding a hindrance in Ernesto's love for another, decides to punish his headstrong nephew by entering himself into marriage and thus disinheriting Ernesto.

His physician Malatesta, Ernesto's friend, pretends to have discovered a suitable partner for him in the person of his (Malatesta's) sister, an "ingénue," educated in a convent and utterly ignorant of the ways of the world.

Don Pasquale maliciously communicates his intentions to the young widow Norina, telling her to distrust Malatesta. The latter, however, has been beforehand with him, and easily persuades Norina to play the part of his (Malatesta's) sister, and to endeavor, by the beauty of her person and the modesty of her demeanor, to gain the old man's affections. Should she succeed in doing so, Don Pasquale and Norina are to go through a mock form of marriage—a notary, in the person of a cousin named Carlo, has already been gained for the purpose—after which Norina, by her obstinacy, extravagance, capriciousness and coquetry, is to make the old man repent of his infatuation and ready to comply with their wishes.

Urged on by her love for Ernesto, Norina consents to play the part assigned to her, and the charming simplicity of her manners, her modesty and loveliness so captivate the old man that he falls into the trap and makes her an offer of his hand. The marriage takes place, and one witness failing to appear, Ernesto, who happens to be near, and who is aware of the plot, is requested to take his place. Besides appointing Norina heiress of half his wealth, Don Pasquale at once makes her absolute mistress of his fortune. Having succeeded in attaining her aim, Norina throws aside her mask, and by her self-willedness, prodigality and waywardness drives her would-be husband to despair. She squanders his money, visits the theatre on the very day of their marriage, ignoring the presence of her husband in such a manner that he wishes himself in his grave, or rid of the termagant who has destroyed the peace of his life. The climax is reached on his discovering among the accounts, all giving proof of his wife's reckless extravagance, a billet-doux, pleading for a clandestine meeting in his own garden. Malatesta is summoned, and cannot help feeling remorse on beholding the wan and haggard appearance of his friend. He recommends prudence, advises Don Pasquale to assist, himself unseen, at the proposed interview, and then to drive the guilty wife from the house. The jealous husband, though frankly confessing the folly he had committed in taking so young a wife, at first refuses to listen to Malatesta's counsel, and determines to surprise the lovers and have them brought before the judge. Finally, however, he suffers himself to be dissuaded and leaves the matter in Malatesta's hands.

In the last scene the lovers meet, but Ernesto escapes on his uncle's approach, who is sorely disappointed at having to listen to the bitter reproaches of his supposed wife, instead of being able to turn her out of doors.

Meanwhile Malatesta arrives, summons Ernesto, and in his uncle's name gives his (Don Pasquale's) consent to Ernesto's marriage with Norina, promising her a splendid dowry.

Don Pasquale's wife, true to the part she has undertaken to play, of course opposes this arrangement, and Don Pasquale, too happy to be able to thwart his wife, hastens to give his consent, telling Ernesto to fetch his bride. His dismay on discovering that his own wife, whom he has only known under the name of Sophronia, and his nephew's bride are one and the same person may be easily imagined. His rage and disappointment are, however, somewhat diminished by the reflection that he will no longer have to suffer from the whims of the young wife, who had inveigled him into the ill-assorted marriage, and he at length consents, giving the happy couple his blessing.

DON QUICHOTTE

Comic Opera in five acts by JULES MASSENET

Text based on the famous tale by CERVANTES

This work was first seen in Monte Carlo, 1910. The scene of the opera is Spain.

Act I. It is a gay holiday. On a public square before the house of Dulcinea are assembled a number of her admirers, among them Don Quichotte with his squire, Sancho Panza, at whose appearance there is great laughter. When Don Quichotte ventures to serenade his mistress, Juan, another of the damsel's suitors, provokes a quarrel. Dulcinea herself prevents a duel, being only highly amused at the gaunt knight's antics. But to encourage him she says he may think of her as much as he pleases if he will first restore to her the precious necklace stolen by robbers.

Act II. Don Quichotte with his squire on the road seeking adventures, the master on his sorry mare Rosinante, the other on his donkey. Sancho is making fun of his master's achievements. He scatters a herd of swine, and next fights windmills, being caught by one of the wings and cast about in the air.

Act III. A mountain scene. Brigands are encountered, and Sancho uses the better part of valor. But the Don defies his assailants, ending as their captive. While waiting for the death stroke, he keeps on repeating the name of Dulcinea. The robbers are impressed with his courage and constancy, and end by turning over to him Dulcinea's necklace.

Act IV. A festival at the house of Dulcinea. She tires of the meaningless gallantries of her wooers, when Don Quichotte and Sancho enter and restore her necklace. She embraces and thanks him. He renews his declaration of love to her, but she admits that she is not fit to be a cavalier's wife. Nevertheless, Don Quichotte affirms his undying affection.

Act V. This passes in a forest, where the noble-hearted knight is dying. As a priceless legacy the knight leaves to his faithful servant an island—"the most beautiful island there is," The Island of Dreams.

LE DONNE CURIOSE

A Comic Opera in three acts by E. WOLF-FERRARI

The text is by LUIGI SUGANA, based on a comedy by CARLO GOLDONI

The first production was at Munich, 1903. The scene is Venice, in the eighteenth century.

The curtain rises showing the quarters of a fashionable social club, where a number of Venetian gentlemen are quietly amusing themselves. Women are excluded from the clubhouse by the strict rules of its members. This fact is even proclaimed by a sign over the entrance door, reading: "No women admitted." The wives of the club members are aware of this prohibition and are chafing at it. For some time their dissatisfaction has found vent in gossip among themselves and in all sorts of surmises as to the mysteries of the club. They are unable to credit the statement of their husbands that no secret doings occur at the club, but suspect the most dreadful things. The plain truth is that nothing more reprehensible is indulged in there than the playing of chess and the giving of dinners, and that the presence of women is only forbidden to allow the men to be among themselves now and then. Thus, Pantalone issues an invitation to a score of his friends for a dinner, and instructs his servant to attend to all the details.

In the next scene there is shown a room in Ottavio's house, where his wife, Beatrice, his daughter, Rosaura, and Lelio's wife, Eleonora, are intensely interested in a discussion as to what there is concealed within the walls of this awful club that is the bugbear of all the women.

Each fair one indulges in a guess. Columbine, the maid, swears that the club members are really only combined to uncover buried treasure. Arlecchino, Columbine's good friend, surmises a lot of ridiculous things. Ottavio, who opportunely drops in on the confabulation, is made to undergo a rigid cross-examination, but is unable to reveal anything of value. As the last one Florindo, the young cavalier who is the favored suitor of Rosaura, the daughter of the house, is made to appear before this dread court of investigation. He is so hard pressed by mistress and maid that at last he cannot help betraying the password of the club,—"Here's to friendship."

In the second act Eleonora, in a room in Lelio's house, gets hold of her husband's breeches, and searches in the pockets for the keys of the clubhouse. But Lelio, a stern man who disapproves even of the indulgence of this connubial prerogative, surprises his wife at this examination. He mercilessly covers her with confusion, and then he leaves for the club. There is a change of scene to Ottavio's house, where one learns from Rosaura and Columbine that the password has been discovered. Columbine now proves her skill by changing the keys in her master's coat for others of similar pattern, and thus possesses herself of the keys to the clubhouse. Next, she elaborately plans to put on male attire and then proceed on her way to the club. This the other ladies also do, setting forth on their travels with all the delicious anticipation of unheard-of adventures. Even Rosaura, first forbidden by her mother to join on the plea of being yet too young for "such things," manages to have Florindo, her suitor, lend her his keys, and she also is on the way to that terrible den of infamy, as they suspect it to be.

The third act first shows the street outside the clubhouse, where a great confusion of missing or wrong keys takes place. Eleonora drops her own key, stolen from her husband's pockets. Then Columbine, although armed with the right key, meets Pantalone, who forces her to deliver it up. Then one and all of the legitimate owners of the keys, to wit, the club members, on arriving at the door, discover that their keys have been stolen. Pantalone, though this thing seems weird to him, nevertheless lets them in with his own key. Florindo detects Rosaura in the throng and tears off her mask. Thus, one by one, despite the cunning of the wives and sweethearts, the men find their way into the clubhouse. And then the women, although somewhat ashamed of the part they have played, appear once more on the square, and at last, by bribing Arlecchino, are admitted to the clubhouse.

The concluding scene takes place in the dining-room of the clubhouse. There is in the rear a door having semi-transparent glass panes in its upper portion. And one by one, with much shoving and screaming, the curious wives are permitted to peep through the glass at the interior of the handsome hall. But they are enormously disappointed, for there is nothing more sensational to see than a body of men peaceably eating a good dinner amid occasional bursts of laughter. But the women are so eager to see the supposed mysteries hidden from them so far that they tumble over each other, and burst open the door, breaking into the room amongst the merry diners. A good dinner, however, predisposes to leniency and good nature, and so the overcurious wives are forgiven, and the women are at last easy in their minds about the real nature of this much-suspected club. There is a dance in which all join. Arlecchino weds his Columbine, and Florindo his Rosaura, and the world goes wagging on.

Dino Borgioli as Alfredo, Claudia Muzio as Violetta and Lawrence Tibbett as Germont in "Traviata"

LES DRAGONS DE VILLARS

(THE BELL OF THE HERMIT)

Comic Opera in three acts by LOUIS AIME MAILLART

Text after the French by G. ERNST

Maillart, who studied under Halévy in Paris, and received the Roman prize (prix de Rome) in the year 1841, composed six operas, all of which are now almost forgotten with the single exception of "Les Dragons de Villars" (in 1856), which found favor in Germany by virtue of its wit and grace.

The music sparkles with French charm and gaiety of the most exquisite kind and these are the merits by which this unpretentious opera has kept its place by the side of its grander and more pompous sisters.

The tale is clever and amusing.

The scene is laid in a French mountain village near the frontier of Savoy, towards the close of the war in the Cevennes, in 1704.

In the first act peasant women in the service of Thibaut, a rich country Squire, are collecting fruit. Georgette, Thibaut's young wife, controls their work. In compliance with a general request she treats them to a favorite Provençal song, in which a young girl, forgetting her first vows made to a young soldier, gives her hand to another suitor. She is interrupted by the sound of trumpets. Thibaut, hurrying up in great distress, asks the women to hide themselves at once, because soldiers are marching into the village. He conceals his own wife in the pigeon-house. A detachment of dragoons arrives, and Belamy, their corporal, asks for food and wine at Thibaut's house. He learns that there is nothing to be had, and in particular that all the women have fled, fearing the unprincipled soldiers of King Louis XIV., sent to persecute the poor Huguenots or Camisards, who are hiding in the mountains—further that the "Dragons de Villars" are said to be an especially wild and dissolute set.

Belamy is greatly disgusted, and, after having had his dinner and a sleep in Thibaut's own bed, decides to march on. The Squire gladly offers to accompany the soldiers to St. Gratient's grotto, near the hermitage, where they have orders to search for Huguenot refugees.

While Belamy is sleeping, Thibaut calls his servant Silvain and scolds him because, though his best servant, he has now repeatedly been absent over-long on his errands; finally orders him to saddle the mules.

Stammering, Silvain owns that they have gone astray in the mountains, but that he is sure of their being found in due time. While Thibaut expresses his fear that they may be stolen by the fugitives, Rose Friquet, an orphan girl, brings the mules, riding on the back of one of them. Thibaut loads her with reproaches, but Silvain thanks her warmly, and though she mockingly repudiates his thanks, he discovers that she has taken the mules in order not to let the provost into Silvain's secret. The fact is that Silvain carries food every day to the refugees, and Rose Friquet, the poor goat-keeper, who is despised and supposed to be wicked and malicious, protects him in her poor way, because he once intercepted a stone which was meant for her head.

While the soldiers are dining, Belamy, who has found Georgette's bonnet, demands an explanation.

Thibaut, confused, finds a pretext for going out, but Rose betrays to Belamy first the wine-cellar and then Georgette's hiding-place. The young wife cries for help, and Rose runs in to fetch Thibaut. Belamy is delighted with the pretty Georgette, but she tells him, rather anxiously, that all the wives of the village must needs remain entirely true to their husbands, for the hermit of St. Gratien, though dead for two hundred years, is keeping rigid watch, and betrays every case of infidelity by ringing a little bell, which is heard far and wide.

Belamy is somewhat desirous to try the experiment with Georgette, and asks her to accompany him to the hermitage instead of her husband.

After having found the other women in the village, the soldiers, to Thibaut's great vexation, decide to stay and amuse themselves. Silvain rejoices, and, after a secret sign from Rose, resolves to warn the refugees in the evening.

In the second act Rose and Silvain meet near St. Gratien. Rose, after telling him that all the paths are occupied by sentries, promises to show him a way for the refugees, which she and her goat alone knows. Silvain, thanking her warmly, endeavors to induce her to care more for her outward appearance, praising her pretty features. Rose is delighted to hear for the first time that she is pretty, and the duet ensuing is one of the most charming things in the opera. Silvain promises to be her friend henceforth, and then leaves, in order to seek the Camisards. After this Thibaut appears, seeking his wife, whom he has seen going away with Belamy. Finding Rose, he imagines he has mistaken her for his wife, but she laughingly corrects him, and he proceeds to search for Georgette. Belamy now comes and courts

Thibaut's wife. But Rose, seeing them, resolves to free the path for the others. No sooner has Belamy tried to snatch a kiss from his companion, than Rose draws the rope of the hermit's bell, and she repeats the proceeding, until Georgette takes flight, while Thibaut rushes up at the sound of the bell. Belamy reassures him, intimating that the bell may have rung for Rose (though it never rings for girls), and accompanies him to the village. But he soon returns to look for the supposed hermit, who has played him this trick, and finds Rose instead, who does not perceive him. To his great surprise, Silvain comes up with the whole troop of refugees, leading the aged clergyman who had been a father to them in his childhood. Silvain presents Rose to them as their deliverer, and vows to make her his wife. Rose leads them to the secret path, while Silvain returns to the village, leaving Belamy triumphant at his discovery.

In the third act we find the people, on the following morning, speaking of nothing but Silvain's wedding with Rose and of the hermit's bell. Nobody knows who has been the culprit, but Thibaut slily calculates that the hermit has rung beforehand, when Rose, the bride, kissed the dragoon. Having learned that the soldiers had been commanded to saddle their horses in the midst of the dancing, the night before, and that Belamy, sure of his prey, has come back, he believes that Rose has betrayed the poor Camisards in order to win the price set on their heads, and this opinion he now communicates to Silvain.

To keep Belamy away from Georgette, the sly Squire has conducted him to the wine-cellar, and the officer, now half drunk, admits having had a rendezvous with Rose. When Thibaut has retired, Belamy again kisses Georgette, and, lo, the bell does not ring this time!

Meanwhile Rose comes down the hill, neatly clad, and glowing with joy and pride, and Georgette, disregarding Thibaut's reproofs, offers her the wedding garland. The whole village is assembled to see the wedding, but Silvain appears with dark brow, and when Rose radiantly greets him, he pushes her back fiercely, believing that she betrayed the refugees who are, as he has heard, caught. Rose is too proud to defend herself, but when Georgette tries to console her she silently draws from her bosom a paper containing the information that the refugees have safely crossed the frontier. Great is Silvain's shame, and heartfelt his repentance. Suddenly Belamy enters, beside himself with rage, for his prey has escaped, and he has lost his patent as lieutenant, together with the remuneration of 200 pistoles, and he at once orders Silvain to be shot. But Rose bravely defends her lover, threatening to reveal the dragoon's neglect of duty. When, therefore, Belamy's superior appears to hear the important news of which the messenger told him, his corporal is only able to stammer out that nothing in particular has happened, and so, after all, Georgette is saved from discovery, and Rose becomes Silvain's happy bride.

THE EGYPTIAN HELEN

Opera in two acts by RICHARD STRAUSS

Libretto by HUGO VON HOFMANNSTHAL

This opera was first given in America at the Metropolitan Opera House, New York, on Nov. 6, 1928.

"Die Ægyptische Helena," or in English "The Egyptian Helen," shows some of the Strauss mastery of the orchestra, but little of the creative genius of "Salome," "Electra," or "Rosenkavalier," and its history in America was a short one, it receiving but four performances when it was given at the Metropolitan Opera House in New York during the season of 1928-29.

Menelaus, after the fall of Troy, takes back with him on his ship, his erring wife, Helen. He decides he must kill her as an expiation to the countless heroes who died for his sake before the walls of Troy. His ship is wrecked on an island ruled over by Æthra. Menelaus is just about to kill Helen, when Æthra, hidden behind a curtain, takes pity on the world's most beautiful woman, and has her elves make a warlike noise which causes Menelaus to believe that he is hearing again the Trojan war-cries and the voice of the dead Paris again challenging him to battle. He rushes out to the ghostly combat. Alone with Helen Æthra causes her to drink a potion which makes her sleep, and forget. When Menelaus returns Æthra tells him a tale which she makes him believe, that for ten years he has been the victim of a phantom, and that the Helen he has taken with him is that phantom. She makes him drink a potion, and then tells him that the real Helen, the Helen who was taken from him ten years before, had been taken to Egypt to the palace of Æthra's father, where she had slumbered ever since. A curtain is raised and Helen is discovered sleeping on a couch. She opens her eyes and comes to Menelaus, who believing Æthra's story, takes his wife tenderly in his arms. Helen whispers to Æthra to waft them to a country where no one has ever heard of the Trojan War, and Æthra consents.

Borne through the air on Æthra's magic mantle, Helen and Menelaus awake at the foot of Mount Atlas. Æthra's deceit has restored only half of Menelaus to his wife, and when he awakes he believes that the woman at his side is the phantom, and that he has killed the real Helen. Two sheiks of the desert, father and son, come upon the two strangers and both sheiks fall in love with Helen. But Helen wishes only Menelaus, and strives to remove from his spirit the darkness that has fallen over it. Æthra comes to her aid, and through her power Menelaus recognizes his wife. Now again the avenger, he raises his dagger to kill her, but his love and her beauty overpowers him and he forgives her. Together they go their way to rule as King and Queen in Sparta.

ELECTRA

Tragic opera in one act by RICHARD STRAUSS

This opera, by Richard Strauss, produced after much preparation by Mr. Oscar Hammerstein, at the Manhattan Opera House, in the season of 1909-10, aroused such a difference of opinion as to its musical merits, that critics in England, Germany, and America carried on quite an animated discussion for many weeks. Mr. Bernard Shaw praised it highly; Mr. Ernest Newman condemned it. Be opinion, however, what it may, the opera is remarkably effective in its dramatic power, and an astonishing musical feat. It was first performed in Dresden, on January 25, 1909.

The text of the opera is by Hugo Von Hofmannsthal, a young Austrian poet. It deals with the tragic incident in Electra's life which makes her the avenger of her father's death on both her mother Clytemnestra, and on her mother's paramour, Ægisthus. The entire action takes place in one act in an inner court of the palace of the King of Mycene.

When the curtain rises serving-women at the well are discussing Electra's whereabouts. As one of them remarks that it is the hour when she cries out upon her father, Electra comes running out of a door and springs back like a wild beast into its lair. The servants continue their remarks, telling how Electra lives and how she is behaving madly towards them. The overseer now comes in and dismisses them into the palace, he going with them.

Electra then comes out of the house. She appears in the red flickerings of light which fall through the branches of the fig trees. She bewails her father's loss in a speech of passionate feeling, and swears to avenge his death with the help of Orestes, her brother. When she and he and her sister Chrysothemis shall have done this, then the three of them will dance about their graves. Chrysothemis enters and looks anxiously for Electra, calling on her softly. Electra turns round like a night wanderer and staggers as she sees her sister's face. She asks Chrysothemis what she wants, and Chrysothemis tells her that Clytemnestra and Ægisthus intend to shut Electra up in a dark tower. Electra laughs and is not afraid. Chrysothemis blames Electra for what is happening to them both. But for her hate and immitigable mind they would have let them out of this prison. She will not sleep in the place every night until she come to die. She will endure no more to herd with menials. Electra answers her that she will wrest the axe out of her mother's hand and kill her. She it was who, from her breast, sent bad dreams to their mother. She will yet drive her before her and kill her. They hear a noise as of some people approaching, and Chrysothemis fears it is her mother coming. She begs Electra not to cross her mother's path if only but for this one day. Electra answers that she has a mind to speak to her mother as she has never spoken to her before.

Against the brightly lighted corridor shuffles and clatters a hurrying procession. There is a tugging and hauling of beasts, a smothered chiding, a quickly stifled cry, the swish of a whip, a pulling back and staggering forward. Chrysothemis, in fear, leaves by the door of the court, and Clytemnestra appears in the wide window. She leans on her waiting-woman, her sallow and bloated face looking whiter above her scarlet dress in the glare of the torches. She is bedecked all over with precious stones and talismans. Electra stands rigid and still, her face turned toward the window. Clytemnestra suddenly opens her eyes, and, trembling with anger, points with her staff at Electra. She rails at her for her conduct; she calls her a serpent rearing its tongue at her, and calls on the immortal gods asking them why is this done to her. A splendidly powerful and dramatic dialogue follows between Electra and her mother, in which Clytemnestra, with royal dignity, and Electra, with terrible hate, lay bare the tragedy of Agamemnon's death by the hand of Ægisthus. Electra, to the speechless horror of her mother, pictures to her the terrible state in which she must live with Ægisthus. Mated to this man, she cries, the bitter gall-drops must fall on her heart. She, Electra, stands before her so that she may see in her face the mingled features of her father and her own. Her silent presence has brought to nought her last word, and her soul has hanged itself within its self-slung noose. They stand eye to eye, Electra in the wildest intoxication, Clytemnestra breathing horribly with fear. At this moment a waiting-woman comes running and whispers some words into Clytemnestra's ear. At first Clytemnestra seems not to understand, but the waiting-woman repeating the message, they both hurriedly run into the house. Electra wonders what was said to Clytemnestra, and Chrysothemis comes running to the door of the court, crying aloud that Orestes is dead. The news renders Electra almost speechless. She had been expecting Orestes, for whom she had sent, to help her in carrying out her scheme for vengeance. She will not believe the news, but when there seems to be no doubt about it she tells her sister that the work must now fall on the two left. She and Chrysothemis must kill "the woman and her husband." Chrysothemis is speechless with horror at the idea of killing her mother, and thinks Electra is beside herself. Electra tells her she is strong, and with a knife or an axe she could easily do it. Chrysothemis recoils in horror and will have nothing to do with Electra's plans. Electra begs on her knees for her help, but Chrysothemis says she simply cannot. When she runs away from Electra through an inner door, Electra sends a curse after her.

Realizing at last that she alone must do the deed, she says, "Then, alone!" She begins to dig hurriedly at the wall of the house, like an animal. As she goes on digging, Orestes stands at the door of the court and sees her. He had been banished from the court from fear of what he might do. Clytemnestra has been living in daily dread of his return. What the waiting-woman had whispered into Clytemnestra's ear was the information that two messengers, an old man and a youth, had arrived in the palace bringing the news that Orestes was dead. It was this news that had made Clytemnestra's face take on its glad look when she met Electra. Orestes stands now looking at his sister. She sees him, but does not recognize him in his disguise. She tells him she has nothing to give him, but he tells her he is come with another with an errand for a lady. She begs him to go away and leave her. He is a herald of misfortune. When, later, he tells her that Orestes lives, she flings herself round and cries aloud to know where he is. When he reveals himself, she flings herself into his arms, sobbing. Eagerly she returns to her thoughts of vengeance, and asks him if he will do it. Yes, the doer shall be he, he answers. Orestes leaves later with his foster-father, who is the old messenger, to perform the act of revenge. Electra is left alone in intolerable suspense. She runs to and fro before the door, with bowed head, like a wild beast in its cage. Suddenly from within is heard the cry of Clytemnestra. Electra shrieks like a demon. "Strike again!" she cries. A second cry is heard from within, and Chrysothemis enters from the servants' door and sees Electra standing with her back against the door. Chrysothemis is followed by the servants and they beg her to let them pass through, to find out what is happening. A waiting-woman runs out to bring help, but she quickly returns, announcing the coming of Ægisthus. Ægisthus enters, demanding why it is there is no one to light the way for him. Electra takes the torch out of the ring, and, running toward him, bows before him. She offers to light him. Then, circling him in a weird dance, she makes him a deep bow as he goes into the house. He has barely got into the house when his cry is heard, shouting, "Murder! Murder!" and his face appears at a little window. He is dragged away, but he reappears, asking if no one hears him. "Agamemnon hears you!" cries Electra, drawing herself up. As Ægisthus is again dragged away, crying, "Woe is me!" Electra stands back, breathing fearfully, her face turned toward the door. Women come running wildly out, Chrysothemis among them. She begs Electra to come away with them, because Orestes has done it. The women leave, while the noise without increases.

Chrysothemis is alone with Electra, who lies crouching on the threshold. She cries shriekingly to Electra to listen to the weeping. Electra raises herself and steps down, her head thrown back like a Mænad.

She lifts her knees, stretches out her arms, and begins her incredible dance. Chrysothemis, who appears against the door with a throng of men and women, cries out against Electra. Electra bids them be silent and dance. She bears the burden of joy, she cries, and she will dance before them there. Only one thing remains for all who are as happy as she is—to be silent and dance. She does a few more steps of tense triumph, and falls a-heap. Chrysothemis runs to her, but Electra lies motionless.

L'ELISIR D'AMORE

An Italian Buffa in two acts by GOETANO DONIZETTI

Text by ROMANI

This graceful little opera was first presented in Milan in 1832. It is bright and gay in its construction, and the music throughout is melodious and pleasing, especially the charming romanza in the second act ("Una furtiva lacrima"), which is one of the most popular songs in light opera.

Adina, a wealthy and capricious young country girl, is devotedly loved by Nemorino, a handsome, but poor, young peasant. She looks rather favorably upon his suit until Belcore, the dashing sergeant of the village garrison, begins to pay her attention. Nemorino, in despair at the success of his rival, visits Doctor Dulcamara, a quack physician, and purchases from him the Elixir of Love, by which he hopes to win back Adina. The mountebank gives him a bottle of Bordeaux wine, which the simple peasant drinks at a gulp, and, becoming tipsy, so enrages Adina, that she promises to marry Belcore on the morrow. The gallant sergeant unexpectedly receiving orders to leave the village, urges Adina to marry him immediately. Nemorino is in despair upon hearing this, for the Elixir was not to take effect until the following day. He therefore goes again to the mountebank, imploring him for another vial, but having no money the Doctor refuses to supply him.

In despair, Nemorino enlists in the army on the advice of Belcore, thereby securing the pay of twenty crowns, with which he purchases a second bottle of the famous Elixir.

In the meantime the maidens in the village have learned that Nemorino's rich uncle has died, leaving him all his property. They crowd about him, showing him the greatest respect and attention, which Nemorino naturally attributes to the Elixir, knowing nothing of the death of his uncle. Adina seeks Doctor Dulcamara, and hearing from him of Nemorino's devotion, is filled with remorse. She goes at once to Belcore, and announcing her change of mind, pays off Nemorino's ransom, which releases him from his obligations to the sergeant. She then bestows her hand upon her happy lover, who is firm in his belief that he owes his good fortune to the magic influence of the Elixir of Love.

THE EMPEROR JONES

Opera in two acts, a Prologue, and an Interlude from EUGENE O'NEILL'S play

Libretto by EUGENE O'NEILL, music by LOUIS GRUENBERG

The Emperor Jones was first presented on January 7, 1933, at the Metropolitan Opera House, New York. The opera caused some difference of opinion among the critics, but the general opinion seems to be that though it had some skillful writing the music added little or nothing to the original play. Yet because of the dramatic force of the libretto the opera had for a time a certain vogue.

Jones, an ex-Pullman porter, has made himself Emperor of an island in the West Indies, but when the scene opens in the palace the Emperor's entourage has all disappeared. Smithers, a Cockney trader and the Emperor's right-hand man, discovers this fact, and, with mean satisfaction, hints to Jones what has occurred. Jones seats himself on his throne, and though he is really worried by the disappearance of his followers pretends it is nothing. Smithers, who hears the tom-toms beating far away in the jungle, realizes that something is afoot, and tries to taunt the Emperor, but is speedily silenced when Jones draws a revolver and threatens him. They talk about Jones's making himself Emperor, and Smithers reminds him that it became possible only when Jones persuaded the bush niggers that he bore a charmed life and that nothing but a silver bullet could kill him. Jones tells Smithers that he has such a bullet which he has made for himself, and that when the time comes he will kill himself with it, as no one but himself is big enough to do it.

Smithers returns to hinting about where Jones's followers are, and asks him if he has noticed any guards about the place for the last few hours. Jones takes up his bell and rings for his servants. When no one answers Jones realizes that his day of power is up. But he brazens it out and declares that he resigns his job. He tells Smithers that he has made all preparations for flight, and that he has hidden food in the jungle, which will support him in his flight to the seacoast where there is a French gunboat which will take him to Martinique with the bank-roll he has saved. Also that he has four lead bullets for the bush-niggers, and the silver bullet for himself, if he fails to reach safety. From the distant hills again comes the beat of the tom-toms. Jones shudders at the sound, but pulling himself together starts for the jungle.

It is the jungle, and it is night. Jones, famished and weary, has arrived at the spot where he thinks he has hidden the food, but he cannot find it. He is in despair, and searches desperately and in vain. Again the tom-toms, and now little formless shapes, his own fears, creep out of the darkness and encircle him. Terrified he draws his revolver and fires at them. They disappear.

The figure of a negro porter, Jeff, whom he had killed in the states in a crap game appears, and begins to throw ghostly dice on the ground. Jones fires at the figure, which vanishes. Louder the tom-toms. In growing terror Jones runs about wildly, then falls with exhaustion. A gang of negro convicts appears guarded by a prison guard, his gun on his shoulder. The negroes start swinging their shovels, digging ghostly earth. The guard motions to Jones to take a shovel, and Jones fires his second bullet. The convicts vanish. Now a band of Southern planters appear and an Auctioneer. The Auctioneer motions to Jones to the auction block, and the planters look at him appraisingly. Jones fires one shot at the Auctioneer, and another at a Planter, and at once they vanish. Jones begins to run, but soon can run no longer. The tom-toms beat ever louder. A Witch-Doctor appears and begins to dance. Soldiers appear and close in on Jones. Jones has only his silver bullet left, and at length terrified above all manner he shoots himself.

L'ENFANT PRODIGUE

(THE PRODIGAL SON)

One-act interlude by CLAUDE DEBUSSY

The text is anonymous

This was first presented in 1910 at London.

As the sun rises Simeon and Leah mourn their long-lost prodigal son, Azael. Youths and maidens bring gifts of fruits and flowers, when Azael enters. He is in tattered raiment, repentant, and utterly exhausted from wandering in a famished condition. He sinks to the ground. Both father and mother forgive him, and kneel down to render thanks to God for his safe return.

ERNANI

Tragic Opera in four acts by GIUSEPPE VERDI

Text by COUNT PIAVE

The story of this opera was taken from Victor Hugo's tragedy "Hernani." It was received with enthusiasm when first presented in Venice in 1844, though later productions gave the composer much trouble on account of the hostility of Victor Hugo, who demanded that the libretto should be changed. Later the poet was appeased and the opera became immensely popular. The music is full of that genuine passionate warmth and dramatic power which characterizes all the works of this composer.

The action takes place in Aragon, Spain, in the year 1519. Ernani, the son of the Duke of Segorbia, has been outlawed by the King, and has become chief of a band of noted brigands. He is deeply in love with Elvira, a noble Spanish lady, and on hearing that she is betrothed to Don Gomez de Silva, an aged grandee of Spain, determines to intervene, and to carry her off if possible.

During the preparations for the marriage, Don Carlos, King of Spain, enters Elvira's chamber, and, declaring his passion, tries to steal her away from the castle. Her cries for help bring Ernani and Silva to her rescue, and the latter, after challenging both of his rivals, recognizes his King, and, falling on his knees, craves pardon, which is granted.

As the wedding nuptials are about to be solemnized, Ernani makes his appearance, disguised as a pilgrim, and, believing Elvira to be false to him, discards his disguise in the presence of Silva, and scornfully demands to be given up to the King. Silva at first refuses to betray his guest, but, on finding that Ernani and Elvira still love each other, swears to be revenged.

The King again appears, and demands the arrest of Silva if he does not give up Ernani, but Elvira pleads so strongly for them that he relents and takes her away as a hostage of the faith of Silva. Silva at once challenges Ernani, who refuses to fight with his aged protector, but promises to give himself up to the King if he may be permitted to see Elvira again before he dies. On hearing that the King has carried her off, Ernani determines on revenge, and promises Silva that he will forfeit his life at any time if he will assist him in his vengeance. To bind the contract Ernani presents him with a horn, which he is to sound when he wishes the promise fulfilled.

The King hears of the plot against his life, and conceals himself in the Catacombs in Aquisgrana, knowing that the assassins are to gather there. During the meeting of the conspirators the King suddenly appears in their midst, condemning all the commoners to prison and the nobles to execution. Ernani, by right of birth, demands to be sentenced with the nobles, but the King, wishing to reign by love rather than by fear, magnanimously pardons all the conspirators, and consents to the union of Ernani and Elvira.

This enrages the jealous Silva, who appears in disguise at the wedding festivities, and blows a blast upon the fatal horn. Ernani, true to his promise, stabs himself to the heart, and dies in the arms of Elvira.

ERO E LEANDRO

Opera in three acts by LUIGI MANCINELLI

Libretto by BOITO based on the Greek legend

This opera was first produced at Madrid in 1897.

Act I. Leandro, victor in the Aphrodisian games both as swordsman and cytharist, is crowned by Hero, priestess of Venus. Ariofarno, the archon, loves Hero who has given her heart to Leandro. When she prays for an omen from Aphrodite, Hero hears in a sea shell the rushing and surging of waters which presage the tragic ending of her romance. Still unconvinced, she kneels before the altar of Apollo and pleads to know her fate. Ariofarno, concealed behind the statue, answers, "Death!"

Act II. The archon, claiming that he has been commanded by the oracle to reinstate a service in a town by the sea, consecrates Hero to the duty of warning the citizens of approaching storms. He later offers to release her from this task if she will return his love. When she again spurns him, he is attacked by Leandro who is banished to the shores of Asia for his crime.

Act III. Leandro has swum the Hellespont to reach Hero in her lonely tower by the sea. While the lovers sing their ecstasy, a storm arises unobserved. A trumpet flares forth from the tower. Leandro leaps into the sea as Ariofarno and his priests enter to chide Hero for neglecting her sacred duties. A thunderbolt shatters a portion of the tower wall and discloses Leandro's body. Hero falls dead at the sight while the archon rages futilely.

L'ETOILE DU NORD

A three-act Opera by GIACOMO MEYERBEER

Text by CAMILLE MEUNIER

This opera was first performed in Paris in 1854. The scene is laid in Russia and Finland.

Act I. The czar, Peter the Great, is disguised as a carpenter, and as such he meets and loves Catharine, who is on the point of donning male attire to serve in the army in place of her brother George.

Act II. At the Russian camp. Catharine, now a recruit in a dragoon regiment, discovers a plot to murder the czar. She betrays the secret and thus enables the czar to spoil the plot and seize the conspirators.

Act III. This happens at the palace of the czar. Peter longs for Catharine whom he has not met of late and thinks she must be dead, for his inquiries have been in vain. But at last he has news that she is alive but insane. The czar sends for her. To please her he has his garden laid out so as to resemble the one he tended in Viborg, Finland, where he first met her. He also puts on his carpenter's costume, and as she sees him she falls into his arms. He makes her his wife.

EUGEN ONEGIN

Opera in three acts by PETER TSCHAIKOWSKY

Text by MODESTE TSCHAIKOWSKY

The first production was in Moscow in 1879. The setting is Russia during the early part of the nineteenth century.

Act I. Eugen Onegin, a dissolute man about town, is called from the wild life of Petrograd to the bedside of his uncle who is ill at his country estate. The uncle dies and Eugen takes possession of his property. He has brought to the countryside a profound satiety of life's enjoyments and a contempt for the society of the people around him. However, he forms a friendship with Lenski, a fanatical young poet, who introduces him to Madame Larina and her two daughters—Olga, a creature of surface emotions, and Tatiana who dreams over the books her mother read when a girl. Lenski is betrothed to Olga. Tatiana recognizes in Eugen the lover of her dreams and reveals her heart to him in a letter. Although Eugen is touched by her adoration, he well knows that his life has unfitted him for marriage. He gently refuses the young girl's love and does not dream that she continues to cherish him in secret as her ideal.

Act II. Tatiana's birthday is being celebrated with a grand ball. Eugen feels hopelessly out of place in the unsophisticated and narrow-minded company. Finally, bored by the stupidity of those around him and longing to avenge himself on Lenski for bringing him to the festival, he begins to flirt with Olga. The poet is offended and challenges Eugen to a duel. Social considerations force Eugen to accept the challenge in spite of his real affection for Lenski. To his dismay, Eugen kills his friend in the duel and, filled with remorse, he leaves the country.

Act III. Twenty-six years have passed. Eugen has wandered aimlessly over the world and is now back in Petrograd. He is invited to a magnificent ball given by Prince Gremin. There he discovers that the Princess Gremina, a beautiful and accomplished woman of the world, is none other than Tatiana. He promptly falls deeply in love with her but she laughs at his impetuous wooing, declaring that he cares for her only because she is now a brilliant personage. Finally, his ardour dispels her mockery and she admits that she still loves him. Eugen is overjoyed but the Princess hastens to add that she intends to remain faithful to her husband. When Eugen's entreaties fail to weaken her resolution, he takes a broken-hearted leave of her and begins again his restless wanderings over the world.

EURYANTHE

Grand Opera by C. M. VON WEBER

Text by HELMINA VON CHEZY

This opera has not had the success of Oberon or Freischütz, a fact to be attributed to the weakness of its libretto, and not to its music, which is so grand and noble that it cannot but fill the hearer with admiration and pleasure.

The overture is one of the finest pieces ever written, and the choruses and solos are equally worthy of admiration.

The plot is as follows:

Adolar, Count of Nevers and Rethel, is betrothed to Euryanthe of Savoy, and the wedding is to take place, when one day, in the King's presence, Lysiart, Count of Forest and Beaujolais, suggests that all women are accessible to seduction. He provokes Adolar so much that he succeeds in making him stake his lands and everything he possesses on his bride's fidelity. Lysiart, on the other hand, promises to bring a token of Euryanthe's favor.

In the following scene we find Euryanthe in the company of Eglantine de Puiset. This lady is a prisoner who has taken refuge in the castle of Nevers, and has ingratiated herself so much with Euryanthe that the latter tenderly befriends the false woman. Asking Euryanthe why she always chooses for her recreation the dreary spot of the park where Adolar's sister Emma lies buried, she is told by her, in confidence, that she prays for Emma, who poisoned herself after her lover's death in battle. Her soul could find no rest until the ring which contained the venom should be wet with the tears of a faithful and innocent maid, shed in her extreme need. No sooner has Euryanthe betrayed her bridegroom's secret than she repents doing so, foreboding ill to come. Lysiart enters to escort her to the marriage festival, but he vainly tries to ensnare her innocence, when Eglantine comes to his rescue. She loves Adolar, and, her passion not being returned, she has sworn vengeance. Stealing the fatal ring from the sepulchre, she gives it to Lysiart as a token of Euryanthe's faithlessness, and Lysiart, after having brought Euryanthe to Adolar, shows the ring in presence of the whole court, pretending to have received it from Euryanthe. The poor maiden denies it, but as Lysiart reveals the mystery of the grave, she cannot deny that she has broken her promise of never telling the secret.

Adolar, full of despair, surrenders everything to his rival, leading Euryanthe, whom he believes to be false, into the wilderness to kill her. A serpent is about to sting him, when his bride throws herself between. He kills the reptile, but, after her sacrifice, he is unable to raise his arm against her and so leaves her to her fate.

She is found by the King and his hunters, and to them she relates the whole story of her error of confiding in the false Eglantine. The King promises to inform Adolar and takes her back with him. Meanwhile Adolar, returning once more to his grounds, is seen by his people. One of them, Bertha, tells him that Euryanthe is innocent, and that Eglantine, who is about to marry Lysiart and to reign as supreme mistress over the country, has been the culprit.

Eglantine, appearing in bridal attire, led by Lysiart,

suddenly becomes a prey to fearful remorse; she sees Emma's ghost, and in her anxiety reveals the whole plot. Her bridegroom stabs her in his fury, but is at once seized by order of the King, who just then comes upon the scene. Adolar, believing Euryanthe dead, demands a meeting with Lysiart. But the King declares that the murderer must incur the penalty of the laws. He renders up to Adolar his possessions and his bride, who the more easily pardons her repentant bridegroom that she has saved his sister's soul by the innocent tears of her misfortune.

THE EVANGELIMANN

A Musical Drama in two acts

With Text and Music by WILHELM KIENZL

The author has learnt a great deal since the days in which he composed Urvasi. His music has become more original and more independent of great models. The new opera, while not so poetical, is eminently touching and true; the text, founded on fact, runs smoothly and is cleverly done, the verses being well adapted to the music. Like Verga's Cavalleria, the subject is such as to be impressive even without music.

It is necessary to explain the title of this opera, which signifies a man who goes about reciting biblical verse, after the fashion of street singers. This means of earning a livelihood is unknown in Germany, but forms a specialty in Austria.

The music of the first act puts one in mind of the Meistersingers; as a whole it is very captivating, fresh and drastic, especially during the ninepin scene. The orchestra predominates, but there are truly poetic airs, which will linger as much in the heart as in the ear of the hearer. Such is: "O sweet days of my youth," and in the last act: "Blessed are they who are persecuted," from Christ's Sermon on the Mount. Another charming bit of music is the children's waltz, in which the composer has paraphrased one of Lanner's well-known waltz motives.

The first scene is laid in the village of St. Othmar, in Austria, or rather in the court of the convent of the

Benedictines of that place. Mathias, a young clerk of the convent, has an interview with Martha, the niece and ward of Frederic Engel, the rich warden of the convent. John, Mathias's elder brother and the village schoolmaster, sees them together. Being in love with the girl himself, he warns her uncle of his brother's courtship and excites his wrath against the lovers, so that Engel, coming across the young people, gruffly tells Mathias that he has already chosen a rich bridegroom for his ward. In vain, the lovers beseech the old man's pity, for his anger only waxes stronger, and he goes so far as to discharge Mathias, warning him to leave the place altogether. Martha, left alone, bemourns her guardian's hardness, and John, thinking to profit by the occasion, approaches her and asks for her hand. But he is so decidedly rejected by Martha that he swears to have his revenge.

Meanwhile the evening approaches, and the country folk come to the inn next to the convent to play their game of ninepins. During this very animated scene Mathias finds Magdalen, his sweetheart's friend, whom he entreats to take a message to Martha, asking her to meet him at eleven o'clock in the bower near the skittle-ground for a last farewell. John hears this, and when night sets in, and the gates of the convent are closed, he remains outside alone, hiding behind the barn floor. When the clock strikes eleven, Martha and Mathias approach the bower. They swear to remain true to each other, come what may. Their tender words excite John's jealousy to the utmost, and while the lovers are engrossed with their sorrow and make plans for the future, he sets fire to the barn floor. Soon the flames leap up to the sky, but the lovers are oblivious of everything, till they hear the watchman's cry of fire. Mathias persuades

Martha to hide herself; so he is found alone on the place and seized by the crowd and brought before the warden. Engel at once jumps to the conclusion that he has been the incendiary, to revenge himself for Engel's hard-heartedness, and, despite his protestations of innocence, Mathias is put in chains and carried away, while Martha, who comes out from her hiding-place, falls back in a swoon, after proclaiming his innocence.

The second act takes place thirty years later in Vienna. Magdalen sits under a lime-tree, in the court of an old house, and muses sadly over days gone by. After long, lonely years, she has found the schoolmaster John sick unto death, and now finds comfort in nursing him. Nothing has ever been heard of Mathias again, and she wonders sadly what has become of him. Children throng into the court, they dance around the lime-tree, while an old organ grinder plays pretty waltz tunes to their steps. While they are dancing, an Evangelimann comes into the court. He reads and sings to the children the verses from Christ's Sermon on the Mount, and teaches them to repeat the melody. When they are able to sing it faultlessly, he faintly asks for a drink of water, which Magdalen brings him. She asks him whence he comes, and when he tells her that his father's house stood in St. Othmar, she recognizes in him her old friend Mathias. Then he relates his sad story, how he lay imprisoned for twenty years, the real incendiary having never been discovered. When he was set free, he returned home, only to find that his bride had drowned herself. All his efforts to earn a livelihood were fruitless; nobody would employ the convict, until he was at last obliged to become an Evangelimann, and wandered from place to place, preaching the gospel to the poor, and getting such small bounties they could afford to give. Exhausted by hunger and overcome by sad remembrances, Mathias sinks down on the bench half fainting, but is revived by bread and broth brought to him by Magdalen, who earnestly entreats him to return soon, and to bring comfort to the sick man she is nursing.

The last scene takes place a day later in John's sick-room. He is lying on a couch, a prey to bitter thoughts and pangs of conscience, when his brother's voice reaches his ear from below, and dimly awakens sweet memories in him. He bids Magdalen to fetch the singer, and when the latter enters he feels so drawn to him, without recognizing his brother, that he begs leave to unburden his soul to him.

Mathias, soon recognizing his brother, is about to fold him in his arms, but John despairingly shrinks from him, while confessing his guilt in broken words and beseeching his forgiveness. The unfortunate Mathias, whose life has been so utterly ruined by his brother, battles fiercely with his natural feelings. But when he sees the wretched John on his knees before him, so broken down and exhausted, he finally forgives him. With a last faint gasp of thanks, John falls back and dies, while Magdalen prays, "And forgive us our trespasses, as we forgive those that trespass against us." Outside the children's voices are heard once more: "Blessed are they that are persecuted for righteousness' sake; for theirs is the Kingdom of Heaven."

FAIRYLAND

A three-act American allegorical Opera by HORATIO PARKER

Libretto by BRIAN HOOKER

This work was first performed at Los Angeles, 1915. The scene is supposed to be a picturesque valley in a hilly district of Europe, about 1300 A.D.

The dwellers in a charming valley are wending homewards one autumn eve, their way leading them past the abbey. Rosamund, a novice, all clad in white, is gazing out afar from a balcony and longing to mingle with the world. Eagerly she stretches out her arms towards that unknown region. In the distance she spies a horseman and she implores him in her thoughts to bear her away to scenes of action. The angelus is tolled, she crosses herself and goes within. Corvain, striding over a frail bridge, pauses at the gate of the abbey. Robin coming from the woods, is hailed by Corvain who inquires which way the king went. Robin's answer is given tauntingly, and he insinuates that Corvain harbors plots against the king. The nuns of the abbey come forth in a procession, walking slowly by twos and threes, Rosamund last. They carry garlands with which to wreathe the shrine near-by. Corvain blocks the path, and Myriel, the abbess, demands to know what is his object there. Corvain rejoins curtly, betraying contempt for his saintly brother. He speaks of taking the king's place. While talking together, Corvain points to the approaching figure of Auburn, the king. Corvain asks the thoughtful monarch who is to bear rule in his absence, and Auburn feels indifferent about it. The abbess claims the rule for the Church and drives Corvain to flight. At Myriel's demand Auburn destroys the bridge leading across the chasm. Auburn prays by the shrine for a clear answer as to the real meaning of life, but in the gathering gloom of night Corvain has stolen up by crooked paths, and now strikes Auburn senseless and seizes the crown. At this moment the red rose within the shrine gleams brightly, and fairy voices are heard singing. Conscience wakes within Corvain, who now flings away the stolen crown and disappears. A fairy scene ensues. Robin comes in, scatters the last drops of wine out of his cup, after drinking to the health of the king and queen of Fairyland, and the unconscious king awakes. He sees Rosamund enthroned on the shrine, in lieu of the Virgin, and they both avow their love and know they are in Fairyland.

At the opening of the second act Corvain stands in his castle attired in garments of royalty, granting audience to Robin and his fellows, all of whom ask for justice. They are driven away, and Rosamund is brought in footsore and in hard plight. She says she is seeking the king in Fairyland. He invites her to stay with him, making love to her, but she rejects his wooing and sings the song of the rose. Robin hears it, and is followed in by Auburn clad as a pilgrim. Rosamund instantly recognizes him, though Auburn has forgotten her and merely stares at her uncomprehendingly. Rosamund collapses at his feet. Auburn lays claim to kingship in the palace, but Rosamund tells him his real rule is in Fairyland. She attempts to make Auburn recall the past and his rulership in Fairyland, until Myriel, the abbess, appears and puts a stop to the growing confidences of these two, telling them to forbear. Myriel and the nuns drag Rosamund away, despite the protests of Auburn. Corvain comes on the scene with a body of stout followers and tries to claim Rosamund for himself, but Myriel disputes his right, and Auburn suddenly interferes and stands confessed as the king. Corvain in turn denies this and the two contend against each other, Corvain resting his claim on the weapons of his men-at-arms, while Auburn relies on the masses of the people. The latter, however, are led astray by the specious eloquence of Corvain, and disown Auburn. When he summons the light of the rose to his aid, that, too, fades away.

The last act shows Rosamund tied to a stake ready for death, and the abbey bell rings, Myriel approaching Rosamund with sympathy and help. Rosamund is endeavoring to explain to Myriel the reasons for the choice she has made, but the abbess fails to understand her. Myriel, however, offers to the girl life, absolution and sainthood, if only she will repent. Rosamund refuses, whereupon Myriel sadly goes away, and Auburn stealthily comes up, and vainly makes an attempt to free her. He acknowledges that it was she who in the past was his friend when all the world reviled him and he kneels to her. Then memory returns to both, and Auburn murmurs happily: "My Queen of Fairyland!" Meanwhile day has come, people wander about; there is life and noise in the tavern, and when Auburn asks Robin to proclaim him the rightful king, Robin is ready to do so. But Corvain comes now with strong armed support, and after a struggle between him and Auburn, the latter is seized and condemned to share the fate of Rosamund. Auburn is fastened to the stake alongside of the girl. At the last moment when Rosamund in sympathy and pity lays her hand upon Auburn's, the fairy rose blooms afresh, the common people change to fairies, and before them the soldiers retreat, the nuns lay down the crozier, and the flames of the fagots, already kindled to consume those two, die down. Their chains fall away, and they are placed on a throne and clad in costly robes. They have attained rulership in Fairyland and are forever happy.

FALSTAFF

A lyric Comedy in three acts by GUISEPPE VERDI

Text by ARRIGO BOITO

Nobody who hears this opera would believe that it has been written by a man in his eightieth year. So much freshness, wit and originality seem to be the privilege of youth alone. But the wonder has been achieved, and Verdi has won a complete success with an opera which runs in altogether different lines from his old ones, another wonder of an abnormally strong and original mind.

Falstaff was first represented in Milan in February, 1893; since then it has made its way to all theatres of renown, and it is now indisputable that we have in it a masterpiece of composition and orchestration. Those who only look for the easy-flowing melodies of the younger Verdi will be disappointed; art is predominant, besides an exuberant humor, full of charm for every cultivated hearer. The numbers which attract most are the gossiping scene between the four women in the first act, Falstaff's air "Quand'ero paggio del Duca di Norfolk era sottile" in the second, and the fairy music in the last act.

The text is so well known to all readers of Shakespeare, that it may be recorded quite briefly. It is almost literally that of "The Merry Wives of Windsor." The first scene is laid in the Garter Inn of that town. After a quarrel with the French Physician Dr. Cajus, who has been robbed while drunk by Falstaff's servants Bardolph and Pistol, Falstaff orders them off with two love-letters for Mrs. Alice Ford and Mrs. Meg Page. The knaves refusing indignantly to take the parts of go-betweens, Falstaff sends them to the devil and gives the letters to the page Robin.

In the second act the two ladies, having shown each other the love-letters, decide to avenge themselves on the fat old fool.

Meanwhile Falstaff's servants betray their master's intentions towards Mrs. Ford to her husband, who swears to guard his wife, and to keep a sharp eye on Sir John. Then ensues a love scene between Fenton and Mr. Ford's daughter Anna, who is destined by her father to marry the rich Dr. Cajus, but who, by far, prefers her poor suitor Fenton.

After a while, the merry wives assemble again, in order to entice Falstaff into a trap. Mrs. Quickley brings him an invitation to Mrs. Ford's house, in absence of the lady's husband, which Sir John accepts triumphantly.

Sir John is visited by Mr. Ford, who assumes the name of Mr. Born, and is nothing loath to drink the bottles of old Cyprus wine which the latter has brought with him. Born also produces a purse filled with sovereigns, and entreats Falstaff to use it in order to get admittance to a certain Mrs. Ford, whose favor Born vainly sought. Falstaff gleefully reveals the rendezvous which he is to have with the lady, and thereby leaves poor disguised Mr. Ford a prey to violent jealousy.

The next scene contains Falstaff's well-known interview with mischievous Alice Ford, which is interrupted by Mrs. Meg's announcement of the husband.

Falstaff is packed into a washing basket, while husband and neighbors search for him in vain. This scene, in which Falstaff, half suffocated, alternately sighs and begs to be let out, while the women tranquilly sit on the basket and enjoy their trick, is extremely comic. The basket, with Falstaff, wash and all, is turned over into a canal, accompanied by the women's laughter.

In the third act Mrs. Quickley succeeds once more in enticing the old fool. She orders him to another rendezvous in the Park at midnight, and advises him to come in the disguise of Herne, the black hunter. The others hear of the joke, and all decide to punish him thoroughly for his fatuity. Ford, who has promised Dr. Cajus to unite Anna to him that very night, tells him to wear a monk's garb, and also reveals to him that Anna is to wear a white dress with roses. But his wife, overhearing this, frustrates his designs. She gives a black monk's garb to Fenton, while Anna chooses the costume of the Fairy Queen Titania. When Falstaff appears in his disguise he is attacked on all sides by fairies, wasps, flies and mosquitoes, and they torment him long, until he cries for mercy. Meanwhile Cajus, in a gray monk's garb, looks for his bride everywhere, until a tall veiled female, in flowing white robes (Bardolph), falls into his arms; on the other side Anna appears with Fenton. Both couples are wedded, and only when they unveil is the mistake discovered. With bitter shame the men see how they have all been duped by some merry and clever women, but they have to make the best of a bad case, and so Ford grants his benediction to the happy lovers, and embraces his wife, only too glad to find her true and faithful.

FAUST

Opera in five acts by CHARLES GOUNOD

The subject of this piece is taken from the first part of Goethe's greatest drama, "Faust."

Faust, a celebrated old doctor, is consumed by an insatiable thirst for knowledge, but, having already lived through a long life devoted to the acquirement of learning and to hard works as a scholar, without having his soul-hunger appreciably relieved, is dissatisfied, and in his disappointment wishes to be released from this life, which has grown to be a burden to him. At this moment Mephistopheles, the incarnation of the Evil One, appears and persuades him to try life in a new shape. The old and learned doctor has only known it in theory; Mephisto will now show it to him in practice and in all the splendor of youth and freshness. Faust agrees, and Mephisto endows him with youth and beauty. In this guise he sees earth anew. It is Easter-time, when all is budding and aglow with freshness and young life, and on such a bright spring day he first sees Margaretha, and at once offers her his arm.

But this lovely maiden, pure and innocent, and well guarded by a jealous brother, named Valentin, refuses his company somewhat sharply. Nevertheless she cannot help seeing the grace and good bearing of the fine cavalier, and the simple village-maiden is inwardly pleased with his flattery. A bad fate wills it that her brother, Valentin, who is a soldier, has to leave on active service, and after giving many good advices and warnings for his beautiful sister's welfare, he goes, and so

Mephisto is able to introduce Faust to the unprotected girl by means of a message, which he is supposed to have received for an old aunt of Margaretha's, Frau Marthe Schwertlein. This old gossip, hearing from Mephisto that her husband has been killed in battle, lends a willing ear to the flatteries of the cunning Devil; and Margaretha is left to Faust, who wins her by his love and easy manners. She is only a simple maiden, knowing nothing of the world's ways and wiles, and she accepts her lover's precious gifts with childish delight.

By and by her brother Valentin returns victorious from the war, but alas! too late. He challenges his sister's seducer; Mephisto, however, directs Faust's sword, and the faithful brother is, much against Faust's own will, slain, cursing his sister with his last breath.

Now Margaretha awakes to the awful reality of her situation, and she shrinks from her brother's murderer. Everybody shuns her, and she finds herself alone and forsaken. In despair she seeks refuge in church, but her own conscience is not silenced; it accuses her more loudly than all the pious songs and prayers. Persecuted by evil spirits, forsaken and forlorn, Margaretha's reason gives way, and she drowns her new-born child.

Meanwhile Mephisto has done everything to stifle in Faust the pangs of conscience. Faust never wills the evil; he loves Margaretha sincerely, but the bad spirit urges him onward. He shows him all the joys and splendors of earth and antiquity in its most perfect form in the person of Helena, but in the midst of all his orgies Faust sees Margaretha. He beholds her, pale, unlike her former self, in the white dress of the condemned, with a blood-red circle round the delicate neck. Then he knows no rest; he feels that she is in danger, and he bids Mephisto save her.

Margaretha has actually been thrown into prison for her deed of madness, and now the executioner's axe awaits her. She sits on the damp straw, rocking a bundle, which she takes for her baby, and across her poor, wrecked brain there flit once more pictures of all the scenes of her short-lived happiness. Then Faust enters with Mephisto, and tries to persuade her to escape with them. But she instinctively shrinks from her lover, loudly imploring God's and the Saints' pardon. God has mercy on her, for, just as the bells are tolling for her execution, she expires, and her soul is carried to Heaven by angels, there to pray for her erring lover. Mephisto disappears into the earth.

LA FAVORITA

Grand Opera in four acts by GOËTANO DONIZETTI

Text by ROYER and WAETZ

This opera is most powerful in its dramatic effect, and the score contains some marvelous melodies, not only in passion and fury, but also in pathos and solemnity. It was first presented at the Académie Royale de Musique, Paris, December 2, 1804.

The action of the opera is supposed to take place in Spain in the year 1340. Ferdinand, a novice in the convent of St. James, is about to assume vows, when he sees and falls in love with Leonora di Gusman, who, unknown to him, is the favorite of Alfonso XI, King of Castile. Ferdinand leaves the convent in pursuit of Leonora, and succeeds in obtaining access to her at her beautiful home on the Isle of St. Leon. He declares his love for her, and finds it purely reciprocated, Leonora being careful not to reveal her real position. Ferdinand urges her to fly with him; this she cannot do, but secures for him a commission in the army, and tells him to go to the wars and prove himself worthy of her hand.

King Alfonso wishes to divorce his Queen and marry Leonora, but the Papal throne is so openly opposed to this that he dares not do it. At this juncture, Ferdinand returns from the wars, where he has gallantly defeated the Moors and practically saved the kingdom from ruin. The King heaps rewards upon him, and, fearing the Papal malediction, consents to his marriage with Leonora. Ferdinand, still ignorant of Leonora's relations to the King, presses his suit, and is accepted, she believing that her lover knows all and has forgiven.

After his marriage the nobles taunt him of the stain upon his honor, and even his beloved friend Balthazar, superior of the convent, recoils from him. Finally, learning the truth, he renounces his bonds, and madly cursing the King and Leonora, returns once more to the convent. The heartbroken Leonora, disguised as a novice, goes to the convent of St. James, where she is forgiven by Ferdinand, who, overcome by his great love, again urges her to fly with him. It is too late, however, for with a prayer of thanksgiving at her absolution, the repentant Leonora expires in the arms of her grief-stricken lover.

FEDORA

Opera in three acts by UMBERTO GIORDANO

Text by COLAUTTI after SARDOU'S drama

This work was first given in Milan in 1898. The action takes place in St. Petersburg, Paris and Switzerland during the latter part of the nineteenth century.

Act I. While the beautiful Princess Fedora awaits the coming of her betrothed, the dissolute Count Vladimir, a titled police spy, he is brought in by De Siriex, mortally wounded. It is thought that Nihilists have assassinated him and Fedora resolves to devote her life to discovering the murderer.

Act II. Fedora suspects Count Loris who has fallen in love with her. At a reception in her home, she succeeds in drawing from him a confession of his guilt and plans to have him taken by Grech, a police officer, after her other guests have departed. Later Count Loris explains that he killed her fiancé because he had betrayed Loris' young wife and brought about her untimely death. Fedora, who first pities then loves Loris, renounces her vengeance and together they escape from the trap she had prepared for him.

Act III. Loris and Fedora are married and living in a mountain villa in Switzerland. She learns that because of Loris' connection with Count Vladimir's murder, his brother has been thrown into prison and dies there. Loris' mother dies of the shock. This weighs upon Fedora's mind as she is responsible for the brother's arrest. When Loris discovers that it was Fedora who set the secret service on his track, he is about to kill her when she, in despair, swallows poison. He now pleads with her to live but she dies in his forgiving arms while a country lad off stage sings, "My mountain maid returns no more!"

LA FÊTE CHEZ THÉRÈSE

Operatic comedy in two acts by VICTOR HAHN

Text after a Parisian vaudeville

This was first produced in Paris, 1910.

Act I. A charming young duchess during a visit at her modiste's, accidentally meets an attractive young man, but in a wholly informal manner. While waiting for the appearance of her dressmaker, she casually inspects the contents of the room, and in doing so she peeps around a long mirror. Her eyes meet those of the young man, evidently admiring her. But the young duchess does not feel like adventures that day, and so she hurries away without further ado.

Act II. But she has not reckoned with the young man, for he has become enamored of her, and therefore introduces himself at a masquerade ball. She, however, still pursues the same tactics: she runs away from him. He is persistent, and in a second disguise prevails upon the duchess to grant him at last a meeting. But now that things begin to be serious the modiste herself takes a hand. She calls upon the duchess, and although the latter is her best customer, she successfully appeals to her, making it plain that the young man is her betrothed. The duchess relinquishes him.

FIDELIO

Opera in two acts by L. van BEETHOVEN

This opera, the only one by the greatest of German composers, is also one of the most exquisite we possess. The music is so grand and sublime, so passionate and deep, that it enters into the heart of the hearer. The libretto is also full of the highest and most beautiful feeling.

Florestan, a Spanish nobleman, has dared to blame Don Pizarro, the governor of the state prison, a man as cruel as he is powerful. Pizarro has thus become Florestan's deadly foe; he has seized him secretly and thrown him into a dreadful dungeon, reporting his death to the Minister.

But this poor prisoner has a wife, Leonore, who is as courageous as she is faithful. She never believes in the false reports, but, disguising herself in male attire, under the name of Fidelio, resolves not to rest until she has found her husband.

In this disguise we find her in the first act; she has contrived to get entrance into the fortress where she supposes her husband imprisoned, and by her gentle and courteous behavior and readiness for service of all kinds has won not only the heart of Rocco, the jailer, but that of his daughter Marcelline, who falls in love with the gentle youth, and neglects her former lover, Jacquino. Fidelio persuades Rocco to let her help him in his office with the prisoners. Quivering with mingled hope and fear, she opens the prison gates, to let the state prisoners out into the court, where they may for once have air and sunshine.

But, seek as she may, she cannot find her husband, and, in silent despair, she deems herself baffled.

Meanwhile Pizarro has received a letter from Sevilla announcing the Minister's forthcoming visit to the fortress. Pizarro, frightened at the consequences of such a call, resolves to silence Florestan for ever. He orders the jailer to kill him, but the old man will not burden his soul with a murder, and refuses firmly. Then Pizarro himself determines to kill Florestan, and summons Rocco to dig a grave in the dungeon, in order to hide all traces of the crime.

Rocco, already looking upon the gentle and diligent Fidelio as his future son-in-law, confides to him his dreadful secret, and, with fearful forebodings, she entreats him to accept her help in the heavy work. Pizarro gives his permission, Rocco being too old and feeble to do the work quickly enough if alone; Pizarro has been rendered furious by the indulgence granted to the prisoners at Fidelio's entreaty, but a feeling of triumph overcomes every other when he sees Rocco depart for the dungeon with his assistant.

Here we find poor Florestan chained to a stone; he is wasted to a skeleton, as his food has been reduced in quantity, week by week, by the cruel orders of his tormentor. He is gradually losing his reason: he has visions, and in each one beholds his beloved wife.

When Leonore recognizes him she well-nigh faints, but, with a supernatural effort of strength she rallies, and begins her work. She has a piece of bread with her, which she gives to the prisoner, and with it the remainder of Rocco's wine. Rocco, mild at heart, pities his victim sincerely, but he dares not act against the orders of his superior, fearing to lose his position, or even his life.

While Leonore refreshes the sick man, Rocco gives a sign to Pizarro that the work is done, and bids Fidelio leave; but she only hides herself behind a stone pillar, waiting with deadly fear for the coming event and decided to save her husband or to die with him.

Pizarro enters, secretly resolved to kill not only his foe but also both witnesses of his crime. He will not kill Florestan, however, without letting him know who his assailant is. So he loudly shouts his own much-feared name, but while he raises his dagger, Leonore throws herself between him and Florestan, shielding the latter with her breast. Pizarro, stupefied like Florestan, loses his presence of mind. Leonore profits by it, and points a pistol at him, with which she threatens his life should he attempt another attack. At this critical moment the trumpets sound, announcing the arrival of the Minister, and Pizarro, in impotent wrath, is compelled to retreat. They are all summoned before the Minister, who is shocked at seeing his old friend Florestan in this sad state, but not the less delighted with, and full of reverence for, the noble courage of Leonore.

Pizarro is conducted away in chains, and the faithful wife with her own hands removes the fetters which still bind the husband for whom she has just won freedom and happiness.

Marcelline, feeling inclined to be ashamed of her mistake, returns to her simple and faithful lover Jaquino.

LA FIGLIA DEL REGGIMENTO

Comic Opera in two acts by GAETANO DONIZETTI

Text by ST. GEORGE and BAYARD

This opera is one of the few of Donizetti's numerous works which still retain their attraction for the theatre visitor; the others are his Lucrezia Borgia and Lucia di Lammermoor.

The "Daughter of the Regiment" happily combines Italian richness of melody with French "esprit" and French sallies, and hence the continued charm of this almost international music.

The libretto can be accounted good.

The scene in the first act is laid near Bologna in the year 1815, the second act in the castle of the Marchesa di Maggioriviglio.

Mary, a vivandière, has been found and educated by a French sergeant named Sulpice, and therefore belongs in a sense to his regiment, which is on a campaign in Italy. She is called the "daughter" of the regiment, which has adopted her, and she has grown up, a bright and merry girl, full of pluck and spirit, the pet and delight of the whole regiment.

Tonio, a young Swiss, who has fallen in love with Mary, is believed by the grenadiers to be a spy, and is about to be hanged. But Mary, knowing that he has only come to see her, tells them that he lately saved her life, when she was in danger of falling over a precipice. This changes everything, and on his expressing a desire to become one of them the grenadiers suffer the Swiss to enlist into their company. After the soldiers' departure he confesses his love to Mary, who returns it heartily. The soldiers agree to give their consent, when the Marchesa di Maggiorivoglio appears, and by a letter once affixed to the foundling Mary, addressed to a Marchesa of the same name, and carefully kept by Sulpice, it is proved that Mary is the Marchesa's niece. Of course this noble lady refuses her consent to a marriage with the low-born Swiss, and claims Mary from her guardian. With tears and laments, Mary takes leave of her regiment and her lover, who at once decides to follow her. But he has enlisted as a soldier, and is forbidden to leave the ranks. Sulpice and his whole regiment curse the Marchesa who thus carries away their joy.

In the second act Mary is in her aunt's castle. She has masters of every kind for her education, in order to become a lady *comme il faut,* but she cannot forget her freedom and her dear soldiers, and instead of singing solfeggios and cavatinas she is caught warbling her "Rataplan," to the Marchesa's grief and sorrow. Nor can she cease to think of Tonio, and only after a great struggle has she been induced to promise her hand to a nobleman, when she suddenly hears the well-beloved sound of drums and trumpets. It is her own regiment, with Tonio as their leader, for he has been made an officer on account of his courage and brave behavior. Hoping that his altered position may turn the Marchesa's heart in his favor, he again asks for Mary, but his suit is once more rejected. Then he proposes flight, but the Marchesa, detecting his plan, reveals to Mary that she is not her niece, but her own daughter, born in early wedlock with an officer far beneath her in rank, who soon after died in battle. This fact she has concealed from her family, but, as it is now evident that she has closer ties with Mary, the poor girl dares not disobey her, and, though broken-hearted, consents to renounce Tonio.

The Marchesa invites a large company of guests to celebrate her daughter's betrothal to the son of a neighboring duchess. But Mary's faithful grenadiers suddenly appear to rescue her from those hateful ties, and astonish the whole company by their recital of Mary's early history. The obedient maiden, however, submissive to her fate, is about to sign the marriage contract, when, at last, the Marchesa, touched by her obedience and her sufferings, conquers her own pride and consents to the union of her daughter with Tonio. Sulpice and his soldiers burst out into loud shouts of approbation, and the high-born guests retire silently and disgusted.

LA FILLE DE MADAME ANGOT

Comic Opera in three acts by LECOCQ

Book by GIRARDIN, CLAIRVILLE and KONAG

The first production took place in Brussels, 1872. Scene, Paris, and time, 1797, during the French Directorate.

The first act takes place at a corner of the central market in Paris. Madame Angot is a politically influential leader of the Dames des Halles, who during the horrors of the Revolution played quite a part. She with her following is in opposition to the present government of which Barras is the head. Her daughter, Clairette, is on the point of being married to Pomponnet, a smirking hairdresser whom she does not love, since her fickle heart is for the time being in the keeping of Ange Pitou, a young and enterprising poet and author of popular ballads. Ange just then has written a song in which he has ridiculed the recognized mistress of Barras, the actress Mademoiselle Lange, who is also the pet of the Paris audiences, and in which he dwells on this young lady's desperate flirtations with a citizen of substance, M. Larivaudière. Clairette is much opposed to wedding Pomponnet, and sees only one way out of it,—to get herself locked up for the grave offense of singing this lampooning song of Ange's making. So she goes out into the street and sings the ballad.

The second act occurs in the drawing-room of Mlle. Lange. That young woman is the owner of a lively sense of humor, and so being informed of the attack made upon her reputation and of the arrest of Clairette, she has the prisoner brought before her. Pomponnet, who is waiting on her as one of his most valued customers, is anxious to shield Clairette, assuring the theatrical star that she is innocent, and that only the anonymous author of the scurrilous sheet is the culprit. When Clairette is brought before her, the actress at once identifies her as a friend of her childhood, with whom she attended school and perpetrated impish tricks. So Mlle. Lange, out of the goodness of her heart, takes an interest in the lively girl, and tries to procure not alone her freedom, but also promises to bestir herself in her behalf, so that the girl will marry the man of her own choice, not knowing, however, that that would be Ange Pitou, in which young man she herself is more than slightly interested. It so happens that Ange Pitou, who frequently pays visits to the actress, is an invited guest of hers that day. He arrives while Mlle. Lange is still engaged in retrospect and conversation with Clairette. Another guest is Larivaudière, to quell whose instantly aroused jealousy, she invents the fiction that Ange Pitou has come to pay his addresses to Clairette, and that he, too, is to join a body of conspirators who are to meet at her house at midnight in a plot to overturn the existing government. Then Pomponnet, although wholly harmless, is arrested for having on his person a copy of the prohibited ballad. At the appointed hour the conspirators all arrive at the place of meeting, and then it is discovered that this house is surrounded by a detachment of hussars who have through a private source received trustworthy information of the dark plot. But at a previously agreed signal all the conspirators hide their insignia, and Mlle. Lange herself fools the soldiers sent out to bag all those present by pretending that what is going on is a wedding ball and reception in honor of Clairette and Ange Pitou. In the course of the festivity, however, Clairette and the actress find out that they both love the same man, namely, Ange Pitou.

In Belleville, a suburb of Paris, a garden party is given, the grounds being splendidly lit up for a ball. Clairette, who, after all, had to serve a short term in jail, has obtained her liberty, and now is trying to ascertain whether Mlle. Lange and the young poet are really in love with each other or merely coquetting. So she has despatched three letters, whereof one is supposed to be from Ange Pitou to the actress, the other from the latter to the poet, and a third to Larivaudière, appointing for them all as meeting-place this very rustic fête. So the young poet meets Mlle. Lange and is caught by Clairette. There is a short-lived quarrel between the young ladies for the possession of the poet, which winds up sensibly enough by Clairette's abandoning all hope of securing Ange, and rewarding the steady-going and ever faithful hairdresser with her hand.

DIE FLEDERMAUS

(THE BAT)

Comic Opera by JOHANN STRAUSS

The delightful music of Johann Strauss's comic opera has always been welcome to the music lovers of Germany, where "Die Fledermaus" is a regular piece in opera houses. In this country and in England, however, it has been only within the past three years that people have had many opportunities to hear it. In England, indeed, it has never been given as Grand Opera. In New York its enthusiastic reception has assured it a place in every season's programme. It was first performed in Vienna in 1874.

The plot of the libretto, written by Meilhac and Halévy, is rather a complicated one, owing to the many situations in which the leading characters are placed. The pivot, so to speak, on which the whole plot revolves is Eisenstein, a banker, who, when the curtain rises, is about to go to prison for five days for an indiscretion which his quick temper made him commit. Eisenstein's friend, Dr. Falke, a notary, invites the banker to a supper to be given by Prince Orlofsky, a young and rich Russian, to the members of the Ballet and Dramatic corps. He does this in order to pay back Eisenstein for a practical joke the latter once played on him. Eisenstein accepts the invitation, telling his wife that he is going to deliver himself up to justice to serve his sentence.

The first act opens with a serenade sung by Alfred, a rather persistent lover of Rosalind Eisenstein, which is listened to by Adèle, Mrs. Eisenstein's maid, but which is really intended for her mistress. Adèle has just received an invitation from her sister Ida, a member of the ballet, to go to a splendid party to be given by a Russian prince, and is most anxious to be present. When Mrs. Eisenstein comes in Adèle begs for leave of absence for the evening in order to see her aunt, who, she says, is very ill. The leave is refused, and Adèle goes off the stage in a sulky dudgeon. Rosalind, left alone, is suddenly met by her lover, Alfred, who comes in through the window. Her weakness for tenors causes her to promise to permit him to return later when her husband is gone. Eisenstein comes in with Dr. Blind, his lawyer, who has conducted the case badly, and now receives Eisenstein's upbraidings. Blind is turned out in anger, and Rosalind tries to comfort her husband by promising him a good supper. Falke comes in and invites Eisenstein to the Prince's supper party, and, before Rosalind returns, he has joyfully accepted Falke's invitation. He declines his wife's supper and tells her he must go to prison at once. He dresses himself in his evening clothes, takes a tender farewell of his wife, and leaves with Falke. Adèle then comes in, and Rosalind, in order to have her out of the way for her reception of Alfred, gives her permission to go to see her sick aunt. Adèle goes out in high glee, to make room for Alfred's reappearance. The tenor prepares to make himself at home by going into Eisenstein's room and coming back in the banker's dressing-gown. The supper prepared for Eisenstein by his wife is now partaken of by Alfred, much to the chagrin and vexation of Rosalind, who only wants to hear the tenor sing. Alfred, however, finds the place so comfortable that he partakes freely of wine, becomes somewhat hilarious, and is ready to remain all night. Rosalind, in distress, knows not what to do. Just then a ring is heard at the door, and Franke, the governor of the prison, appears. He is come to take Eisenstein to prison. Rosalind, terrified to be found in so compromising a position with the tenor, introduces Alfred to the governor as her husband, and Alfred, in good humor, allows himself to be carried off to gaol in Eisenstein's place. The curtain goes down here on the first act.

The second act represents the garden of a café, where Prince Orlofsky is giving the banquet. Adèle enters, attired in her mistress's best dress, and looking smart and roguish. Eisenstein recognizes her at once, and begins to make love to her. She pretends to be very angry with him for mistaking her for his wife's maid and flirtingly repulses his advances. Prince Orlofsky now comes in and tells Eisenstein that Dr. Falke has promised him much fun in a practical joke he intends to play on the banker. Eisenstein, not knowing what is about to happen, is rendered very uncomfortable. Falke, in the meantime, has sent for Rosalind, who just then enters unrecognized because of her mask. Falke introduces her as a Hungarian Countess who, because of her rank, desires to remain unknown. Rosalind quickly finds her husband flirting with Adèle and determines to punish him, not only for making love to her maid, but for deceiving her by saying he was going to prison. Eisenstein, on his part, is much attracted by the magnificence of the dress and charming figure of the supposed Countess, and transfers his attentions to her. He makes such violent love to her that he even counts her heart-beats with the aid of a watch which he promises to give her. He irritates Rosalind by withholding the present, but she manages to get possession of it and slips away before he can recover it from her. The entire party now sit down to supper, and Eisenstein, partaking rather freely of wine, tells the company the practical joke he once played on his friend Falke. He once attended with his friend a masquerade ball to which Falke had gone in the costume of a bat. He had made his friend drink more than was good for him, so that Falke had gone to sleep in the street, where Eisenstein had left him all night. When Falke woke up in the morning he found himself surrounded by a great crowd of jeering people, who had nicknamed him "Die Fledermaus." The story Eisenstein told with great glee is received by the company with much laughter. Falke, however, only smiles, and says simply that he laughs best who laughs last. Dancing follows the supper, and when the clock strikes six Eisenstein remembers he ought to be in prison. He therefore takes leave of the company and goes out with Franke, the governor of the prison, who was present at the banquet as the Chevalier Chagrin, but who is not known to Eisenstein as the prison governor.

The curtain rises on the third act, showing the prison-governor's office. Franke returns and is received by his jailer, Frosch, who has taken advantage of his master's absence to get thoroughly drunk. Frosch's play as a drunken man trying to find his lamp is highly amusing. Franke, musing over the night's entertainment, becomes drowsy and falls asleep. He is awakened, however, by the entrance of Adèle and her sister Ida, who have come from the party to ask the supposed Chevalier to intercede for Adèle with his friend Eisenstein. Adèle confesses to him that she is not what she pretends to be, being only a lady's maid, but that she has talents for the stage. She proceeds to show by demonstration how well she can dance. She is interrupted by a ring at the door, and Franke, to get the two women out of the way, orders Frosch to put them into a cell to wait until his visitors have gone. Frosch conducts them to cell number 13, next to the one in which the supposed Eisenstein is confined. The ring at the door came from Eisenstein, who now enters to give himself up. He recognizes in Franke the Chevalier Chagrin he had met at Orlofsky's party, and each is surprised to meet the other in this place. Dr. Blind now enters to shield the supposed Eisenstein and meets the real Eisenstein, who again hustles him out and, possessing himself of Blind's cap, coat, and spectacles, returns to interview the man who has been locked up in his stead. As Alfred is being brought from his cell Rosalind enters ready to revenge herself on her husband. She has her husband's watch with her. Seeing Alfred, she and he begin to vent their grievances to the disguised Eisenstein, who, when he learns of Alfred's visit to his wife at his house, becomes greatly enraged. Throwing off his disguise, he reveals himself as Rosalind's husband and turns on her in righteous anger. She, on her part, scorns him for his treachery and deception. The mutual recriminations between husband and wife are interrupted by the entrance of Dr. Falke, accompanied by all those who were present at Prince Orlofsky's banquet. Falke clears up the misunderstanding and explains that the whole affair is a stupendous practical joke on his part, played on Eisenstein by way of revenge for the joke Eisenstein had played on him. The prince had been aware of his intention and had entered into the spirit of the joke. Eisenstein, seeing the turn matters have taken, and, convinced of his wife's innocence, embraces Rosalind, and all toast each other in champagne.

DER FLIEGENDE HOLLÄNDER

(THE FLYING DUTCHMAN)

Romantic Opera in three acts by WAGNER

This fine opera is Wagner's second work, which he composed in direst need, when living at Paris with his young wife. The songs, which so well imitate the hurricane and the howling of the ocean, he himself heard during an awful storm at sea. The whole opera is exceedingly characteristic and impressive. Wagner arranged the libretto himself, as he did for all his operas which succeeded this one. He found the substance of it in an old legend that dates from the 16th century. The Flying Dutchman is a sort of wandering Jew, condemned to sail for ever on the seas, until he has found a woman whose love to him is faithful unto death.

In the first act we find ourselves on the high seas. Daland, a Norwegian skipper, has met with several misfortunes on his way home, and is compelled to anchor on a deserted shore. There he finds the Flying Dutchman, who vainly roves from sea to sea to find death and with it peace. His only hope is doomsday. He has never found a maiden faithful to him, and he knows not how often and how long he has vainly tried to be released from his doom. Once every seven years he is allowed to go on shore and take a wife. This time has now come again, and hearing from Daland that he has a daughter, sweet and pure, he begins to hope once more, and offers all his wealth to the father for a shelter under the Norwegian's roof and for the hand of his daughter Senta. Daland is only too glad to accept for his child what to him seems an immense fortune, and so they sail home together.

In the second act we find Senta in the spinning-room. The servants of the house are together, spinning and singing. Senta is amongst them, but her wheel does not turn—she is dreamily regarding an old picture. It is that of the Flying Dutchman, whose legend so deeply touches her that she has grown to love its hero, without having in reality seen him.

Senta has a wooer already in the person of Erick the hunter, but she does not care much for him. With deep feeling she sings to the spinning maidens the ballad of the doomed man, as she has heard it from Mary, her nurse.

An old captain wanted to sail round the Cape of Good Hope, and as the wind was against him he swore a terrible oath that he never would leave off trying. The devil heard him, and doomed him to sail on to eternity, but God's angel had pity on him, and showed him how he could find deliverance through a wife, faithful unto the grave.

All the maidens pray to God to let the maiden be found at last, when Senta ecstatically exclaims: "I will be his wife!" At this moment her father's ship is announced. Senta is about to run away to welcome him, but is detained by Erick, who tries to win her for himself. She answers evasively; then Daland enters and with him a dark and gloomy stranger. Senta stands spell-bound; she recognizes the hero of her picture. The Dutchman is not less impressed, seeing in her the angel of his dreams and, as it were, his deliverer, and so, meeting by the guidance of a superior power, they seem created for each other, and Senta, accepting the offer of his hand, swears to him eternal fidelity.

In the third act we see the Flying Dutchman's ship; everybody recognizes it by its black mast and its blood-red sail. The Norwegian sailors call loudly to the mariners of the strange ship, but nothing stirs—everything seems dead and haunted. At last the unearthly inhabitants of the Dutch ship awake; they are old and gray and wrinkled, all doomed to the fate of their captain. They begin a wild and gloomy song, which sends a chill into the hearts of the stout Norwegians.

Meanwhile Erick, beholding in Senta the betrothed of the Dutchman, is in despair. Imploring her to turn back, he calls up old memories and at last charges her with infidelity to him.

As soon as the Dutchman hears this accusation he turns from Senta, feeling that he is again lost. But Senta will not break her faith. Seeing the Dutchman fly from her, ready to sail away, she swiftly runs after him and throws herself from the cliff into the waves.

By this sacrifice the spell is broken, the ghostly ship sinks for ever into the ocean, and an angel bears the poor wanderer to eternal rest, where he is reunited to the bride who has proved faithful unto death.

LA FORZA DEL DESTINO

Opera in four acts by GIUSEPPE VERDI

Book by PLAVE, after DE RIVAS' drama, "Don Alvaro o La Fuerza del Sino"

This opera was first performed at Petrograd in 1862. The scenes are laid in Spain and Italy, during the middle of the eighteenth century.

Act I. In Seville, Don Alvaro is about to elope with Donna Leonora, daughter of the Marquis di Calatrava, when the latter comes upon them. The father forces Don Alvaro to draw his rapier and in the fight, the Marquis is fatally wounded. He curses his daughter with his dying breath and invokes the vengeance of his son, Don Carlo, upon her and her lover. Don Alvaro escapes.

Act II. Believing that she has been deserted, Leonora flees, disguised as a man. She establishes herself as a hermit, Father Raphael, near a monastery. In the meantime, Don Alvaro, under the name of Don Federigo, enters the Italian army where he meets Don Carlo whom he does not recognize as Leonora's brother. The two become devoted friends. However, Don Carlo eventually learns the identity of Don Federigo and challenges him to a duel. Alvaro is forced to accept and wounds Don Carlo. Thinking the brother dead, Alvaro leaves the country, finally becoming a monk in the monastery near Leonora's hermitage.

Act III. Don Carlo, who has recovered from his wound, has been searching for five years for his father's slayer. One day he encounters Alvaro near Father Raphael's grotto and recognizes him. Don Alvaro refuses to accept his challenge to resume the duel until Don Carlo has repeatedly insulted him. The two fight and again the brother is wounded. Don Alvaro hastens into the hermit's cave to ask the holy friar to come to the dying man. Leonora recognizes her lover but there is no time for reconciliations. She hurries out to Don Carlo. As she bends over him, he stabs her to the heart and dies cursing her. Father Guardiano from the monastery supports her into her grotto. She absolves Alvaro who kneels beside her as her soul ascends to heaven. Monks enter, singing the Miserere and Don Alvaro throws himself over a precipice.

FRA DIAVOLO

Comic Opera in three acts by AUBER

Text by SCRIBE

This is a nice little opera; though not equal in beauty and perfection to the Muette de Portici, by the same author, it is, notwithstanding, a happy invention of Auber's, particularly because the local tints are so well caught. The banditti are painted with bright and glowing colors, and the part of the heroine Zerline is one of the most grateful ever written for a soubrette. The text by Scribe abounds in happy sallies and lively details. It is laid at Terracina in Italy. Fra Diavolo is a celebrated and much feared chief of brigands. The Roman court of justice has set a price of 10,000 piastres on his head. In the first act we meet with the Roman soldiers who undertake to win the money. Their captain, Lorenzo, has a double aim in trying to catch the brigand. He is Zerline's lover, but, having no money, Zerline's father Matteo, the owner of a hotel, threatens to give her to a rich farmer's son. Meanwhile Fra Diavolo has forced his society on a rich English lord, Cookburn by name, who is on his wedding-tour with his fair young wife Pamela. Lord Cookburn looks jealously at Fra Diavolo, though he does not recognize in him a brigand. The English are robbed by Diavolo's band. Disgusted with the insecurity of "la bella Italia" they reach the inn at Terracina, where the dragoons, hearing the account of this new robbery, believe that it was Fra Diavolo with his band, and at once decide to pursue him.

Shortly afterwards Fra Diavolo arrives at the inn, disguised as the Marquis of San Marco, under which name the English lord has already made his acquaintance. He is not enchanted by the arrival of this Marquis; he fears a new flirtation with his own fair wife. Pamela wears most valuable diamonds, and these strike the eye of Fra Diavolo.

He sees that the English have been clever enough to conceal the greater part of their wealth, and resolves to put himself speedily into possession of it.

He is flirting desperately with Pamela, and looking tenderly at the pretty Zerline, when the soldiers return, having captured twenty of the brigands and retaken the greater part of Lord Cookburn's money and jewels. Lorenzo, the captain of dragoons, is rewarded by the magnanimous lord with 10,000 lire, and may now hope to win Zerline's hand. But Fra Diavolo vows to avenge the death of his comrades on Lorenzo.

In the second act he conceals himself behind the curtains in Zerline's sleeping-room, and during the night he admits his two companions, Beppo and Giacomo. Zerline enters and is about to retire to rest, after praying to the Holy Virgin for protection. During her sleep Giacomo is to stab her, while the two others are to rob the English milord.

But Zerline's prayer and her innocence touch even the robbers, the deed is delayed, and this delay brings Lorenzo upon them. Fra Diavolo's two companions hide themselves, and the false Marquis alone is found in Zerline's room. He assures Lorenzo that he had a rendezvous with his bride, and at the same time whispers into milord's ear that he came by appointment with milady, showing her portrait, of which he had robbed her the day before, as proof. The consequence of these lies is a challenge from Lorenzo, and a meeting with Diavolo is fixed. The latter is full of triumphant glee; he has arranged a deep-laid plan with the surviving members of his band, and hopes to ensnare not only Lorenzo but his whole company. Ordinarily Diavolo is a noble brigand; he never troubles women, and he loads poor people with gifts, taking the gold out of rich men's purses only, but now he is full of ire, and his one thought is of vengeance.

Finally he is betrayed by the carelessness of his own helpmates. Beppo and Giacomo, seeing Zerline, recognize in her their fair prey of the evening before, and betray themselves by repeating some of the words which she had given utterance to. Zerline, hearing them, is now able to comprehend the wicked plot which was woven to destroy her happiness. The two banditti are captured, and compelled to lure their captain into a trap. Diavolo appears, not in his disguise as a Marquis, but in his own well-known dress, with the red plume waving from his bonnet, and, being assured by Beppo that all is secure, is easily captured. Now all the false imputations are cleared up. Milord is reconciled to his wife, and Lorenzo obtains the hand of the lovely Zerline.

FRANCESCA DA RIMINI

Tragic Opera in five acts. The book based on the drama by GABRIELE D'ANNUNZIO

Music composed by R. ZANDONAI

This work was first produced in 1914, at Turin, and the scene is laid in Ravenna and Rimini, during the thirteenth century.

The first act occurs at Ravenna. Four female attendants of Francesca are conversing with a jester who has arrived at the castle of the Polentani. He is told that their master, Guido da Polenta, intends to give his beautiful daughter, Francesca, to one of the sons of Malatesta of Verucchio. The jester replies that he is to sing at the wedding festivities. Ostasio is heard approaching, and the women save themselves. Ostasio is accompanied by the notary, to whom he explains his plans. Francesca is to wed Gianciotto Malatesta, a cripple of evil mind and looks, since the handsome brother, Paolo, is already married. But Paolo is to be sent to represent his brother, and Ostasio, who knows his high-spirited sister well, urges haste before Francesca learns the full truth. The notary falls in with the scheme, and they further discuss the political advantages to accrue to the Polentani family by means of this projected union. But Ostasio is not quite satisfied with the terms, for he considers them unfair. After they leave Francesca and her sister Samaritana enter, and the former gives expression to her forebodings. News is brought of the arrival of Francesca's betrothed, and in fear and trembling she goes to meet him. It is, of course, Paolo, and they look upon each other in silence, Francesca finally plucking a red rose and handing it to him as a love token.

On a strong tower of the Malatesta fortalice the Malatesta are preparing for battle with their Ghibelline foes. Francesca has meanwhile become the spouse of Giovanni, the cripple, and now lives with the latter and his young brother, the one-eyed Malatestino, at Rimini. She treasures wrath at Paolo for his part in misleading her into her first belief that he, Paolo, was to be her husband, and feels she cannot forgive him for what she deems his deception. Paolo enters, and despite her attempts to avoid him, follows her steps, and makes a confession to the effect that he feels bitter shame at the part he was forced to play in deceiving her. Francesca, as punishment, exacts from him a promise that he will fight without helmet or shield, thus leaving the issue of the ordeal to God. Fighting begins, and when imminent danger threatens Paolo because of his agreement with her, Francesca rushes out to shield him with her own body, love for him having suddenly entered her heart. After the fighting has ceased, it is found that Paolo is uninjured, and to Francesca this seems like a message from on high that she may now hold Paolo in her bosom as immaculate. His brother Gianciotto enters, upbraiding his men fiercely for what he holds their lack of valor. He announces to his brother that envoys from Florence have come to summon Paolo there, since he has been chosen for a high post of command in that city, and that therefore he must leave at once.

Francesca within the security of her sumptuously furnished chamber is discovered in the third act reading aloud to her women the story of Lancelot and Queen Guinevere, and after dismissing them Paolo enters.

Paolo has been driven there from Florence by his unappeased longing for Francesca. While they make every effort to suppress their mutual passion, it is constantly felt by both of them. Finally they begin to read together the story of Guinevere, each taking the corresponding part. When they reach the passage: "She takes him by the chin and slowly kisses him on the mouth," they suit the action to the words.

In the next act, the fourth, the young brother, Malatestino, is seen talking with Francesca, and suddenly he owns to an overwhelming passion for her. Knowing that she hates her husband, he offers to get rid of him for her by poison. Francesca is aghast at the youth's schemes, but in pity for his tender years is willing to forgive him. She hears a terrible cry, and the young man informs her it comes from an imprisoned foe, one who is waiting to be ransomed. Malatestino goes out, saying he will silence the noise. He returns and finds his brother Gianciotto who asks what he is concealing under the folds of a cloth. It is the head of the foe, whom he has decapitated. When his elder brother reproaches him for this act and shows besides some suspicion of him, Malatestino tries to save himself by making dark insinuations against Paolo and Francesca. Gianciotto's jealousy is roused and he decides on a plan by which he hopes to surprise his brother and his wife, and to lull the latter's uneasiness he tenderly bids her farewell, and then starts out ostensibly for Pesaro.

The fifth act takes place in Francesca's apartments, where her women are watching and she herself is fitful and restless. At last she dismisses all attendants, and after they are gone she opens her door to Paolo. The lovers embrace, and later on read and talk together. But without warning the deformed husband is heard shouting for admission, and Paolo hastily seeks a hiding-place, going down a few steps to a trapdoor. The angry husband discovers him, however, and flings himself with a naked sword upon him. Francesca rushes between them to save Paolo and is mortally hurt in doing so. Paolo receives her in his arms and Gianciotto stabs him likewise. Then Gianciotto breaks his own sword.

FRAUENLOB

Opera in three acts by REINHOLD BECKER
Text by FRANZ KOPPEL ELLFELD

Becker, the well-known Dresden composer, has long won name and fame by his beautiful songs, which may be heard all over the Continent. He is a first-rate "Liedermeister," and great was the excitement with which his friends looked forward to his first opera.

Their expectations were not deceived, for the opera was put on the stage in Dresden on December 8, 1892, and was received with unanimous applause.

Becker is not one of those high-flown artists who elevate us to the skies; he rather lacks dramatic strength; the lyric element is his strong point. By the *Lied* he finds his way direct to the hearts of his hearers, and wherever this could be woven into the action of his opera he has done it with subtle taste. Tilda's dancing-air in the first act, the evening song—sung while the people are gliding down the Rhine in boats, whose lovely variations remind us of quaint old airs of bygone days—the chorus of the stone-masons in the second act, and the love duet in the third are brilliant gems in Becker's music.

The libretto rivals the best of its kind.

The scene is laid near and in Maintz in the year 1308; it takes place during the reign of Ludwig, Emperor of Bavaria.

Heinrich Frauenlob, the famous minstrel, who had won his name by his songs in women's praise, is by birth a knight, Dietherr zur Meise. Years ago he slew the

Truchsess of Maintz in self-defence, and having, therefore, become an outlaw, had entered the service of the Emperor. In the beginning of the opera we find him, however, near Maintz, where he stays as a guest at his friend Wolf's castle. He takes part in the people's festival on Midsummer Day, deeming himself unknown.

When the customary St. John's fire is lighted, no one dares leap over it, for fear of an old gipsy's prophecy which threatened with sudden death the first who should attempt it. Frauenlob, disregarding the prophecy, persuades Hildegund, Ottker von Scharfenstein's fair ward, to venture through the fire with him. Hildegund is the slain Truchsess's daughter, and has sworn to wed the avenger of her father's death; but each lover is unconscious of the other's name. The gipsy Sizyga alone, who had been betrayed in her youth by Frauenlob's father, recognizes the young knight, and though he has only just saved the old hag from the people's fury, she wishes to avenge her wrongs on him. To this end she betrays the secret of Frauenlob's birth to Hildegund's suitor, Servazio di Bologna, who is highly jealous of this new rival, and determines to lay hands on him as soon as he enters the gates of Maintz. Frauenlob, though warned by Sizyga, enters Maintz, attracted by Hildegund's sweet graces; he is determined to confess everything, and then to fly with her, should she be willing to follow him.

The second act opens with a fine song of the warder of the tower. The city awakes; the stone-masons assemble, ready to greet the Emperor, whose arrival is expected. Tilda, Hildegund's friend, and daughter of Klas, chief of the stone-masons, is going to church, but on her way she is accosted by the knight Wolf, who has lost his heart to her, and now, forgetting his plan to look for Frauenlob, follows the lovely damsel. When Frauenlob comes up and sees again the well-known places of his youth, he is deeply touched; but seeing his lady-love step on the balcony and soon after come down to enter the dome, he accosts her, imploring her to fly with him. At this moment Servazio, who has lain in wait, steps forth with officers, who capture Frauenlob. Servazio now reveals the singer's secret, and Hildegund hears that her lover is her father's murderer. Though Frauenlob tells Hildegund that he killed her father in self-defence, she turns from him shuddering. Feeling that all hopes of his future happiness are at an end, he wishes to atone for his deed by death, refusing the help of Wolf, who comes up with his men to release him. But the stone-masons, having recognized the celebrated minstrel, with whose song they are about to greet the Emperor, decide to invoke the latter's clemency.

In the third act the citizens of Maintz hail the Emperor, after which Frauenlob's cause is brought before him. The whole population demands his pardon, and the monarch, who loves the singer, would fain liberate him, had not Servazio roughly insisted on the culprit's punishment. Uncertain what to do, the Emperor receives a long procession of ladies, with Tilda at its head, who all beseech pardon for Frauenlob. At last the Emperor calls for Hildegund, leaving in her hands the destiny of the prisoner. Left alone with him, the latter, prepared to die, only craves her pardon. After a hard struggle with her conscience, love conquers, and she grants him pardon. When the Emperor re-enters with his suite, to hear the sentence, they find the lovers in close embrace. To the joy of everybody, the monarch sanctions the union and orders the nuptials to be celebrated at once. Another pair, Wolf and Tilda, are also made happy. But Servazio vows vengeance. Sizyga having secretly slipped a powder into his hands, he pours it into a cup of wine, which he presents to Frauenlob as a drink of reconciliation. The Emperor, handing the goblet to Hildegund, bids her drink to her lover. Testing it, she at once feels its deadly effect. Frauenlob, seeing his love stagger, snatches the cup from her, emptying it at one draught. He dies, still praising the Emperor and women, breathing the name of his bride with his last breath. Servazio is captured; and while Hildegund's body is strewn with roses, the wailing women of Maintz carry their beloved minstrel to his grave.

DER FREISCHÜTZ

Romantic Opera in three acts by C. M. VON WEBER
Text by FRIEDRICH KIND

This charming opera, done at Dresden 1820, is the most favored of Weber's compositions. It is truly German, being both fantastic and poetic. The libretto is an old German legend, and runs thus:

A young huntsman, Max, is in love with Agathe, daughter of Cuno, the chief ranger of Prince Ottocar of Bohemia. Max woos her; but their union depends on a master shot which he is to deliver on the following morning.

During a village festival he has all day been unlucky in shooting, and we see him full of anger and sorrow, being mocked at by peasants more lucky than he.

His comrade, Caspar, one of the ranger's older huntsmen, is his evil genius. He has sold himself to the devil, is a gloomy, mysterious fellow, and hopes to save his soul by delivering some other victim to the demon. He wants to tempt Max to try enchanted bullets, to be obtained at the cross-road, during the midnight hour, by drawing a magic circle with a bloody sword and invoking the name of the mysterious huntsman. Father Cuno, hearing him, drives him away, begging Max to think of his bride and to pray to God for success.

But Max cannot forget the railleries of the peasants; he broods over his misfortunes, and when he is well-nigh despairing, Caspar, who meanwhile calls Samiel (the devil in person) to help, encourages him to take refuge in stimulants. He tries to intoxicate the unhappy lover by pouring drops from a phial into his wine. When Max has grown more and more excited, Caspar begins to tell him of nature's secret powers, which might help him. Max first struggles against the evil influence, but when Caspar, handing him his gun, lets him shoot an eagle soaring high in the air, his huntsman's heart is elated, and he wishes to become possessed of such bullet. Caspar tells him that they are enchanted, and persuades him to a meeting in the Wolf's Glen at midnight, where the bullets may be moulded.

In the second act Agathe is with her cousin Annchen. Agathe is the true German maiden, serious and thoughtful almost to melancholy. She presents a marked contrast to her gay and light-hearted cousin, who tries to brighten Agathe with fun and frolic. They adorn themselves with roses, which Agathe received from a holy hermit, who blessed her, but warned her of impending evil. So Agathe is full of dread forebodings, and after Annchen's departure she fervently prays to Heaven for her beloved. When she sees him come to her through the forest with flowers on his hat, her fears vanish, and she greets him joyously. But Max only answers hurriedly that, having killed a stag in the Wolf's Glen, he is obliged to return there. Agathe, filled with terror at the mention of this ill-famed name, wants to keep him back, but ere she can detain him he has fled. With hurried steps Max approaches the Wolf's Glen, where Caspar is already occupied in forming circles of black stones, in the midst of which he places a skull, an eagle's wing, a crucible, and a bullet mould. Caspar then calls on Samiel, invoking him to allow him a few more years on earth. Tomorrow is the day appointed for Satan to take his soul, but Caspar promises to surrender Max in exchange. Samiel, who appears through the cleft of a rock, agrees to let him have six of the fatal balls, reserving only the seventh for himself.

Caspar then proceeds to make the bullets, Max only looking on, stunned and remorseful at what he sees. His mother's spirit appears to him; but he is already under the influence of the charm; he cannot move. The proceeding goes forward amid hellish noise. A hurricane arises, flames and devilish forms flicker about, wild and horrible creatures rush by, and others follow in hot pursuit. The noise grows worse, the earth seems to quake, until, at length, after Caspar's reiterated invocations, Samiel shows himself at the word, "seven." Max and Caspar both make the sign of the cross, and fall on their knees more dead than alive.

In the third act we find Agathe waiting for her bridesmaids. She is perturbed and sad, having had frightful dreams, and not knowing what has become of Max. Annchen consoles her, diverting her with a merry song until the bridesmaids enter, bringing flowers and gifts. They then prepare to crown her with the bridal wreath, when, lo! instead of the myrtle, there lies in the box a wreath of white roses, the ornament of the dead.

Meanwhile everybody is assembled on the lawn near Prince Ottocar's tent, to be present at the firing of the master shot. The Prince points out to Max a white dove as an object at which to aim. At this critical moment Agathe appears, crying out: "Don't shoot, Max, I am the white dove!" But it is too late; Max has fired, and Agathe sinks down at the same time as Caspar, who has been waiting behind a tree, and who now falls heavily to the ground, while the dove flies away unhurt. Everybody believes that Max has shot his bride, but she is only in a swoon; the bullet has really killed the villain

Caspar. It was the seventh, the direction of which Samiel reserved for himself, and Satan having no power over the pious maiden, directed it on Caspar, already forfeited to him. Max confesses his sin with deep remorse. The Prince scornfully bids him leave his dominions for ever. But Agathe prays for him, and at last the Prince follows the hermit's advice, giving the unhappy youth a year of probation, during which to prove his repentance and grow worthy of his virtuous bride.

GENOVEVA

Opera in four acts by ROBERT SCHUMANN

Text after HEBBEL and TIECK

The music of this opera is surpassingly delightful. Though Schumann's genius was not that of a dramatist of a very high order, this opera deserves to be known and esteemed universally. Nowhere can melodies be found finer or more poetical and touching than in this noble musical composition, the libretto of which may also be called interesting, though it is faulty in its want of action.

It is the old legend of Genoveva somewhat altered. Siegfried, Count of the Palatinate, is ordered by the Emperor Charles Martell to join him in the war with the infidels who broke out of Spain under Abdurrahman. The noble Count recommends his wife Genoveva and all he possesses to the protection of his friend Golo, who is, however, secretly in love with his master's wife. After Siegfried has said farewell, she falls into a swoon, which Golo takes advantage of to kiss her, thereby still further exciting his flaming passion. Genoveva finally awakes and goes away to mourn in silence for her husband.

Golo being alone, an old hag, Margaretha, whom he takes for his nurse, comes to console him.

She is in reality his mother, and has great schemes for her son's future happiness. She insinuates to him that Genoveva, being alone, needs consolation, and will easily be led on to accept more tender attentions, and she promises him her assistance. The second act shows Genoveva's room. She longs sadly for her husband, and sees with pain and disgust the insolent behavior of the servants, whose wild songs penetrate into her silent chamber.

Golo enters to bring her the news of a great victory over Abdurrahman, news which fills her heart with joy.

She bids Golo sing and sweetly accompanies his song, which so fires his passion that he falls upon his knees and frightens her by glowing words. Vainly she bids him leave her; he only grows more excited, till she repulses him with the word "bastard." Now his love turns into hatred, and when Drago, the faithful steward, comes to announce that the servants begin to be more and more insolent, daring even to insult the good name of the Countess, Golo asserts that they speak the truth about her. He persuades the incredulous Drago to hide himself in Genoveva's room, the latter having retired for the night's rest.

Margaretha, listening at the door, hears everything. She tells Golo that Count Siegfried lies wounded at Strassbourg; she has intercepted his letter to the Countess, and prepares to leave for that town, in order to nurse the Count and kill him slowly by some deadly poison. Then Golo calls quickly for the servants, who all assemble to penetrate into their mistress's room. She repulses them, full of wounded pride, but at last she yields, and herself taking the candle to light the room, proceeds to search, when Drago is found behind the curtains and at once silenced by Golo, who runs his dagger through his heart. Genoveva is led into the prison of the castle.

The third act takes place at Strassbourg, where Siegfried is being nursed by Margaretha. His strength defies her perfidy, and he is full of impatience to return to his loving wife, when Golo enters, bringing him the news of her faithlessness.

Siegfried, in despair, bids Golo kill her with his own sword. He decides to fly into the wilderness, but before fulfilling his design, he goes once more to Margaretha, who has promised to show him all that passed at home during his absence. He sees Genoveva in a magic looking-glass, exchanging kindly words with Drago, but there is no appearance of guilt in their intercourse. The third image shows Genoveva sleeping on her couch, and Drago approaching her. With an imprecation Siegfried starts up, bidding Golo avenge him, but at the same instant the glass flies in pieces with a terrible crash, and Drago's ghost stands before Margaretha, commanding her to tell Siegfried the truth.

In the fourth act Genoveva is being led into the wilderness by two ruffians, who have orders to murder her. Before this is done, Golo approaches her once more, showing her Siegfried's ring and sword, with which he has been bidden to kill her. He tries hard to win her, but she turns from him with scorn and loathing, preferring death to dishonor. At length relinquishing his attempts, he beckons to the murderers to do their work, and hands them Count Siegfried's weapon. Genoveva, in her extreme need, seizes the cross of the Saviour, praying fervently, and detains the ruffians, till at the last moment Siegfried appears, led by the repentant Margaretha. There ensues a touching scene of forgiveness, while Golo rushes away to meet his fate by falling over a precipice.

GERMANIA

Dramatic Opera in four acts by ALBERTO FRANCHETTI

The libretto is by LUIGI ILLICA

This work was first produced at Milan, in 1902. The action is supposed to take place in various parts of Germany. The time is 1806.

Act I shows an old mill in Nuremberg, which has been dismantled and fitted up by a band of men, secretly organized to resist the power of Napoleon, as a printing plant to distribute propaganda. Palm, the leader in these attempts to resist Napoleon's sway, is being hotly pursued by the French police, but has so far escaped them. He goes on writing pamphlets against Napoleonic rule. The printed matter is surreptitiously sent out in sacks in the guise of flour. Worms, who has charge of the printing press, is accused by Ricke, his sweetheart, of being a traitor to the cause of liberating Germany. Loewe, Ricke's former lover, is expected back almost immediately, and Worms by fierce threats attempts to cow the girl into submission to his plans.

In Act II the scene changes to the Black Forest, where Loewe, Ricke, and some of their friends seek shelter in a deserted mountain cabin. Loewe has been added to the list of proscribed felons after Napoleon's most recent victories. Ricke, who has not the courage to speak of her past relations with Worms, has promised to marry Loewe. But just as the simple wedding ceremony has been performed by the clergyman, Worms mysteriously appears and summons Loewe to an important rally of the fraternity. Ricke fears evil consequences from this summons; she disappears and in a note begs her young husband not to try and find her hiding-place. In casting about for an explanation for all this mystery, Loewe accidentally is told by Ricke's small sister of the true state of the case.

Act III transpires at a secret hall in Koenigsberg, where those opposed to Napoleonic supremacy hold an important meeting. They discuss plans to defeat the invader of their country. One man alone, who stands at a distance closely masked, takes no part. This intruder is Loewe and he threatens Worms with a violent death. The quarrel, however, is stopped by others.

Act IV takes place on the battlefields of Leipsic. The whole plain is covered with the bodies of the slain. Ricke is there among those who seek their loved ones and finds at last not only the corpse of her husband, Loewe, but also that of Worms, her lover.

GIANNI SCHICCHI

One-act comic opera by GIACOMO PUCCINI

Libretto by ADAMI

The first performance took place in New York in 1918. Florence at the end of the thirteenth century provides the setting.

The sweet breath of life has barely left Donati when his relatives begin a frantic search for his will. Donati was wealthy but it has been rumored in Florence that he will bequeath everything to a convent. The relatives find the will and to their dismay learn that the rumors were well-founded for all goes to the convent. What can be done? Renuccio remembers that Neighbor Schicchi, father of Lauretto whom Renuccio loves, is versed in the tricks of lawyers. Neighbor Schicchi is called. As no one outside the family knows yet that Donati is dead, Gianni proposes that he be allowed to impersonate their uncle and dictate a new will. They agree enthusiastically. He reminds them that the penalty for forging wills is the loss of an arm and banishment from Florence. This does not deter them for who among them would betray the secret?

A notary is called and Gianni, muffled in the bedclothes in Donati's darkened room, dictates the new will making "his beloved friend, Gianni Schicchi" chief beneficiary! The relatives fume impotently since they cannot betray him without implicating themselves. When the notary departs all save Renuccio berate the astute Schicchi and then steal everything they can carry away with them. As for Renuccio, he is happy for Gianni provided a legacy sufficient for him to marry Lauretto.

LA GIARA

Ballet opera in one act by ALFREDO CASELLA

Libretto by LUIGI PIRANDELLO

The first production was given in Rome in 1925. The setting is Sicily at the end of the nineteenth century.

Don Lolló has a magnificent oil jar of which he is very proud. One day the servants find it broken. As the irascible temper of Don Lolló is notorious, no one dares to tell him of the catastrophe. Finally he discovers the broken jar and flies into a rage. His young daughter, Nela, assures him that Zi 'Dima, an old mender famous for his great skill, can make the vessel look like new. He is called in haste by the peasant, and, after examining the jar, agrees to repair it. They leave him alone with his tools and his melancholy. Finally when the fragments are ready to be put into place, the servants return and Zi 'Dima asks them to help him climb into the jar as he will be able to work better from the inside. Soon the mending is complete and the peasants are enthusiastic in their praise of the old man's skill. But Zi 'Dima has reckoned without his hump which now prevents his climbing out of the neck of the jar. Don Lolló arrives and emphatically refuses to let the jar be broken again to let the mender escape. Declaring that Zi 'Dima can live in the vessel as a bird lives in a cage, Don Lolló dismisses the servants and himself departs.

Night comes. The moon rises and from the neck of the jar curls a ribbon of smoke from the pipe of the philosophic Zi 'Dima. Nela slips out of her father's house and approaches the imprisoned mender. She calls the servants who drink to the health and deliverance of Zi 'Dima. They dance around the jar and gradually the dance becomes an orgy. Don Lolló is awakened and furious at being disturbed, with one stupendous effort he hurls the massive jar down the hillside where it is broken against an olive tree. As the peasants rush to aid Zi 'Dima, Don Lolló retires discomfited into his house.

LA GIOCONDA

Grand Opera in four acts by PONCHIELLI

This opera, by Ponchielli, for which Tobio Gorrio wrote the libretto, was first produced in America at the Metropolitan Opera House, New York, on December 20, 1883. The scene of the play is laid in Venice in the seventeenth century.

The first act, titled in the story "The Lion's Mouth," takes place in the Grand Courtyard of the Ducal Palace. On one side of the courtyard is seen one of the historical "lion's mouths," in which letters were dropped by any person who desired to inform the Inquisition as to any plot, or conspiracy, or person dangerous to the State.

As the curtain rises a chorus, by sailors, monks, and masquers, is sung in praise of the Doge and the Republic. Barnaba, a spy in the employ of the Inquisition, jeers in moody meditation at the people singing. Pointing to the gratings of the subterranean prisons, he says they are dancing on their graves. He is longing to make captive the wayward Gioconda, a ballad singer, with whom he is in love. Gioconda now enters, leading her blind mother, Cieca. Barnaba, seeing them coming, hides himself behind one of the columns, and listens to their conversation. Gioconda tells her mother that she is going to look for Enzo, a Genoese noble, and will return with him. Cieca calls down Heaven's blessings on her footsteps, and Gioconda is about to leave when Barnaba steps forward and commands her to remain. He loves her, he says, and will bar her way if she return not his love. She repulses his advances. He seizes her to prevent her running away, but she escapes. Barnaba is now determined to revenge himself on her. With that end in view he plans to persecute Cieca, her mother, place the blind woman in a position where she will have no means to escape, and prevail on Gioconda by reason of his power over the mother. Barnaba thereupon tells Zuane, the defeated contestant at the regatta, that Cieca practiced witchcraft on him, and because of this he lost the race. The ignorant boatman and his equally ignorant friends seize on the excuse and, for a time, the life of Cieca is in grave danger. The people cry to burn her, and they are about to carry their suggestions into execution when Gioconda rushes in with Enzo, who prevents the immediate execution of the old woman. Alvise, chief of the Council of Ten, and Laura, his wife, now enter. Gioconda begs Alvise to save her mother's life, and Enzo commands his sailors to help him to protect her. Laura, hearing Enzo's voice, is arrested by it, and looks at him curiously. She seems to know him. Enzo recognizes Laura as the woman who was once betrothed to him. Barnaba does not miss the looks each is giving the other, and feels that he is being foiled. Alvise pardons Cieca, who, when Laura approaches her, gives her a rosary.

The recognition between Laura and Enzo is now mutual. All leave, at the command of Alvise, for the church, except Enzo, and Barnaba, who is watching Enzo closely. Barnaba knows Enzo to be the Prince of Santa Fior, and suspecting that he loves Laura, tells him that Laura will be on his ship at nightfall. Enzo, filled with delight at the news, leaves to go on board to wait for her coming. Barnaba has done this on purpose to get Enzo out of the way of meeting Gioconda, and to further a new scheme of villainy he has conceived. Being assured that the unsuspecting Enzo will fall into his trap, he dictates a letter to Alvise in which he informs the Chief of the State Inquisition that his wife is about to elope with Enzo. Gioconda, behind a column, overhears Barnaba dictating the letter. She is sunk in despair at the perfidy of Enzo. From the church is heard the vesper hymn sung by the monks and people, and the curtain falls as Gioconda and Cieca leave, the mother endeavoring to comfort her broken-hearted daughter.

The second act, entitled "The Rosary," takes place on board Enzo's brigantine, lying by the deserted bank of an uninhabited island in the Fusina Lagoon. The curtain rises discovering sailors, some seated on the deck, other standing in groups. Remaining thus, they sing a *marinaresca.* Barnaba enters with Isepo, both disguised as fishermen. Barnaba sends Isepo to summon three war galleys. Enzo comes on deck and sends his sailors below, remaining alone on deck in expectation of Laura's arrival. Laura enters, and the two lovers determine to sail that night. Enzo goes to make preparations for their departure. Laura is alone, but Gioconda steals in and is about to kill her, but stays her hand when she sees the rosary Laura is holding. She recognizes her as the lady who saved her mother's life. Gioconda is now determined to save Laura. She lends her her own mask, and, calling two boatmen, she places Laura in their boat and bids her leave before Alvise and Barnaba come and find her there. The war galleys summoned by Barnaba attack Enzo's yacht, but Enzo sets fire to his ship as the curtain falls.

The third act, bearing, in the libretto, the title, "The House of Gold," takes place in a chamber of Alvise's residence. It is the night after Laura's escapade on board Enzo's yacht. Alvise is alone, meditating on Laura's perfidy, and has determined to kill her. He summons her to him and tells her that she must drink the phial of poison he gives her before the last note of the serenade is sung that some passing gondoliers are singing. He leaves Laura standing with the poison in her hand, while the chorus is singing the serenade. Gioconda now enters, bringing a flask containing a powerful sleeping draught. She persuades Laura to drink this instead of the poison her husband gave her. Then, pouring into the empty flask the poison contained in the phial, she departs, leaving the empty phial behind her. Alvise enters, and, seeing the empty phial, is convinced that Laura has done what he commanded her to do. "All now is over," he says. He believes he is revenged.

The scene now changes to a hall magnificently adorned for a festivity. Cavaliers, ladies, and masquers enter and Alvise greets them. Gioconda also enters, but her arrival is unperceived. A charming ballet, "The Dance of the Hours," is now executed. Barnaba then enters, dragging Cieca, whom he found in one of the adjoining rooms. Cieca excuses her presence by saying that she came to pray for the lady who is just dead. The guests are astonished to hear that Alvise's wife is no longer living. Enzo, who is also present, masked, learning that Laura is dead, tears off his mask and denounces Alvise. Alvise orders him to be seized by the guards, and holds Barnaba responsible if Enzo shall escape. Gioconda, seeing that Enzo's fate is doomed, begs Barnaba to set him free, promising to become his wife if he will give Enzo his liberty. Barnaba accepts her offer. The act comes to a close as Alvise opens the curtain at the back, revealing Laura, laid out on her bier. He declares he has killed her to avenge his honor.

The fourth act takes place in the vestibule of a ruined palace on the island of Giudeca. On the right of the scene is a long and dimly lighted street. At the back is a large porch, through which can be seen the Lagoon and the brilliantly lighted square of St. Mark. Gioconda is alone, buried in thought. Two men come along the street, bearing the body of a woman between them. It is Laura they are bringing. When they knock at the entrance of the palace, Gioconda opens the door and bids them enter. They place Laura on a bed behind a screen. Gioconda then pays them, and begs them to try and find her mother, and, when they do find her, to bring her to Canreggio, where Gioconda will be waiting, because she is soon to leave Giudeca. Gioconda, alone once more, determines on suicide, and is tempted to kill Laura. While she is hesitating, Enzo arrives. He is deeply grateful to her for having obtained for him his liberty, but is resolved to end his life. Laura, now waking up from the effects of the drug Gioconda gave her, calls for Enzo, and comes from behind the screen. The lovers meet in a transport of joy, and, with gratitude to their deliverer, they leave the palace and escape in a boat. Gioconda now realizes the price she has paid for her love. She remembers her promise to Barnaba, and resolves to run away. She prays to the Virgin Mary to deliver her from the foul demon, as she calls Barnaba. Barnaba overhears her from behind a half-open door and confronts her, as she is about to leave. Determined to outwit him, she assumes a gay demeanor and tells him that she is going to adorn herself in order to do him honor. Barnaba is delighted. As Gioconda is putting on her jewels she manages to seize a dagger and stab herself, crying, in her death throes. "Take me, I am thine!"

THE GIRL OF THE GOLDEN WEST

A Sentimental Opera in three acts by GIACOMO PUCCINI
Text by DAVID BELASCO

This opera was performed for the first time on any stage in New York, in 1910. The book is based on an Italian drama by Zangarini and Civinini. The scene of the action is a mining camp in California, during the gold fever of 1849-50.

When the curtain rises a number of miners are seen in a barroom, among them Jack Rance, the sheriff. Ashby, agent of the Wells-Fargo Company, appears and declares that he is on the track of Ramirez, chief of a band of Mexican outlaws who committed a big robbery some time before. Rance in talking with the other men brags of his relations with Minnie, saying she is on the point of marrying him. A miner takes exception to this, and there is a brawl when Minnie herself enters and stops it. Minnie with the aid of an assistant, runs the barroom, as she is the orphan child of a man who had started the place and died there. When Rance tries to make good his claim on her, Minnie scorns him, threatening her importunate suitor with a revolver. A stranger enters, giving his name as Dick Johnson, from Sacramento. The sheriff suspects him, but Minnie takes his part, alleging that she met him before. The stranger in reality is none other than the sought-for Ramirez and has come to rob the saloon. Minnie does not know this and rehearses with Dick the events of their first meeting when they both fell in love with each other. Dick, who is not without some good points, becomes more and more enamored of the girl and makes up his mind to relinquish his plan of robbing the place. After Minnie and the others have gone to the dance hall, José Castro, a member of Ramirez' band, is brought in a prisoner, captured by Ashby's men. The men are in favor of "stringing up" Castro, who volunteers to lead them to the hiding-place of his chief, Ramirez, for he has recognized the latter's horse and saddle. A strange body of men go in search of Dick, or Ramirez, and meanwhile they leave their hoard of gold dust in Minnie's charge, with only Nick, the bartender, and Billy Jackrabbit, the Indian, to help protect it. Minnie says that anyone wishing to steal the gold of the miners must do so over her dead body. Dick (Ramirez) admires her courage. Minnie invites him to pay her a visit at her "shack" later on, when the miners shall have returned, and he accepts and walks out.

In Act II while the Indian squaw is rocking her baby, Minnie and the Indian, Billy, enter the cabin, and Minnie adorns herself as best she may in honor of the visitor whom she graciously entertains. They plight their troth, and when a sudden snowstorm surprises them, she invites her lover to spend the night at the cabin. Suddenly in the darkness outside shots are heard. Dick swears they shall not take him alive. Nick, the bartender, is searching for Minnie and calls out her name. She hides Dick and then admits Nick, Rance, Ashby, and a number of miners. They are looking for Dick, whom they know to be near and whom they have discovered to be Ramirez. Minnie, however, declines the protection of any men against the robber chief and the men all leave. Then she faces Ramirez—Dick—

with the revelations the men have made, and Dick acknowledges the facts, but explains how he drifted into his lawless life. Minnie cannot overlook his having deceived her after confessing his love and sends him out of the cabin into the night. He goes in a desperate mood and soon after shots are heard outside. Minnie opens her door and drags in Dick, seriously wounded, hiding him in a hayloft under her roof. The sheriff follows in search of the fugitive, and Minnie has almost overcome his suspicions, when a drop of blood falls on his hand from the wounded man above his head, and he discovers Dick. As a last resort Minnie, knowing Rance to be a desperate gambler, offers to play with him at a game of draw-poker, the stakes to be either Dick and her own hand, or else Dick's freedom. They play, and Minnie cleverly cheats and wins the hand. Rance is as good as his word, and leaves her in possession of the field.

The last act is on the fringe of the great California forest, it being early dawn, and Rance, Ashby, and Nick waiting. Rance stands telling how Dick has been nursed back to life and health by his faithful Minnie, when Dick is brought in by Ashby's men. He is fettered, in soiled and tattered clothing, and the men now surround him and cruelly jest about the fate awaiting him. Dick nevertheless is defiant and prepares to die. As the only favor he requests that they never tell Minnie how he died. But Minnie herself rushes in on horseback just when the lynchers are about to draw the noose of the rope taut. She gets in front of the condemned man and with her drawn gun holds the crowd at bay, while Rance chafes and foams in impotent rage. She strongly appeals to them all, reminds them how she has always cared for them faithfully, and how they must not fail her now in their turn. Her natural eloquence wins them at last to her side, and despite the sheriff's objections they cut the rope, turn Dick loose and restore him to Minnie, who bids them farewell.

LES GIRONDINS

Tragic Opera in four acts by YVES LE BORNE

Text by P. CHABRIER and A. PETIT

The first performance of this opera took place at Lyons, France, 1905.

The first act discloses a plot at the home of Jean Duclos, one of the leading deputies of the Gironde to the French national convent at Paris, its object being to punish Varlet, a traitor to the cause of his party. Varlet has meanwhile secured the aid of the terrorist section, especially of Robespierre, whose agents force their way into the house. Duclos is arrested and carried off to prison. Varlet seeks Laurence, the mistress of Duclos, for it was to possess himself of her that he caused Duclos's arrest, but he assures her if she will give up Duclos, he will be liberated forthwith.

During the second act Varlet confers with Robespierre as to the arrest of the whole Girondist faction in the convention. Varlet counsels that all of them be gathered in, and Robespierre, with a fatal smile, decides to that effect. Richard, a Jacobin of the extreme wing, accompanied by Laurence is sent with an order from Robespierre freeing Duclos. Varlet corroborates the order that Duclos is to be discharged. Snatching away the document and hiding it in her bosom, Laurence instantly shoots down Varlet.

Duclos and Fonfrède, Girondist leaders, together are looking for Laurence. The Jacobin Richard, informs them of Laurence's call on Varlet. Duclos's suspicion is aroused that he owes his freedom to Laurence's sacrifice, and he purposely insults Robespierre, seeking death thereby. Richard returns, saying that Varlet is merely wounded, not killed. The rabble of Paris cries out against the Girondists, demanding their destruction. Laurence, meeting at last her lover Duclos, affirms her fidelity and offers to go with him to the scaffold. Varlet appoints Richard chief jailer, while Artemise, the mistress of Richard, begs of him the release of Duclos and Laurence.

The fourth act occurs at the Bastille prison, whither Laurence has been permitted to go by Richard, with his secret connivance in case she wants to save Duclos, whom she finds there. They perfect their arrangements for flight from the place, but on the point of escaping they both hear the farewell hymn sung by the chorus of Girondists and they consider it ignoble to flee. Thus they remain to die for their country with their comrades.

GÖTTERDÄMMERUNG

By RICHARD WAGNER

This is the end of the great and beautiful tragedy, and really it may be called both a sublime and grand conclusion, which unites once again all the dramatic and musical elements of the whole, and presents to us a picture the more interesting and touching, as it is now purely human. The Gods who, though filled with passions and faults like mortals, never can be for us living persons, fall into the background and human beings, full of high aspirations, take their places. The long and terrible conflict between the power of gold and that of love is at last fought out, and love conquers.

In Götterdämmerung we see again the curse which lies on gold, and the sacred benediction of true love. Can there be anything more noble, more touching, than Brünnhilde's mourning for Siegfried and the grand sacrifice of herself in expiation of her error?

The third day opens with a prelude, in which we see three Norns, weaving world's fate. When the cord breaks, they fly; the dawn of another world is upon them.

In the first act Siegfried bids Brünnhilde farewell. His active soul thirsts for deeds, and Brünnhilde, having taught him all she knows, does not detain him. He gives her the fatal ring in token of remembrance, confiding her to the care of Loge. Then we are transported to the Gibichung's hall on the Rhine. Gunther and his sister Getrune sit there, together with their gloomy half-brother Hagen. The latter advises his brother to marry, telling him of the beautiful woman guarded by the flames. When he has sufficiently excited Gunther's longing, he suggests that, as Siegfried is the only one able to gain Brünnhilde, Gunther should attach him to his person by giving him Gutrune as wife. This is to be achieved by a draught which has the power of causing oblivion. Whoever drinks it forgets that ever a woman has existed beside the one who has tended the potion. Hagen well knows of Siegfried's union with Brünnhilde, but Gunther and Gutrune are both ignorant of it.

Siegfried arrives and is heartily welcomed. All turns out as Hagen has foretold. By the fatal potion Siegfried falls passionately in love with Gutrune, so that he completely forgets Brünnhilde. He swears blood brothership to Gunther; and promises to win Brünnhilde for him. Then the two depart on their errand.

Meanwhile the Walkyrie Waltraute comes to Brünnhilde and beseeches her to render Siegfried's ring to the Rhine daughters, in order to save the Gods from destruction. Brünnhilde refuses to part with the token of her husband's love, and hardly has Waltraute departed than fate overtakes her in the person of Siegfried, who ventures through the flames in Gunther's shape. She vainly struggles against him, he snatches the ring from her, and so she is conquered. Siegfried holds vigil through the night, his sword separating him and the woman he wooed, and in the early dawn he leads her away to her bridegroom, who takes Siegfried's place unawares.

In the second act Alberich appears to Hagen. He tells his son of the story of the ring and bids him kill Siegfried and recover the stolen treasure for its owner.

Siegfried appears, announcing Gunther's and Brünnhilde's arrival. The bridal pair is received by all their men, but the joy is soon dampened by Brünnhilde recognizing in the bridegroom of Gutrune her own husband. Siegfried does not know her, but she discovers her ring on his hand, and asserting that Gunther won it from her, this hero is obliged to acknowledge the shameful rôle he played. Though Siegfried swears that his sword Northung guarded him from any contact with Gunther's bride, Brünnhilde responds in a most startling manner, and both swear on Hagen's spear that it may pierce them should their words prove false. All this makes a dreadful impression on the weak mind of Gunther.

When Siegfried has withdrawn in high spirits with his bride Gutrune, Hagen, hoping to gain the ring, offers to avenge Brünnhilde on the faithless Siegfried. Brünnhilde, in her deadly wrath, betrays to him the only vulnerable spot beneath Siegfried's shoulder. Gunther consents reluctantly to their schemes.

The third act opens with a scene on the Rhine. The Rhine daughters try to persuade Siegfried to render them the ring. He is about to throw it into the water, when they warn him of the evil which will befall him should he refuse their request. This awakens his pride, and, laughing, he turns from them, he, the fearless hero. His fellow hunters overtake him, and while he relates to them the story of his life, Hagen mixes a herb with his wine which enables him to remember all he has forgotten. Hagen then treacherously drives his spear into Siegfried's back, killing him. He dies with Brünnhilde's praise on his lips. The funeral march which here follows is one of the most beautiful ever written. When the dead hero is brought to the Gibichung's hall,

Gutrune bewails him loudly. A dispute arises between Hagen and Gunther about the ring, which ends by Hagen slaying Gunther. But, lo, when Hagen tries to strip the ring off the dead hand, the fingers close themselves, and the hand raises itself, bearing testimony against the murderer. Brünnhilde appears to mourn for the dead; she drives away Gutrune, who sees too late that, under the influence of the fatal draught, Siegfried forgot his lawful wife, whom she now recognizes in Brünnhilde. The latter, taking a long farewell of her dead husband, orders a funeral pile to be erected. As soon as Siegfried's body is placed on it she lights it with a firebrand, and when it is in full blaze she mounts her faithful steed, leaping with it into the flames.

When the fire sinks, the Rhine daughters are seen to snatch the ring, which is now purified from its curse by Brünnhilde's death. Hagen, trying to wrench it from them, is drawn into the waves and so dies.

A dusky light, like that of a new dawn, spreads over heaven, and through a mist, Walhalla, with all the Gods sleeping peacefully, may be perceived.

GRISELIDIS

Romantic Opera in three acts by J. MASSENET

Text based on chronicles of the Provence

This work was first presented at Paris, 1901. The scene is the south of France.

Act I. Time, 14th century. The shepherd Alain and the shepherdess Griselidis, herding their flocks and piping their lays together, are vastly in love with each other. But the powerful and wealthy Marquis de Saluzzo comes between them, and Griselidis listens to his voice, and jilts her Alain. In due time a son is born to her, who is christened Loys. Just at this time the marquis feels an overpowering desire to fight the infidels. The priest tries hard to dissuade him from this adventure, but he will not heed. In his arguments with the marquis the priest has much to say about the devil and his cunning schemes for leading men and particularly women astray. Long absence of her lord would not be good for Griselidis. However, the marquis goes forth to fight the Saracens and leaves his charming wife to all the temptations the devil can devise. So sure of his wife is the marquis that he even hands the devil his wedding ring, a very foolish thing for a departing husband to do.

Act II. The scene changes to a pretty garden overlooking the sea. The devil and his wife (Fiamina) argue with Griselidis that the latter should become housekeeper during the absence of the marquis. After settling this point Fiamina facilitates the appearance at the castle of Alain, one-time wooer of Griselidis, who makes good use of his opportunity. But in the nick of time Loys, the baby son of Griselidis, saves his mother from infidelity and perdition. At this the devil is so wroth that he seizes the little fellow and runs off with him to parts unknown.

Act III. However, his satanic majesty keeps on tempting the pretty grass widow. His next move is an offer from him to return the child to the mother if she will but give him a kiss, one measly little kiss. Griselidis is in doubt; she hesitates. But again chance favors her, for her truant husband, the marquis, returns from fighting the Saracens precisely at the time when the devil has left to the young wife only the above alternative. The marquis is mightily aggrieved at the disappearance of his son and heir and makes up his mind to search for him high and low. The devil, however, causes his weapons to vanish without which in those days searching parties could not get along. Thereupon he and his wife, scenting something fiendish, begin to pray earnestly. Then the triptych over the altar opens, and lo! the boy walks out of it.

GWENDOLINE

Tragic Opera in two acts by EMANUEL CHABRIER

Text by MARTEAU and SIMON

This opera was first performed at Paris, in 1893.

Act I. Harald, king of the Vikings, has made war upon the Saxons under Armel whom he has conquered and condemned to execution. But the victor sees Armel's fair daughter, Gwendoline, the first woman he has ever beheld, and to him, matchless. Instantly his savage nature undergoes a radical change. He feels a deep and pure affection for Gwendoline and asks her to wed him. With her father's consent Gwendoline accepts Harald as her future husband. But Armel secretly gives instructions to his men to slaughter the Danes at the marriage feast when they will be disabled by drink.

Act II. This transpires in the bridal chamber, whither Armel has followed the bride. He hands her a sharp dagger, exacting a promise that she will slay the sleeping Harald as the foe of her people. She refuses to comply, and at the cry of the Danes she gives the weapon to her husband and remains by his side. But in the last scene, at sea, the Saxons kill all the Danes and Harald falls by the hand of Armel. Gwendoline stabs herself over his corpse.

LA HABAÑERA

Tragic Opera in three acts by JUAN LAPARRA

Text by C. PETIT and M. BOISVENT

This work was first heard at Paris, 1908. The scene is Spain.

Act I. At a tavern. There is first a noisy drinking scene and next a love duet between Pedro and his betrothed, Pilar. Then Pilar hurries off to join a group of dancers in the street who are performing the Habañera. Ramon, brother of Pedro, secretly infatuated with his brother's fiancée, provokes a violent quarrel with Pedro and finally stabs him to death.

Act II. The murder has remained a mystery, for nobody suspects Ramon. In a courtyard are assembled the father of the two brothers, Pilar, Ramon, and several neighbors, all of them speaking of the young man's death with deep regret. Ramon, in order to hide his guilt the better, has sworn to his father to avenge the death of his brother. Again the company dance the Habañera, and in the midst of them appears Pedro's ghost, but visible only to the murderer, to whom he whispers that if the truth is not confessed by the following day, his sweetheart Pilar, madly beloved by Ramon, shall die.

Act III. This act occurs in a cemetery. Flowers are placed on the tombs by a number of mourners. Pilar and Ramon are among them. After the others are gone Ramon is courting Pilar, who wavers in her mind. But suddenly the remembrance of the day before comes back to Ramon, and he finally confesses that he killed his brother Pedro. Pilar is unable to bear the truth and sinks dead on the grave of her dead lover, Pedro. Ramon himself rushes madly off the scene as the curtain falls.

HAMLET

Grand Opera in five acts by AMBROISE THOMAS

Text taken from SHAKESPEARE
by MICHEL CARRÉ and JULES BARBIER

Hamlet was first reproduced in Paris in 1868, a year after the representation of Mignon, but it never reached the latter's popularity. This is not due to the music, which is very fine, and even nobler than in Mignon, but to the horrid mutilation of Shakespeare's glorious tragedy, which almost turns into ridicule the most sublime thoughts.

The text is soon explained. We find the Shakespearian names with their thoughts and deeds turned into operatic jargon.

The first act shows Hamlet's disgust and pain at his mother's early wedding with Claudius, King of Denmark, only two months after her first husband's death. Ophelia vainly tries to divert his sombre thoughts; he finds her love very sweet, however, and when her brother Laertes, before starting on a long journey, commends her to his friend's protection, Hamlet swears to be true to her unto death.

In the interview at midnight with his father's ghost, Hamlet experiences great revulsion of feeling when he discovers that his mother's second husband is his father's murderer. The ghost urges Hamlet to avenge his parent, which he swears to do.

In the second act we find Hamlet quite changed. He not only avoids his father and mother, but also shuns

Ophelia, who vainly tries to understand his strange behavior. Determined to find out the truth about Claudius's guilt, Hamlet has paid some actor to play the old tragedy of Gonzaga's murder. When the actor pours the poison into the sleeping King's ear, Claudius sinks back half fainting, and Hamlet, keenly observant, loudly accuses him of his father's death. But he is unable to act, and after the King's escape he seeks his mother's room to ponder on his wrongs. Hidden behind a pillar, he overhears from Claudius' own lips that Ophelia's father, old Polonius is the King's accomplice. This destroys the last spark of his belief in humanity. Thrusting the weeping Ophelia from him, he advises her to shut herself in a convent and to bid farewell to all earthly joys. Left alone with his mother, he wildly reproaches her, and at last so far forgets himself that he is about to kill her, had not his father's ghost appeared once more, exhorting him to take vengeance, but to spare his mother.

This scene is very powerful, the music of strange and weird beauty.

In the fourth act poor demented Ophelia takes part in the plays of the village maidens. The Swedish song she sings to them is full of sweet pathos. When her playmates leave her, she hides among the willows, enticed into the water by the "Neck" (Swedish for Sirens), whose own song she has sung. Slowly floating out on the waves, her voice dies away softly. With her death the interest in the opera ends; however, a fifth act takes us to her grave, where the whole funeral procession arrives. The ghost once more appeals to Hamlet for vengeance, until he rouses himself and runs his sword through Claudius, after which the ghost disappears, while Hamlet is elected King of Denmark on the spot.

The audience in German theatres is spared this last piece of absurdity, and the play is brought to a more appropriate close by Hamlet's stabbing himself on his bride's bier.

HANSEL AND GRETEL

A Fairy tale in three pictures by ADELHEID WETTE
Music by ENGELBERT HUMPERDINCK

After a long period of "Sturm und Drang," we have an opera so fresh and simple that any child will delight in it. It not only captivates children and people of simple tastes, but the most *blasé* must acknowledge its charms. No thrilling drama, but a simple fairy tale, known in every nursery, has achieved this wonder. It is a revelation. True music finds its way to the heart, and how wonderfully refreshing are these simple nursery songs, recalling days of sweet childhood, how droll and truly realistic are these children in their natural and *naïve* sauciness! Here is no display of human passions; simply and clearly the old fairy tale goes on, embellished by the masterly way in which the musician handles the modern orchestra.

The first act represents the miserable little hut of a broom-maker. Hansel is occupied in binding brooms, Gretel is knitting and singing old nursery songs, such as "Susy, dear Susy, what rattles in the straw?" Both children are very hungry, and wait impatiently for the arrival of their parents. Hansel is particularly bad-tempered, but the merry and practical Gretel, finding some milk in a pot, soon soothes his ruffled feelings by the promise of a nice rice-pap in the evening. Forgetting work and hunger, they begin to dance and frolic, until they roll on the ground together. At this moment their mother enters, and seeing the children idle, her wrath is kindled, and she rushes at them with the intention of giving them a sound whipping. Alas, instead of Hansel, she strikes the pot and upsets the milk. The mother's vexation cools, and only sorrow remains, but she quickly puts a little basket into Gretel's hands, and drives the children away, bidding them look for strawberries in the woods. Then sinking on a chair, utterly exhausted, she falls asleep. She is awakened by her husband, who comes in singing and very gay. She sees that he has had a drop too much, and is about to reproach him; but the words die on her lips when she sees him unfold his treasures, consisting of eggs, bread, butter, and coffee. He tells her that he has been very fortunate at the church ale (Kirmes), and bids her prepare supper at once. Alas, the pot is broken, and the mother relates that, finding the children idle, anger got the better of her, and the pot was smashed to pieces. He good-naturedly laughs at her discomfiture, but his merriment is changed to grief when he hears that their children are still in the forest, perhaps even near the Ilsenstein, where the wicked fairy lives who entices children in order to bake and devour them. This thought so alarms the parents that they rush off to seek the children in the forest.

The second act is laid near the ill-famed Ilsenstein. Hansel has filled his basket with strawberries, and Gretel is winding a garland of red hips, with which Hansel crowns her. He presents her also with a bunch of wild-flowers and playfully does homage to this queen of the woods. Gretel, enjoying the play, pops one berry after another into her brother's mouth; then they both eat, while listening to the cuckoo. Before they are aware of it, they have eaten the whole contents of the basket and observe with terror that it has grown too dark either to look for a fresh supply or to find their way home. Gretel begins to weep and to call for her parents; but Hansel, rallying his courage, takes her in his arms and soothes her, until they both grow sleepy. The dustman comes, throwing his dust into their eyes, but before their lids close they say their evening prayer; then they fall asleep and the fourteen guardian angels, whose protection they invoked, are seen stepping down the heavenly ladder to guard their sleep.

In the third act the morning dawns. Crystal drops are showered on the children by the angel of the dew: Gretel opens her eyes first and wakes her brother with a song. They are still entranced by the beautiful angel dream they have had, when suddenly their attention is aroused by the sight of a little house, made entirely of cake and sugar. Approaching it on tiptoe, they begin to break off little bits, but a voice within calls out "Tip tap, tip tap, who raps at my house?" "The wind, the wind, the heavenly child," they answer, continuing to eat and to laugh, nothing daunted. But the door opens softly, and out glides the witch, who quickly throws a rope around Hansel's throat. Urging the children to enter her house, she tells her name, Rosina Sweet-tooth. The frightened children try to escape, but the fairy raises her staff, and by a magic charm keeps them spellbound. She imprisons Hansel in a small stable with a lattice door, and gives him almonds and currants to eat; then turning to Gretel, who has stood rooted to the spot, she breaks the charm with a juniper bough, and compels her to enter the house and make herself useful.

Believing Hansel to be asleep, she turns to the oven and kindles the fire; then, breaking into wild glee, she seizes a broom and rides on it round the house singing,

Gretel all the while observing her keenly. Tired with her exertions, the witch awakes Hansel and bids him show his finger, at which command Hansel stretches out a small piece of wood. Seeing him so thin, the witch calls for more food, and while she turns her back, Gretel quickly takes up the juniper bough, and speaking the formula, disenchants her brother. Meanwhile the witch, turning to the oven, tells Gretel to creep into it, in order to see if the honey-cakes are ready, but the little girl, affecting stupidity, begs her to show how she is to get in. The witch impatiently bends forward, and at the same moment Gretel, assisted by Hansel, who has escaped from his prison, pushes her into the hot oven and slams the iron door. The wicked witch burns to ashes, while the oven cracks and roars and finally falls to pieces. With astonishment the brother and sister see a long row of children, from whom the honey-crust has fallen off, standing stiff and stark. Gretel tenderly caresses one of them, who opens his eyes and smiles. She now touches them all, and Hansel, seizing the juniper bough, works the charm and recalls them to new life. The cake children thank them warmly, and they all proceed to inspect the treasures of the house, when Hansel hears their parents calling them. Great is the joy of father and mother at finding their beloved ones safe and in the possession of a sweet little house. The old sorceress is drawn out of the ruins of the oven in the form of an immense honey-cake, whereupon they all thank Heaven for having so visibly helped and protected them.

HENRY VIII

Opera in four acts by CAMILLE SAINT-SAËNS

The libretto is based on English sources

This interesting opera was first produced in Paris, in 1883, but for unknown reasons has not often been given elsewhere.

The first act shows a hall in Westminster. The Spanish ambassador, Gomez, acknowledges to the Duke of Norfolk that he is insanely enamored of Anne Boleyn, a fact of which Queen Catherine is aware. He adds that he has in his possession a letter from Anne wherein she confesses her love for him. Norfolk tells him to beware, for King Henry himself is smitten with the charms of the fair Anne. News comes that King Henry has condemned the Duke of Buckingham to die. When the king enters all save Gomez, Norfolk, and Surrey leave the hall. Henry speaks of the new maid of honor, Anne Boleyn, to the great consternation of Gomez. There is a change of scene. Henry converses with Surrey concerning the Pope's unwillingness to grant him a divorce. Catherine is summoned and dares to intercede for Buckingham. The king refuses; she chides him for his lack of consideration towards herself, whereupon he retorts that morally their married union has been wrong from the first. When Anne Boleyn presents herself, the king is assiduous in his attentions to her and makes her Marchioness of Pembroke. From outside come the sounds of the funeral march for Buckingham, who has just been executed. Anne says this is a fateful omen.

Act II takes place at Richmond Park, where Gomez appears, soon followed by Anne, who is accompanied by a number of ladies. She expresses her love for Gomez. But the king pursues her and to his wooing Anne makes reply that she will marry him if he will make her queen. The king promises. Queen Catherine strongly reproves Anne for her godless ambition, but she is obdurate and turns to King Henry asking him to help her out of her straits. A royal messenger arrives in great haste from Rome,—the bearer of evil news. However, Henry postpones receipt of his message until the next day and bids those present to enjoy the moment with dancing and banqueting.

In the third act Henry confers with the legate from Rome, who upholds the spiritual suzerainty of the Pope, which is met by Henry with bold defiance. Anne Boleyn enters and Henry betrays jealousy of her very palpably. After more talk with the papal legate Henry threatens to make a direct appeal to his subjects, announces himself head of the Church in England, and makes Anne his wife.

The fourth act passes in the apartments of the new queen, where Norfolk and Surrey are discussing the suspicions which the king has of her. Gomez brings a singular letter to the king from the former queen, Catherine, who is still in possession of the compromising letter from Anne. Henry rages and bids Anne to quit his presence and Gomez to leave England. A change of scene. Catherine, who is dying, with her last strength casts Anne's love letter into the fire.

HERODIAS

A Biblical Opera in four acts by JULES MASSENET

The libretto of this opera, by Jules Massenet, was written by Messrs. Milliet, Grémont, and Zanardini, and the opera itself completed by the composer in 1880. Its first performance took place in Brussels, on December 19, 1881.

The first act takes place in the large outer court of Herod's palace, overlooking the valley of Jerusalem, and affording a view in the distance of the Dead Sea. The dawn is about breaking, though it is still dark, and caravans of Jewish merchants and chieftains are seen sleeping on the ground near the outer gate, waiting for the daylight to come ere entering the palace to present Herod with the gifts they are bringing him. As the day dawns the chiefs awake and call to the merchants to rise, for the palace is open. Two groups of merchants begin quarrelling as to the merit of their horses when Phanuel, a young Jew, enters and puts a stop to the dispute. He rails at them for fighting with each other when the times are such that they ought to prepare for a more serious fight, for a revolt against Rome is at hand. The merchants go down to the city, while the chiefs, with the presents for the king, borne by the slaves enter the palace.

As they disappear Salomé comes out, looking anxiously about her. Phanuel asks her what fate has brought her to the palace. She tells him she is still looking for her mother. She is come to Jerusalem because the prophet is here, and he is kind and good. She was sick and alone, but her heart grew peaceful when she heard his tender and musical voice. Phanuel bids her go, and assures her that a faithful friend will watch over her while she is here. Distant voices are heard shouting, "Jerusalem! Jerusalem! Hail!" As Phanuel watches Salomé leaving, the slaves of the king appear and go toward the palace.

Herod now enters suddenly by the door through which Salomé had passed and cries out excitedly for Salomé: "Thee I adore, Salomé!" he cries. "Return once more." Herodias, pale and distraught, comes in and demands of him to avenge her for a deep insult given her. She had been walking that morning in the desert, when a half-naked man had followed her with threats, and calling her "Jezebel!" The man was John. When Herod asks her what he can do, she tells him he can give her his head. Herod says he cannot do this. The man is revered by the Jews, and he would lose their good opinion if he granted her devilish wish. She tells him he no longer loves her, and that she will accomplish her own vengeance. "John!" she cries, "I will strike you down!"

John enters at that moment, and, overhearing these last words, bids her strike, then. Herod and Herodias start back with a cry at his sudden appearance. John curses Herodias and fills her with fear. Herod drags his wife away with him into the palace, both flying from John as if in terror. Salomé appears and, seeing John, she rushes up to him, and falling at his feet, cries, "John! I have found thee!" John asks her kindly what it is she wants of him. She tells him she loves him and that she belongs to him. He pities her and asks what place her beauty can have in his gloom of life.

He bids her kindly to go and leave him. She will not leave him. Her love is no blasphemy, she cries; she loves him only, and would spread the glory of her hair upon his knees. She embraces him passionately. John, as if inspired, bids her love him then, but her love must be the love of dreams and not the unholy love of the body. He bids her to raise up her soul till it shall soar, and realize the new faith. Salomé tells him that the light of his eyes is to her more splendid than the sun, and falls at his feet in an ecstasy of passion. He leaves her, pointing to the sky, while the curtain falls.

The first scene of the second act shows us Herod's chamber in the palace. Herod is seen reclining on his couch, with his slaves about him. He cannot sleep, and is restless for thinking of Salomé. He bids the slaves dance. A Babylonian dance follows. A young woman offers him a love draught, which he no sooner drinks than an ecstasy of passion seizes him. He believes Salomé is with him, and appeals to her to come to him. Tired out, he falls asleep. Phanuel comes in and speaks of Herod as a man blasted by the delirium of his love. Herod awakes and begs Phanuel to cure him of his passion for Salomé, but Phanuel upbraids him for thinking of a woman at a time when his kingdom is in danger of destruction. Herod retorts that he will conquer the prophets of the people when the Romans have been driven out, and as the people without are heard crying, "Hail to the Tetrarch," Herod turns to Phanuel, encouraged by the cry, and tells him he would face all dangers.

The scene changes to the great square in Jerusalem, showing on the right the principal entrance to Herod's palace. The city itself can be seen in the distance, with Solomon's temple on Mount Moriah. A motley crowd of priests, Jews, sailors, merchants, soldiers, chieftains, and ambassadors are surging beneath the shade of the trees awaiting the arrival of Herod. The square is most animated. Herod enters, descending the steps of the palace, and is cheered by the people, who promise him their aid in gaining independence.

A fanfare of Roman trumpets is heard in the distance, and Herodias appears on the top of the steps and motions for silence. She announces the coming of Vitellius, the Proconsul. The trumpets are heard more distinctly, and the people rush about distractedly in fear of the coming of the Roman soldiers. The Proconsul arrives, preceded by torchbearers and the Roman Standard bearers. Vitellius asks the people what it is they want. The Jewish priests ask that the Temple be given back to Israel. Vitellius answers them that Tiberius will grant their reasonable request. A great cheering follows, and the Proconsul is hailed with Caesar. Herodias invites Vitellius to enter the palace, and while the soldiers make ready again to march, Salomé and John appear on the scene, followed by the Canaanite women. They sing "Hosanna! Hosanna! Hosanna!" Vitellius stops in surprise at the honor done to John, while Herod, seeing Salomé, points her out to Phanuel, Herodias looking on the scene in jealous anger. John addresses the people and Vitellius and prophesies against Vitellius. The women with Salomé take up the chant again, while the people hail the Proconsul. Herodias and Vitellius go into the palace, and Phanuel leads away Herod, whose eyes are riveted on Salomé.

The first scene of the third act takes us to Phanuel's home, at the back of which is a large opening overlooking Jerusalem. It is a fine, starlit night. Phanuel apostrophizes the city and wonders who this John is who is come into its life. As he remains wrapt in thought Herodias enters, greatly agitated. She is come seeking revenge. At her request he reads her horoscope and tells her that the star of Salomé is continually eclipsing her star. She bids him look again, and he sees her star quenched by blood. He leads her to the opening at the back and points to Salomé as she is going to the Temple: "Your child!" he says. "My daughter!" she cries. "She? My rival!" Phanuel bids her go. "You are but a woman," he says; "a mother, never!"

The scene changes to the interior of the Temple, that part of it before the Sanctuary. Voices of women are heard off the stage, singing in praise of Herod and his Queen. Salomé enters, almost fainting, and scarcely able to support herself. John has been thrown into prison and his fate is causing her to suffer. She prays that he may be saved, and falls down before the bars of his prison. Herod enters, preoccupied, soliloquizing as to John's fate and determined to save him. He sees Salomé and declares his love for her, begging her to go with him. Salomé is indignant that he should speak to her thus, and repulses his advances. She despises him and his love and his power, and calls him a disgusting brute. Herod leaves her threateningly, as Salomé sinks before the Sanctuary. The priestly nobles now enter and the people follow quietly and reverently. As the high priest himself finally comes in the people fall prostrate. Worship is conducted by the high priest, at the end of which a sacred dance is danced by the daughter of Manahim. Herodias, Herod, Vitellius, and Phanuel now enter, followed by the Romans, and later by John and Salomé. The priests demand that John be put to death. When John is brought in Herod questions him and then answers that the man cannot be condemned because he is mad. Herodias would have the impostor crucified, and the people, incited by the priests, cry aloud for his death. At a signal from the priests the guards of the Temple advance to seize John, when Salomé breaks suddenly through the crowd and rushes to John, crying that she be allowed to share his fate. She falls at John's feet. Herod, consumed by jealousy, denounces both John and Salomé, and condemns them both to death. The Temple guards then advance and seize them.

The opening scene of the fourth and last act represents the dungeon in the Temple, a circular vault arched at the top. John is sitting in the middle, and a funeral lamp sheds a faint light beside him. John, soliloquizing, dedicates himself to God. He will die for justice and liberty. A luminous glow now fills the dungeon and Salomé appears in it. He is astonished to see her in this place and bids her go. The priests in the Temple are heard shouting "Death to the Prophet!" John again implores her to leave him, but she will not go. In his arms she will die, she cries, as she embraces him. The chief priest now comes in, followed by the slaves of Herod, and tells John his hour is come. Herodias has commanded that he be put to death. The slaves seize Salomé, tearing her away from John, and John places himself voluntarily in the hands of the guards of the Temple, whom he follows, while Salomé is being dragged away.

The scene changes to the great hall in the palace of the Proconsul, in which a festival is about to take place. Herod, Herodias, Vitellius, and a number of Romans enter, the last singing a chorus in praise of their arms.

Vitellius is acclaimed as Caesar's representative, and a ballet is enacted by women of Egypt, Babylonia, Gaul, and Phoenicia. At the conclusion of the ballet Salomé enters, her hair dishevelled, endeavoring to free herself from the slaves who are holding her. Phanuel and people also enter. She asks Herod why she is refused the last favor of dying with John. She implores him to let John live. She turns to Herodias and makes the same supplication. Herodias is indignant that she should so curse her mother, and Herod again offers her his love. Salomé's pleading seems to have some effect on her mother, who is about to give way, when the executioner appears at the back with his sword dripping with blood. Salomé utters a loud cry and the people exclaim: "The Prophet is dead!" Salomé, drawing a dagger from her girdle, turns on the Queen and accuses her of having slain John. In a rage of hate for her mother she stabs herself and dies.

HERRAT

Grand Opera in three acts by FELIX DRAESEKE

The first representation of Herrat took place in Dresden on the 10th of March, 1892.

The Amelungenlied, a translation of which has appeared from Simrock, bears great likeness to the Nibelungen; we even find in part the same persons. The subject is a bloody one; love and heroism are the poles which move it. The music is grand, stern, sometimes sublime, but we look vainly for grace and sweetness. The libretto is rather poor, the rhymes unmelodious and uneven; nevertheless the musical effect is deep and lasting; the breath of a master genius has brought it to life.

The first scene is laid in Etzel's (Attila's) Castle Gran. The King of the Hun's best vassal, Dietrich von Bern, has been severely wounded, and sent by his Sire to Gran, that he might be tended by Queen Helke, Etzel's wife. Instead of taking care of the hero, she leaves him to her maid Herlinde, who has naught but water at her disposition, while the Queen nurses her kinsman Dietrich der Reusse, a prisoner of war. The consequence of this is that Etzel, coming home, finds his friend sicker than before, while his enemy is well and strong. Full of wrath, he orders the Queen to keep Dietrich der Reusse prisoner, without leaving her any guards; should he escape, she is to be beheaded.

After Etzel's departure to the army Dietrich der Reusse escapes, notwithstanding the Queen's entreaties.

In her distress Helke turns to the sore wounded Dietrich von Bern, who, though bitterly cursing her ingratitude, rises from his sick-bed in order to pursue the fugitive.

In the second act Dietrich der Reusse arrives on foot at Saben's castle in Esthonia. (Saben is a usurper, who has dispossessed King Nentwin and taken possession of his castle and his daughter Herrat.) Dietrich's steed is dead; but hearing his pursuer close upon his heels, he takes refuge in an adjacent wood. Herrat, standing on a balcony, has recognized him. She sees him vanish with regret, because prediction told her that a Dietrich would be her deliverer; but when another hero comes up she directs him to the wood to which Dietrich has flown. She hears the combat going on between the two, and soon the pursuer comes back, telling her that his enemy is dead and begging for rest and shelter. When he tells her his name, she starts back, well knowing that Saben, who has slain Dietrich's relatives, will not receive him graciously. She, however, accompanies him to a room, and, determined to protect him against Saben's wiles, she binds up his wounds and nurses him tenderly. Saben, entering, recognizes the Berner by his celebrated helmet; he leaves the room, telling Herrat to look well after such a famous guest. But Herrat's mind misgives her; she tries to rouse the hero, who has sunk into the sleep of exhaustion, and, not succeeding, places his arms well within his reach. When she is about to withdraw, she sees Saben return with a band of assassins. Their murmurs rouse Dietrich, who defends himself bravely, slaying one after another. But his strength is failing, when suddenly a disguised youth rushes to his assistance with eight well-armed companions. Saben's men are slain; Saben himself falls a victim to Dietrich's sword. When the youth unmasks, Dietrich recognizes in his deliverer Herrat, his sweet nurse, whose likeness to his own dead wife, Gotlinde, has moved him from the first. She offers him her father's kingdom, which he, though full of love and gratitude, is loath to accept, as he only claims her heart and hand. But ambition urges him to accept her offer, and so he not only obtains her hand, but is proclaimed King of Esthonia.

The third act presents the camp of the Huns, pitched southwards of Gran, near the Danube. Etzel has already twice granted respite to the Queen; but as there is no trace of the two Dietrichs, Helke is now to be executed. Old Hildebrand, one of the Berner's followers, is particularly inimical to her, because he believes her to be the cause of his beloved master's death.

Suddenly everybody's attention is attracted to a ship approaching the camp. Hildebrand, perceiving on it a hero in disguise, wearing Dietrich's helmet, with Waldemar and Ilias, Etzel's enemies, on his side, calls the people to arms. But when the foreign knight disembarks and, unmasking, shows the face of Dietrich von Bern, everybody is full of joy. He brings the two hostile kings as prisoners to Etzel, and lays the two crowns of Esthonia and of the Wiking country at his feet.

Etzel's brow, however, remains sombre; he sternly asks after Dietrich der Reusse. The Berner, unwilling to sing his own praise, is silent, when his wife, Herrat, steps forth, relating how her hero killed his antagonist in Saben's woods. Now, at last, Etzel relents; he draws his wife to his breast in forgiveness, and all sing hail to Etzel and Dietrich and to their Queen.

L'HEURE ESPAGNOLE

Comic Opera in one act by MAURICE RAVEL

Text by NOHAIN

This opera was first produced in Paris in 1911. The setting is eighteenth century Toledo.

Ramiro, a Herculean muleteer, comes to the shop of old Torquemada, an absent-minded clock-maker of Toledo, to have his watch repaired. Torquemada persuades the muleteer to tend shop for an hour while he goes to regulate the town clock. This annoys Concepçion, Torquemada's young wife, for she has planned to entertain her lovers during the clock-maker's absence. How now can she get rid of Ramiro? Equally embarrassed—for he is more at home with mules than with pretty young women—Ramiro offers to carry to Concepçion's room one of the large clocks which her husband has declared too heavy for him to lift.

While he is gone, Concepçion's lover Gonzalve arrives and is hidden in a large grandfather's clock which the unsuspecting muleteer is instructed to exchange for the other one in the wife's room. Shortly afterward Inigo, a gallant banker enamoured of Concepçion, enters the shop and he, too, is hidden in a clock. Another exchange of timepieces effects a change in lovers. But the strength of the muleteer has won Concepçion's admiration and she transfers her flirtation to him. They disappear into another room. Torquemada, returning, finds the two forgotten philanderers moping in their clocks and releases them with a philosophic sigh. Ramiro and Concepçion enter and all join in the sparkling quintet which concludes the opera.

LES HUGUENOTS

Grand Opera in five acts by GIACOMO MEYERBEER

Text by SCRIBE

This is the best opera of this fertile composer, and one with which only his "Robert le diable" can compare.

The music is not only interesting, but highly dramatic; the "mise en scène," the brilliant orchestration, the ballet, everything is combined to fascinate the hearer. We find such an abundance of musical ideas, that we feel Berlioz but spoke the truth when he said that it would do for twenty others of its kind.

The scene is laid in France, at the time of the bloody prosecutions of the Protestants or Huguenots by the Catholics. The Duke of Medics has apparently made peace with Admiral Coligny, the greatest and most famous of the Huguenots; and we are introduced into the castle of Count Nevers, where the Catholic noblemen receive Raoul de Nangis, a Protestant, who has lately been promoted to the rank of captain. During their meal they speak of love and its pleasures, and everybody is called on to give the name of his sweetheart. Raoul begins by telling them that once, when taking a walk, he surprised a band of students molesting a lady in a litter. He rescued her, and as she graciously thanked him for his gallant service, he thought her more beautiful than any maiden he had ever before seen. His heart burnt with love for her, though he did not know her name. While Raoul drinks with the noblemen, Marcel, his old servant, warns him of the danger of doing so.

Marcel is a strict old Protestant; and sings a ballad of the Huguenots to the young people, a song wild and fanatic. They laugh at his impotent wrath, when a lady is announced to Count Nevers, in whom Raoul recognizes the lady of his dreams.

Of course, he believes her false and bad, while, as a matter of fact, she only comes to beseech Nevers, her destined bridegroom, to set her free. Nevers does so, though not without pain. When he returns to his companions, he conceals the result of the interview, and presently Urbain, a page, enters with a little note for Raoul de Nangis, in which he is ordered to attend a lady unknown to him. The others recognize the seal of Queen Margarita of Valois, and, finding him so worthy, at once seek to gain his friendship.

In the second act we find Raoul with the beautiful Queen, who is trying to reconcile the Catholics with the Protestants. To this end the Queen has resolved to unite Raoul with Valentine, her lady of honor, and daughter of the Count of St. Bris, a staunch Catholic. Valentine tells her heart's secret to her mistress for to her it was that Raoul brought assistance, and she loves him. The noble Raoul, seeing Margarita's beauty and kindness, vows himself her knight, when suddenly the whole court enters to render her homage. Recognizing her at last to be the Queen, Raoul is all the more willing to fulfil her wishes, and offers his hand in reconciliation to the proud St. Bris, promising to wed his daughter. But when he perceives in her the unknown lady whom he believes to be so unworthy, he takes back his word. All are surprised, and the offended father vows bloody vengeance.

In the third act Marcel brings a challenge to St. Bris, which the latter accepts, but Maurevert, a fanatical Catholic nobleman, tells him of other ways in which to annihilate his foe. Valentine, though deadly offended with her lover, resolves to save him. Seeing Marcel, she bids him tell his master not to meet his enemy alone. Meanwhile Raoul is already on the spot, and so is St. Bris with four witnesses. While they fight, a quarrel arises between the Catholic and the Protestant citizens, which is stopped by Queen Margarita. The enemies accuse each other, and when the Queen is in doubt as to whom she shall believe, Valentine appears to bear witness. Then Raoul hears that her interview with Nevers had been but a farewell, sought for but to loosen forever the ties which her father had formed for her against her will; but the knowledge of his error comes too late, for St. Bris has once more promised his daughter to Nevers, who at this moment arrives with many guests, invited for the wedding. The presence of the Queen preserves peace between the different parties, but Raoul leaves the spot with death in his heart.

In the fourth act the dreadful night of St. Bartholomew is already beginning.

We find Valentine in her room despairing. Raoul comes to take a last farewell; but almost immediately St. Bris enters with a party of Catholics, and Raoul is obliged to hide in the adjoining room. There he hears the whole conspiracy for the destruction of the Protestants, beginning with their leader, Admiral Coligny. The Catholics all assent to this diabolical plot. Nevers alone refuses to soil his honor, and swears only to fight in open battle. The others, fearing treason, decide to bind and keep him prisoner until the next morning. Raoul prepares to save his brethren or die with them. Vain are Valentine's entreaties; though she confesses to her love for him, he yet leaves her, though with a great effort, to follow the path of duty.

In the last act Raoul rushes pale and bloody into the hall, where Queen Margarita sits with her husband, Henry of Navarre, surrounded by the court.

He tells them of the terrific events which are going on outside, and beseeches their help. It is too late, however; Coligny has already fallen, and with him most of the Huguenots.

Raoul meets Valentine once more. She promises to save him if he will go over to her faith. But Marcel reminds him of his oath, and Valentine, seeing that nothing can move her lover's fortitude and firmness, decides to remain with him. She accepts his creed, and so they meet death together, Valentine falling by the side of her deadly wounded lover, both praising God with their last breath.

IDOMENEUS

Opera in three acts by W. A. MOZART

Text by ABBATE GIANBATTISTA VARESCO

This opera, which Mozart composed in his twenty-fifth year for the Opera-seria in Munich, was represented in the year 1781, and won brilliant success.

It is the most remarkable composition of Mozart's youthful age, and though he wrote it under Gluck's influence, there is many a spark of his own original genius, and often he breaks the bonds of conventional form and rises to heights hitherto unanticipated. The public in general does not estimate the opera very highly. In consequence, Idomeneus was represented in Dresden, after the long interval of twenty-one years, only to find the house empty and the applause lukewarm. But the true connoisseur of music ought not to be influenced by public opinion, for though the action does not warm the hearer, the music is at once divinely sweet and harmonious; no wild excitement, no ecstatic feelings, but music pure and simple, filling the soul with sweet content.

The scene takes place in Cydonia, on the isle of Crete, soon after the end of the Trojan war.

In the first act Ilia, daughter of Priam, bewails her unhappy fate; but, won by the magnanimity of Idamantes, son of Idomeneus, King of Crete, who relieves the captive Trojans from their fetters, she begins to love him, much against her own will. Electra, daughter of Agamemnon, who also loves Idamantes, perceives with fury his predilection for the captive princess and endeavors to regain his heart.

Arbaces, the High-priest, enters, to announce that Idomeneus has perished at sea in a tempest. All bewail this misfortune and hasten to the strand to pray to the gods for safety.

But Idomeneus is not dead. Poseidon, whose help he invoked in his direst need, has saved him, Idomeneus vowing to sacrifice to the god the first mortal whom he should encounter on landing. Unfortunately, it is his own son, who comes to the strand to mourn for his beloved father. Idomeneus, having been absent during the siege of Troy for ten years, at first fails to recognize his son. But when the truth dawns on both, the son's joy is as great as his father's misery. Terrified, the latter turns from the aggrieved and bewildered Idamantes. Meanwhile the King's escort has also safely landed, and all thank Poseidon for their delivery.

In the second act Idomeneus takes counsel with Arbaces, and resolves to send his son away, in order to save him from the impending evil. The King speaks to Ilia, whose love for Idamantes he soon divines. This only adds to his poignant distress. Electra, hearing that she is to accompany Idamantes to Argos, is radiant, hoping that her former lover may then forget Ilia. They take a tender farewell from Idomeneus, but just when they are about to embark, a dreadful tempest arises, and a monster emerges from the waves, filling all present with awe and terror.

In the third act Idamantes seeks Ilia to bid her farewell. Not anticipating the reason of his father's grief, which he takes for hate, he is resolved to die for his country, by either vanquishing the dreadful monster sent by Poseidon's wrath, or by perishing in the combat.

Ilia, unable to conceal her love for him any longer,

bids him live, live for her. In his newfound happiness Idamantes forgets his grief, and when his father surprises the lovers, he implores him to calm his wrath, and rushes away, firmly resolved to destroy the monster.

With terrible misgivings Idomeneus sees Arbaces approach, who announces that the people are in open rebellion against him. The King hastens to the temple, where he is received with remonstrances by the High-priest, who shows him the horrid ravages whch Poseidon's wrath has achieved through the monster; he entreats him to name the victim for the sacrifice and to satisfy the wishes of the god. Rent by remorse and pain, Idomeneus finally names his son.

All are horror-stricken, and falling on their knees, they crave Poseidon's pardon. While they yet kneel, loud songs of triumph are heard, and Idamantes returns victorious from his fight with the monster.

With noble courage he throws himself at his father's feet, imploring his benediction and—his death. For, having heard of his father's unhappy vow, he now comprehends his sorrow, and endeavors to lessen his grief.

Idomeneus, torn by conflicting feelings, at last is about to grant his son's wish, but when he lifts his sword, Ilia throws herself between, imploring him to let her be the victim. A touching scene ensues between the lovers, but Ilia gains her point. Just when she is about to receive her death-stroke, Poseidon's pity is at last aroused. In thunder and lightning he decrees that Idomeneus is to renounce his throne in favor of Idamantes, for whose spouse he chooses Ilia.

In a concluding scene we see Electra tormented by the furies of hate and jealousy. Idomeneus fulfils Poseidon's request, and all invoke the god's benediction on the happy royal house of Crete.

INGRID

Opera in two acts by KARL GRAMMANN

Text by T. KERSTEN

Helga is to wed Godila, her cousin, but loves Erhard. Ingrid saves Erhard's life in a coach accident, and falls in love with him, but discovers that he is in love with Helga. Old Father Wandrup tells Ingrid that she was found a babe on his threshold twenty-five years before, and that nobody knows who she is. Codila discovers that Helga loves Erhard and is about to elope with him on a ship. Godila furiously jealous drags Helga toward the Ljora bridge and is preparing to throw her over, when Ingrid who witnesses the scene calls Erhard, who is on the ship. Erhard grapples with Godila who lets Helga go, and is himself accidently precipitated into the water. Erhard tries to save him, but is prevented by Ingrid, who knows he will only drown himself.

Helga is carried fainting to the house and Wandrup when he hears that Erhard has killed Godila turns on him and brands him as his murderer. Ingrid, however, tells the truth of what happened and pleads for Helga's union with Erhard. The lovers leave on the ship, and Ingrid resolves to destroy herself. She takes a last look at a miniature of Erhard's mother that he had given her in gratitude at saving his life, when Wandrup sees it and recognizes it as his own dead love, and confesses that Ingrid is his daughter, and that now he knows Erhard is his son and Ingrid's brother. Ingrid decides to live because of her Father.

IPHIGENIA IN AULIS

Grand Opera in three acts by GLUCK

Text of the original rearranged by R. WAGNER

This opera, though it does not stand, from the point of view of the artist, on the same level with Iphigenia in Tauris, deserves, nevertheless, to be represented on every good stage. It may be called the first part of the tragedy, and Iphigenia in Tauris very beautifully completes it. The music is sure to be highly relished by a cultivated hearer, characterized as it is by a simplicity which often rises into grandeur and nobility of utterance.

The first scene represents Agamemnon rent by a conflict between his duty and his fatherly love; the former of which demands the sacrifice of his daughter, for only then will a favorable wind conduct the Greeks safely to Ilion. Kalchas, the High-priest of Artemis, appears to announce her dreadful sentence. Alone with the King, Kalchas vainly tries to induce the unhappy father to consent to the sacrifice.

Meanwhile Iphigenia, who has not received Agamemnon's message, which ought to have prevented her undertaking the fatal journey, arrives with her mother, Klytemnestra. They are received with joy by the people. Agamemnon secretly informs his spouse that Achilles, Iphigenia's betrothed, has proved unworthy of her, and that she is to return to Argos at once. Iphigenia gives way to her feelings. Achilles appears, the lovers are soon reconciled, and prepare to celebrate their nuptials.

In the second act Iphigenia is adorned for her wedding, and Achilles comes to lead her to the altar, when Arkas, Agamemnon's messenger, informs them that death awaits Iphigenia.

Klytemnestra, in despair, appeals to Achilles, and the bridegroom swears to protect Iphigenia. She alone is resigned in the belief that it is her father's will that she should face this dreadful duty. Achilles reproaches Agamemnon wildly, and leaves the unhappy father a prey to mental torture. At last he decides to send Arkas at once to Mykene with mother and daughter, and to hide them there until the wrath of the goddess be appeased. But it is too late.

In the third act the people assemble before the royal tent and, with much shouting and noise, demand the sacrifice. Achilles in vain implores Iphigenia to follow him. She is ready to be sacrificed, while he determines to kill any one who dares touch his bride. Klytemnestra then tries everything in her power to save her. She offers herself in her daughter's stead, and finding it of no avail, at last sinks down in a swoon. The daughter, having bade her an eternal farewell, with quiet dignity allows herself to be led to the altar. When her mother awakes, she rages in impotent fury; then she hears the people's hymn to the goddess, and rushes out to die with her child. The scene changes. The High-priest at the altar of Artemis is ready to pierce the innocent victim. A great tumult arises; Achilles with his native Thessalians makes his way through the crowd, in order to save Iphigenia, who loudly invokes the help of the goddess. But at this moment a loud thunder-peal arrests the contending parties, and when the mist, which has blinded all, has passed, Artemis herself is seen in a cloud with Iphigenia kneeling before her.

The goddess announces that it is Iphigenia's high mind which she demands, and not her blood; she wishes to take her into a foreign land, where she may be her priestess and atone for the sins of the blood of Atreus.

A wind favorable to the fleet has risen, and the people, filled with gratitude and admiration, behold the vanishing cloud and praise the goddess.

IPHIGENIA IN TAURIS

Opera in four acts by GLUCK

Text by GUILLARD

Gluck's Iphigenia stands highest among his dramatic compositions. It is eminently classic, and so harmoniously finished that Herder called its music sacred.

The libretto is excellent. It follows pretty exactly the Greek original.

Iphigenia, King Agamemnon's daughter, who has been saved by the goddess Diana (or Artemis) from death at the altar of Aulis, has been carried in a cloud to Tauris, where she is compelled to be High-priestess in the temple of the barbarous Scythians. There we find her, after having performed her cruel service for fifteen years. Human sacrifices are required, but more than once she has saved a poor stranger from this awful lot.

Iphigenia is much troubled by a dream in which she saw her father deadly wounded by her mother, and herself about to kill her brother Orestes. She bewails her fate in having, at the behest of Thoas, King of the Scythians, to sacrifice two strangers who have been thrown on his shores. Orestes and his friend Pylades, for these are the strangers, are led to death, loaded with chains.

Iphigenia, hearing that they are her countrymen, resolves to save at least one of them, in order to send him home to her sister Electra. She does not know her brother Orestes, who, having slain his mother, has fled, pursued by the furies, but an inner voice makes her choose him as a messenger to Greece. A lively dispute arises between the two friends. At last Orestes prevails upon Iphigenia to spare his friend, by threatening to destroy himself with his own hands, his life being a burden to him. Iphigenia reluctantly complies with his request, giving the message for her sister to Pylades.

In the third act Iphigenia vainly tries to steel her heart against her victim. At last she seizes the knife, but Orestes' cry: "So you also were pierced by the sacrificial steel, O my sister Iphigenia!" arrests her; the knife falls from her hands, and there ensues a touching scene of recognition.

Meanwhile Thoas, who has heard that one of the strangers was about to depart, enters the temple with his body-guard, and though Iphigenia tells him that Orestes is her brother and entreats him to spare Agamemnon's son, Thoas determines to sacrifice him and his sister Iphigenia as well. But his evil designs are frustrated by Pylades, who, returning with several of his countrymen, stabs the King of Tauris. The goddess Diana herself appears, and helping the Greeks in their fight, gains for them the victory. Diana declares herself appeased by Orestes's repentance, and allows him to return to Mykene with his sister, his friend, and all his followers.

IRIS

A Tragic Opera in three acts by PIETRO MASCAGNI
Book by LUIGI ILLICA

This work was first performed at Rome, in November, 1898, and was revised a year later. The scene of the opera is Japan and the time is the present.

The first act shows a Japanese garden, where a hymn is sung to the sun, as the cause of all life. Iris and her blind father are there. The latter listens with pleasure to the prattle of the little girl, who is playing with her doll. There enters Osaka, a libertine, who desires the young girl for his evil purposes. Kyoto is bribed by him to arrange for the abduction of Iris. She is attracted away from her other companions, who are washing soiled linen by the river front, in order to attend a puppet show gotten up by Kyoto, and then is seized by men and carried off, while a sum of money is left behind for the father to bind the bargain and make it legal. Geishas are fluttering all about Iris during the scene of abduction, and her father, the blind old man, is given strong evidence that Iris really went voluntarily to Kyoto's house of shame. The deserted father, forced to believe this, pronounces a solemn curse on the head of his daughter, and becomes a strolling vagabond upon the face of the earth.

In the second act the scene is a yoshiwara, and Iris, slumbering while other geishas strum the lute and softly sing a plaintive melody, Osaka makes his entrance, and bargains with Kyoto for possession of Iris. Kyoto demands a high figure for Iris, and after some haggling Osaka agrees to the terms, because, as he puts it, Iris is a "creature with a soul." When Iris wakes she finds herself in a wonderful, a lovely place, where all is perfume and song. And as Osaka first approaches her she is unaware of his purpose and salutes him as a son of light. Kyoto becomes wearied of the poor girl's complete innocence and bids the keeper of the place to take her away. Besides, he also orders his geishas to robe Iris in transparent veils and thus to expose her to the gaze of the passers-by. Osaka's pity is aroused and he promises Kyoto his own price. During this auction the victim herself still remains completely ignorant of its true meaning. And towards its end her blind father appears as one of the crowd surrounding the show window, and his daughter shouts with joy at seeing him, but the blind man hurls mud at her and heaps curses upon her. Iris, not having the key to it all, sinks to the ground with despair, and flings herself down a precipice, being thought to be killed by the fall.

In Act III is seen a huge heap of garbage, on the outskirts of the city. In rummaging through it the rag-pickers discover the body of Iris, clothed in its finery, and the men scatter and run away in fright. But Iris is not yet dead. Voices seem to come to her from a distance and murmur phrases that she is dimly aware to have heard before but not understood. She hears Osaka telling her that she is perishing as a flower that sheds its fragrance only in death. She hears her father justifying himself. She wonders what it all means. She remembers her own hymn to the sun, as the cause of all life, and thus she passes away—the refuse becomes a flowery path, and her soul hovers over it all in light and gladness.

ISABEAU

Opera in three acts by PIETRO MASCAGNI

Libretto by ILLICA, based upon the story of Lady Godiva

The first performance was given in Buenos Aires in 1911. The setting is Italy of the eleventh century.

The Princess Isabeau is as renowned for her aversion to marriage as for her beauty which is always veiled in a snow white mantle. King Raimondo is eager for his daughter to take a husband and arranges a tournament of love at which she is to award her hand to the knight who wins her favor. She rejects all the gallant and noble contendents and for her obstinacy, is condemned by her father to ride unclad through the streets at noon. At the urging of the shocked populace, the king modifies the sentence so far as to announce that no one shall remain in the streets or look out of the windows while she rides through the city.

All obey the order save Folco, a guileless youth, who showers the Princess with flowers and sings her charms from the battlements. Escaping mayhem from the vulgar mob, he is imprisoned under sentence of death. Isabeau visits him in gaol and, convinced of his purity of mind, she promptly falls in love with him. While she is on her way to tell her father that she is ready to marry, the populace, incited by the Chancellor, murder Folco. Isabeau returns, and commits suicide over his body.

JEAN DE PARIS

Comic Opera in three acts by ADRIEN BOIELDIEU

Text by ST. JUST

After a lapse of many years this spirited little opera has again been put upon the stage, and its success has shown that true music never grows old.

Next to the "Dame blanche" "Jean de Paris" is decidedly the best of Boieldieu's works; the music is very graceful, fresh, and lively, and the plot, though simple and harmless, is full of chivalric honor and very winning.

The scene takes us back to the seventeenth century, and we find ourselves in an inn of the Pyrenees.

The young and beautiful Princess of Navarre, being widowed, and her year of mourning having passed, is induced by her brother, the King of Navarre, to marry again. The French Crown Prince has been selected by the two courts as her future husband, but both parties are of a somewhat romantic turn of mind, and desire to know each other before being united for life.

For this purpose the Prince undertakes a journey to the Pyrenees, where he knows the Princess to be.

In the first scene we see preparations being made for the reception of the Princess, whose arrival has been announced by her Seneschal. In the midst of the bustle there enters a simple page to demand rooms for his master. As he is on foot, the host treats him spitefully, but his daughter Lorezza, pleased with his good looks, promises him a good dinner. While they are still debating, the numerous suite of the Prince comes up and, without further ado, takes possession of the house and stables which have been prepared for the Princess and her people. The host begins to feel more favorably inclined towards the strange Seigneur, though he does not understand how a simple citizen of Paris (this is the Prince's incognito) can afford such luxury.

By the time "Monsieur Jean de Paris" arrives the host's demeanor has entirely changed, and seeing two large purses with gold, he abandons the whole house to the strange guest, hoping that he shall have prosecuted his journey before the arrival of the Princess. But he has been mistaken, for no sooner are Jean de Paris's people quartered in the house than the Seneschal, a pompous Spanish Grandee, arrives to announce the coming of the Princess. The host is hopelessly embarrassed, and the Seneschal rages at the impudence of the citizen, but Jean de Paris quietly intimates that the house and everything in it are hired by him, and courteously declares that he will play the host and invite the Princess to his house and dinner.

While the Seneschal is still stupefied by such unheard-of impudence, the Princess arrives, and at once takes everybody captive by her grace and loveliness. Jean de Paris is fascinated, and the Princess, who instantly recognizes in him her future bridegroom, is equally pleased by his appearance, but resolves to profit and to amuse herself by her discovery.

To the Seneschal's unbounded surprise she graciously accepts Jean's invitation.

In the second act the preparations for the dinner of the honored guests have been made. Olivier, the page, shows pretty Lorezza the minuets of the ladies at court, and she dances in her simple country fashion, until Olivier seizes her, and they dance and sing together.

Jean de Paris, stepping in, sings an air in praise of God, beauty, and chivalry, and when the Princess appears, he leads her to dinner, to the unutterable horror of the Seneschal. Dinner, service, plate, silver, all is splendid, and all belongs to Jean de Paris, who sings a tender minstrel's song to the Princess. She sweetly answers him, and telling him that she has already chosen her knight, who is true, honest, and of her own rank, makes him stand on thorns for a while, lest he be too late, until he perceives that she only teases in order to punish him for his own comedy. Finally they are enchanted with each other, and when the people come up, the Prince, revealing his true name, presents the Princess as his bride, bidding his suite render homage to their mistress. The Seneschal humbly asks forgiveness, and all unite in a chorus in praise of the beautiful pair.

JESSONDA

Opera in three acts by LOUIS SPOHR

Text by HENRY GEHE

Spohr wrote this opera by way of inauguration to his charge as master of the court chapel at Cassel, and with it he added to the fame which he had long before established as master of the violin and first-rate composer. His music is sublime, and sheds a wealth of glory on the somewhat imperfect text.

The story introduces us to Goa, on the coast of Malabar, at the beginning of the sixteenth century.

A Rajah has just died, and is bewailed by his people, and Jessonda, his widow, who was married to the old man against her will, is doomed to be burnt with him, according to the country's laws. Nadori, a young priest of the God Brahma, is to announce her fate to the beautiful young widow. But Nadori is not a Brahmin by his own choice; he is young and passionate, and though it is forbidden to him to look at women, he at once falls in love with Jessonda's sister Amazili, whom he meets when on his sad errand. He promises to help her in saving her beloved sister from a terrible death.

Jessonda meanwhile hopes vainly for the arrival of the Portuguese General, Tristan d'Acunha, to whom she pledged her faith long ago, when a cruel fate separated her from him. She knows that the Portuguese are at this moment besieging Goa, which formerly belonged to them. Jessonda is accompanied by her women through the Portuguese camp, to wash away in the floods of the Ganges the last traces of earthliness. She sacrifices a rose to her early love.

Turning back into the town, she is recognized by Tristan, but, alas, a truce forbids him to make an assault on the town in order to deliver his bride. Jessonda is led back in triumph by the High-priest Daudon, to die an untimely death.

In the third act Nadori visits Tristan in secret, to bring the welcome news that Daudon himself broke the truce, by sending two spies into the enemy's camp to burn their ships. This act of treachery frees Tristan from his oath. Nadori conducts him and his soldiers through subterranean passages into the temple, where he arrives just in time to save Jessonda from the High-priest's sword. She gives him hand and heart, and Nadori is united to her sister Amazili.

THE JEWELS OF THE MADONNA

Dramatic Opera in three acts. Music by ERMANNO WOLF-FERRARI

Book by C. ZANGARINI and E. GOLISCIANI

First performance at Berlin, 1911. The scene is Naples of the present day. The plot is simple, hinging on a popular superstition of the lower class Neapolitans, and on the jealousy between a wayward girl's two lovers.

In Act I it is the afternoon of a great procession in honor of the Holy Virgin. Maliella, beautiful and high-spirited, but a creature of impulse alone, escapes from her quiet home, with dress disordered and hair flying, in order to join a joyous crowd dancing and shouting on a small public square near the sea, and awaiting the passing of the festival procession. Gennaro, her foster-brother, who secretly adores her, has followed her from his home, and endeavors to induce her to come back with him. She indulges in banter and flatly refuses to obey, then sings a song of challenge, in which she dares the youths present to rob her of a kiss. She resents Gennaro's interference, and he vainly tries to control her reckless gaiety. On the square meanwhile a dance is improvised, and Maliella rushes into the crowd where she disappears for the moment from view. Raffaelle, one of the chief Camorrists of Naples, notices the girl as she goes whirling in the mazes of the dance, and tries to seize and subdue her. She pushes him back, however, and when he uses physical force to make her do his bidding, she stabs him with her silver hairpin, wounding him in the hand. Instead of reproaching her, the Camorrist chief laughs, kisses the wound, and then picks up a flower and flings it so it falls into her bosom. But Maliella takes out the flower and casts it on the ground, trampling on it. Now the procession comes in sight, and while the others kneel Raffaelle remains by the side of the girl, pleading his love with her. As the image of the Madonna passes by, adorned and loaded with precious stones, he whispers to her that to win her love he is even ready to risk his soul by snatching the jewels of the Madonna from its neck and placing it around her own fair shoulders. But Maliella is terrified at the thought, and shrieks out her horror. Raffaelle and his criminal followers merely laugh her to scorn, while she runs off towards home. He follows and as she is about to enter the house again, he throws another flower at her, which this time she receives in thoughtful mood, places between her lips and goes within.

The second act passes at the house of Carmela, mother of Gennaro and Maliella's foster-mother, on the evening of the same day. The festival is not yet over, and Carmela soon leaves them to retire. Gennaro left alone with Maliella, pleads his passion to her and vows his devotion. But the girl is wearied with it. She complains of the monotonous life she is condemned to lead in her humble home, and taunts Gennaro with the daring and generosity shown by the Camorrist lover, telling him at last of the supreme proof of affection offered by him to her, namely, the purloining of the very jewels of the Madonna for her sake. She threatens to leave her home for good. Gennaro begs for a farewell kiss, but the girl scornfully denies it, and speaks once more in high praise of Raffaelle. To cut short his weary plaints the girl escapes from him, and Gennaro now indulges his bitter reflections. It seems to him that nothing can win the love of Maliella save the very thing the Camorrist boasted of in advance, and he reaches the resolution to forestall Raffaelle and do the thing himself which the other merely meant to do. Maliella comes back, and he takes keys and his blacksmith tools with him, locks the garden gate, and leaves. Raffaelle arrives at the outside of the house to serenade the girl, bringing with him a host of his friends and fellow-Camorrists. The music and the words draw the girl into the garden, and the two embrace through the bars of the garden enclosure, avowing their mutual love. But Gennaro returns, pallid and sombre, and Raffaelle leaves the field to him. When she asks him the meaning of it all, Gennaro places the jewels of the Madonna around her neck, and after a moment's hesitation Maliella looks at the glittering gems admiringly in the pale moonlight, and rejoices at possession of them.

The last act occurs the next day, at the rendezvous of the Camorrists where men and women are holding high revel. Some are asleep; and others are one by one returning from some secret expedition. Raffaelle appears with some of his close friends, and is greeted with shouts of applause. A while after he sings a song in praise of Maliella and her charms, whereat the women grow furious. Dancing follows, which degenerates into a wild orgy. Maliella, invited to join Raffaelle there, now rushes in in desperation, and on being asked the reason, confesses to the ownership of the far-famed jewels of the Madonna. All are horror-struck and call her accursed. When Raffaelle hears that Gennaro is the malefactor he summons his men and tells them to bring him in dead or alive,—to capture him at all costs. Then Gennaro himself enters, half demented, and is spurned alike by the girl and the band of criminals. The girl, in an access of despair, casts herself into the sea, and Gennaro, after adorning afresh the image of the Madonna with the stolen jewels, stabs himself to death at the altar.

LE JONGLEUR DE NOTRE DAME

(THE JUGGLER OF NOTRE DAME)

Opera by JULES MASSENET

The plot of the libretto of this opera is similar to that employed by the writers of the miracle plays of the Middle Ages. Not that the story is in any way the story of one of these miracle plays, but a miracle is employed to give dramatic value to the dénouement. Maurice Lena, the writer of the book of the libretto, calls it "a miracle play," and, in a sense, the phrase is applicable; but the old miracle plays were altogether interpretative in their character and were acted to satisfy the demand of the time for a more objective presentation of religious ideas.

In this sense "Le Jongleur de Notre Dame" is not a miracle play, but a play with a miracle. This opera, by Jules Massenet, was first produced in Paris, in 1903.

The first act takes place in one of the squares of Cluny—a suburb of Paris—some time in the fourteenth century. It is the first day of the month of Marie, or May Day, and the people are about to celebrate the occasion in front of the monastery. Citizens and their wives, knights and their squires, peasants, priests, women, and common people are seen coming and going through the marketplace. Among those to arrive is Jean, a poor juggler, who performs his tricks for their gratuities, and who makes the people laugh by his remarks and performances. He is asked to sing a drinking song, and Jean, loth to do it, yet anxious to earn his day's expenses, asks pardon of the Virgin before he complies with the people's request. Jean barely gets through three of the verses of his parody on the Paternoster, Ave, and Credo, when the door of the convent opens violently and the Prior steps out in anger. The people run away in fear, leaving Jean, alone and amazed, with the Prior. The Prior turns on Jean and scolds him for his wicked ways, threatening him with the fires "of formidable hell" if he mend not his life. Jean, terrified, falls to the ground in an agony of supplication and craves pardon at the foot of the Virgin's statue. The Prior, seeing Jean humbling himself, thinks that a convert may be made of the man. He promises Jean pardon if he will change his life, and asks him to become a monk, instead of going about as a vagabond. Jean pleads for his liberty. While he is still young liberty, the "careless fay of the golden smile," is very dear to his heart. The two are interrupted by the entrance of Boniface, the cook of the monastery, mounted on a donkey which carries also the provisions for the monks' refectory. The sight of the provisions does for Jean what all the Prior's arguments failed to do. He consents to become a monk, and follows Prior and Boniface into the monastery, though not before he has retained possession of his juggler's outfit.

The second act takes place in the Abbey's study room, which opens on the garden of the monastery. A picture of the Virgin is well in sight, on which a monk is at work finishing it in colors. The Musician Monk is rehearsing a hymn to the Virgin with a number of other monks who are grouped around him. It is the morning of Assumption Day. Jean, musing sadly by himself, is bewailing that he cannot sing praises to the Virgin in Latin, because he does not know that language, and she would not understand him if he spoke to her in common French. He knows nothing but the refectory, and begs the Prior to turn him away for fear he bring ill-luck. The monks beg Jean to take to their arts. One asks him to be a painter, another a sculptor, still another a musician. They quarrel with each other over the merits of their respective arts, and almost come to blows in the heat of their discussions. The Prior intervenes and orders them all to chapel, there to practice humility. Jean gets into a conversation with Boniface and deplores his ignorance and bewails the fact that he can do nothing to please the Virgin. Boniface, to comfort and encourage him, tells him that the Virgin understands French also and that she is as good as a sister. He tells him a story of how a common sage plant saved the life of Jesus when he was being pursued by the bloody cavalier of the King, the child-killer. Jean is much moved, and finally is convinced that his prayers, even if offered in vulgar French, may reach as high as the King's. Advancing toward the picture, Jean lifts his eyes toward Heaven and prays, remaining in an attitude of ecstatic devotion as the curtain falls, the orchestra playing, the while, the mystic pastorale that unites the two acts.

The curtain rises on the third act discovering the chapel of the Abbey. On the altar, and plainly visible, is the painted picture of the Virgin. Jean is present with his juggler's outfit, but so placed that he can be seen without his perceiving those who see him. In the distance the monks are singing the hymn to the Virgin. In front of the picture, and alone, is the Painter Monk. He gives a last look at his handiwork, and, noticing Jean entering, hides behind a column. Jean enters on tiptoe and approaches the altar. He tells the picture that, knowing naught else but his trade by which to do her honor, he will go through the performance of his craft under her eyes, in order that she may take it as an expression of his devotion. Dropping his monk's robe, he shows himself in the vest of a juggler. Then, spreading his carpet, he takes out his playing instrument and plays the same tune he played in the market-place of Cluny. The Painter Monk, thinking Jean has gone crazy, runs off to bring the Prior. Jean, bowing to the Virgin, begins his performance, interrupting himself to tell her that some of his songs are hardly fit for her ears. Still, he intends to be entirely respectful toward her. He then sings the pastoral. While he is singing, the Prior, led by the Painter Monk, arrives on the scene with Boniface, the cook. They are unseen by Jean, who still continues with his juggling performance, but the Prior and his monks can easily see him. Several times the scandalized Prior attempts as if to rush forward and put a stop to the sacrilege that is taking place; but he is withheld by Boniface. Jean, in the meantime, has arrived at that stage of his performance when it is his business to dance. He begins the dance of a country step, with tapping of feet and exclamations of enjoyment. Faster and faster he dances until, tired out, he falls at the feet of the Virgin and prostrates himself in profound adoration. The monks, who have, in the meantime, come in, seeing this performance, cry "Sacrilege!" Just when they can no longer restrain themselves, the face of the Virgin in the picture is seen to become animated; her arms extend towards the praying and worshipping Jean. It is Boniface who draws the attention of the monks to this wonder, and when they see it they cry, "Oh, miracle!" Voices of invisible angels are heard singing "Hosannah!" and the monks, led by the Prior, approach the prostrate Jean. Jean rises, and, seeing himself surprised in the costume of the juggler, falls on his knees before the Prior for pardon. The Prior bids him rise. " 'Tis for me to be at your knees," he says to Jean. "You are a great saint; pray for us." Jean, thinking he is being mocked, begs to be punished, but the Prior asks him how can he mock the honor of the monastery when he sees with his own eyes the Virgin bless him. The altar, until now dimly lighted, is illumined by an intense light, while the nimbus of the chosen, detaching itself from the hands of the Virgin, sparkles over the head of Jean. Jean, as if stricken to the heart, dies in an ecstasy of exaltation, while the monks recite litanies. The final scene shows the Virgin mounting slowly to Heaven.

JONNY SPIELT AUF

An Opera in two Parts. Book and music by ERNST KRENEK

Ernst Krenek's satiric jazz-opera, first performed at the Leipsic *Opernhaus* on Feb. 11, 1927, in the words of the composer endeavours "to interpret the rhythms and atmosphere of modern life in this age of technical science." In short, this is the effort of a Continental European to write an opera inspired by American jazz. In Central Europe the opera was very popular for several seasons, where it was accepted as a telling satire on American materialism, but when the work was produced at the Metropolitan Opera House in 1929, the American audience realized that the jazz was inferior to the native product, and that Kranek's melodic invention was extremely slender.

Max, an idealistic composer, and Anita, an opera-singer, are lovers, and Anita leaves for Paris to create the title-rôle in one of Max's operas. Jonny, the jazz-band leader of the Paris hotel where Anita is staying, wants to get hold of a violin belonging to Daniello, a celebrated virtuoso. Jonny tries to make love to Anita, but is rescued by Daniello, who buys Jonny off. Daniello then makes love to Anita, who succumbs, and they go together into her room, whereupon Jonny enters Daniello's room and steals his violin. Daniello, discovering his loss, makes a scene, which is intensified because Anita has refused to remain with him after the one night they have spent together. The Hotel Manager fires his chambermaid, Yvonne, for negligence in allowing the violin to be stolen, and Yvonne is hired by Anita. Daniello in revenge gives Yvonne the ring Anita has given him, telling her to give it to Max, with his greetings.

Jonny has concealed the stolen violin in Anita's banjo case, and goes to Anita's home to get it. Meanwhile Yvonne has given Max Anita's ring, and in despair he rushes out to a glacier whose voice advises him to make the best of his lot. A radio-speaker from a nearby hotel projects Jonny's jazz-band, and Daniello, recognizing the tone of his violin, telegraphs the police. Jonny, fleeing from the police, puts the violin on Max's luggage in a railway station where he has gone to meet Anita at the suggestion of the glacier. The police discover the violin and arrest Max. Anita asks Daniello to explain that Max is not the thief, but Daniello refuses, and Daniello in trying to prevent Anita from going herself to the police, is pushed off the platform by Yvonne and killed by a train. Jonny knocks the chauffeur of the police wagon unconscious, and abducts Max and the violin. Max escapes and goes off to America with Anita and Yvonne. In the final apotheosis Jonny appears as the genius of Jazz. The clock in the station is transformed into a revolving globe, and Jonny, standing on the North Pole, plays his violin while the world starts a wild jazz-dance.

JOSEPH IN EGYPT

Opera in three acts by ÉTIENNE HENRY MEHUL

Text after ALEXANDER DUVAL

This opera, which has almost disappeared from the French stage, is still esteemed in Germany, and always will be so, because, though clad in the simplest garb, and almost without any external outfit, its music is grand, noble, and classic; it equals the operas of Gluck, whose influence may be traced, but it is free from all imitation. Here we have true music, and the deep strain of patriarchal piety, so touching in the Biblical recital, finds grand expression.

Joseph, the son of Jacob, who was sold by his brothers, has by his wisdom saved Egypt from threatening famine; he resides as governor in Memphis under the name of Cleophas. But though much honored by the King and all the people, he never ceases to long for his old father, whose favorite child he was.

Driven from Palestine by this same famine, Jacob's sons are sent to Egypt to ask for food and hospitality. They are tormented by pangs of conscience, which Simeon is hardly able to conceal, when they are received by the governor, who at once recognized them. Seeing their sorrow and repentance, he pities them, and promises to receive them all hospitably. He does not reveal himself, but goes to meet his youngest brother Benjamin and his blind father, whose mourning for his lost son has not been diminished by the long years. Joseph induces his father and brother to partake in the honors which the people render to him. The whole family is received in the governor's palace, where Simeon, consumed by grief and conscience-stricken, at last confesses to his father the selling of Joseph. Full of horror, Jacob curses and disowns his ten sons. But Joseph intervenes. Making himself known, he grants full pardon and entreats his father to do the same.

The old man yields, and together they praise God's providence and omnipotence.

LA JOTA

Tragic Opera in two acts by MANUEL LAPARRA

Text by an anonymous Spanish writer

The first performance of this work occurred at Paris in 1911. The theme of the text is taken from the Carlist wars in Northern Spain, and the name of the opera is that of a well-known Spanish dance.

The scene of the first act is Anso, a place in the Spanish Pyrenees, and the time is 1835. Juan Zumarragua is a Basque, and though he is the lover of Soledad, a Spanish girl, he will not deny his race for love of her. They argue and quarrel on this point, and are about to separate, but finally there is a reconciliation, and they embrace. Juan, however, is summoned to arms, as the Carlist War has broken out. He follows the call, intending to do his duty as a soldier. So the two dance a last jota together and then bid each other good-by. Soledad, however, has bewitched Mosen Jago, a curate, who in vain attempts to save himself from the enthralment of her beauty.

In the second act the Carlist forces have reached Anso, and the church building itself has been destroyed. The curate and his flock are crowded within around the shrine of the Virgin, but outside Soledad leads the attack, and the curate is defeated with his men. Among the victorious Carlists is also Juan. He has had to fight against his own brothers and friends. Soledad herself meets her lover in the throng, and there is a reunion. The curate is nailed to the cross by the Carlists.

LA JUIVE (THE JEWESS)

Grand Opera in five acts by HALÉVY

Text by EUGENE SCRIBE

This opera created a great sensation when it first appeared on the stage of the Grand Opera at Paris in the year 1835, and it has never lost its attraction. It was one of the first grand operas to which brilliant mise en scène, gorgeous decorations, etc., added success.

Halévy's great talent lies in orchestration, which is here rich and effective; his style, half French, half Italian, is full of beautiful effects of a high order.

The libretto is one of the best which was ever written by the dextrous and fertile Scribe.

The scene of action is laid in Constance, in the year 1414, during the Council.

In the first act the opening of the Council is celebrated with great pomp.

The Catholics, having gained a victory over the Hussites, Huss is to be burnt, and the Jews, equally disliked, are oppressed and put down still more than before. All the shops are closed, only Eleazar, a rich Jewish jeweller, has kept his open, and is therefore about to be imprisoned and put to death, when Cardinal de Brogni intervenes, and saves the Jew and his daughter Recha from the people's fury. The Cardinal has a secret liking for Eleazar, though he once banished him from Rome. He hopes to gain news from him of his daughter, who was lost in early childhood. But Eleazar hates the Cardinal bitterly. When the mob is dispersed, Prince Leopold, the Imperial Commander-in-Chief, approaches Recha. Under the assumed name of Samuel he has gained her affections, and she begs him to be present at a religious feast, which is to take place that evening at her father's house. The act closes with a splendid procession of the Emperor and all his dignitaries. Ruggiero, the chief judge in Constance, seeing the hated Jew and his daughter amongst the spectators, is about to seize them once more, when Prince Leopold steps between and delivers them, to Recha's great astonishment.

In the second act we are introduced to a great assembly of Jews, men and women, assisting at a religious ceremony. Samuel is there with them. The holy act is, however, interrupted by the Emperor's niece, Princess Eudora, who comes to purchase a golden chain, which once belonged to the Emperor Constantine, and which she destines for her bridegroom, Prince Leopold. Eleazar is to bring it himself on the following day. Samuel, overhearing this, is full of trouble. When the assembly is broken up and all have gone, he returns once more to Recha, and finding her alone, confesses that he is a Christian. Love prevails over Recha's filial devotion, and she consents to fly with her lover, but they are surprised by Eleazar. Hearing of Samuel's falseness, he first swears vengeance, but, mollified by his daughter's entreaties, he only bids him marry Recha. Samuel refuses, and has to leave, the father cursing him, Recha bewailing her lover's falseness.

In the third act we assist at the Imperial banquet. Eleazar brings the chain, and is accompanied by Recha, who at once recognizes in Eudora's bridegroom her lover, Samuel. She denounces the traitor, accusing him of living in unlawful wedlock with a Jewess, a crime which is punishable by death.

Leopold (alias Samuel) is outlawed, the Cardinal Brogni pronounces the anathema upon all three, and they are put into prison.

In the fourth act Eudora visits Recha in prison, and by her prayers not only overcomes Recha's hate, but persuades her to save Leopold by declaring him innocent. Recha, in her noblemindedness, pardons Leopold and Eudora, and resolves to die alone.

Meanwhile the Cardinal has an interview with Eleazar, who tells him that he knows the Jew who once saved the Cardinal's little daughter from the flames. Brogni vainly entreats him to reveal the name. He promises to save Recha, should Eleazar be willing to abjure his faith, but the latter remains firm, prepared to die.

In the fifth act we hear the clamors of the people, who furiously demand the Jew's death.

Ruggiero announces to father and daughter the verdict of death by fire. Leopold is set free through Recha's testimony. When in view of the funeral pile, Eleazar asks Recha if she would prefer to live in joy and splendor and to accept the Christian faith, but she firmly answers in the negative. Then she is led on to death, and she is just plunged into the glowing furnace when Eleazar, pointing to her, informs the Cardinal that the poor victim is his long-lost daughter; then Eleazar follows Recha into the flames, while Brogni falls back senseless.

A KING AGAINST HIS WILL

(DER KÖNIG WIDER WILLEN)

Comic Opera in three acts by EMANUEL CHABRIER

Text after a comedy written by ANCELOT from EMILE DE NAJAC and PAUL BURANI

The composer has recently become known in Germany by his opera Gwendoline, performed at Leipsic a short time ago. His latest opera, "A King Against His Will," was represented at the Royal Opera in Dresden, April 26, 1890, and through its wit, grace, and originality won great applause. Indeed, though not quite free from "raffinement," its melodies are exquisitely interesting and lovely. Minka's Bohemian song, her duet with De Nangis, her lover, as well as the duet between the King and Alexina, are masterpieces, and the national coloring in the song of the Polish body-guard is characteristic enough.

The libretto is most amusing, though the plot is complicated. The scene is laid at Cracow in the year 1574. Its subject is derived from a historical fact. Henry de Valois has been elected King of Poland, through the machinations of his ambitious mother, Caterina de' Medici, to whom it has been prophesied that all her sons should be crowned.

The gay Frenchman most reluctantly accepts the honor, but the delight of his new Polish subjects at having him is not greater than his own enchantment with his new kingdom.

The first act shows the new King surrounded by French noblemen, gay and thoughtless like himself, but watching all his movements by order of his mother, who fears his escape. By chance the King hears from a young bondwoman, Minka, who loves De Nangis, his friend, and wishes to save him a surprise, that a plot had been formed by the Polish noblemen, who do not yet know him personally, and he at once decides to join the conspiracy against his own person. Knowing his secretary, Fritelli, to be one of the conspirators, he declares that he is acquainted with their proceedings and threatens him with death should he not silently submit to all his orders. The frightened Italian promises to lead him into the house of Lasky, the principal conspirator, where he intends to appear as De Nangis. But before this, in order to prevent discovery, he assembles his guard and suite, and in their presence accuses his favorite De Nangis with treachery, and has him safely locked up in apparent deep disgrace.

The second act opens with a festival at Lasky's, under cover of which the King is to be arrested and sent over the frontier. Now the King, being a total stranger to the whole assembly, excepting Fritelli, presents himself as De Nangis and swears to dethrone his fickle friend, the King, this very night. But meanwhile De Nangis, who, warned by Minka's song, has escaped from his confinement through the window, comes up, and is at once presented by the pretended De Nangis as King Henry. The true De Nangis, complying with the jest, at once issues his Kingly orders, threatening to punish his antagonists and proclaiming his intention to make the frightened Minka his Queen. He is again confined by the conspirators, who, finding him so dangerous, resolve to kill him. This is entirely against King Henry's will, and he at once revokes his oath, proclaiming himself to be the true King, and offering himself, if need shall be, as their victim. But he is not believed; the only person who knows him, Fritelli, disowns him, and Alexina, the secretary's wife, a former sweetheart of the King in Venice, to whom he has just made love again under his assumed name, declares that he is De Nangis. Henry is even appointed by lot to inflict the death-stroke on the unfortunate King. Determined to destroy himself rather than let his friend suffer, he opens the door to De Nangis's prison, but the bird has again flown. Minka, though despairing of ever belonging to one so high-born, has found means to liberate him, and is now ready to suffer for her interference. She is, however, protected by Henry, who once more swears to force the King from the country.

The third act takes place in the environs of Cracow, where preparations are made for the King's entry. No one knows who is to be crowned, Henry de Valois or the Archduke of Austria, the pretender supported by the Polish nobles, but Fritelli, coming up, assures the innkeeper that it is to be the Archduke. Meanwhile the King enters in hot haste, asking for horses, in order to take himself away as quickly as possible. Unfortunately, there is only one horse left and no driver, but the King orders this to be got ready, and declares that he will drive himself. During his absence Alexina and Minka, who have proceeded to the spot, are full of pity for the unfortunate King, as well as for his friend De Nangis. Alexina resolves to put on servant's clothes, in order to save the fugitive, and to drive herself. Of course Henry is enchanted when recognizing his fair driver, and both set about to depart.

Minka, left alone, bewails her fate and wants to stab herself, whereupon De Nangis suddenly appears in search of the King. At the sight of him, Minka quickly dries her tears, being assured that her lover is true to her. Fritelli, however, who at first had rejoiced to see his wife's admirer depart, is greatly dismayed at hearing that his fair wife was the servant-driver. He madly rushes after them to arrest the fugitives. But the faithful guard is already on the King's track, and together with his Cavaliers, brings them back in triumph.

Finding that, whether he will or no, he must abide by his lot, and hearing further that the Archduke has renounced his pretensions to the crown of Poland, the King at last submits. He unites the faithful lovers De Nangis and Minka, sends Fritelli as Ambassador to Venice, accompanied by his wife Alexina, and all hail Henry de Valois as King of Poland.

THE KING'S HENCHMAN

Lyric Opera in three Acts by DEEMS TAYLOR

The libretto, by EDNA ST. VINCENT MILLAY, is based on early English legends

The first performance of this opera was given at the Metropolitan Opera House in New York in 1927. The action takes place in England during the tenth century.

Act I. The rising curtain shows Eadgar, the masterful Saxon king of England, carousing with his nobles at a royal banquet. While the wine flows and the minstrels sing, the king dreams of a queen to grace his throne. Aethelwold, beloved friend and henchman of Eadgar, arrives at the feast in time to hear the king tell of his loneliness and his desire for a lovely woman for his queen. Such a one, men say, is Aelfrida, daughter of the Thane of Devon. Engrossed with kingly problems, Eadgar sends his henchman to see if Aelfrida be as fair as men report. Aethelwold accepts the commission and departs for Devon, accompanied by the minstrel, Maccus.

Act II. It is the eve of All Hallows. Aethelwold and Maccus, weary and craving sleep, stumble and crash through the underbrush of a Devon wood. Exhausted, they fling themselves under an oak tree and are soon fast asleep. A light approaches from the back of the "wood bewitched with mist" and Aelfrida appears with her serving woman, Ase. The maiden has come to the forest to practice certain charms which she hopes will bring her a lover. As she murmurs her incantations, the mist clears and moonlight discloses Aethelwold asleep beneath an oak. Aelfrida, filled with wonder at the efficacy of her magic runes, stoops to kiss the youth. He awakes and is enraptured by Aelfrida's beauty. They avow their love in a duet of ecstatic lyricism. Then the lovers tell their names and Aethelwold learns with horror that he has unwittingly betrayed his friend and king. He tries to flee from the enchanted wood, but Aelfrida's voice calls him back. His loyalty dissolved by his love for Aelfrida, Aethelwold sends Maccus to the king with the message that the Maid of Devon was nothing fair, but that since her father was rich in lands and kine while he, the henchman, had little beside the king's love, he would stay and wed Aelfrida.

Act III. Aethelwold and his stolen bride settle down in her father's home on the bleak Devon coast. Aelfrida, bored with the monotonous round of housework and fretted by the cold sea winds, is impatient to escape to a more pleasant land. Aethelwold declares that they will leave that night for Ghent. But it is too late, for the king is at the gates, come on a friendly visit to his henchman. In sudden panic, Aethelwold confesses his duplicity to his wife and commands her to retire and dim her beauty before the king sees her. When Aelfrida has departed to do her husband's bidding, a throng of villagers burst into the castle, followed by the king and his retinue. Eadgar greets his beloved henchman warmly. Aelfrida enters, treacherous and beautiful, dazzling in her jewels and cloth of gold. The truth dawns on the king who rebukes Aethelwold. The henchman, overcome with remorse for the betrayal of his king, plunges a dagger into his heart.

KOENIGSKINDER

Fairy Opera in three acts by ENGELBERT HUMPERDINCK

Book by ERNEST HOSMER

First production in New York, 1910. The scene is at Hellabrunn, in the mountains of Germany, and the time is the Middle Ages.

Act I. The hut and garden of the witch, situated in a secluded valley. A young girl is kept prisoner there who knows nothing of her parentage. A spell has been cast over the valley by the witch, so that the girl may not run away. She simply tends her flock of geese, and dreams of the unknown world. Because of this the witch charges her with idleness, and orders her to knead the dough for the magic bread which never grows stale and will some day bring death to whosoever eats it. The girl reluctantly obeys. Next the girl returns to the open, and there she meets a man, a stranger, the first one who ever succeeded in coming so far. He turns out to be the prince, son of the king sent into exile. The two recognize each other as "King's Children." When he invites her to come with him into the big world outside, she finds she cannot follow him because of the spell cast on her and the valley. But the prince is unable to fathom the girl's meaning and hence goes away in angry mood. The king has died, and a delegation from Hellabrunn arrives inquiring of the witch who is to be the next ruler. "He who at noon to-morrow shall knock first at the city gate," she replies. One of the delegation, the fiddler, lingers and takes the goose girl with him, although the witch curses him for doing it.

Act II. At the gates of Hellabrunn the municipal authorities are waiting for the fulfilment of the prophecy. In the crowd is also the king's son, clad in rags, for he has been toiling at common labor. At the stroke of noon the goose girl with her geese demands admittance at the gate. Seeing her the prince bounds forward with the cry: "My queen!" But the magistrates laugh these two to scorn, and turn them away.

Act III. It is winter, and the hut of the witch is all buried in snow and desolate, for the people in their rage have burned the witch herself. Only the fiddler, lame and decrepit, has there found a refuge. The prince and his goose girl, after having vanished for so long, appear together and apply at the hut for admittance. It is denied them by a woodcutter, who sells them a loaf of bread, the same poisoned loaf which never grows stale. The two "King's Children" die from it. They are buried together, and now they lie in a grave dug on the summit of the mountain. There they dream of those other "King's Children" who, almost every day in the week, perish because they go unrecognized.

KUHREIGEN
(RANZ DE VACHES)

Two-act Opera by WILHELM KIENZL

This work was first performed in Vienna in 1911

Act I. During the French revolution the army was forbidden to sing a certain Swiss air—the Kuhreigen, or Ranz de Vaches—which often caused the desertion of Swiss volunteers in the ranks of the French, since it made them homesick and melancholy. One of the Swiss soldiers is about to be shot for disobeying the order, when a powerful marquise takes an interest in his case and brings about his pardon, making him overseer of her estates.

Act II. Later on, when under the Terror both the marquise and her husband are sentenced by the Revolutionary tribunal to be beheaded, the grateful overseer exerts himself to the utmost to save his benefactress, but she scorns such plebeian aid and prefers to mount the scaffold with a mocking smile.

LADY MACBETH OF MIZENSK

or

KATERINA IZMAILOVA

Opera in four acts by DMITRI SHOSTAKOVICH

Text by D. SHOSTAKOVICH and A. PREIS, based on a novel by N. LESSKOV

This is one of the first of the Soviet operas, and has won considerable favor in Russia, though it was less enthusiastically received when it was given in New York.

Katerina, the wife of Zinovi Iznailova, a well-to-do merchant, is bored with the idleness of her life and the tyrannical nagging of her father-in-law, Boris. As the opera opens she bids her husband farewell and he leaves her in the care of her father-in-law, after having hired a new clerk, Sergei.

Sergei, who is the favorite of the servants, is the instigator of a prank to put the cook, Aksinia, into a barrel without a bottom, rolling her around the yard. Katerina enters and rescues the cook, and in fun, wrestles with Sergei. Her father-in-law puts a stop to it, threatening to tell her husband.

Katerina, preparing for bed, is told by her father-in-law not to waste the candle but to get right to sleep. Sergei comes to the door and on the pretext of borrowing a book enters the room. Katerina considers it useless to resist as the door has been locked by Boris. Boris catches Sergei leaving Katerina's room and flogs him, whereupon Katerina poisons her father-in-law with a dish of mushrooms.

Sergei is sleeping in Katerina's bedroom when Zinovi, her husband, returns and the lovers strangle the husband.

Drunken peasants searching for plunder discover the body of Zinovi when they break in the cellar. The peasants hurry to the police station, where the police are resenting the fact that they have not been bidden to the feast at the Izmailov home, and tell of the finding of the body.

Katerina and Sergei are at their wedding feast when the police enter and lead them away for the murder of Zinovi.

On the highway to Siberia the convicts are getting settled for the night. Katerina manages to get over to the men's side to speak to Sergei, but he repulses her. Then he speaks to Sonetka, a beautiful girl whom he is courting, and she demands that he get her a pair of stockings from Katerina, which he does, and in front of everyone presents them to Sonetka. The convicts all jeer at Katerina, and before they leave she pushes Sonetka into the water drowning her, and jumps in herself. The convicts continue the march to Siberia.

LAKMÉ

Romantic Opera in three acts by LEO DELIBES

Text by GONDINET and PH. GILLE

This opera was adapted from the romance "Le Mariage de Loti," and was first given in Paris in 1883. Delibes is at his best in light opera and ballets. The composition which is Oriental in character, lacks the dramatic interest which the libretto demands, nevertheless, it is attractive when performed by good artists, because of its charming love songs and graceful duets.

The scene is laid in India in a locality recently subdued by the English. The first act presents the private gardens of Nilakantha, an Indian priest, who has a great dislike for all foreigners. A small party of English ladies and British officers, including Gerald and Frederick, intrude upon his sacred grounds while strolling about in search of amusement. They discover some magnificent jewels, which Lakmé, daughter of Nilakantha, has left upon a shrine, and Gerald is so struck by their beauty that he remains to make a sketch of them for his fiancée, Ellen, while the others, realizing the impropriety of their intrusion, retire unnoticed. Lakmé soon returns, and on seeing Gerald immediately falls in love with him, and warns him of the death penalty which will result if his presence is discovered. Gerald hastily conceals himself as Nilakantha enters, but the wily priest discovers his footprints, and declares that he must be captured, and suffer the penalty for his rashness.

In the second act, Lakmé and her father, disguised as Penitents, appear in the public square, where a grand

Lily Pons in "Lakme"

festival is taking place in honor of the Gods of India. Many English people are present, and the priest commands his daughter to sing before them, hoping she will be recognized by the intruder, and that he will thus be induced to disclose himself. The plan succeeds, and Nilakantha, determined on revenge, steals up behind Gerald and stabs him in the back. Lakmé, who witnesses the deed, hurries to the assistance of her lover, and with aid of Hadji, her slave, removes him to a hut in the forest, where he is seen in the third act being nursed back to life and strength by the faithful Lakmé, who, knowing the secret properties of the Indian plants, soon restores him to perfect health. Under her tender care and affection Gerald forgets his former love and duties, and swears eternal love for Lakmé. To prove his constancy, he begs her to procure a draught of the sacred water which possesses the property of making earthly love eternal. While she is absent in search of it, Frederick appears on the scene, urges his friend to leave Lakmé and his present mode of living and to return to his fiancée and his duties in the army. Gerald reluctantly consents on hearing that his regiment is about to be ordered into action, and Frederick leaves just as Lakmé returns with the magic potion. She lovingly offers it to him, but as she does so the fifes and drums of his troop are heard in the distance preparing for their departure, and the love of duty overmastering him, Gerald refuses to drink. The heart-broken Lakmé immediately sees they are estranged forever, and in despair she takes a deadly poison, and falls dying in the arms of her lover as the angry priest and his Hindoo followers arrive on the scene. With her last breath Lakmé urges her father to forgive him, and, the request being granted, Gerald is allowed to depart unharmed.

THE LEGEND

Lyric opera in one act by JOSEPH BREIL

Libretto by BYRNE

This opera was first performed in New York in 1919. The setting is the mythical country of Muscovadia in the Balkans during the nineteenth century.

Count Stackareff, a penniless nobleman by day, Black Lorenzo the bandit by night, lives with his daughter Carmelita at his hunting lodge in Muscovadia. It is a stormy night. Stackareff tells his daughter of having captured a wealthy merchant whose ransom is expected to arrive by messenger at any moment. If it does not come, Stackareff intends to kill the prisoner. Carmelita fears not only for the safety of her father but that her lover, Stephen Pauloff, will discover the Count's double life and cast her off. As she is praying before a statue of the Virgin, Marta, an old servant, enters and says that she has seen Stephen in the forest. Carmelita is overjoyed but Marta warns her that on this night the Evil One walks abroad and knocks at doors. He who opens the door dies within a year. Carmelita laughs at the old woman's superstitions and asks her to tell her fortune. The ace of spades is drawn at every cutting. Marta refuses to explain the significance of the death card and leaves her young mistress bewildered.

Above the sound of the rising storm, Carmelita hears a knock at the door and runs to open it, thinking Stephen has come. No one is there.

Later Stephen arrives, explaining that he has been

sent to capture the murderous bandit, Black Lorenzo, dead or alive. While the two are planning to elope, Stackareff enters. When he learns of Stephen's mission, he shouts that he is the bandit and leaps through the door to escape. The young soldier starts after him and when Carmelita's prayers fail to keep him from following her father, she stabs him. Two soldiers enter with the body of Stackareff and seeing that Carmelita has killed their captain, they fire upon her, the fatal shot ringing out through the music of the finale.

A LIFE FOR THE TSAR

Russian Historical Opera in four acts and an epilogue by M. I. GLINKA

Text after Mérimée's "Les Faux Démétrius"

When Dehn, Glinka's teacher, told the latter: "Go and write Russian music," the Russian opera did not exist. Glinka not only composed real Russian music for this opera, but also took his facts for the book from Russian history. The period of Russian history ensuing on the death of Ivan the Terrible and lasting until the accession of Michael Romanov, is known as the Time of Trouble, culminating in the reign of the usurper Boris Godounov. Russia was beset on all sides by cruel foes, of whom the Poles were the most formidable. It is on this state of affairs that the curtain rises.

The first act occurs in a village where Ivan Soussanin, a simple but heroic peasant, lives with his daughter Antonida and his son Vanya. A celebration is going on to mark the approaching end of the long struggle with Russia's enemies. Antonida rapturously gazes in the direction whence she expects the return from the wars of her lover Sobinin. The father, however, is still oppressed with fear that all is not going well. Sobinin arrives and gives an account, from which it seems that a Tsar has been chosen at last. Thereupon Soussanin consents to the marriage, long delayed, of his daughter with the warrior Sobinin.

The second act takes us to Poland, where the nobles, confident of vanquishing the Russians, are reveling. Towards the close of the feasting, however, a messenger arrives bearing news of the retreat of the Polish forces and of the election of a national Russian for Tsar.

The third act strikes a high note of patriotism, although its background is humble. In the izba, or hut, of the peasant Soussanin we see in progress general rejoicings. A chorus of peasants, singing some wonderful folksongs, Soussanin, Vanya, and the pair of lovers, all participate in the merrymaking. This scene is interrupted by the noise of approaching soldiers. It is a detachment of approaching Polish soldiers, and these burst into the izba a moment later. The intruders are on the march to Moscow whence they reckon on bringing back the newly elected Tsar as a prisoner. Being, however, unacquainted with the road they force Soussanin to act as their guide. The latter, scenting the imminent danger to his new sovereign, resolves to lead the Polish forces astray. Lulling the foes into false security, he seizes an opportunity before leaving his cabin to whisper instructions to his son Vanya, telling him to hasten with all speed to the retreat of the Tsar and acquaint him with the circumstances, enabling him to forestall the danger. Soussanin then leaves with the Poles. Antonida's young playmates enter singing a nuptial song and find her in deep grief. Sobinin, on arriving, is also made acquainted with the state of things, and at once determines on pursuit of the enemy forces.

The fourth act is divided into three scenes. Sobinin and his men are seen hunting for traces of the enemy. The second scene discovers young Vanya at the monastery of Kostroma, where Michael Romanov, the newly chosen Tsar, has taken refuge. Help is summoned to warn the Tsar and his followers of the approaching enemy. Then the Polish band is seen led by Soussanin. He has taken them to a marshy forest where snow is falling fast. The night is beginning to close in, and the Poles suspect that they have been betrayed by their guide. They encamp while the sleepless Soussanin prepares for death. A storm arises and during its roar the patriotic peasant prays. He now scorns to dissemble any longer, feeling sure that his lord, the Tsar, must now have attained shelter from his foes. At the first dawn, therefore, he boldly owns up to having betrayed the enemies of his country, whereupon they fall upon him and put an end to his life.

The epilogue is acted on the famous Red Square of Moscow. A crowd of jubilant Russians sing the magnificent "Slavsya" chorus, acclaiming the newly crowned monarch. Among them are Antonida and Vanya. Together they intone one of the finest pieces of music in the opera, the unrivaled trio. The curtain drops amid loud acclaims.

LINDA DI CHAMOUNIX

Opera in three acts by GAETANO DONIZETTI

Book by PROCH after ROSSI

The first production was given in 1842 at Vienna. The scenes are laid in Chamounix and Paris, during the reign of Louis XV, about 1760.

Act I. Antonio and Madeline, poor Savoyard farmers in the village of Chamounix, are afraid of being dispossessed by their landlord, the Marquis de Boisfleury. When the opera opens, Antonio has returned from a visit to the Marquis' agent who has given him hope of leniency from his titled landlord. Antonio and Madeline have a daughter, Linda, whose beauty has attracted the Marquis. Linda is in love with an artist, Charles, but does not know that he is the Viscount de Sirval, nephew of the Marquis de Boisfleury. When her parents learn of the wealthy roue's intentions toward Linda, they send her to Paris to stay with the village prefect's brother.

Act II. Linda has been installed by Charles in a handsome apartment in Paris. When she had arrived in the city with her Savoyard companions, she found that the prefect's brother had died, and she was forced to support herself by singing in the streets. Fortunately Charles had discovered her. He had disclosed his identity and they plan to be married as soon as he can obtain his family's consent to the union. Meantime, the Marquis has traced Linda and calls to force his unwelcome attentions upon her. No sooner had he been repulsed than Charles comes to say that his family insists that he marry another. Next appears Linda's father who, seeing the costly surroundings, forms the obvious conclusions and denounces his daughter bitterly. Pierrot, a Savoyard minstrel and friend to Linda, now enters to inform her that Charles' wedding is in progress. Linda's mind gives way before her father's denunciation and what she believes to be Charles' desertion.

Act II. The Savoyards, whom Linda had accompanied to Paris at the end of the first act, are returning to Chamounix after their season's work in the city. Among them is Charles, successful at last in persuading his family to consent to his marriage with Linda. But Linda cannot be found. When she finally comes back to Chamounix, led by the faithful Pierrot, she does not recognize her lover as he tries to explain that there is now no obstacle to their union. But the truth eventually pierces her clouded reason and she swoons. Upon awakening from unconsciousness, her sanity is restored, and the curtain falls on the happy tears of everyone, including the rascally old Marquis whom Linda naïvely greets as her "dear, dear uncle."

Elizabeth Rethberg as Elsa in "Lohengrin"

LOBETANZ

A Fairy Opera in three acts by LUDWIG THUILLE

Text by OTTO JULIUS BIERBAUM

The first production of this work was at Mannheim, Germany, 1898. The scene is laid in Germany, during the Middle Ages.

In the first act a garden, with adjoining palace, is seen. There is a festival of song, on a sunny day of spring, and joy unrestrained reigns. Girls dance, strew roses, and chant pleasant ditties. Lobetanz, a homeless, wandering troubadour, happens along, and drawn by all this gayety, ventures into the garden. His garments are torn, and he himself is famished, but his faithful violin he carries with him, and the joyous maidens, seeing he can play for their dancing, invite him to join in their revel. They tell this strolling musician that the king has set aside this day for singing and general rejoicing, hoping that thus his daughter, who has been ailing with a mysterious complaint, may find a cure. It appears, they say, that all the physicians of the country have been unable to reach the seat of her malady, and that only a song touching her heart may heal her. Therefore the poets and composers and minstrels of the entire realm have been bidden to do their utmost. Lobetanz is urged to attempt a song. He looks down at his tattered clothing, and says that he, alas, is no fit company for royalty. He even tries to hide when a gorgeous procession, headed by the king himself, is seen approaching. The sympathetic damsels, telling him to pluck up courage, hide the minstrel's shabby clothes with garlands of roses, just before the royal party reaches the spot. Courtiers and harpers, flutists and fiddlers, poets and rhymesters do their best, but the princess, indifferent to their efforts, remains listless and melancholy. Still others try their skill, violently quarreling about their precedence. Of a sudden the soft, sweet strains of a violin, coming from a leafy bower, arrest her attention, and she is spellbound by the lay. When the last notes float away, she begs the musician may be brought to her. Lobetanz is dragged out of his hiding place, and the princess is charmed with him. Next she begs him to sing to her, and when he intones a rare melody, the princess faints from sheer excess of delight. There is an uproar, ending with the minstrel's being charged with black art. In the confusion, however, Lobetanz slips off unobserved.

The second act happens in the forest, where Lobetanz has found shelter in the cabin of the gamekeeper. Lobetanz seeks repose in the shade of a far-spreading lime-tree, and while asleep there a raven pounces upon his cap, and carries it off toward hangman's hill. The forester, his friend, tells the waking man of this incident, and augurs ill therefrom, but the laughing minstrel scorns the omen. Then along comes the princess, taking the fresh air in the quiet woods, and instantly recognizes her unknown minstrel, him of whom she has been dreaming all along, ever since the day he sang to her. She shows her delight at finding him, and they confess their mutual love. This scene is cut short by the arrival of the king with his retinue, who have been hunting in the glades. Lobetanz is seized, and the death sentence is passed on him as being a sorcerer, to the utter despair of his sweetheart, the princess.

The first scene of the third act shows the dungeon in

which Lobetanz is chained up securely waiting his doom. Some of his fellow-prisoners mock him for his presumption in daring to aspire to the hand of a princess, but Lobetanz keeps his air of serenity. He even is handed his fiddle, and with his manacled hand he plays a hymn to Death, while the motley crowd about him, one of them assuming the character of the grim destroyer, act a gruesome pantomine. In the midst of the noise the executioner comes in, claiming Lobetanz as his prey.

The last scene is enacted on hangman's hill outside the town, where a great throng has gathered to see the gay minstrel die. The executioner proclaims publicly why Lobetanz is to be put to death, saying that only the delinquent's blood can redeem the princess from the wicked spell that she is suffering under. The princess at this juncture is carried to the foot of the gallows, nearly lifeless, and Lobetanz, seeing her, begs as a last favor that he may play one more tune to her. After some discussion the request is granted, and the effects of the music are marvelous. At the first stroke of the bow she revives, and with every new tone she recovers more and more. When the music ceases, the princess sits up, gazes lovingly at Lobetanz, and finally stretches out her arms to him; she is fully recovered. Her royal father instantly grants a full pardon to the condemned man, gives his consent to the marriage with his daughter. Minstrel and princess join hands and blithely lead in the merry dance that follows, a dance in which even king and hangman take part. And at this moment, too, the solemn raven that had carried off the minstrel's cap, drops it from the top of the gallows. This, the old cronies aver, means the height of good fortune, and no longer shameful death. And so they all meander forth.

LODOLETTA

Opera in three acts by PIETRO MASCAGNI

Words by FORZANO, after OUIDA'S novel, "Two Little Wooden Shoes"

This opera was first performed at Rome in 1917. The scenes are laid in a Dutch village during the Second Empire.

Act I. Lodoletta lives with old Antonio who found her in a basket of flowers beside the lake when she was an infant. When the opera opens, she is begging Antonio for a pair of red wooden shoes, but, alas, he has no money. Then Flammen, a gay young Parisian artist, induces the old villager to sell him a treasured picture of a Madonna. With the gold Antonio buys Lodoletta the red shoes. Soon afterward while picking blossoms for the spring festival, the old man falls from a tree and dies. Lodoretta is left alone in the world.

Act II. Flammen, who has fallen in love with the young girl, persuades her to become his model. This causes gossip among the villagers. After refusing honest Gianetto, Lodoretta begs Flammen to return to Paris since the love he offers is not altogether honorable. He goes, only to find that absence intensifies his passion; and so he comes back to the village. But Lodoretta has disappeared.

Act III. On New Year's eve, Flammen's friends have gathered at his villa to help him forget his love in gaiety. When the celebration is at its height, Lodoretta, who in her turn has been searching for the artist, reaches his garden. Watching the merrymakers through a window, Lodoretta realizes that Flammen is not for her and, exhausted and disillusioned, she swoons in the snow. Here Flammen, after his lively friends have departed, finds her and flinging himself upon her frozen body, he swears to die for love of her.

LOHENGRIN

Romantic Opera in three acts by RICHARD WAGNER

This is the most popular of all Wagner's operas. No need to say more about its music, which is so generally known and admired that every child in Germany knows the graceful aria where Lohengrin dismisses the swan, the superb bridal chorus, etc.

Wagner again took his material from the old legend which tells us of the mystical knight Lohengrin (Veron of Percival), Keeper of the "Holy Grail."

The scene is laid near Antwerp, where "Heinrich der Vogler," King of Germany, is just levying troops amongst his vassals of Brabant to repulse the Hungarian invaders. The King finds the people in a state of great commotion, for Count Frederick Telramund accuses Elsa of Brabant of having killed her young brother Godfrey, heir to the Duke of Brabant, who died a short time ago, leaving his children to the care of Telramund. Elsa was to be Telramund's wife, but he wedded Ortrud of Friesland, and now claims the deserted Duchy of Brabant.

As Elsa declares her innocence, not knowing what has become of her brother, who was taken from her during her sleep, the King resolves to decide by a tourney in which the whole matter shall be left to the judgment of God. Telramund, sure of his rights, is willing to fight with any champion who may defend Elsa. All the noblemen of Brabant refuse to do so, and even the King, though struck by Elsa's innocent appearance, does not want to oppose his valiant and trustworthy warrior.

Elsa alone is calm; she trusts in the help of the heavenly knight, who has appeared to her in a dream, and publicly declares her intention of offering to her defender the crown and her hand. While she prays, there arrives a knight in silver armor; a swan draws his boat. He lands; Elsa recognizes the knight of her dream, and he at once offers to fight for the accused maiden on two conditions: first, that she shall become his wife, and second, that she never will ask for his name and his descent.

Elsa solemnly promises, and the combat begins. The strange knight is victorious, and Telramund, whose life the stranger spares, is, with his wife Ortrud, outlawed.

The latter is a sorceress; she has deceived her husband, who really believes in the murder of Godfrey, while as a matter of fact she has abducted the child. In the second act we see her at the door of the Ducal palace, where preparations for the wedding are already being made. She plans vengeance. Her husband, full of remorse, and feeling that his wife has led him on to a shameful deed, curses her as the cause of his dishonor. She derides him, and rouses his pride by calling him a coward. Then she pacifies him with the assurance that she will induce Elsa to break her promise and ask for the name of her husband, being sure that then all the power of this mysterious champion will vanish.

When Elsa steps on the balcony to confide her happiness to the stars, she hears her name spoken in accents so sad that her tender heart is moved. Ortrud bewails her lot, invoking Elsa's pity. The Princess opens her door, urging the false woman to share her palace and her fortune. Ortrud at once tries to sow distrust in Elsa's innocent heart.

As the morning dawns, a rich procession of men and women throng to the Münster, where Elsa is to be united to her protector. Telramund tries vainly to accuse the stranger; he is pushed back, and silenced. As Elsa is about to enter the church, Ortrud steps forward, claiming the right of precedence. Elsa, frightened, repents, too late, having protected her. Ortrud upbraids her with not even having asked her husband's name and descent. All are taken aback, but Elsa defends her husband, winning everybody by her quiet dignity.

She turns to Lohengrin for protection, but, alas! the venom rankles in her heart.

When they are all returning from church, Telramund once more steps forth, accusing Lohengrin, and demanding from the King to know the stranger's name. Lohengrin declares that his name may not be told excepting his wife asks. Elsa is in great trouble, but once more her love conquers, and she does not put the fatal question.

But in the third act, when the two lovers are alone, she knows no rest. Although her husband asks her to trust him, she fears that he may leave her as mysteriously as he came, and at last she cannot refrain from asking the luckless question. From this moment all happiness is lost to her. Telramund enters to slay his enemy, but Lohengrin, taking his sword, kills him with one stroke. Then he leads Elsa before the King, and loudly announces his secret. He tells the astounded hearers that he is the Keeper of the Holy Grail. Sacred and invulnerable to the villain, a defender of right and virtue, he may stay with mankind as long as his name is unknown. But now he is obliged to reveal it. He is Lohengrin, son of Percival, King of the Grail, and is now compelled to leave his wife and return to his home.

The swan appears, from whose neck Lohengrin takes a golden ring, giving it to Elsa, together with his sword and golden horn.

Just as Lohengrin is about to depart Ortrud appears, triumphantly declaring that it was she who changed young Godfrey into a swan, and that Lohengrin would have freed him, too, had Elsa not mistrusted her husband. Lohengrin, hearing this, sends a fervent prayer to Heaven, and loosening the swan's golden chain, the animal dips under water, and in his stead rises Godfrey, the lawful heir of Brabant. A white dove descends to draw the boat in which Lohengrin glides away, and Elsa falls senseless in her brother's arms.

LORELEY

Romantic Opera in three acts by ALFREDO CATALANI

Libretto by A. ZANARDINI and CARLO D'ORMVILLE

This opera was first heard in Chicago, April, 1919. The scene is laid on the banks of the Rhine, during medieval times.

In the first act Walter, the governor of Oberwesel, meets the Loreley wandering the shores of the river, and although betrothed to Anna of Rehberg, niece of the margrave, he is smitten with a sudden passion for the alluring stranger. He confides the facts to his friend, Herman, who solemnly urges him to remain faithful to Anna, although he himself is deeply in love with the latter and has merely yielded to his friend heretofore because Anna favored him in her love. But Loreley coming in search of Walter, hears that he is already betrothed to another, and swoons at the news. Herman, lamenting that he has yielded up Anna to another, appeals to the god of the Rhine to avenge Anna's wrongs. Loreley seeks the nymphs of the river and the spirits of the air, who all are singing in praise of Thor, and of the river god, bemoaning her lost chastity and foretelling revenge. The spirits tell her that Alberich, the cunning, godlike dwarf, can assist her by rendering her irresistible and thus capable of torturing the faithless one with new pangs of love. But she must swear fidelity. She does so and rises instantly, transformed, with golden hair and wearing the golden comb of the Loreley.

The second act transpires in front of the castle of the

margrave. When Walter and Anna are both on their way to church to be married, they are confronted by Loreley, who appears in a mystic light, and who sings her song of love to Walter. He casts Anna from him, and as he rushes into the arms of Loreley, she eludes him, plunging into the Rhine and leaving Walter forlorn on its bank. As Anna falls lifeless, Loreley reappears on the rock.

The third act shows the obsequies of Anna. Walter meets the mourning procession, and being informed it is that in honor of Anna, he falls in a swoon by the river, and as he wakes he sees Loreley on her rock, singing her song of love to him. As she is about to embrace him, threatening voices from the deep remind her of her oath to the river god. She tears herself from Walter and returns to her rock. Walter, in a frenzy, throws himself into the river, and Loreley sings her song of enticement for the last time.

LOUISE

Opera in four acts by GUSTAVE CHARPENTIER

Both libretto and music of this opera are by Gustave Charpentier, who took for his subject matter the French law, which requires the consent of the parents for a child of either sex to marry. Charpentier endeavors to show how cruelly this law works when a genuine love inspires the child and when the parent, acting from motives of prudence and foresight, refuses to recognize the profounder impulse which brings young people of different sexes together. A young working girl, Louise by name, falls in love with a young man, Julien, the poet of Montmartre. Her beauty and sweetness of character have wrought a similar feeling in him for her. The father of Louise, however, refuses his consent to Louise's marriage with Julien because he does not approve of the poet's way of life. This is the beginning of the tragedy of the lives of the young people. The opera was performed for the first time in Paris, in 1900.

The first act introduces us to Louise's garret room in her father's home, which is an ordinary workman's lodging in Paris. Roofs of houses are to be seen, and a terrace fronting an artist's studio is opposite to the window of Louise's chamber. Julien, standing on the terrace, discusses with Louise at her window the refusal, Julien's letter to her father for her hand had met with. They are both much depressed, but comfort each other with expressions of love. Louise advises Julien to write again to her father, and, in the event of a second refusal, promises to run away from her home and live with him. The mother then comes in and overhears part of what has been said by the young lovers. She is angry with Louise for listening to "a rascal, a starveling, a dissipator." It is of no avail for Louise to plead that he is "so good, so courageous"; in her mother's eyes he is "the pillar of a wine shop." The mother becomes furiously angry with Louise and attempts to chastise her, but Louise avoids her by running behind the table. They cease their quarrelling on hearing steps on the stairs, and listen, frightened, for the arrival of the father, who comes in bearing a letter in his hand. On his entrance the mother leaves for the kitchen. The father sits down, opens the letter, and reads it. After he has read it he looks at his daughter and opens his arms for her embrace. She rushes into them. The mother, in the meantime, has been preparing the supper, and when it is ready they all sit down and partake of it. After the meal the father promises Louise to look into Julien's prospects and antecedents; but the mother still remains implacable and resents his attitude towards a marriage with a good-for-nothing who laughs in her face when he meets her. He is a debauchee, and she could tell some dreadful things about him. Louise indignantly denies her mother's insinuations, and is slapped in the face. The father interferes, but the mother continues with her jibes, singing mockingly a song of Julien's. The father tries to comfort Louise and gives her the newspaper to read to him. They all seat themselves at the table, the mother sewing, while Louise reads: "The Spring Season is most brilliant. All Paris is in holiday garb." Louise stops for a moment in her reading and sobs: "Paris—," as the curtain slowly descends.

The second act consists of two scenes. The first scene represents the meeting-place of several streets in the Montmartre quarter of Paris. On the left of the stage is seen a shed, and on the right a house and a drinking shop. People are going and coming, shopping during the early morning hours. Various types of the district are introduced chatting and joking with each other. Julien enters with his companions of the café. He has come to waylay Louise on her way to work. Prior to her arrival Julien and his Bohemians make fun and horseplay after the usual manner of students and night-walkers. Julien is left waiting and watching for Louise. When she does come she is accompanied by her mother, who leaves her, after making sure no one is about, and after Louise has entered the house. Julien comes in quietly and then rushes into the house, reappearing again, dragging Louise with him. He wants to know what is the answer to his letter written to her father. Louise tells him that it is not favorable. He then reminds her of her promise to go with him, but Louise refuses to go with him. He begs and implores her, but Louise remains firm in her refusal. She knows she will break her father's heart if she goes away with Julien. He tries to drag her with him, but she struggles in resistance. Finally she embraces him, after promising to be his wife, and goes back into the house, leaving Julien filled with despondency. The second scene of this act shows a workroom for sewing girls, with a number of girls sitting at work, Louise being among them. They are gossiping together and busy with their labors. Some of the girls twit Louise on being in love. Their teasing is interrupted by some one singing from the courtyard below. It is Julien serenading Louise, determined to show her his love in every way he can. The girls in the room throw him pennies and kisses by way of gratuity. Julien, enraged at this reception, still continues with his serenade, but the girls, getting tired of him, ask him to stop. He still goes on, and the girls, becoming angry, shout to the musicians in the street to play. The musicians obey and a great din ensues, during which Louise, no longer able to stand the trying situation, takes up her hat and goes out. The girls are astonished at her behavior, and rush to the window to see what she is going to do. They find her walking away with Julien. The work-girls are highly amused, and the curtain falls on their hilarious laughter.

The curtain of the third act rises and reveals a small house and garden situated at the apex of the Butte Montmartre. This is the home to which Julien has brought Louise to live with him, she having at last consented to leave her parents and keep her promise. The two are in the midst of the enjoyment of their happiness in each other, and a very charming and tender love scene is enacted. Their friends, having prepared a surprise for them, now come to crown Louise as the Muse of Montmartre. They come in by twos and threes—Bohemians, grisettes, urchins, carriers, loafers, and others—and decorate the house with flowers, garlands, and lanterns. A chorus in procession arrives and greets Louise as the Muse, presenting her with the black and silver shawl as the badge of her office. Singing and dancing follow as part of the ceremonial, and a great concourse of people arrive to assist in the joyful celebration. As the crowd gives way, Louise sees her mother, and flies to the arms of Julien in fear. The mother comes forward humbly, and tells Julien that she is come not as an enemy. She is come to tell Louise that her father is suffering, and that she alone can save him.

Julien looks incredulous, but the mother assures him of her husband's pitiable condition. On the mother's promise that Louise shall be allowed to return, he gives his permission for her to go and see her father. Louise takes off the shawl of her office and hands it to Julien. The mother goes to the garden gate and Louise follows. She returns for a tender separation from Julien, and the curtain goes down as she goes out backward, with her finger on her lips, as Julien spreads his arms toward her.

The scene of the fourth and last act is the same as that of the first, except that the terrace of Julien's studio is not there. It is nine o'clock of a summer's evening. Louise's father is seated near the table, while Louise can be seen through a glass door, in her room. The mother comes in from the kitchen and invites the father to drink. He seems not to hear her, as he keeps his eyes fixed on Louise. He becomes peevish as his wife tries to comfort him, and talks bitterly of the ingratitude of children, who forget all that their parents have done for them, who leave father and mother at the first sight of an attractive face, and become lost to all sense of decency and honor. The mother calls to Louise and asks for her help in the house. Louise rises, arranges her sewing, and puts out her lamp. As she opens her door to come in her father opens his arms for an embrace, but she passes him by without noticing his appeal, and disappears in the kitchen. Her mother scolds her for her behavior and begs her to be reasonable and good to her father, who is suffering so much. Louise replies that she was promised leave to go back to her lover—to a love that is free. The mother mocks her—"free love," she cries; "that's a fine story." Louise comes back and goes up to her father, bids him good night, and offers her forehead for a kiss. The father embraces her passionately, but Louise is cold and unresponsive. She tries to go, but he restrains her, begging her to remain as in the old days. He and her mother, he says, only live for her happiness. They argue with each other, Louise for her love and freedom, he from his fear for her life in the city. The mother comes in and Louise turns on her also. Finally the parents become angry, and their anger arouses in Louise a passion for her lover, on whom she calls. She wants only Julien and Paris—Paris the beautiful. As she cries the words aloud, the City becomes gradually lighted up. The father, enraged, attempts to strike her, but, changing his mind, throws open the door and bids her go, dragging her to the exit. "Here's your pleasure, ladies," he cries, pointing to the brightening City; "they'll dance till they die, they'll laugh till they cry." Louise, trembling, runs round the room in deadly fear of her father. The mother begs her husband to cease raging, but the father, now maddened into a fury, rushes at Louise. Louise escapes with a cry and is gone. The father, dazed, looks about him for a moment, then, realizing that she is gone, he runs to the staircase crying aloud his daughter's name. "Louise! . . . Louise!" He returns and looks for a moment through the window; then, shaking his fist in a rage at the City, he cries: "Oh, Paris!"

LOVE'S BATTLE

(DER LIEBESKAMPF)

Opera in two acts

Music and Text by ERICK MEYER-HELMUND

Pietro, a sailor, returns from a long voyage only to find his promised bride, Maritana, the wife of another.

After having waited three years for his return, she fell into dire distress, which was augmented by the report that Pietro's ship "Elena" had been wrecked and her lover drowned. An innkeeper, Arrigo, came to her aid, and not only rescued her from misery, but also adopted her child, the offspring of Maritana's love for Pietro, after which she promised him her hand in gratitude.

Not long after their marriage the "Elena" returns with Pietro, who never doubts his sweetheart's constancy. Great is his dismay when he hears from Arrigo and his father that Maritana is lost to him. Pietro endeavors to persuade Maritana to fly with him, but the young wife, although conscious of her affection for him, denies that she ever loved him.

The second act begins with the wedding festival of Giovanni and Giulietta, Arrigo's niece. After the charming love duet Pietro once more offers his love to Maritana but in vain.

In the midst of the turmoil of frolic, in which Pietro seems one of the wildest and gayest, Arrigo takes him aside, whispering: "There is no room here for both of us unless you leave Maritana in peace. Quit this place; there are more girls in the world to suit you." Pietro promises, and in his passion he at once turns to the bride Giulietta, whom he embraces. Of course her bridegroom, Giovanni, is not willing to put up with this piece of folly; a violent quarrel ensues, in which the men rush upon Pietro with daggers drawn.

Maritana, willing to sacrifice herself in a quarrel for which she feels herself alone responsible, rushes between the combatants. Then Pietro, fully awake to her love, but seeing that she is lost to him, quickly ascends a rock, and calling out, "O Sea eternal, I am thine; farewell, Maritana, we shall meet in heaven!" he precipitates himself into the waves, while Maritana falls back in a faint.

LUCIA DI LAMMERMOOR

Tragic Opera in three acts by GAETANO DONIZETTI
Text from SCOTT'S romance by SALVATORE CAMMERANO

This opera is Donizetti's masterpiece, and, except his "Figlia del Reggimento" and "Lucrezia Borgia," is the only one of his fifty operas which is still given on all stages abroad. The chief parts, those of Lucia and Edgardo, offer plenty of scope for the display of brilliant talent, and Lucia in particular is a tragic heroine of the first rank.

In the libretto there is not much left of Scott's fine romance. Edgardo, the noble lover, is most sentimental, and, generally, English characteristics have had to give place to Italian coloring.

Henry Ashton, Lord of Lammermoor, has discovered that his sister Lucia loves his mortal enemy, Sir Edgardo of Ravenswood. He confides to Lucia's tutor, Raymond, that he is lost if Lucia does not marry another suitor of his (her brother's) choice.

Lucia and Edgardo meet in the park. Edgardo tells her that he is about to leave Scotland for France in the service of his country. He wishes to be reconciled to his enemy, Lord Ashton, for though the latter has done him all kinds of evil, though he has slain his father and burnt his castle, Edgardo is willing to sacrifice his oath of vengeance to his love for Lucia. But the lady, full of evil forebodings, entreats him to wait, and swears eternal fidelity to him. After having bound himself by a solemn oath, he leaves her, half distracted with grief.

In the second act Lord Ashton shows a forged letter to his sister, which goes to prove that her lover is false. Her brother now presses her more and more to wed his friend, Arthur, Lord Bucklaw, declaring that he and his party are lost, and that Arthur alone can save him from the executioner's axe. At last, when even her tutor Raymond beseeches her to forget Edgardo, and, like the others, believes him to be faithless, Lucia consents to the sacrifice. The wedding takes place in great haste, but just as Lucia has finished signing the marriage contract, Edgardo enters to claim her as his own.

With grief and unabounded passion he now sees in his bride a traitoress, and tearing his ring of betrothal from her finger, he throws it at her feet.

Henry, Arthur, and Raymond order the raving lover to leave the castle, and the act closes in the midst of confusion and despair.

The third act opens with Raymond's announcement that Lucia has lost her reason, and has killed her husband in the bridal room. Lucia herself enters to confirm his awful news; she is still in bridal attire, and in her demented condition believes that Arthur will presently appear for the nuptial ceremony. Everybody is full of pity for her, and her brother repents his harshness. Too late, alas!—Lucia is fast dying, and Eliza leads her away amid the lamentations of all present.

Edgardo, hearing of these things while wandering amid the tombs of his ancestors, resolves to see Lucia once more. When dying, she asks for him, but he comes too late. The funeral bells toll, and he stabs himself, praying to be united to his bride in heaven.

LUCREZIA BORGIA

Tragic Opera in three acts by DONIZETTI

Text by FELICE ROMANI, after VICTOR HUGO'S drama

Donizetti's Lucrezia was one of the first tragic operas to command great success, notwithstanding its dreadful theme and its light music, which is half French, half Italian. It is in some respects the predecessor of Verdi's operas, "Rigoletto," "Trovatore," etc., which have till now held their own in many theatres because the subject is interesting and the music may well entertain us for an evening, though its value often lies only in the striking harmonies. The libretto cannot inspire us with feelings of particular pleasure, the heroine, whose part is by far the best and most interesting, being the celebrated murderess and poisoner, Lucrezia Borgia. At the same time she gives evidence, in her dealings with her son Gennaro, of possessing a very tender and motherly heart, and the songs in which she pours out her love for him are really fine, as well as touching.

Lucrezia, wife of Don Alfonso, Duke of Ferrara, goes to Venice in disguise to see the son of her first marriage, Gennaro. In his earliest youth he was given to a fisherman, who brought him up as his own son. Gennaro feels himself attracted towards the strange and beautiful woman who visits him, but hearing from his companions, who recognize and charge her with all sorts of crimes, that she is Lucrezia Borgia, he abhors her. Don Alfonso, not knowing the existence of this son of an early marriage, is jealous, and when Gennaro comes to Ferrara, and in order to prove his hatred of the Borgias tears off Lucrezia's name and 'scutcheon from the palace gates, Rustighello, the Duke's confidant, is ordered to imprison him. Lucrezia, hearing from her servant Gubetta of the outrage to her name and honor, complains to the Duke, who promises immediate punishment of the malefactor.

Gennaro enters, and terror-stricken Lucrezia recognizes her son. Vainly does she implore the Duke to spare the youth. With exquisite cruelty he forces her to hand the poisoned golden cup to the culprit herself, and, departing, bids her accompany her prisoner to the door. This order gives her an opportunity to administer an antidote by which she saves Gennaro's life, and she implores him to fly. But Gennaro does not immediately follow her advice, being induced by his friend Orsini to assist at a grand festival at Prince Negroni's.

Unhappily all those young men who formerly reproached and offended Lucrezia so mortally in presence of her son are assembled there by Lucrezia's orders. She has mixed their wine with poison, and herself appears to announce their death. Horror-stricken, she sees Gennaro, who was not invited, among them. He has partaken of the wine, like the others, but on her offering him an antidote he refuses to take it; its quantity is insufficient for his friends, and he threatens to kill the murderess. Then she reveals the secret of his birth to him, but he only turns from this mother, for whom he had vainly longed his whole life, and dies. The Duke, coming up to witness his wife's horrible victory, finds all either dead or dying, and Lucrezia herself expires, stricken down by deadly remorse and pain.

LUISA MILLER

Opera in three acts by GIUSEPPE VERDI

Based on SCHILLER'S play, "Kabale and Liebe"

This opera was first given in 1849 at Naples. The setting is the Wurtemberg Court in 1874.

Act I. Rodolfo, Count Walter's son, refuses to marry the Duchess of Ostheim, his father's choice, because he loves Luisa, daughter of the old soldier, Miller. Luisa is unaware of Rodolfo's nobility as he has wooed her in the guise of a peasant. Count Walter, enraged at his son's obstinacy in preferring a union with Luisa, is about to consign her and her father to prison when Rodolfo deters him with a threat to reveal that the Count, aided by his steward Wurm, assassinated his predecessor to obtain his title and estates.

Act II. Luisa's father has been imprisoned by Count Walter. To save his life, Luisa consents to write a letter, declaring that she had never loved Rodolfo but had encouraged him on account of his rank and fortune of which she said she had always been aware and, finally offering to fly with Wurm, the Count's evil steward. This letter is shown Rodolfo who then consents to marry the Duchess Frederica but resolves to kill Luisa and himself.

Act III. Luisa has also determined to end her life. When Rodolfo comes to her home to ask if she wrote the letter, she admits that she did. He poisons the wine which she unwittingly offers him to quench his thirst. At his request, she also drinks of the poison and feeling that approaching death releases her from her vow of secrecy, she tells her lover the truth about the letter. He forgives her and the two then die before their horror-stricken parents.

THE MACCABEES

Opera in three acts by ANTON RUBINSTEIN

Text by MOSENTHAL, taken from OTTO LUDWIG'S drama of the same name

This opera when it appeared created a great sensation in the musical world. In it the eminent pianist and composer has achieved a splendid success. The music belongs to the noblest and best, and is in most masterly fashion adapted to the Jewish character. Ludwig and Mosenthal, both names of renown in Germany, have given a libretto worthy of the music.

The hero is the famous warrior of the Old Testament. The scene takes place 160 years before Christ, partly at Modin, a city in the mountains of Judah, and partly in Jerusalem and its environs.

The first act shows Leah with three of her sons, Eleazar, Joarim and Benjamin. Eleazar is envious of Judah, the eldest son, whose courage and strength are on everybody's lips, but his mother consoles him by a prophecy that Eleazar shall one day be High-priest and King of the Jews.

The fête of the sheep-shearing is being celebrated, and Noëmi, Judah's wife, approaches Leah with garlands of flowers, asking for her benediction. But she is repulsed by her mother-in-law, who is too proud to recognize the low-born maid as her equal, and slights her son Judah for his love. She tries to incite him into rebellion against the Syrians, when Jojakin, a priest, appears. He announces the death of Osias, High-priest of Zion, and calls one of Leah's sons to the important office. As Judah feels no vocation for such a burden, Eleazar, his mother's favorite, is chosen, and so Leah sees her dream already fulfilled. They are about to depart, when the approaching army of the Syrians is announced. Terror seizes the people as Gorgias, the leader of the enemy, marches up with his soldiers, and loudly proclaims that the Jews are to erect an altar to Pallas Athene, to whom they must pray henceforth. Leah seeks to inflame Eleazar's spirit, but his courage fails him. The altar is soon erected, and as Gorgias sternly orders that sacrifices are to be offered to the goddess, Boas, Noëmi's father, is found willing to bow to the enemy's commands. But the measure is full; Judah steps forth and striking Boas, the traitor to their faith, dead, loudly praises Jehova. He calls his people to arms, and repulses the Syrians, and Leah, recognizing her son's greatness, gives him her benediction.

The second act represents a deep ravine near Emaus; the enemy is beaten, and Judah is resolved to drive him from Zion's walls, but Jojakim warns him not to profane the coming Sabbath.

Judah tries to overrule the priests and to excite the people, but he is not heard, and the enemy is able to kill the psalm-singing soldiers like lambs.

The next scene shows us Eleazar with Cleopatra, daughter of King Antiochus of Syria.

They love each other, and Eleazar consents to forsake his religion for her, while she promises to make him King of Jerusalem.

In the next scene Leah, in the city of Modin, is greeted with acclamations of joy, when Simei, a relative of the slain Boas, appears to bewail Judah's defeat: other fugitives coming up confirm his narrative of the massacre. Leah hears that Judah fled and that Antiochus approaches, conducted by her own son Eleazar. She curses the apostate. She has still two younger sons, but the Israelites take them from her to give as hostages to the King Antiochus. Leah is bound to a cypress tree by her own people, who attribute their misfortunes to her and to her sons. Only Noëmi, the despised daughter-in-law, remains to liberate the miserable mother, and together they resolve to ask the tyrant's pardon for the sons.

In the third act we find Judah, alone and unrecognized, in the deserted streets of Jerusalem. Hearing the prayers of the people that Judah may be sent to them, he steps forth and tells them who he is, and all sink at his feet, swearing to fight with him to the death. While Judah prays to God for a sign of grace, Noëmi comes with the dreadful news of the events at Modin, which still further rouses the anger and courage of the Israelites. Meanwhile Leah has succeeded in penetrating into Antiochus's presence to beg the lives of her children from him. Eleazar, Gorgias and Cleopatra join their prayers to those of the poor mother, and at last Antiochus consents, and the two boys are led into the room.

But the King only grants their liberty on condition that they renounce their faith. They are to be burnt alive should they abide by their heresy. The mother's heart is full of agony, but the children's noble courage prevails. They are prepared to die for their God, but the unhappy mother is not even allowed to share their death. When Eleazar sees his brothers' firmness his conscience awakens, and notwithstanding Cleopatra's entreaties he joins them on their way to death. The hymns of the youthful martyrs are heard, but with the sound of their voices there suddenly mingles that of a growing tumult. Antiochus falls, shot through the heart, and the Israelites rush in, headed by Judah, putting the Syrians to flight. Leah sees her people's victory, but the trial has been too great—she sinks back lifeless. Judah is proclaimed King of Zion, but he humbly bends his head, giving all glory to the Almighty God.

MADAME BUTTERFLY

A Musical Tragedy in three acts by GIACOMO PUCCINI

The plot of this opera is founded on the book by John Luther Long and the play by David Belasco. The scene is laid in Nagasaki, Japan, and the action of the drama takes place in our own time. The music, by Puccini, if not of the excellence of the composer's "La Bohème," is yet of so beautifully melodious a quality and so richly colored by the spirit of the place, which Puccini has felt, that "Madame Butterfly" will undoubtedly remain a standard opera. The opera was first performed in Milan, in 1904.

The story is the old story of a lover loving a maid and then forsaking her. In this particular instance, however, the novelty lies in the maid being a Japanese lady and the man a lieutenant in the American navy.

The curtain rises discovering Goro, the matchmaker, showing Lieutenant Pinkerton over the house the latter had just purchased. Pinkerton is to occupy it as soon as he has been married to Cho-Cho-San, the beautiful Japanese girl, who is better known as Butterfly. Goro, who sold Pinkerton the house, also sold him Cho-Cho-San, and the first scene is occupied with Goro's enjoyment and Pinkerton's delight in the place. Suzuki, Butterfly's maid, and two other servants are then introduced to Pinkerton, who is patiently awaiting the arrival of his bride.

Sharpless, the American Consul at Nagasaki, is heard climbing the hill, and comes on the scene to dissuade his friend Pinkerton from the step he is about to take. He begs Pinkerton to think seriously of what he is doing, because what may be a passing fancy for him may be a serious affair for the girl. Pinkerton, who is much in love with the girl, laughs at his friend's arguments, and their talk is interrupted by the arrival of Butterfly and her friends. In the midst of the general greetings Sharpless enters into a conversation with Butterfly and finds that his reading of her attitude to Pinkerton is correct. She tells Sharpless her history, and informs him that, owing to the death of her father, she has had to support herself and her mother by becoming a Geisha. After the relatives of the girl have made their formal greetings to Pinkerton, Butterfly and Pinkerton go over the house alone, and in a charming conversation the girl's love for the American sailor is laid bare in all its simple sincerity. More relatives arriving, as well as the proper officials, the ceremony of the marriage contract is duly gone through. In the midst of the joyous toasts an interruption occurs in the coming of Butterfly's uncle, the Bonze, or Japanese priest, who, learning that his niece has renounced the faith of her ancestors in order to wed the foreigner, has come to curse her. He urges all her relatives to forsake her for what she has done, and they rush from her in horror. Butterfly, weeping bitterly, is consoled by Pinkerton, who brings her back to smiles and joy. The scene between the two is most charming. The act closes on the happiness of the strangely assorted pair who have thus entered on their life together.

When the curtain goes up on the second act, three years are supposed to have elapsed, during which time Pinkerton has gone back to America, after promising his wife to return "when the robins nest." Butterfly is alone with her maid, Suzuki, who invokes the gods for the return of the faithless Pinkerton. Butterfly, in spite of the three years' waiting, is still firm in her faith in her husband. She refuses the Prince Yamadori, who has loved her for years, and who sues her now. In declining the Prince's offer of marriage she tells him that, though she might consider herself a free woman according to the law of Japan, she has married an American, and must abide by the laws of his country. "How can I marry him," she cries, "when I am married already?" Yamadori leaves and Sharpless enters, bearing a letter from Pinkerton. He is afraid to tell her immediately what the letter says, so he prepares the way by warning her that Pinkerton will never come back. He advises her to accept Prince Yamadori's offer. Butterfly will not listen to him. She points to her little baby, a boy with the blue eyes and fair hair of Pinkerton, and asks, "Can such as this well be forgotten?" She begs Sharpless to write to her husband and tell him what a fine child is waiting for him. Sharpless, much touched, leaves Butterfly without showing her the letter. Suzuki then enters, screaming and denouncing Goro for spreading a report that the child's father is not known. Butterfly, goaded almost to madness by this calumny, seizes a knife to kill Goro, but, suppressing her anger, she throws the knife away, spurning the wretched man with her foot.

Cannon shots are just then heard announcing the arrival of a man-of-war ship. Butterfly rushes to the terrace with her maid Suzuki, and both find that it is the *Abraham Lincoln* come back again. Immediately Butterfly is transported with joy. She has proved her faith and her husband is coming back to her. It is her reward for her fidelity. She bids Suzuki gather flowers from the garden, and spreads these round the room in honor of Pinkerton's home-coming. Then the child is brought in, and while Suzuki is combing his hair Butterfly rouges her face to make ready for the meeting with her husband. They all sit down behind a partition, in which they have made holes so as to watch and see Pinkerton's arrival. Night falls and Pinkerton does not come. Suzuki and the baby fall asleep, but Butterfly stands motionless, looking and waiting. The curtain falls on this moving picture of the loving and faithful wife waiting in loving expectation the return of the lover who has left her alone.

The curtain rises on the third act and discovers Butterfly in the same position in which she was when the second act closed. Suzuki and the child are still asleep, and Butterfly is still gazing through the holes of the *shosi,* or partition. Suzuki awakes and, seeing it is morning, she begs her mistress to lie down and take some rest herself. Butterfly then turns to her child, takes it into her arms, and retires into an inner room. Butterfly has barely retired when a loud knock causes Suzuki to bestir herself. She opens the *shosi* and sees Sharpless and Pinkerton standing before her. Pinkerton motions to her not to disturb Butterfly, and Suzuki, in her joy at seeing him back again, shows him the room decorated with flowers for his arrival. Suddenly she notices a strange lady walking in the garden, and learns that she is Pinkerton's American wife.

Sharpless takes Suzuki aside and asks her to prepare Butterfly for what is coming, telling her that the lady is come to adopt the little boy. Pinkerton, realizing Butterfly's faith and life, is overcome by remorse. He begs Sharpless to comfort her as best he can, and leaves the house in tears. Mrs. Pinkerton also comes forward and urges her desire to take the child with her. Suzuki has barely time to act in the situation when Butterfly returns from her room expecting to see her husband.

She finds instead Sharpless, a foreign lady, and Suzuki in tears. The truth then suddenly overwhelms her. "Is he alive?" she asks, and Suzuki answers he is. The answer and the manner in which it is given tells Butterfly the terrible truth. She now knows that her husband has forsaken her. She listens dumbly and pathetically to Mrs. Pinkerton's offer to take the boy and bears the news with a gentle and touching dignity. When her answers comes it is said quietly: "I will give up my child to him only; let him come and take him. I shall be ready in half an hour." Sharpless and Kate Pinkerton then leave her. When they have gone Butterfly asks Suzuki to go into another room with the child. She then takes her father's long knife and, throwing a white veil over the folding screen she kisses the blade, noticing as she does so the inscription engraved on it: "He dies in honor who no longer lives in honor." Raising the knife to her throat, she is about to kill herself, when the door opens and her child runs towards her with outstretched arms. She snatches the little one to her bosom and covers him with kisses. She then sends him into the garden. Then, seizing the knife again, she rushes behind the screen, and a little later the sound of the knife falling to the ground is heard.

Pinkerton returns and calls for Butterfly. She hears him and drags herself from behind the screen to the door, but her strength fails her, and when Pinkerton comes in he finds her lying dead.

MADAME CHRYSANTHÈME

A Romantic Opera in four acts, with epilogue and prologue, by F. MESSAGER

Text based on PIERRE LOTI'S tale of the same name

The lieutenant and his faithful Yves are on board their ship, and the former tells of his intention of contracting a temporary marriage with one of the pretty girls at Nagasaki, a region famed for its lovely women. This is the prologue.

Act I. Pierre meets Madame Chrysanthème for the first time. M. Kangourou, a matrimonial agent, arranges matters and the bridal veil is handed to Chrysanthème.

Act II. Pierre and his bride are enjoying themselves at Mme. Prune's sunny cottage, and his comrades arrive with their own feminine charmers and serenade him. All of them, including Mmes. Strawberry, Daffodil and Cowslip, stop for luncheon.

Act III. There is a festival going on at the house of Lieut. Pierre, and little Chrysanthème is singing her best. But he becomes jealous, thinking she is flirting with Yves and flies into a tremendous rage, which results in a serious quarrel with her.

Act IV. A peace is patched up between the couple, and their happiness restored, when the boom of guns aboard ship calls the lieutenant to duty. The epilogue is again between the lieutenant and Yves, who both mourn for little Chrysanthème.

MADAME SANS-GÊNE

Historical Opera in four acts by UMBERTO GIORDANO

Text by RENATO SIMONI, after a play by VICTORIEN SARDOU

The first production of this work, which is really a "musical comedy," so colorful and interesting is the plot, occurred at the Metropolitan Opera House, New York, in 1915. The scene is laid partly in Paris and partly in Compiègne, and the action stretches over a period of nineteen years, from August 10, 1792, to September, 1811. The opera is also unique in that it brings the great figure of Napoleon on the stage with an important singing part.

The first act takes place in the Paris laundry of Catherine Huebscher, the Madame Sans-Gêne of history, a pretty, frank and courageous figure of the Napoleonic era. Although the French revolution is at its height and the royal château, the Tuileries is being stormed by the people, work goes on as usual at the laundry. Catherine enters, followed by an amused crowd, because one of the soldiers in the streets has kissed her against her will. Triumphant shouts are heard outside. The royal residence has just been taken, and both king and queen made prisoners. Catherine gives her laundry girls a holiday to rejoice in the popular victory. Fouché, then an officer in the National Guards, but later police minister under Napoleon, is in the place to get his linen. There is conversation about the political outlook, Catherine's sweetheart, Sergeant Lefèbvre, and a third customer of Catherine's, the poverty-stricken artillery lieutenant, Napoleon Buonaparte. Outside the noise of the street fighting increases. Catherine, from pity, finally admits a wounded royalist, Count de Neipperg and sends him to her own room in the rear. Her lover, Lefèbvre rushes in precipitately with a squad of soldiers, searching for a royalist fugitive, the very one who is in hiding there. Catherine treats the guests to wine, but the sergeant accidentally discovers the wounded royalist in Catherine's chamber. His jealousy is roused at first, but he soon convinces himself that there is no reason for it.

The second act is in Compiègne, in September, 1811, and Catherine, although still as "free and easy" as ever, has become the wife of Lefèbvre, now one of Napoleon's great generals and created Duke of Danzig. She, however, is too unceremonious for these changed times, and Napoleon has found fault with Lefèbvre for disgracing his court by the many blunders of his wife regarding court etiquette. Lefèbvre and Catherine talk things over and resolve not to separate in any event. Catherine is just taking a belated lesson in dancing and bowing from Despreaux, but dismisses the dancing master for more important affairs. Fouché, now at the head of the imperial police, comes and advises Catherine and her husband to show more circumspection in dealing with high personages, such as the emperor's sisters, Queen Caroline and Princess Elisa, who are to be her guests that day. Count Neipperg pays a clandestine visit and asks advice. He says he is in love with Napoleon's wife, Marie Louise, and has been banished from court on that account by Napoleon. He is told to forget her, but he insists on paying her a farewell call before leaving for good. Meanwhile the guests begin to arrive, and Catherine, delayed by Neipperg, comes late in receiving them.

Napoleon's sisters are especially angry at this supposed slight, and treat their outspoken hostess with much hauteur, but are paid back in kind. The two sisters lay their complaint before the emperor, who summons Catherine to exculpate herself.

This she does in the third act. Catherine is at first received with rigor by Napoleon. But she tells him precisely how she was provoked by his sisters into paying them in their own coin, and the emperor admits she was justified. Then she draws forth from her bosom a soiled and creased bit of paper and presents it to Napoleon. It is an old bill of his for laundry work done by her for him, left unpaid during the days when he was half starving in a Paris garret. He remembers the debt and its circumstances, and recognizes her as the Madame Sans-Gêne of those days. She next tells him of her experience as Lefèbvre's wife, how she followed him and the army in several campaigns as vivandière, and was even wounded, exhibiting the scar. The emperor kisses the scar and says the Lefèbvre ought to be proud of such a wife, promising that she shall in future find full recognition at his court. But while still talking, they both notice a man secretly approaching the apartments of the empress. It turns out to be Neipperg, he who was banished by Napoleon for suspicious behavior. The intruder is seized and sentenced to be shot at dawn of day, although he is the Austrian ambassador.

At the beginning of the last act Napoleon is seen pacing his chamber restlessly when Catherine requests audience with him. She furnishes proof that Neipperg is, after all, only suspected, not convicted, of any serious misconduct, while there is not even a shadow of evidence against the empress herself. She proposes a test of

Marie Louise's own feelings in the matter. Napoleon adopts her stratagem, and the empress proves herself innocent. Neipperg is freed and sent home to Vienna, and Catherine herself earns the emperor's high praise.

MADELEINE

A Lyric Opera in one act by VICTOR HERBERT

Text by GRANT STEWART, being based on a French play

This was first produced in New York, 1914. The scene is Paris, on New Year's Day, 1760.

At her luxurious apartments Madeleine Fleury, the great diva of the Paris opera, remembers suddenly, when a load of costly gifts from her admirers is brought in, that it is New Year's Day. She enjoys these attentions, but the thought occurs to her where and with whom she can dine that day in a manner satisfactory to herself. One by one her friends decline her invitation. Her lover, the Chevalier de Mauprat, is unable to do so because on that day he must be with his mother at home. The Duke d'Esterre pleads the same excuse, and even her threat, to turn to his rival, Fontanges, does not alter his decision. She carries out this intention and hastily scribbles off a note to Fontanges. But that means simply another refusal. Even her own maid, coquettish Nichette, else always so pliant, at the risk of offending her generous mistress, says that she cannot stay that day, because she has previously promised her mother to dine with her.

Madeleine is in real despair. All her blandishments to obtain the presence of someone to keep her company on the most joyous day of the whole year are wasted, and she feels chagrined and outraged. She throws herself on the divan in a fit of sobbing and disgust, and there her old schoolmate and protégé, the impecunious painter Didier, finds her in a tearful mood. When she tells him the cause he replies that he is sorry, for he, too, must dine on that day with his poor old mother. He invites her, however, as his guest. Madeleine declines, and when Nichette soon after comes back, saying that her mother has sent her to keep her mistress company, she again declines. Instead the operatic star takes down from the wall a speaking likeness of her own mother, dead some time ago, places it opposite her plate on the dining table, and thus also finds somebody she loves to dine with.

THE MAIDENS OF SCHILDA

Comic Opera in three acts by ALBAN FÖRSTER

Text by RUDOLF BUNGE

The Prince of Dessau calls all the youngsters of Schilda to arms. The chief magistrate, who has already given to the town so many wise laws—as, for instance, the one which decrees that the Schilda maidens under thirty are not allowed to marry—now demonstrates to his two nieces, Lenchen and Hedwig, the benefit of his legislation, inasmuch as they might otherwise be obliged to take leave of their husbands. He wants to marry one of them himself, but they have already given their hearts to two students. This tyrant now orders all the maidens to be locked up in a place of safety every evening.

The Marquis de Maltracy, enters, imploring the Burgomaster to hide him from the Prussian pursuers. He promises a cross of honor to Rüpelmei, who hides him in the Town Hall. Meanwhile a chorus of students approaches, who have left Halle to avoid being enlisted in the army. Lenchen and Hedchen, recognizing their sweethearts among them, greet them joyfully.

A lively scene of student life ensues, in which the maidens join.

Rüpelmei, returning, orders the police to seize the students; but instead of doing so they thrust him into the very barrel which he has invented for the punishment of male citizens.

In the second act he has been liberated by his faithful citizens; the students have escaped, and the maidens are waiting to be locked up. Berndt and Walter return and are hidden by their sweethearts among the other maidens after having put on female garments. The Prince of Dessau arrives with his Grenadiers to seize the students and orders his soldiers to search the houses, beginning with the Town Hall. Rüpelmei, remembering the Marquis, implores him to desist from his resolution, the Town Hall being the nightly asylum for Schilda's daughters, but in vain. Schlump, the snoring guardian, is awakened and ordered to open the door to the room where the maidens are frolicking with their guests. The Marquis de Maltracy has also introduced himself, and when the Prussian Grenadiers are heard, they hide him in a large trunk.

The Prince, finding all those pretty girls, is quite affable, and a general dancing and merry-making ensues, during which the students vainly try to escape, when suddenly two of the Grenadiers perceive that their respective beauties have beards. The students are discovered and at once ordered to be put into the uniform.

When the third act opens, drilling is going on in the town. Lenchen and Hedwig arrive with the other girls to free the students. They flatter the drill-sergeant, and soon the drilling is forgotten, and they are dancing merrily, when the Prince of Dessau arrives. While the maidens are entreating him to be merciful, Berndt tells the Prince that they have captured a French Marquis. The Prince promising to set them free if that proves to be true, the Marquis is conducted before the Prince, and the latter discovers that he is a messenger to the King of France, and that his letter is to show how the French army might attack the Russians unawares.

The students are set free, and each of them obtains an office and the hand of his maiden besides, and the luckless Rüpelmei is also liberated.

THE MAGIC FLUTE

(DIE ZAUBERFLÖTE)

Opera in two acts by MOZART
Text by SCHIKANEDER

This last opera of Mozart's, written only a few months before his death, approaches so near to perfection that one almost feels in it the motion of the spirit-wings which were so soon, alas! to bear away Mozart's genius from earth, too early by far, for he died at the age of thirty-five, having accomplished in this short space of time more than other great composers in a long life.

The Magic Flute is one of the most remarkable operas known on the stage. It is half fictitious, half allegorical. The text, done by the old stage-director, Schikaneder, was long mistaken for a fiction without any common sense, but Mozart saw deeper, else he would not have adapted his wonderful music to it. It is true that the tales of old Egypt are mixed up in a curious manner with modern Freemasonry, but nobody, except a superficial observer, could fail to catch a deep moral sense in the *naïve* rhymes.

The incidents of the opera are the following: Prince Tamino, a youth as valiant as he is noble and virtuous, is implored by the Queen of Night to save her daughter, whom the old and sage High-priest Sarastro has taken from her by force. The bereaved mother pours forth her woe in heart-melting sounds and promises everything to the rescuer of her child. Tamino is filled with ardent desire to serve her. On his way he meets the gay

Scene from the Chicago Civic Opera's production of "The Magic Flute"

Papageno, who at once agrees to share the Prince's adventures. Papageno is the gay element in the opera; always cheerful and in high spirits, his ever-ready tongue plays him many a funny trick. So we see him once with a lock on his mouth by way of punishment for his idle prating. As he promises never to tell a lie any more, the lock is taken away by the three ladies of the Queen of Night. Those ladies present Tamino with a golden flute, giving at the same time an instrument made with little silver bells to Papageno, both of which are to help them in times of danger. The Queen of Night even sends with them three boy-angels. These are to point out to them the ways and means by which they may attain their purpose.

Now the young and beautiful Princess Pamina is pursued by declarations of love from a negro servant of Sarastro. Papageno comes to her rescue, frightening the negro Monostatos with his feathery dress. Papageno, on the other hand, fears the negro on account of his blackness, believing him to be the devil in person. Papageno escapes with Pamina, but the negro overtakes him with his servants. Then Papageno shakes his bells, and lo! all, forgetting their wrath, forthwith begin to dance.

Meanwhile Tamino reaches Sarastro's castle, and at once asks for the High-priest, poor Pamina's bitter enemy. The Under-priests do not allow him to enter, but explain that their master Sarastro is as good as he is sage, and that he always acts for the best. They assure Tamino that the Princess lives and is in no danger. Full of thanks, the Prince begins to play on his flute; and just then he hears Papageno's bells. At this juncture Sarastro appears, the wise Master, before whom they all bow. He punishes the wicked negro; but Tamino and his Pamina are not to be united without first having given ample proof of their love and constancy. Tamino determines to undergo whatever trials may await him, but the Queen of Night, knowing all, sends her three ladies to deter Tamino and his comrade from their purpose. But all temptation is gallantly set aside; they have given a promise to Sarastro which they will keep.

Even the Queen of Night herself is unable to weaken their strength of purpose; temptations of every kind overtake them, but Tamino remains firm. He is finally initiated into the mysteries of the goddess Isis.

In the interval Pamina deems Tamino faithless. She would fain die, but the three celestial youths console her by assuring her that Tamino's love is true, and that he passes through the most severe trials solely on her behalf.

On hearing this, Pamina at once asks to share in the trials, and so they walk together through fire and water, protected by the golden flute, as well as by their courage and constancy. They come out purified and happy.

Papageno, having lost his companion, has grown quite melancholy, and longs for the little wife that was promised to him and shown to him only for a few moments. He resolves at last to end his life by hanging himself, when the celestial youths appear, reminding him of his bells. He begins to shake them, and Papagena appears in feathery dress, the very counterpart of himself. All might now be well, were it not that the Queen of Night, a somewhat unreasonable lady, broods vengeance. She accepts the negro Monostatos as her avenger, and promises to give him her daughter. But already Sarastro has done his work; Tamino is united to his Pamina, and before the sunny light of truth everything else vanishes and sinks back into night!

MANON

Opera in five acts by JULES MASSENET

Text by H. MEILHAC and P. GILLE

Massenet possesses the foresight to always select subjects for his operas which are eminently suited to his peculiar genius, and this is especially true in the adoption of Manon from Abbé Prevost's famous romance "Manon Lescaut." The music, which is full of poetry and refinement, suits the story admirably. It was first presented with great success at the Opera Comique, Paris, in 1884, and is considered to be one of the best of modern French operas.

The action takes place in the year 1721, the first act presenting the Inn at Amiens, where Guillot Monfontain, Minister of Finance, and a roué, is making merry with a party of friends. In the midst of their festivities, Manon, a vain and beautiful adventuress, arrives at the Inn, in company with her cousin, Lescaut, of the Royal Guards. Guillot, struck with the beauty of Manon, leaves his friends, and tries to entice her to go with him, but is rebuked by her, and is finally compelled to retreat. Lescaut, after warning his cousin against Guillot, leaves her for a short time on business, and during his absence the Chevalier Des Grieux arrives at the Inn, and immediately falls in love with Manon on account of her beauty and seeming simplicity. Although about to take holy orders, he becomes so infatuated with her that he consents to her plan of making use of Guillot's carriage to elope, and they drive to Paris, where they are found in the second act, comfortably established in cozy apartments in the Rue Vivienne. They are interrupted by the entrance of the enraged Lescaut and his friend De Bretigny, a nobleman who is in love with Manon. The two men are pacified on hearing that Des Grieux has written to his father for consent to his marriage with Manon, but it so happens that the Count, his father, refuses to give his consent, and Des Grieux is seized by men in his father's employ, and is taken away from his love and placed in captivity.

The third act reveals the fête of Cours la Reine where Manon is under the protection of De Bretigny. They encounter Count Des Grieux, who informs De Bretigny that his son has entered the Seminary of St. Sulpice, as a priest, on account of the conduct of Manon. On hearing this, all Manon's love for the Chevalier returns, and she flies from De Bretigny to rejoin her lover. After a great struggle with himself Des Grieux finally succumbs to the entreaties of Manon, and renouncing the priesthood, goes forth again into the gay world.

The fourth act is the interior of a fashionable gambling house in Paris. Des Grieux and Manon enter, and, after much persuasion, the Chevalier consents to play, in hopes of winning riches for the pleasure-loving Manon. He plays in remarkable luck, and after winning continually from Guillot, is unjustly accused by him of cheating, and trouble ensues. The Chevalier and Manon are both on the point of being arrested when the Count Des Grieux appears and releases his son, but Manon is captured and condemned to exile.

In the last act, Lescaut and Des Grieux are seen hiding in a lonely spot on the road to Havre, where Manon is to pass on her way to exile. By bribing a soldier, the unhappy lover succeeds in obtaining an interview with Manon. He urges her to try and escape with him, but she is too weak from fatigue, and, after praying him to forgive her for unworthiness, the repentant Manon dies in the arms of the grief-stricken Chevalier.

MANON LÉSCAUT

Opera in four acts by GIACOMO PUCCINI

The plot of this opera, by Giacomo Puccini, is founded on the famous story by the Abbé Prevost, entitled "Manon Léscaut." The opera was first produced in 1893, in Milan.

The first act takes place at Amiens. The scene is a large square near the Paris Gate. On the right is an avenue, and on the left an inn, under whose porch are tables for customers. An outer staircase leads to the upper floor of the inn. A mixed crowd of students, citizens, women, and soldiers are strolling about the square and along the avenue. Some are gaming. Edmund enters with some other students, followed later by Des Grieux. The students act as a chorus to Edmund's "Hail, beautiful night!" When Des Grieux enters in melancholy mood the students joke him. The girls, for whom the students have been waiting, now enter from their work. They turn away from Des Grieux, and Edmund begs his friends to leave him alone. A postillion's horn is heard and a diligence arrives, from which Léscaut, Geronte, and Manon alight. Des Grieux is enchanted with Manon's beauty, and when Léscaut goes into the inn, approaches Manon, and obtains her consent to meet him later. Léscaut comes back with Geronte. He has brought his sister Manon to enter her in a convent. Geronte, who is enamored of the girl, tells Léscaut that his pretty little sister seems unhappy. He invites Léscaut to sup with him, and Léscaut accepts the invitation. Léscaut is attracted by the gamblers and takes part in their gaming. Geronte, seeing Léscaut absorbed in the game, determines to run away with Manon. He tells the innkeeper he will want horses and a carriage in an hour, and that he must keep silent if he sees a man and a maiden go off. Edmund overhears the conversation, and suggests to Des Grieux that he should run away with Manon and take Geronte's place in the carriage. Manon keeps her assignation with Des Grieux, and the two go off as Léscaut and Geronte appear on the scene. Geronte is then told by Edmund that Manon has gone off with the young student. In disgusted astonishment, Geronte disturbs Léscaut in his play and tries to prevail upon him to follow the flying pair. Léscaut, however, will have the supper promised him, and says he will go after Manon in the morning. The curtain falls to the sound of loud laughter from the students.

In the second act the scene changes from Amiens to Paris. The curtain goes up discovering a handsomely furnished room in Geronte's house, in which Manon is now living as his mistress. She had left Des Grieux when his money was gone. Manon is seated at her toilet-table, waited on by the hair-dresser with two assistants. She is instructing the hair-dresser to be careful in the work of doing her hair. Léscaut now enters and congratulates his sister on her change in life. Manon keeps instructing the hair-dresser, and, when the toilet is finally completed, steps forward to be admired by her brother. In spite of her brother's praise of her beauty and position, Manon is sad at having left Des Grieux. She is always thinking of him. Geronte is old, and bad, and a bore. Singers now enter, sent by Geronte to amuse Manon, and they sing a madrigal in praise of Manon's beauty. Manon gives her brother money with which to pay the singers, but Léscaut pockets the purse, saying he could not insult them by offering them money. He bids them farewell in the name of glory, and the singers bow themselves out. Geronte now enters, bringing with him a dancing-master, musicians, and some old friends. Manon is bored by them all. Under Geronte's instructions a minuet is danced, in which Manon takes part, led by the dancing-master.

Geronte now suggests that it is time to take a stroll on the boulevards, and begs Manon to join them there later. He leaves, kissing Manon's hand, and all depart with him. Manon is alone, and busies herself arranging her toilet for the promenade, while waiting for the sedan chair Geronte has gone to order. Des Grieux suddenly appears, and they renew their love vows in a charming duet. They have barely finished embracing each other when Geronte comes back. They separate hurriedly, in surprise at being discovered. Des Grieux makes a menacing step forward towards Geronte, but Manon places herself between them. Geronte jeers at her and reminds her of all that he has done for her. She answers him by placing a mirror in his hand and bids him look there and he will see why she cannot love him. Geronte controls his anger and leaves the two together, smiling in sarcasm, and promising them that they will meet again quickly. The lovers are overjoyed at being left alone. They determine to go away together. Manon, however, is loth to leave her jewels and pretty dresses. Des Grieux is bitter at her disposition, which can be so easily led by the allurements of pretty things rather than by love. Manon is moved by his despair and begs forgiveness. She swears to be true and faithful to him. Léscaut now enters hurriedly and entreats them to get away at once. The vile old scoundrel, as he calls Geronte, has called the guards, and these must be now on their way. Manon quickly seizes her jewels, and she and Des Grieux make for the door. They find it locked. Léscaut pushes Manon and Des Grieux into an alcove and follows after them. A scream from Manon is heard, and immediately after she rushes out of the alcove, followed by Des Grieux and her brother. From the open curtains of the alcove come soldiers. The door is now burst open and soldiers rush in to arrest Manon. In trying to escape, Manon lets fall the jewels. She is dragged away by the soldiers, who will not permit Des Grieux to go with them.

An Intermezzo is now played, during which Des Grieux declares his intention to follow Manon even to the end of the world.

The third act takes place in Havre. The scene is a square near the harbor. On the left is a soldiers' prison, showing a window protected by iron bars. On the side looking towards the square is a large closed gate, at which a sentinel stands guard. In the distant harbor a man-of-war ship is partly visible. Manon is in prison, and Des Grieux and Léscaut have come to Havre to be near her. Des Grieux is distracted with grief. Léscaut tells Des Grieux he has bribed an archer, who will take the guard's place when the latter is relieved. As the dawn breaks Léscaut approaches the barracks, and, exchanging a sign with the new sentinel, goes up to the barred window and taps cautiously. Manon appears at the window, and is overjoyed at seeing Des Grieux. She tells them she is to be taken to America. They attempt a rescue, but they are disturbed in their efforts by the firing of shots. They are compelled to leave. A guard appears, bringing a number of women who are to sail to America; Manon is one of them. As they pass by, Léscaut points out his sister to one of the citizens, who have come to watch the embarkation, and tells him that he knows her story. She was abducted from her young lover. Des Grieux attempts to walk by Manon's side, but the sergeant of the guard pushes him aside roughly. Des Grieux threatens him, and entreats Manon to cling to him. Urged on by Léscaut, the citizens take Des Grieux's part. The captain of the vessel suddenly appears, and, learning what the trouble is, takes pity on Des Grieux and permits him to go on board with the rest for America. Des Grieux is overcome with joy, and Manon, realizing the help that is come to her, opens her arms to her lover, who embraces her. Léscaut, astonished at the turn things have taken, shakes his head and walks away.

The fourth act takes us to America. The scene is a great plain near New Orleans. The sky is overcast, and night is falling. Manon and Des Grieux enter, poorly clothed and evidently worn out from fatigue. Manon is exhausted and leans heavily on Des Grieux. They do not know where to find either food or shelter, or even water to drink. Manon is in the last stages of weakness, and Des Grieux is beside himself with despair. He finds a resting place for her, and goes off to look for water. Manon, thinking he has forsaken her entirely, feels there is now no hope for her at all. Only the tomb, she cries, can release her from her burden. Des Grieux comes back in time to be present at her last moments. She dies, declaring her love for him. Des Grieux falls senseless on her body.

MANRU

Romantic Opera in three acts by I. J. PADEREWSKI

Text by ALFRED NOSSIG

The plot of this opera is Paderewski's own conception. It was first presented under his direction at the Court Theatre, Dresden, May 29, 1901. The opera as a piece of real musical workmanship proves conclusively the author's right to recognition as a composer, as well as a musician. He skilfully introduces the violin and other musical instruments, and there is a delicacy and beauty throughout the score which secures a distinct success for the opera.

The scene is laid in the Tatra Mountains, between Galicia and Hungary. The first acts presents a village scene in the mountains where Hedwig is seen bemoaning the loss of her daughter Ulana, who has run away with gypsy Manru. Ulana suddenly appears in the village, and coming to her mother's cottage begs forgiveness for herself and her lover. Hedwig promises to forgive her if she will renounce Manru forever, but this the girl persistently refuses to do, and finally her mother in a rage drives her from the door with curses. Ulana then seeks the assistance of Urok, a dwarf and reputed sorcerer, who has often confessed his love for her. From him she obtains a magic potion with which she hopes to win back the love of Manru, who has already begun to tire of his exile, and to long for the old roving life of the Gypsies.

The second act shows a hut in the mountains, where Ulana is singing a lullaby to her infant, while Manru is struggling between his love and his desire to join the Gypsies. Urok enters the hut, and suddenly beautiful violin music is heard in the distance, which Manru recognizes as coming from the Gypsy fiddler, Jogu. The charm of the music proves too much for him, and he rushes from the hut and disappears in the forest. Jogu tries to persuade him to rejoin the band and be their chief, telling him that the beautiful Gypsy maiden Asa is pining with love for him. In the midst of his temptation Ulana appears and finally persuades him to return to the hut, where she gives him a drink of the magic potion. This has the effect of temporarily winning back his love.

The third act reveals a lake in the mountains, where Manru is seen wandering in the moonlight. He hears strange voices echoing through the mountains, and, becoming weary, falls asleep beneath the trees, where he is found shortly after by the band of Gypsies. The maiden Asa recognizes him immediately, and begs Oros, the Gypsy chief, to forgive him and receive him back into the tribe. Oros refuses to comply with her wishes, and finding his people ready to forgive Manru, leaves the band in anger. Manru is finally persuaded by Asa to accept the position of chief in Oros' stead. Urok suddenly appears in their midst and pleads with Manru not to desert Ulana and his child, but all in vain, as Manru finally succumbs to the alluring smiles of Asa and disappears in the mountains with the Gypsy band.

On hearing of her desertion, Ulana, maddened with grief, throws herself into the lake and is drowned. Manru and Asa, walking down the mountain path with their arms about each other, are suddenly confronted by Oros, who, grappling with Manru, hurls him into the abyss, thereby regaining his position as chief of the Gypsies.

MARGA

Opera in one act by GEORG PITTRICH

Text by ARNO SPIESS

The first performance of this highly interesting little opera took place in Dresden in February, 1894.

The scene is laid in a Bulgarian village at the foot of the Schipka Pass. Marga, the heroine, a Roumanian peasant-girl, has had a sister, Petrissa, who, suffering cruel wrong at the hands of Vasil Kiselow, has cursed her seducer and sought death in the waves. Marga, who had vowed to avenge her sister, is wandering through the world in vain search of Vasil. When the curtain opens she has just reached the village where Vasil occupies the most conspicuous position of judge. Thoroughly exhausted she sinks down at the foot of a cross, and falls asleep.

Vasil's son, Manal, finding her thus, detects a wonderful likeness between the sleeping beauty and a picture which he had found some time ago in the miraculous Sabor Cave, and which for him is the ideal of love and beauty. This picture, a likeness of Petrissa, had been hung there by Vasil, in order to exorcise the curse of the unhappy virgin, but Manal has no knowledge of his father's misdeed.

When Marga awakes the young people of course fall in love with each other; and Marga discovers too late that Manal is the son of her sister's destroyer. Hesitating between love and her vow of vengeance she wildly reproaches Vasil, who falls at her feet in deep contrition, beseeching her forgiveness, which she grants at last. Full of penitence, he relinquishes his property to the young people, and exhorting Manal to be a just and clement judge, he betakes himself to the mountains, resolved to join in the war against the Turks.

MARITANA

Romantic Opera in three acts by ROBERT C. WALLACE

This tuneful and interesting work was first seen in London, in 1845, and then on every stage elsewhere, particularly America.

The scene of the first act is Madrid. Charles, the Spanish King, has fallen desperately in love with a charming young gypsy, who with her band sings in the open squares of the city. The royal minister of state, in order to promote dark plans of his own, heats the King's fancy still more, dwelling enthusiastically on the girl's extraordinary beauty and verve. Don Caesar, a Spanish noble and formerly an intimate friend of José, the minister, is seen reeling out of a tavern. In his inebriated condition he espouses the cause of Lazarillo, an unfortunate waif, and this involves him in a duel for which he is arrested and sentenced to death. He is incarcerated. During this time Don José has been exercising his arts on Maritana, the gypsy girl, telling her wonderful tales of wealth and a great marriage, and thus spurring on her ambition.

In the second act Don Caesar is seen in the dungeon, with his devoted Lazarillo asleep beside him. He is to be executed at seven in the morning, and it is now five. Don José, his false friend, enters and offers his services. Caesar wishes to die a soldier's death, and wants to escape the gallows. After appearing to hesitate, Don José accedes to this plea, but insists that the condemned must first marry. Don Caesar declines, but is finally persuaded to do as José has urged. Although royal clemency has not yet been vouchsafed and Don Caesar has, therefore, but two more hours to live, the nuptial banquet is prepared, and everything got ready for the wedding ceremony. Then Lazarillo enters, bearing the king's pardon. He is, however, waylaid by the cunning Don José, and prevented from handing the document to Don Caesar. The bride, Maritana, who is to be made a wife of convenience, but in reality the mistress of the monarch, enters, and just as the priest pronounces Don Caesar and Maritana duly wedded, soldiers come in for the carrying out of the death penalty on Don Caesar. However, Lazarillo, his humble friend, has by a ruse managed to draw the bullets from the rifles, and when the shots are fired Don Caesar falls apparently lifeless. Don Caesar, after escaping from prison, goes away in a reckless mood to attend a gorgeous ball given by the Marquis de Montefiori. Maritana is there palmed off, under instructions from Don José, as his niece. When Don Caesar demands Maritana as his lawful wife, the minister manages to spirit her away.

The last act shows Maritana in the royal palace, where she has been taken in ignorance. Don José, in the belief that Don Caesar will at least not dare to present himself in the royal palace, introduces the king, whom he attempts to play off as Maritana's husband. The girl resents this, while the king in vain flatters and woos her. Caesar at this juncture breaks into the royal closet and demands his wife, the Countess de Bazan, that being the name given Maritana by the Marquis de Montefiori on instructions from Don José. The king retorts: "I am Don Caesar." And Don Caesar tops this by saying "I am the king." Then comes word from the queen that she is waiting for the king. The latter hastens away, leaving for the moment Don Caesar and Maritana together. Explanations follow, and Don Caesar resolves to ask the queen for her intervention. As he is waiting for the appearance of the queen, he hears in the next room Don José telling her that the king is to meet his mistress that evening. At this Don Caesar breaks in, confronts Don José, exposes his treachery, and kills him on the spot. Then he hurries back to Maritana, with whom he finds the king. Don Caesar boldly proclaims what he has just done, and says: "I myself have safeguarded the king's honor. Will the king in return deprive me of my own honor?" The king sees the point, makes Don Caesar the governor of Valencia, and yields Maritana up to his rival.

MAROUF, LE SAVETIER DU CAIRE

Opera in five acts by HENRI RABAUD

Book by NEPOTY after the story of Aladdin and the Wonderful Lamp in "The Thousand and One Nights"

The first performance took place in Paris in 1914. The scenes are laid in Cairo, Khaitan and a city "somewhere between China and Morocco."

Act I. Marouf, the cobbler, is unhappy. His wife, Fatimah, has the temper of a shrew. When he brings her a cake made of sugar instead of honey, she flies into a rage and accuses him before the credulous Cadi of brutally beating her. The Cadi, notwithstanding the protests of Marouf's neighbors, orders 200 stripes for the luckless cobbler. But Marouf joins a party of sailors and suddenly disappears from Cairo. The ship is wrecked in a tempest and Marouf alone is saved.

Ali, his friend whom he has not seen in twenty years and who is now a prosperous trader, takes him to the city of Khaitan and bids him play the rôle of a wealthy merchant whose caravan will arrive soon. Marouf so overplays his part that the Sultan, wandering through the bazaars in disguise, is impressed by his fabled riches and invites him to the palace.

Inspired by the splendors around him, Marouf delights the Sultan with increasingly fabulous accounts of his wealth. The avaricious sovereign desires a rich son-in-law, so he offers the hand of the Princess Saamcheddine to the runaway cobbler. When Marouf pleads poverty until his caravan arrives, the Sultan places his treasury at his command. The wedding, accordingly, is celebrated and for forty days Marouf lives in luxury with the beautiful Princess. By this time he has emptied the royal treasury—yet his caravan has not arrived. The suspicious Vizier urges the Sultan to have his daughter question Marouf, and the latter laughingly admits to his wife that he is a penniless cobbler. They decide upon flight, the Princess disguising herself as a boy.

At an oasis in the desert, the runaways are sheltered by a poor peasant. While he goes to prepare food for them, Marouf guides his plow. The plowshare catches in a ring attached to a flat stone hidden in the soil. When the Princess rubs the ring, the peasant is transformed into a serviceable *djinn* who discloses a hidden treasure. The Sultan and his guards, in pursuit of the fugitives, now appear and Marouf's execution has been ordered when the sounds of an approaching caravan are heard. Marouf, no less surprised than the Sultan, counts a thousand camels and fourteen hundred mules, laden with rich stuffs, jewels and rare perfumes. The ruler apologizes and the rejoicing lovers depart to the music of the bastinado which the hateful Vizier receives at the Sultan's orders.

Marouf, the cobbler, is no longer unhappy.

MARTHA

Comic Opera in four acts by FLOTOW

Text by W. FRIEDRICH

This charming opera finally established the renown of its composer, who had first found his way to public favor through Stradella. It ranks high among our comic operas, and has become as much liked as those of Lortzing and Nicolai.

Not the least of its merits lies in the text, which Friedrich worked out dexterously, and which is amusing and interesting throughout.

Lady Harriet Durham, tired of the pleasures and splendors of Court, determines to seek elsewhere for a pastime, and, hoping to find it in a sphere different from her own, disguises herself and her confidant Nancy as peasant girls, in which garb they visit the Fair at Richmond, accompanied by Lord Tristan, who is hopelessly enamored of Lady Harriet, and unwillingly complies with her wish to escort them to the adventure in the attire of a peasant. They join the servant girls who are there to seek employment, and are hired by a tenant, Plunkett, and his foster brother, Lionel, a youth of somewhat extraordinary behavior, his air being noble and melancholy, and much too refined for a country squire, while the other, though somewhat rough, is frank and jolly in his manner.

The disguised ladies take the handsel from them, without knowing that they are bound by it, until the sheriff arrives to confirm the bargain. Now the joke becomes reality, and they hear that they are actually hired as servants for a whole year.

Notwithstanding Lord Tristan's protestations, the ladies are carried off by their masters, who know them under the names of Martha and Julia.

In the second act we find the ladies in the company of the tenants, who set them instantly to work. Of course they are totally ignorant of household work, and as their wheels will not go round, Plunkett shows them how to spin. In his rough but kind way he always commands and turns to Nancy, with whom he falls in love, but Lionel only asks softly when he wishes anything done. He has lost his heart to Lady Harriet, and declares his love to her. Though she is pleased by his gentle behavior, she is by no means willing to accept a country squire, and wounds him by her mockery. Meanwhile Plunkett has sought Nancy for the same purpose, but she hides herself, and at last the girls are sent to bed very anxious and perplexed at the turn their adventure has taken. But Lord Tristan comes to their rescue in a coach, and they take flight, vainly pursued by the tenants. Plunkett swears to catch and punish them, but Lionel sinks into deep melancholy, from which nothing can arouse him.

In the third act we meet them at a Court-hunt, where they recognize their hired servants in two of the lady hunters. They assert their right, but the ladies disown them haughtily, and when Lionel, whose reason almost gives way under the burden of grief and shame which overwhelms him at thinking himself deceived by Martha, tells the whole story to the astonished Court, the ladies pronounce him insane, and Lord Tristan sends him to prison for his insolence, notwithstanding Lady Harriet and Nancy's prayer for his pardon.

Lionel gives a ring to Plunkett, asking him to show it to the Queen, his dying father having told him that it would protect him from every danger.

In the fourth act Lady Harriet feels remorse for the sad consequences of her haughtiness. She visits the prisoner to crave his pardon. She tells him that she has herself carried his ring to the Queen, and that he has been recognized by it as Lord Derby's son, once banished from Court, but whose innocence is now proved.

Then the proud lady offers hand and heart to Lionel, but he rejects her, believing himself duped. Lady Harriet, however, who loves Lionel, resolves to win him against his will. She disappears, and dressing herself and Nancy in the former peasant's attire, she goes once more to the Fair at Richmond, where Lionel is also brought by his friend Plunkett. He sees his beloved Martha advance toward him, promising to renounce all splendors and live only for him; then his melancholy vanishes, and he weds her, his name and possessions being restored to him, while Plunkett obtains the hand of pretty Nancy, alias Julia.

DER MAURER

(THE MASON)

Opera in three acts by AUBER

Text by SCRIBE

This charming little work is one of the best semi-comic operas ever composed; from the time of its first representation in Paris until now it has never lacked success.

The libretto is founded on a true anecdote, and is admirably suited to the music.

The scene is laid in Paris in the year 1788.

The first act represents the merry wedding of Roger, a mason, with Henrietta, sister of Baptiste, a locksmith. A jealous old hag, Mistress Bertrand, who would fain have married the nice young man, is wondering whence the poor mason has the money for his wedding, when suddenly a young nobleman, Léon de Mérinville, appears, greeting Roger warmly. He relates to the astonished hearers that Roger saved his life, but would not take any reward, nor tell his name. Roger explains that the nobleman put so much money into his pocket, that it enabled him to marry his charming Henrietta, but Mérinville is determined to do more for him. Meanwhile Roger tries to withdraw from the ball with his young wife; but Henrietta is called back by her relations, according to custom. Roger, being left alone, is accosted by two unknown men, who, veiling his eyes, force him to follow them to a spot unknown to him, in order to do some mason-work for them. It is to the house of Abdallah, the Turkish ambassador, that he is led. The latter has heard that his mistress Irma, a young Greek maiden, is about to take flight with a French officer, who is no other than de Mérinville.

The lovers are warned by a slave, named Rica, but it is too late; Abdallah's people overtake and bind them. They are brought into a cavern, the entrance to which Roger is ordered to wall up. There, before him, he finds his friend and brother-in-law, Baptiste, who was likewise caught, and is now forced to help him.

Recognizing in the officer his benefactor, Roger revives hope in him by singing a song which Léon heard him sing at the time he saved his life.

Meanwhile, Henrietta has passed a dreadful night, not being able to account for her husband's absence. In the morning Mistress Bertrand succeeds in exciting the young wife's sorrow and jealousy to a shocking degree, so that when Roger at last appears, she receives him with a volley of reproaches and questions.

Roger, unhappy about Mérinville's fate and ignorant of where he has been in the night, scarcely listens to his wife's complaints, until Henrietta remarks that she well knows where he has been, Mistress Bertrand having recognized the carriage of the Turkish ambassador, in which he was wheeled away.

This brings light into Roger's brain, and without more ado he rushes to the police, with whose help the poor prisoners are delivered. Roger returns with Mérinville to his wife's house, where things are cleared up in the most satisfactory manner.

MEFISTOFELE

Grand Opera in prologue, four acts, and epilogue

Music and text by ARRIGO BOITO

This is one of the strongest Italian operas, and the composer is often called the "Italian Wagner." It was first presented in Milan in 1868. The libretto is a paraphrase of Goethe's Faust, and is treated from a dramatic, rather than a philosophical, point of view. The music, which is a combination of Italian and German styles, is strikingly powerful and original in character.

The scene of the Prologue is laid in the regions of space, where Mefistofele makes a wager with the Deity that he will gain a victory over the powers of Heaven by enticing Faust to commit evil.

The first act is in the city of Frankfort-on-the-Main, where Faust and his pupil, Wagner, are seen amid the crowd, followed continually by a Gray Friar, who is Mefistofele in disguise. Faust returns to his laboratory, still pursued by the Friar, who conceals himself in an alcove. The sight of Faust reading the Bible brings Mefistofele out with a shriek, and throwing off his disguise appears in the dress of a knight, and reveals his real identity. Faust promises to serve him under certain conditions, and the compact being made the demon spreads his cloak and both disappear through the air.

The second act discloses Faust (under the name of Henry) and Margaret, Mefistofele and Martha strolling through a rustic garden, chatting and love-making. The scene suddenly changes to the heights of the

Brocken, where, amid the celebration of the Witches' Sabbath, Mefistofele discloses to Faust a vision of the sorrowful Margaret, fettered in chains.

In the third act, Margaret is seen in prison, lying upon a heap of straw, where she has been committed for poisoning her mother and killing her babe. Mefistofele and Faust appear, and the latter urges Margaret to escape with him, but Mefistofele recalls to her the reality of her situation, and she shrinks away from her lover and falls dying. The voices of angels are soon heard in the distance, announcing that her soul has been received in Heaven.

In the fourth act, Mefistofele takes Faust to the beautiful banks of the Peneus, in the vale of Tempe, during the night of the Classic Sabbath. Faust pays court to Helen of Troy, and pledging their love and devotion, they wander in ecstasy amid the beauties of their surroundings.

In the Epilogue which follows, the aged Faust is seen in his laboratory mourning over his past life and praying for a happier one to come. Mefistofele, fearing to lose him, urges him to fly once more, but he resists the temptation. As a last resort, Mefistofele summons a vision of beautiful sirens, and Faust, though sorely tempted, again resists the demon by turning to his Bible and praying for help.

His prayer is answered, and, as he dies, the celestial choir announces his salvation.

DIE MEISTERSINGER VON NÜRNBERG

Opera in three acts by WAGNER

This opera carries us back to the middle of the sixteenth century, and the persons whom we meet are all historical.

Amongst the tradesmen whose rhyme-making has made them famous, Hans Sachs, the shoemaker, is the most conspicuous.

The music is highly original, though not precisely melodious, and is beautifully adapted to its characteristically national subject.

In the first act we see St. Catherine's church in Nuremberg, where Divine Service is being celebrated, in preparation for St. John's Day. Eva, the lovely daughter of Master Pogner, the jeweller, sees the young knight, Walter Stolzing, who has fallen in love with Eva, and who has sold his castle in Franconia to become a citizen of Nuremberg. She tells him that her hand is promised to the winner of the prize for a master-song, to be sung on the following morning.

We are now called to witness one of those ancient customs still sometimes practised in old German towns. The master-singers appear, and the apprentices prepare everything needful for them. Walter asks one of them, called David, an apprentice of Sachs, what he will have to do in order to compete for the prize. He has not learned poetry as a profession like those worthy workmen, and David vainly tries to initiate him into their old-fashioned rhyming. Walter leaves him, determined to win the prize after his own fashion.

Pogner appears with Beckmesser the clerk, whom he wishes to have as son-in-law. Beckmesser is so infatuated that he does not doubt of his success. Meanwhile Walter comes up to them, entreating them to admit him into their corporation as a master-singer.

Pogner consents, but Beckmesser grumbles, not at all liking to have a nobleman among them. When all are assembled, Pogner declares his intention of giving his daughter to the winner of the master-song on the day of St. John's festival, and all applaud his resolution. Eva herself may refuse him, but never is she to wed another than a crowned master-singer. Sachs, who loves Eva as his own child, seeks to change her father's resolution, at the same time proposing to let the people choose in the matter of the prize, but he is silenced by his colleagues. They now want to know where Walter has learned the art of poetry and song, and as he designates Walter von der Vogelweide and the birds of the forest, they shrug their shoulders.

He begins at once to give a proof of his art, praising Spring in a song thrilling with melody. Beckmesser interrupts him; he has marked the rhymes on the black tablet, but they are new and unintelligible to this dry verse-maker, and he will not let them pass. The others share his opinion; only Hans Sachs differs from them, remarking that Walter's song, though new and not after the old use and wont rules of Nuremberg, is justified all the same, and so Walter is allowed to finish it, which he does with a bold mockery of the vain poets, comparing them to crows oversounding a singing-bird. Sachs alone feels that Walter is a true poet.

In the second act David the apprentice tells Magdalene, Eva's nurse, that the new singer did not succeed, at which she is honestly grieved, preferring the gallant younker for her mistress, to the old and ridiculous clerk. The old maid loves David; she provides him with food and sweets, and many are the railleries which he has to suffer from his companions in consequence.

The evening coming on, we see Sachs in his open workshop; Eva, his darling, is in confidential talk with him. She is anxious about tomorrow, and rather than wed Beckmesser she would marry Sachs, whom she loves and honors as a father. Sachs is a widower, but he rightly sees through her schemes, and resolves to help the lovers.

It has now grown quite dark, and Walter comes to see Eva, but they have not sat long together when the sounds of a lute are heard.

It is Beckmesser trying to serenade Eva, but Sachs interrupts him by singing himself, and thus excites Beckmesser's wrath and despair. At last a window opens, and Beckmesser, taking Magdalene for Eva, addresses her in louder and louder tones, Sachs all the time beating the measure on a shoe. The neighboring windows open, there is a general alarm, and David, seeing Magdalene at the window apparently listening to Beckmesser, steals behind this unfortunate minstrel, and begins to slap him. In the uproar which now follows, Walter vainly tries to escape from his refuge under the lime-tree, but Sachs comes to his rescue, and takes him into his own workshop, while he pushes Eva unseen into her father's house, the door of which has just been opened by Pogner.

In the third act we find Sachs in his room. Walter enters, thanking him heartily for the night's shelter. Sachs kindly shows him the rules of poetry, encouraging him to try his luck once more. Walter begins, and quite charms Sachs with his love-song. After they have left the room, Beckmesser enters, and reading the poetry, which Sachs wrote down, violently charges the shoemaker with wooing Eva himself. Sachs denies it, and allows Beckmesser to keep the paper. The latter, who has vainly ransacked his brains for a new song, is full of joy, hoping to win the prize with it.

When he is gone, Eva slips in to fetch her shoes, and she sees Walter stepping out of his dormitory in brilliant armor. He has found a third stanza to his song, which he at once produces. They all proceed to the place where the festival is to be held, and Beckmesser is the first to try his fortunes, which he does by singing the stolen song. He sadly muddles both melody and words, and being laughed at, he charges Sachs with treachery; but Sachs quietly denies the authorship, pushing forward Walter, who now sings his stanzas, inspired by love and poetry. No need to say that he wins the hearers' hearts as he has won those of Eva and Sachs, and that Pogner does not deny him his beloved daughter's hand.

MERLIN

Opera in three acts by CHARLES GOLDMARK

Text by SIEGFRIED LIPINER

This creation of the talented composer at once proved itself a success when produced for the first time in the Opera House in Vienna.

Merlin surpasses the Queen of Sheba in dramatic value, and is equal to it in glowing coloring and brilliant orchestration. Goldmark is quite the reverse of Wagner. Though equally master of modern instrumentation, he abounds in melodies. Airs, duets, and choruses meet us of surpassing beauty and sweetness. The text is highly fantastic, but interesting and poetical.

King Artus is attacked by the Saxons and almost succumbs. In his need he sends Lancelot to Merlin, an enchanter and seer, but at the same time the King's best friend and a knight of his table.

Merlin, offspring of the Prince of Hell and of a pure virgin, has power over the demons, whom, however, he only employs in the service of Heaven, his good mother's spirit protecting him. Merlin calls up a demon, whom he forces to blind the heathen Saxons, so that the Britons may be victorious. The demon obeys unwillingly, and after Merlin's departure he calls up the fairy Morgana, who knows all the secrets of the world. Morgana tells the demon that if Merlin loves an earthly woman, his power will be gone, and the demon resolves to tempt Merlin with the most beautiful woman on earth. He vanishes, and the Britons return

Ernestine Schumann-Heink in "Die Meistersinger"

victorious, Merlin with prophetic insight recognizing the knight who had betrayed his people to the Saxons. While he sings a passionate chant in honor of his King and his country, Vivien, a Duke's daughter, appears, and they are at once attracted to each other. But Merlin vanquishes his love, and refuses to accept the crown of oak-leaves which his King offers him by the hand of Vivien. Then Artus takes his own crown and puts it on Merlin's curls.

The second act begins with a conspiracy headed by Modred, Artus' nephew, against his uncle. Lancelot openly accuses him of treason, and the King sends to Merlin for judgment. But alas! Merlin's love has already blinded his understanding; he fails to detect the culpable Modred, and declares that he is not able to find fault in him. King Artus and his knights depart to seek new laurels, leaving the country in Modred's hands. Merlin stays in his sanctum, to where the demon now leads Vivien, who has lost her way. The doors of the temple open by themselves at Vivien's request, and she finds a rosy, glittering veil, which, thrown into the air, causes various charming apparitions to present themselves. When Merlin comes, the whole charm vanishes into air. Vivien tells him of her delightful adventure, but Merlin, frightened, informs her that whoever is touched by the veil will be in the power of demons, chained to a rock forever. Love conquers, and the short hour succeeding is for both filled with earth's greatest bliss. The news of Modred's treachery to King Artus awakes Merlin from his dream. He tears himself from his love, vowing to shun her forever, and to return to the well of grace. But Vivien, finding all her prayers vain, throws the fatal veil over him to hinder his flight. The dreadful effect becomes instantly apparent; the rose-garden disappears, mighty rocks enclose the vale on all sides, and Merlin is held down by burning chains.

While Vivien is consumed by self-reproach and pain, the fairy Morgana appears, telling her that love, which is stronger than death, can bring Merlin eternal grace. Vivien is led away by her maid, and Lancelot enters with the knights to seek Merlin's help against the treacherous Modred.

Seeing Merlin in this pitiful state, he sadly turns from him, but Merlin in despair promises his soul to the demon, if he but assist to deliver his King and his country. The demon breaks the chains, and Merlin rushes with the knights into battle. During his absence Vivien prepares herself to receive her hero, but though she sees him return victorious, he is wounded to death. The demon comes up to claim his victim, but Vivien, remembering Morgana's words, sacrifices herself, piercing her heart at Merlin's feet. The demon disappears, cursing heaven and earth, while Artus and his knights, though they sadly mourn for their hero, yet praise the victory of true love.

MELUSINE

Romantic Opera in three acts by CARL GRAMMANN

Text after C. CAMP'S poem of the same name

The first act shows a forest, peopled by water-nymphs and fairies. Melusine, their princess, emerges from her grotto. While they sing and dance, Count Raymond appears with Bertram, his half-brother, seeking for their father. Bertram disappears, while Raymond, hearing a cry for help, rushes into the bushes whence it comes, not heeding Melusine's warning, who watches half hidden in her grotto. The nymphs break out into lamentations. Melusine is already in love with Raymond, whose misfortune she bewails. When he hurries back in despair at having slain his father, whose life he tried to save from the tusks of a wild boar—his sword piercing the old man instead of the beast—he finds the lovely nymph. She presents him with a draught from the magic well, which instantly brings him forgetfulness of the past. The Count drinks it, and immediately falls in love with the nymph. Melusine consents to the union under the condition that he pledges himself by a solemn oath never to blame her, nor to spy her out should she leave him in the full-moon nights. Raymond promises, the hunters find him in his bride's company, and he presents their future mistress to them; only Bertram stands scornfully aside.

The first scene of the second act represents the crypt of the Lusignan family. The old Duke has been found dead in the forest, and a choir of monks sings the

Requiem. A hermit, Peter von Amiens, comforts the widowed Duchess and warns them all of Melusine. He relates the legend of the water-fairy, who seduces human beings. The poor mother implores Heaven to save her son, while Bertram invokes Hell to avenge his father on the murderer.

Raymond and Melusine enjoy their nuptial bliss, until the rising of the full-moon awakes in Melusine the longing for her native element. She tears herself from him, and Raymond, mindful of his oath, retires. But Melusine's steps are interrupted by Bertram, who declares his love. She scornfully rejects him, and he threatens to betray Raymond, whose bloody sword he has found at the spot where their father was murdered. Melusine escapes to the temple in the garden, and prophesies that Raymond will be happy as long as he keeps her faith. Bertram remains motionless and stunned, until he hears Raymond's voice. He asks Raymond to surrender all his possessions, Melusine, even his life. But Raymond, oblivious of the deed, draws his sword, when his mother interferes. The Duchess repeats to her son the suspicion expressed by the hermit in regard to Melusine, and Raymond calls for her to refute the accusation. But instead of his wife, sweet songs are heard from the temple; he forgets his oath, spies into its interior and perceives the place of the nixies, with Melusine in their midst.

Melusine, finding the gates of her husband's castle closed, vainly calls for him. His mother answers in his stead, charging her with witchcraft, and refusing to admit her. Melusine, sure of Raymond's love, undauntedly answers that only Raymond's want of faith could undo her. A herald announces the arrival of Crusaders with Peter von Amiens. The latter exhorts Raymond to join the holy army. Raymond is willing to go, when

Melusine entreats him not to leave her. All present press around to insult her, only Bertram steps forth as her protector, once more showing Raymond's bloody sword. She kneels to him in order to save her husband, but Raymond, misunderstanding her movements, accuses her of secret intercourse with Bertram. Melusine throwing her husband's ring at his feet, disappears in the Rhine, Bertram leaping after her; the stream overflows its banks, and lightning destroys the castle. The scene changes to the one of sylvan solitude in the first act. Raymond appears in pilgrim's garb to seek for his lost love. Melusine once more emerges from her grotto to comfort him, but also to bring him death. He dies in her embrace.

THE MERRY WIVES OF WINDSOR

Comic Opera in three acts by OTTO NICOLAI

Text by MOSENTHAL

This charming opera has achieved the fame of its composer, of whom very little is known, except that he is the author of this really admirable musical composition, which is valued not only in Germany but all over Europe. Its overture is played by almost every orchestra, and the choruses and songs are both delightful and original. As may be gathered from the title, the whole amusing story is taken from Shakespeare's comedy.

Falstaff has written love-letters to the wives of two citizens of Windsor, Mrs. Fluth and Mrs. Reich. They discover his duplicity and decide to punish the infatuated old fool.

Meanwhile, Mr. Fenton, a nice but poor young man, asks for the hand of Miss Anna Reich. But her father has already chosen a richer suitor for his daughter in the person of silly Mr. Spärlich.

In the following scene Sir John Falstaff is amiably received by Mrs. Fluth, when suddenly Mrs. Reich arrives, telling them that Mr. Fluth will be with them at once, having received notice of his wife's doings. Falstaff is packed into a washing basket and carried away from under Mr. Fluth's nose by two men, who are bidden to put the contents in a canal near the Thames, and the jealous husband, finding nobody, receives sundry lectures from his offended wife.

In the second act Mr. Fluth, mistrusting his wife, makes Falstaff's acquaintance, under the assumed name of Bach, and is obliged to hear an account of the worthy Sire's gallant adventure with his wife, and its disagreeable issue. Fluth persuades Falstaff to give him a rendezvous, swearing inwardly to punish the old coxcomb for his impudence.

In the evening Miss Anna meets her lover, Fenton, in the garden, and ridiculing her two suitors, Spärlich and Dr. Caius, a Frenchman, she promises to remain faithful to her love. The two others, who are hidden behind some trees, must perforce listen to their own dispraise.

When the time has come for Falstaff's next visit to Mrs. Fluth, who of course knows of her husband's renewed suspicion, Mr. Fluth surprises his wife and reproaches her violently with her conduct. During this controversy Falstaff is disguised as an old woman, and when the neighbors come to help the husband in his search they find only an old deaf cousin of Mrs. Fluth's who has come from the country to visit her. Nevertheless the hag gets a good thrashing from the duped and angry husband.

In the last act everybody is in the forest, preparing for the festival of Herne the Hunter. All are masked, and Sir John Falstaff, being led on by the two merry wives, is surprised by Herne (Fluth), who sends the whole chorus of wasps, flies, and mosquitoes onto his broad back. They torment and punish him till he loudly cries for mercy. Fenton, in the mask of Oberon, has found his Anna in Queen Titania, while Dr. Caius and Spärlich, mistaking their masks for Anna's, sink into each other's arms, much to their mutual discomfiture.

Mr. Fluth and Mr. Reich, seeing that their wives are innocent and that they only made fun of Falstaff, are quite happy, and the whole scene ends with a general pardon.

MIGNON

Opera in three acts by AMBROISE THOMAS

Text by MICHEL CARRÉ and JULES BARBIER

This opera is full of French grace and vivacity, and has been favorably received in Germany. The authors have used for their libretto Goethe's celebrated novel, "Wilhelm Meister," with its typical figure, Mignon, as heroine, though very much altered.

The first two acts take place in Germany.

Lothario, a half-demented old man, poorly clad as a wandering minstrel, seeks his lost daughter, Sperata. Mignon comes with a band of gypsies, who abuse her because she refuses to dance. Lothario advances to protect her, but Jarno, the chief of the troop, only scorns him, until a student, Wilhelm Meister, steps forth and rescues her, a young actress named Philine compensating the gypsy for his loss by giving him all her loose cash. Mignon, grateful for the rescue, falls in love with Wilhelm and wants to follow and serve him, but the young man, though delighted with her loveliness and humility, is not aware of her love. Nevertheless he takes her with him. He is of good family, but by a whim just now stays with a troop of comedians, to whom he takes his protégée. The coquette Philine loves Wilhelm, and has completely enthralled him by her arts and graces. She awakes bitter jealousy in Mignon, who tries to drown herself, but is hindered by the sweet strains of Lothario's harp, which appeal to the nobler feelings of her nature. The latter always keeps near her, watching over the lovely child. He instinctively feels himself attracted towards her; she recalls his lost daughter to him, and he sees her as abandoned and lonely as himself. Mignon, hearing how celebrated Philine is, wishes that the palace within which Philine plays might be struck by lightning, and Lothario at once executes her wish by setting the house on fire.

While the guests rush into the garden, Philine orders Mignon to fetch her a nosegay, the same flowers which the thoughtless youth offered to his mistress Philine. Mignon, reproaching herself for her sinful wish, at once flies into the burning house, and only afterward does her friend Laërtes perceive that the theatre has caught fire too. Everybody thinks Mignon lost, but Wilhelm, rushing into the flames, is happy enough to rescue her.

The third act carries us to Italy, where the sick Mignon has been brought. Wilhelm, having discovered her love, which she reveals in her delirium, vows to live only for her. Lothario, no longer a minstrel, receives them as the owner of the palace, from which he had been absent since the loss of his daughter. While he shows Mignon the relics of the past, a scarf and a bracelet of corals are suddenly recognized by her. She begins to remember her infantine prayers, and recognizes the hall with the marble statues and her mother's picture on the wall. With rapture Lothario embraces his long-lost Sperata. But Mignon's jealous love has found out that Philine followed her, and she knows no peace until Wilhelm has proved to her satisfaction that he loves her best.

At last Philine graciously renounces Wilhelm and turns to Friedrich, one of her many adorers, whom to his own great surprise she designates as her future husband. Mignon at last openly avows her passion for

Wilhelm. The people, hearing of the arrival of their master, the Marquis of Cypriani, alias Lothario, come to greet him with loud acclamations of joy, which grow still louder when he presents to them his daughter Sperata, and Wilhelm, her chosen husband.

THE MIKADO

A Comic Opera in two acts by ARTHUR S. SULLIVAN

The text is by WILLIAM S. GILBERT

First production in London, 1885. The scene is at "Titipu," Japan, and the time is the past.

The first act happens in a street of Titipu. The Mikado's son, Nanki-Poo, rather than wed an elderly charmer, by the name of Katisha, has run away from court and leads the merry though impecunious life of a strolling minstrel youth. He has gone from town to town, hearing all sorts of things, when in Titipu he happens to fall in love head over heels with the charming Yum-Yum. This Yum-Yum is a minor and therefore one of the many wards of Ko-Ko, a high official who has a monopoly on guardianship throughout the empire. Yum-Yum in fact is still a schoolgirl, a naïve young creature, who is home during vacation with two of her equally charming friends. Ko-Ko had had an idea of marrying this particular ward himself, not having much else to do just about this time. But Nanki-Poo's affection is to the full returned by Yum-Yum, and this is the way matters stand when Pooh-Bah drifts in from some other point of the compass, and messes matters up by his arrival. Pooh-Bah is not alone the depositant and purveyor of all state secrets, holding also every office in the gift of the country with the single exception of that of Lord High Executioner, which is the prerogative of his friend Ko-Ko, but he is always loaded with schemes. Ko-Ko had been a tailor by trade, until he was offered this fat office, and he is by no means as bloodthirsty as the Mikado would like him to be, in fact since the day of his inauguration there has not been even one execution. The Mikado has now come out with an ultimatum: if within a month nobody has been beheaded or otherwise disposed of for good, Ko-Ko will lose his remunerative job. It is in this dilemma that Nanki-Poo, having of late found the strolling minstrel business particularly unremunerative, steps forth and offers to serve Ko-Ko as a client at the end of the month if he be allowed to marry Yum-Yum first and live with her for that space. This proposal appears to both Ko-Ko and Pooh-Bah to hit the bull's-eye and they accept it forthwith.

The second act is at the home of little Yum-Yum, where the wedding of the maid with Nanki-Poo is to take place. An unlooked-for complication arises by Ko-Ko's unearthing an obsolete law to the effect that when a man is beheaded his widow also must be buried alive. But Nanki-Poo's chivalry is not to be outdone. Driven by his code, the Japanese *bushido,* the young man offers to solve the difficulty by stabbing himself with neatness and dispatch. But unfortunately this will not serve the need of Ko-Ko, who is driven into a corner and makes up a false statement as to the execution. It is precisely at this juncture that the Mikado himself comes to Titipu, quite accidentally, and learns with exquisite pleasure that after such a long delay an execution, and that a fine sanguinary one, described with much gusto by the old swindler, Ko-Ko, has actually taken place. The Mikado grunts approval of all the horrible things that have been done to the wretched delinquent. But suddenly he learns that the delinquent is his own son, for whom he has been looking high and low, and this, of course, changes the aspect of affairs. He decrees forthwith that the Lord High Executioner shall be boiled in oil for his blunder. But the gods are merciful. Nanki-Poo shows up very much alive just in the nick of time, and the Mikado remits all other penalties to Ko-Ko save only the one of marrying Katisha, the elderly court beauty.

LE MIRÂCLE

Sentimental Opera in four acts by G. A. HÜE

Text based on a legend of Burgundy dating from the fifteenth century

This work was first produced in Paris, 1910.

Act I. A strong town in France is beleaguered by an army of mercenaries, and inside its walls suffering from famine and disease is great. The commander of these troops sends word that he will raise the siege of the place if Alix, a noted courtesan of great beauty, is surrendered to him. He asserts that she has bewitched him by black art. To save her home town Alix agrees to his condition, and the citizens of the freed city, to express their gratefulness to Heaven for the timely rescue, give an order to their best sculptor, Soys, to make a statue of their patron saint, St. Agnes, to be placed in the church devoted to her service in memory of her aid. But Alix is not satisfied with this. She attributes entirely the saving of the city to her great charms and to her spirit of sacrifice, and she conceives a plan by which the artist is to carve the statue in her own likeness, thus immortalizing herself instead of the saint who really had nothing to do with it.

Act II. Meanwhile Soys, the sculptor, having seen and admired Alix, has also been bewitched by her. He is unable to drive her picture from his mind. Night and day it dwells there, despite all his prayers. It glows and glitters in his fancy, and delays his work on the statue of the saint. In desperation, finally, he throws the half-finished figure from his scaffold at the moment when

Alix enters his studio. Her robe clings to her divine form. Her presence is alluring, irresistible. Soys kneels down and worships her.

Act III. The scene shows the Church of St. Agnes, with the veiled statue in one of its cloisters. It is the day when the artist is to turn over the finished statue to the city authorities. The whole populace is astir to do honor to the patron saint, and flags and flowers testify to the general joy. But as Soys slowly withdraws the cloth hiding the figure, it is seen to be a nude representation of Alix. Fanatical rage seizes all. Everybody cries out at the sacrilege. The bishop in his golden vestments threatens to put the whole town under the ban. The crestfallen, humbled artist has nothing to say in his defense. But Alix rejoices. She is proud and satisfied. The governor who now approaches the statue and prepares to destroy it is struck dead by Alix.

Act IV. The outraged church and clergy demand condign punishment. Alix has been removed to a narrow dungeon cell. Soys attempts to save her, but she scorns to be saved. She follows a procession of nuns to the scene of her late triumph, where the statue, again closely veiled, stands mutely in the corner. It falls to her, in atonement for her insolence, to shatter her own image, for only then will Soys be pardoned. Soys, frantic, broken, and yet still under the seductive spell of Alix, is in the procession. Alix approaches the statue, lifts the heavy hammer, and strikes—a bolt of lightning shoots forth from the stone, and she lies dead. Soys tears off the veil. A miracle has been wrought. It is now the calm, sweet image of St. Agnes. And the whole town now blesses the sculptor.

MIREILLE

Romantic Opera in four acts by CH. GOUNOD

Words by PAUL CARRÉ, after the story "Miréo" by FRÉDÉRIC MISTRAL

This dainty work was first seen at Paris, 1878. Its scene is the south of France, in the recent past.

The first act discovers Mireille, the daughter of Ramon, a wealthy farmer, in a mulberry plantation, surrounded by village girls and neighbors, who rally her on her affection for Vincent, a handsome but poor youth. The girl, being very naïve, admits her passion without reservation. Taven, a reputed witch, cautions her not to bare her heart too quickly.

The second act opens with a chorus and dance in the arena at Arles, where Mireille and Vincent meet again. But Taven warns her that she has heard Ourrias, a wealthy but semi-savage cattle owner, boast that he would wed her. Ourrias is repulsed by Mireille and reports these facts to Ramon, who vows that his daughter shall obey him.

In the third act a harvest festival is being celebrated, and Andreloun, a poor shepherd boy, enters playing his bagpipe. Ramon and his whole household are in festive mood, but Mireille cannot shake off her melancholy. News is brought that Ourrias, the suitor favored by her father, has met Vincent and attacked him with a trident, injuring him seriously. Taven nurses Vincent and predicts his recovery, but Mireille wants to implore the aid of heaven, and undertakes a pilgrimage to the shrine at the St. Mary's Church, situated in the Cro, a desert region.

In the last act the two lovers meet at the famous shrine, where Vincent opens his arms to his sweetheart. There is religious music, and the pilgrim's march is chanted. This and the presence of Vincent restore Mireille once more to sanity, and her father, Ramon, at last relents.

THE MISER KNIGHT

Fantastic Opera in three acts by VLADIMIR RACHMANINOFF

This opera was first seen at Moscow, 1905.

A nobleman, who has amassed much wealth, has become extremely penurious. He allows his castle to go to ruin, to save the cost of repairs, and his only son to go about in rags and to suffer from hunger. The youth defeats a rival knight in a duel and then muses as to the causes of his success. He comes to the conclusion that it was owing to his sorry equipment, for once his anger was roused by the shattering of his helmet, he displayed superhuman strength. But further reflecting he feels wrath at his father's miserliness, which deprives him of all enjoyment of life and youth. He thereupon looks up a usurer, who advises him to poison his father and thus come into possession of all his riches.

The second act is peculiar because there appears but one person, the miser, on the stage. It shows him in the lowest cellars of his strong castle, where he is surrounded on all sides by kegs and pouches of gold and silver. He is counting his treasures over and over again, and tells with ecstasy of the thrills of pleasure he gets from the feel of the gold pieces, which he terms his "little friends." He sings in equal measure of the awful struggle going on all over the world for the winning, keeping, and increasing of gold.

The third and last act shows the appalling death agony of the miser, who at last dies with the keys still in a grasp of steel, unlocking his treasures.

MONA

A Dramatic Opera in three acts by HORATIO PARKER

The book by BRIAN HOOKER

The first production was in New York, 1912. The scene is Southwestern Britain in ancient times.

This work earned the prize of $10,000 offered that year by the Metropolitan Opera House, New York.

In the first act the interior of Arth's hut in the dense woodland is seen. The Britons are wroth at tyrannical Roman rule in their island, and the priests are seeking some chieftain of high courage and influence among the warriors of their race to lead them forth again to combat the Roman legions. Mona, last of the royal strain that gave Boadicea to Britain, is chosen by the priests, for they discover in this woman an unbending will and a more than manly ambition. Mona herself has been brought up by Arth and Enya as their foster child. Mona on her part has as a lover Gwynn, one of a party attempting to reconcile Romans and Britons, and throughout a man of peace. She does not know it, but Gwynn is really the son of the Roman proconsul who has been administering Britain for years, while his mother is of British extraction. Naturally the Roman father has steadily been endeavoring to bring about reconciliation between the two races. Gwynn, whose Roman name is Quintus, does his best to wean Mona away from her bellicose ideals and to induce her to marry him. Mona, however, although fond of Gwynn, cannot prevail upon herself to abandon her visions of greatness, and is, besides, convinced that fate calls upon her to imitate the deeds of her ancestress, Boadicea.

The second act reveals a druidic fane in the depth of the forest. The Roman proconsul in command of the island is informed by his spies that the druidical priesthood are once more solemnizing their rude rites, and hence he concludes that a great uprising is near. Gwynn, still pursuing his plan of mutual reconciliation, urges Mona to become his wife. His father, who is rather cynical as to his son's intentions, gives him leave to try his scheme. Gwynn meets Mona after one of the great national ceremonials instigated by the druids, and she yields to his persuasive eloquence and confesses her love for him. But she quickly recants when he owns to his Roman descent, and curses her feminine weakness. She even summons her attendants, and they take Gwynn captive.

The third act reveals a forest in front of a British town with a Roman garrison and a Romanized population. Enya, the foster mother of Mona, and Nial, a half-witted youth, are watching the battle. The besieging Britons are unable to withstand Roman military discipline, and they fall back, Mona among them. Mona is unwounded, but in great danger of being seized by the Romans as a rebel. Gwynn, who has torn his fetters during the engagement, arrives in search of Mona, and again offers her his affection and a peaceful home. He is not recognized by Mona, who sees in him a traitor to his native land. In an access of fury she stabs him to death, while he does not resist her at all. When the Romans next pursue the foe they take Mona a prisoner, and as such she is brought face to face with the Roman ruler of the country, Gwynn's father. He tells her the full truth that Gwynn, the man she slew, was the best friend the country had, and that with him perished all hope of a peaceful settlement. Mona too late becomes conscious that she has overstepped the boundaries set for true womanhood.

MONA LISA

Opera in two acts. Prologue and epilogue by
MAX SCHILLINGS

Libretto by DOVSKY

The first performance was given in Stuttgart in 1915. The action takes place in Florence of Renaissance and modern times.

Prologue. A lay monk of the Certosa order is showing two tourists, an elderly husband and his beautiful young wife, through the mansion that once belonged to the pearl merchant, Francesco del Giocondo. As he recounts the tragic story of Giocondo's lovely wife, Mona Lisa, the stage darkens and when the light returns, the tale is enacted in its Renaissance setting.

Act I. Giocondo's friends are making merry over wine in his magnificent home when Mona Lisa enters. Her jealous husband is racked by her baffling smile whose secret is still a riddle on Leonardo da Vinci's canvas. When Giovanni Salviato arrives, sent by the Pope to buy a great pearl, Giocondo opens the double doors of his jewel closet and shows his guests the lustrous gems in the casket he draws up by windlass from the bed of the Arno, flowing beneath the house. When his friends go and he is locking up, the merchant glimpses Giovanni who has returned in the hope of seeing Mona Lisa, his lost love, married off by her parents during his absence from Rome. After Giocondo has heard his wife promise to fly with Giovanni, he so maneuvers that she hides her lover in the jewel closet, which he then locks. While the youth is strangling within the safe, the husband makes pretended love to the distracted Mona Lisa and finally flings into the Arno the key for which she begs.

Act II. Waking in the grey dawn of Ash Wednesday, Mona Lisa beats despairingly on the door which hides her dead lover. Dionora, Giocondo's daughter by his first wife, enters with the key which had fallen into the boat where she was sitting beneath her father's window. Just as the young wife snatches the key from her stepdaughter, Giocondo returns. Cunningly Mona Lisa leaves him uncertain whether or not Giovanni has escaped and when he opens the closet to get her a pearl necklace which she pretends to want to wear, she pushes him inside with a scream of maniac joy. Giocondo will suffer as her lover did.

Epilogue. As Mona Lisa's voice dies away, the scene reverts to the present. The elderly husband of the prologue reproves his wife's sympathy for the unfortunate woman and the monk, when she drops a spray of white iris at his feet as she goes away, calls longingly after her, "Mona Lisa . . . Mona Lisa!"

MONNA VANNA

Sentimental Grand Opera in four acts by HENRY FÉVRIER
Text by MAURICE MAETERLINCK

The first-night performance of this opera was in Paris, 1909. The action occurs in Pisa, Italy, during the fifteenth century, and is based on an historical incident.

Act I. Made frantic by a long and cruel siege and brought to the verge of actual starvation, the Florentine army investing the city being on the point of enforcing surrender, the clamoring population of Pisa are before the palace of Guido Colonna, commander of the brave garrison, and demand the death of the general, since it was he who brought about the war. Guido Colonna himself is seated inside, wrapt in melancholy thought, and hears the shouts of the maddened crowd. His officers, Borso and Torello, come to him with the report that the ammunition is giving out. He replies that he has already sent his own father, the venerable Marco, to Prinzivalle, commanding the besieging Florentine army, to obtain favorable terms. His father returns, and his report is to the effect that Prinzivalle will deal leniently with Pisa and send them a large convoy of food and ammunition if Guido will accept his terms. These terms, Marco announces, are that in token of submission, Guido himself send his wife, the beautiful Monna Vanna, to the tent of Prinzivalle. The lady, it is conditioned, is to come without arms, nude, wrapped only in a cloak, and is to stay with the general of the foe until dawn of the next day. Guido is shocked and humiliated, and demands to know the reason of such singular conditions. The father replies that Prinzivalle is enamored of Monna. And when Guido remains of the opinion that that cannot be true since Prinzivalle has never seen Monna, Marco answers that Prinzivalle certainly must have met Monna before, and that the latter, having been told by Marco of these conditions, has declared herself ready to carry them out. Vanna is summoned, and hears the ferocious cries of the throng outside, all shouting for the death of her husband, whereupon she reiterates her willingness to fulfil the terms of the victor. Her husband, unable to fathom her motive, and not inclined to put such deep trust in his wife's affection, is roused to insane jealousy, and at first will not agree to the conditions imposed. He protests wrathfully, but finding his wife firm in her resolution, he cannot help believing that her love for him has died, and puts her coldly from him, asserting that his love also is now dead.

In the second act Prinzivalle is awaiting the coming of Monna in his tent, but is told by his secretary, Vedio, that a letter has just been received from Florence in which the general is ordered to storm the beleaguered city of Pisa next morning, in default of which he will be regarded a traitor and taken into custody to await trial. The envoy from Florence, Trivulzio, a venomous enemy of Prinzivalle, enters the tent just as the signal agreed upon, showing that Monna has started for her ordeal, is beginning to flash on the ramparts of Pisa. Prinzivalle has been watching this signal. Trivulzio is confronted by the commander with several letters from partisans in Florence showing clearly that Trivulzio and a number of his fellow-conspirators have resolved on Prinzivalle's death even if the latter should end the siege successfully.

Trivulzio, seeing himself betrayed, treacherously attempts to stab the general with a poniard. But he only wounds him in the face, and is then disarmed and handed over to the guards for safekeeping. Vedio warns his master that his foes in Florence are bent on his destruction, but Prinzivalle laughs at him. Vedio leaves, and Monna enters. The dialogue between these two shows that Monna still cherishes a single purpose in coming, namely, to save the people of Pisa and to redeem her husband. It is also shown that Prinzivalle was her playmate during childhood and has treasured her memory. He behaves toward her with so much delicacy and forbearance that he earns her gratitude and respect, and she allows him to caress her hands in token of these feelings, but no further intimacy is attempted on either side. Vedio at this juncture rushes in to let his principal know that an officer from Florence with a body of soldiers are proclaiming him a traitor throughout the camp. Prinzivalle is urged to flee, and now Monna wants him to come with her to Pisa, where he would be safe. He accepts her offer, and they both go.

The third act opens with Guido's plans for vengeance. Monna Vanna comes acclaimed by the people as their savior. The aged father, Marco, affectionately embraces her, but her husband will have none of her, and drives out the joyful crowd that has followed her to the palace. He notices a man in her wake, and inquires as to his identity. When he hears that it is Prinzivalle, he is seized with a paroxysm of unreasonable rage, but suddenly the assumption comes over him that his wife has brought this man for him to wreak his vengeance on, and then he goes to the other extreme, taking her to his arms and begging her forgiveness for having misconstrued her past behavior. In his mind he is hatching schemes for the torture of Prinzivalle. He calls back the populace and tells them who the stranger is. Vanna makes every endeavor to be heard and to explain the facts in the case, but when at last she is permitted to say something, Guido flatly disbelieves her, and tauntingly parades his incredulity that Prinzivalle did spare her from shame and outrage just because he loved her. He asks her, however, to come to his arms and be caressed, which she coldly refuses to do. Neither do the throng of people whom she has saved by her own sacrifice believe her pure and unsullied because of the deep respect felt for her by Prinzivalle. Guido prepares to feast on the tortures which he has in store for Prinzivalle, and when Monna Vanna thus realizes the truth, she pretends that her husband's surmises have been correct, and claims Prinzivalle as her own victim, to do with as she chooses. Prinzivalle accordingly is cast into a dungeon, manacled and treated cruelly, and the key to his cell is confided to her.

In the last rather short act, Monna Vanna frees Prinzivalle from his bonds, and the two bare their souls to each other. She makes it clear why she can no longer love her husband after the foul suspicions he has had of her, and after the fiendishly cruel instincts shown by him throughout the whole matter. On the other hand she now feels the most enduring affection for Prinzivalle. She opens the doors of the prison to him, and the two go forth to buffet the world together.

LA MUETTE DE PORTICI

Grand Historical Opera in five acts by AUBER

Text by SCRIBE

This opera was first put on the sage in the Grand Opera House at Paris in the year 1828, and achieved for its author universal celebrity, not only because in it Auber rises to heights which he never reached either before or after, but because it is purely historical. The "Muette" is like a picture which attracts by its vivid reproduction of nature. In the local tone, the southern temper, Auber has succeeded in masterly fashion, and the text forms an admirable background to the music. Its subject is the revolution of Naples in the year 1647, and the rise and fall of Masaniello, the fisherman King.

In the first act we witness the wedding of Alfonso, son of the Viceroy of Naples, with the Spanish Princess Elvira. Alfonso, who has seduced Fenella, the Neapolitan Masaniello's dumb sister, and abandoned her, is tormented by doubts and remorse, fearing that she has committed suicide. During the festival Fenella rushes in to seek protection from the Viceroy, who has kept her a prisoner for the past month. She has escaped from her prison and narrates the story of her seduction by gestures, showing a scarf which her lover gave her. Elvira promises to protect her, and proceeds to the altar, Fenella vainly trying to follow. In the chapel Fenella recognizes her seducer in the bridegroom of the Princess. When the newly married couple come out of the church, Elvira presents Fenella to her husband, and discovers from the dumb girl's gestures that he was her faithless lover. Fenella flies, leaving Alfonso and Elvira in sorrow and despair.

In the second act the fishermen, who have been brooding in silence over the tyranny of their foes, begin to assemble. Pietro, Masaniello's friend, has sought for Fenella in vain, but at length she appears of her own accord and confesses her wrongs. Masaniello is infuriated, and swears to have revenge, but Fenella, who still loves Alfonso, does not mention his name. Then Masaniello calls the fishermen to arms, and they swear perdition to the enemy of their country.

In the third act we find ourselves in the market place in Naples, where the people go to and fro, selling and buying, all the while concealing their purpose under a show of merriment and carelessness. Selva, the officer of the Viceroy's bodyguard, from whom Fenella has escaped, discovers her, and the attempt to rearrest her is the sign for a general revolt, in which the people are victorious.

In the fourth act Fenella comes to her brother's dwelling and describes the horrors which are taking place in the town. The relation fills his noble soul with sorrow and disgust. When Fenella has retired to rest, Pietro enters with comrades and tries to excite Masaniello to further deeds, but he only wants liberty and shrinks from murder and cruelties.

They tell him that Alfonso has escaped, and that they are resolved to overtake and kill him. Fenella, who hears all, decides to save her lover. At this moment Alfonso begs at her door for a hiding place. He enters with Elvira, and Fenella, though at first disposed to avenge herself on her rival, pardons her for Alfonso's sake. Masaniello, reëntering, assures the strangers of his protection, and even when Pietro denounces Alfonso as the Viceroy's son he holds his promise sacred. Pietro, with his fellow-conspirators, leaves him full of rage and hatred.

Meanwhile the magistrate of the city presents Masaniello with the royal crown, and he is proclaimed King of Naples.

In the fifth act we find Pietro, with the other fishermen, before the Viceroy's palace. He confides to Moreno that he has administered poison to Masaniello in order to punish him for his treason, and that the King of one day will soon die. While he speaks, Borella rushes in to tell of a fresh troop of soldiers marching against the people, with Alfonso at their head. Knowing that Masaniello alone can save them, the fishermen entreat him to take the command of them once more, and Masaniello, though deadly ill and half bereft of his reason, complies with their request. The combat takes place while an eruption of Vesuvius is going on. Masaniello falls in the act of saving Elvira's life. On hearing these terrible tidings, Fenella rushes to the terrace, from which she leaps into the abyss beneath, while the fugitive noblemen again take possession of the city.

NATOMA

A Romantic Opera in three acts by VICTOR HERBERT

Text by JOSEPH D. REDDING

This opera was first produced at Philadelphia, 1911. The scene is laid in Southern California, and the time is 1820, during the Spanish occupation.

The first act occurs at the island of Santa Cruz. A wealthy Spaniard, Don Francisco, is expecting the return from a convent on the mainland of his daughter Barbara. She has completed her education at the convent, and everybody on Don Francisco's vast estate is impatient to welcome her. Alvarado, a young Spaniard of distinction, has been courting the Señorita Barbara for some time. Natoma, the young lady's Indian maid, is greatly attached to her mistress. And somebody else, too, is anxious to meet her, namely, Lieutenant Merrill, of the U. S. Navy, who happens to be stationed at Santa Cruz at the behest of his government. Without his own knowledge, Natoma, who is quite a superior person for an Indian, is deeply in love with the young officer, whereas he treats her with indulgence, but as a mere child of the wilderness. Nevertheless, Natoma, not fathoming his true state of feelings, harbors hopes of ultimately winning Merrill's affections. And strangely enough, it is owing precisely to Natoma's vivid descriptions of the sweet charms of her mistress that the lieutenant is prepared in advance to fall in love with her. Natoma after some chance remark of his, suddenly realizes this, and from that moment on her feelings are strongly divided between loyalty to her mistress and uncontrollable love for Merrill. When Barbara at last does arrive, and is greeted most enthusiastically by everybody, an attachment between herself and the young officer ripens speedily into love, exactly as Natoma had forebodingly felt would be the case. When in the evening after her arrival a ball is given in Barbara's honor, Alvarado, whose suit has not prospered, becomes aware that a new and formidable obstacle to his aspirations exists in the person of Merrill. When he pleads his cause with Barbara he is definitely repulsed, and he then lays plots with his half-breed servant, Castro, to possess himself of the person of Barbara by abduction. But Natoma becomes aware of Alvarado's criminal designs and conceives a means of foiling them.

The second act opens with a scene on the public plaza of Santa Barbara. A fair is being celebrated in the ancient town, and among the attractions offered there is the presence of a body of American marines. Alvarado invites Barbara to the dance, and despite her reluctance she is told by her father not to refuse, and hence accepts his company. But Alvarado wounds the girl's feelings, and she leaves him to join her father. Alvarado, though, keeps a sharp lookout for her, trying to find a favorable opportunity to get her into his power. He has Castro and some other ruffians to aid him. As part of the plot Castro issues a challenge to all present to share with him in a public display of the dagger dance. He thrusts his dagger deep into the soil, and a crowd of admirers is quickly formed about him. Natoma takes up his challenge, and both then keep on whirling cautiously about, each intent on seizing the other's weapon. Suddenly Natoma leaps forward, pushes Castro's dagger aside, and coming at one bound up to Alvarado, stabs him to the heart, just as he was on the point of seizing Barbara. Merrill and his marines take the side of Natoma, and prevent the crowd of enraged villagers from wreaking vengeance on her. At this moment Father Peralta, appearing on the threshold of the near-by church, offers sanctuary to Natoma. She disappears within.

The interior of the church is seen in the last act. Natoma is kneeling there before the altar, and a conflict of feelings is raging in her bosom. The old instincts of her race have reawakened, and she dreams of the rude freedom of the forest. There is no regret for what she has done, but her love for Merrill is as strong as ever. She still feels loyal towards her beloved mistress, but she does not intend to give up the lieutenant even to her. It is in that frame of mind that the gentle old priest meets her within the church. When he accosts her with authority regarding her deed, she at first scorns him and his teachings. But he speaks with so much persuasion and understands the workings of her heart so well, that gradually he softens her, and finally Natoma sinks on her knees. She renounces all her dreams, and is anxious to enter a convent and lead a penitential life. Worshippers now arrive, unheeded by Natoma, and then mass is celebrated by Father Peralta, and the nuns are seen approaching across the sun-lit gardens of the cloister. At last the Indian maiden takes eternal leave of her beloved mistress, and vanishes through the gate that leads to peace.

LA NAVARRAISE

A two-act Romantic Opera by J. MASSENET

Text after the Spanish

This work was first played in London, 1894. The scene is in Spain, during the Carlist war.

Act I. A poor peasant girl, Anita, (La Navarraise) is in love with Araquil, sergeant in the Spanish army, and he reciprocates. When the curtain rises the Carlists have won the day, and Araquil is anxiously looking for his sweetheart. Their meeting is most tender and touching. Araquil's father, Remigo, also meets his boy; Anita appeals to the father to be lenient in the matter of dowry with her, because while he has two thousand douros,—she has nothing. In another scene there is a battle, and General Garrido, on the Spanish side, offers a fortune to the soldier who will kill or take the redoubted Carlist leader, Zucarraguay, prisoner during the engagement and bring him to the commander. Anita, disguised as a soldier, hears this and rushes off towards the camp of the enemy.

Act II. Night. A camp scene. As day breaks, fighting is resumed. The rumor spreads that Zucarraguay has been stabbed by a woman, a spy. A change. Anita presents herself before General Garrido, and furnishes proof of having killed the Carlist leader. She receives the reward. But at the same time Araquil, her lover, is brought in dying from a wound. He has heard of her visiting the enemy camp, and, unaware of her having killed Zucarraguay, he reproaches her for having sold herself to obtain riches. He curses her and dies. Anita becomes a raving maniac, and expires over the body of her lover.

NERONE

Opera in four acts by ARRIGO BOITO

Libretto by the composer

The first production was given in Milan in 1924. The scenes are laid in Rome during the reign of Nero.

While Simon Magus, a magician, is digging a grave among the tombs on the Appian Way, Nero, carrying an urn containing his murdered mother's ashes, appears and begs the necromancer to save him from his mother's ghost. Asteria, the Roman girl tormented by her passion for the emperor, enters and Nero, thinking her an avenging fury, flees in terror. Simon, after listening to Asteria's wild lamentations, leaves her groveling on the ground.

At dawn the next morning Rubria, a vestal priestess who has been ravished by Nero, comes to the tombs with the apostle Fanuel to place flowers on a grave. Fanuel has won a wide following among the citizens and Simon proposes to the holy man that they unite their powers and so conquer Rome. Fanuel curses the magician and Rubria flees as a procession is heard approaching with the emperor leading.

Simon, in his underground temple devoted to black magic, is weaving his spells when Nero enters and sees Asteria's face reflected in a mirror. He imagines that she is a fury and is first frightened by her glance, then overcome with desire for her. But when he clasps her in his arms, he is enraged to find her a woman and not the supernatural creature of his fears. He smashes the temple idols and orders his guards to seize Asteria and Simon. He then mounts the altar and bursts into song, accompanying himself on the lyre.

While Fanuel is preaching to a crowd in the street, Asteria, who has escaped from the guards, rushes in to warn him that Simon is on his track. The magician appears and has Fanuel arrested.

To the clamoring of a bloodthirsty mob filling the Coliseum, Fanual leads a group of doomed Christians into the arena. As they cross the sands, the building bursts into flame. All is confusion. In the crypt of the Coliseum, Fanuel and Asteria find Simon dead and Rubria dying. The apostle tells the dying girl of Christ and she accepts the salvation he offers. But Asteria, still absorbed in her passion for the dissolute emperor, has a question to ask of Rubria—how did she win Nero's heart? The gentle smile on the peaceful face of the dead girl rebukes her and bidding Rubria sleep in peace, Asteria escapes from the crypt as the roof crumples in the flames.

NORMA

Tragic Opera in two acts by BELLINI

Text by ROMANI

Few operas can boast of as good and effective a libretto as that which Romani wrote for Bellini's Norma. He took his subject from a French tragedy, and wrote it in beautiful Italian verse.

With this work Bellini won his fame and crowned his successes. Again it is richness of melody in which Bellini excels—highly finished dramatic art and lofty style he does not possess—and it is this very richness of melody which makes him, and specially his Norma, such a favorite in all theatres. His music is also particularly well suited to the human voice, and Norma was always one of the most brilliant parts of our first dramatic singers.

The story is as follows:

Norma, daughter of Orovist, chief of the Druids, and High Priestess herself, has broken her vows and secretly married Pollio, the Roman Proconsul. They have two children. But Pollio's love has vanished. In the first act he confides to his companion, Flavius, that he is enamored of Adalgisa, a young priestess in the temple of Irminsul, the Druid's god.

Norma, whose secret nobody knows but her friend Clothilde, is worshipped by the people, being the only one able to interpret the oracles of their god. She prophesies Rome's fall, which she declares will be brought about, not by the prowess of Gallic warriors, but by its own weakness. She sends away the people to invoke alone the benediction of the god. When she also is gone, Adalgisa appears, and is persuaded by Pollio to fly with him to Rome. But remorse and fear induce her to confess her sinful love to Norma, whom she, like the others, adores. Norma, however, seeing the resemblance to her own fate, promises to release her from her vows and give her back to the world and to happiness; but hearing from Adalgisa the name of her lover, who, as it happens, just then approaches, she of course reviles the traitor, telling the poor young maiden that Pollio is her own spouse. The latter defies her, but she bids him leave. Though as he goes he begs Adalgisa to follow him, the young priestess turns from the faithless lover, and craves Norma's pardon for the offence of which she has unwittingly been guilty.

In the second act, Norma, full of despair at Pollio's treason, resolves to kill her sleeping boys. But they awake, and the mother's heart shudders as she thinks of her purpose; then she calls for Clothilde and bids her fetch Adalgisa.

When she appears, Norma entreats her to be a mother to her children, and to take them to their father, Pollio, because she has determined to free herself from shame and sorrow by a voluntary death. But the noble-hearted Adalgisa will not hear of this sacrifice, and promises to bring Pollio back to his first love. After a touching duet, in which they swear eternal friendship to each other, Norma takes courage again. Her hopes are vain, however, for Clothilde enters to tell her that Adalgisa's prayers were of no avail. Norma, distrusting her rival, calls her people to arm against the Romans, and gives orders to prepare the funeral pile for the sacrifice. The victim is to be Pollio, who was captured in the act of carrying Adalgisa off by force. Norma orders her father and the Gauls away, that she may speak alone with Pollio, to whom she promises safety if he will renounce Adalgisa and return to her and to her children. But Pollio, whose only thought is of Adalgisa, pleads for her and for his own death. Norma, denying it to him, calls the priests of the temple, to denounce as victim a priestess who, forgetting her sacred vows, has entertained a sinful passion in her bosom and betrayed the gods. Then she firmly tells them that she herself is this faithless creature, but to her father alone does she reveal the existence of her children.

Pollio, recognizing the greatness of her character, which impels her to sacrifice her own life in order to save him and her rival, feels his love for Norma revive, and stepping forth from the crowd of spectators, he takes his place beside her on the funeral pile. Both commend their children to Norma's father, Orovist, who finally pardons the poor victims.

LA NOTTE DI ZORAIMA

Opera in one act by ITALO MONTEMEZZI

Libretto by MARIO GHISALBERTI

This opera was first given in America at the Metropolitan Opera House, New York, on December 2, 1931.

Montemezzi's L'Amore dei tre Re is one of the few really significant operatic works of the last quarter century, and when this composer's La Notte di Zoraima was produced the world listened expectantly, hoping that a new masterwork would be revealed. Though workmanlike the new opera failed to make any profound impression, and Italo Montemezzi remains up to the present time a man of one opera.

The scene is laid in Peru following the first Spanish conquest. Zoraima, an Inca Princess, betrothed to Muscar, the dethroned king, is living in the ruined city. She pretends madness so as to spy on the Spanish invaders. Muscar is lying in wait for the Spanish convoy, and Zoraima has given orders to set the forest ablaze if the Spaniards discover her lover's hiding-place. Pedrito, the Spanish general, has fallen in love with Zoraima, and Zoraima sends word to Muscar that Pedrito has sworn to kill him and win her love. Muscar arrives to see Zoraima before his attack, and when he leaves Manuela, Pedrito's discarded mistress, asks Zoraima not to allow Pedrito to win her. Zoraima promises her that he never will.

Muscar is shot by Pedrito and flees back to Zoraima, who hides him, just as Pedrito arrives. Pedrito knows that Muscar is there, and tries to make love to Zoraima, who repulses him. The Spanish colonists surge into the house and demand the deaths of Zoraima and Muscar, and Zoraima to save Muscar tells the crowd that Pedrito is her lover. Pedrito orders the crowd to leave, and Zoraima tells him that if he will allow Muscar to escape that she will give him a marvellous gift. Pedrito, thinking she means her love, sets Muscar free. Zoraima takes a tender leave of Muscar, and then whispers to one of her followers to set the forest afire as soon as Muscar is safely away. Pedrito thinking he has won, tries to make love to Zoraima, but she holds him off, until a glare in the distance tells her that Muscar is safe and pursuit cut off by the flames. She turns to Pedrito crying: "Muscar is safe!" Then plunging a dagger into her breast she adds triumphantly: "This is my gift to you!"

LE NOZZE DI FIGARO

Comic Opera in four acts by MOZART

Text by LORENZO DA PONTE

This opera may be said to be the continuation of Rossini's Barbiere di Seviglia. The text, too, is taken from Beaumarchais's Figaroade, and the principal persons in it we find to be old acquaintances. It is the same Count Almaviva, now married to Rosina; Figaro, the cunning barber, has entered the Count's service, and is about to marry Rosina's maid, Susanna. We meet among the others old Doctor Bartolo and Basilio. Even in the management of the subject and in the music we find some resemblance. "Figaro's wedding" has the same character of gaiety; no storms, very few clouds; there prevails throughout an atmosphere of sunshine and brightness. After Don Juan, Figaro was Mozart's darling, and it shines radiantly in the crown of his fame. There is no triviality in it, as we find in most of the comic operas of Offenbach and others; it is always noble, as well as characteristic in every part.

The text may be paraphrased thus:

Count Almaviva, though married to Rosina and loving her ardently, cannot bring himself to cease playing the rôle of a gallant cavalier; he likes pretty women wherever he finds them, and notwithstanding his high moral principles is carrying on a flirtation with Rosina's maid, the charming Susanna. This does not hinder him from being jealous of his wife, who is here represented as a character both sweet and passive. He suspects her of being overfond of her Page, Cherubino. From the bystanders, Doctor Bartolo and Marcellina, we hear that their old hearts have not yet ceased to glow at the touch of youth and love; Bartolo would fain give his affections to Susanna, while Marcellina pretends to have claims on Figaro.

These are the materials which are so dexterously woven into the complicated plot, and which furnish many funny quid pro quos.

In the second act we find Cherubino, the Page, in the rooms of the Countess, who, innocent and pure herself, sees in him only a child; but this youth has a passionate heart, and he loves his mistress ardently. Mistress and maid have amused themselves with Cherubino, putting him into women's dresses. The Count, rendered suspicious by a letter given to him by Basilio, bids his wife open her door. The women, afraid of his jealousy, detain him a while, and only open the door when Cherubino has got safely through the window and away over the flower beds. The Count, entering full of wrath, finds only Susanna with his wife. Ashamed of his suspicions, he asks her pardon and swears never to be jealous again. All blame in the matter of the letter is put on Figaro's shoulders, but this cunning fellow lies boldly, and the Count cannot get the clew to the mystery. Figaro and Susanna, profiting by the occasion, entreat the Count at last to consent to their wedding, which he has always put off. At this moment the gardener Antonio enters, complaining of the spoiled flower beds. Figaro, taking all upon himself, owns that he sprang out of the window, having had an interview with Susanna and fearing the Count's anger. All deem themselves saved, when Antonio presents a document which the fugitive has lost. The Count, not quite convinced, asks Figaro to tell him the contents; but the latter, never at a loss, and discovering that it is the Page's patent, says that the document was given to him by the Page, the seal having been forgotten. The Count is about to let him off, when Bartolo appears with Marcellina, who claims a matrimonial engagement with Figaro. Her claim is favored by the Count, who wishes to see Susanna unmarried. Out of this strait, however, they are delivered by finding that Figaro is the son of the old couple, the child of their early love; and all again promises well. But the Countess and Susanna have prepared a little punishment for the jealous husband as well as for the flighty lover.

They have both written letters in which they ask the men to an interview in the garden. Susanna's letter goes to the Count, Rosina's to Figaro. Under the wings of night the two women meet each her own lover, but Susanna wears the Countess's dress, while Rosina has arrayed herself in Susanna's clothes.

The Countess, not usually given to such tricks, is very anxious. While she awaits her husband, Cherubino approaches, and taking her for Susanna, he, like a little Don Juan as he is, makes love to her. Hearing the Count's steps, he disappears. Almaviva caresses the seeming Susanna, telling her nice things and giving her a ring, which she accepts. They are observed by the other couple and the sly Figaro, who has recognized Susanna, notwithstanding her disguise, denounces the Count to her, vows eternal love and generally makes his bride burn with wrath. In her anger she boxes his ears, upon which he confesses to having known her from the first, and at once restores her good humor.

Seeing the Count approach, they continue to play their former rôles, and the false Countess makes love to

Figaro, till the Count accosts her as "traitress." For a while she lets him suffer all the tortures of jealousy, then the lights appear and the Count stands ashamed before his lovely wife, recognizing his mistake. The gentle Countess forgives him, and the repenting husband swears eternal fidelity. He speedily unites the lovers Figaro and Susanna, and forgives even the little Page Cherubino.

OBERON

Romantic Opera in three acts by WEBER

English text by PLANCHÉ, translated by TH. HELL

Oberon is Weber's last work. In the year 1824 he had the honor of being commissioned to compose this opera for the Covent Garden Theatre. He began at once to study English, but, his health giving way, he progressed slowly. Notwithstanding his illness, however, he worked on and finished the opera in the year 1826. He had the happiness of seeing it crowned with success when he travelled to London in February of that year, but he could not witness its triumphs in Germany, for he died in the following July.

The text is most fantastic, without any strict order of succession either in the matter of time or locality. It is taken from Wieland's fairy tale of the same name.

In the first act we find Oberon, the Elfin King, in deep melancholy, which no gaiety of his subjects, however charming, avails to remove. He has quarrelled with his wife Titania, and both have vowed never to be reconciled until they find a pair of lovers faithful to each other in all kinds of adversity. Both long for the reunion, but the constant lovers are not to be found.

Oberon's most devoted servant is little Puck, who has vainly roved the world to find what his master needs. He has, however, heard of a valiant knight in Burgundy, Hüon, who has killed Carloman, the son of Charlemagne, in a duel, having been insulted by him. Charlemagne, not willing to take his life for a deed of defence, orders him to go to Bagdad, to slay the favorite sitting to the left of the Calif, and to wed the Calif's daughter Rezia. Puck resolves to make this pair suit his ends. He tells Oberon the above-mentioned story, and by means of his lily sceptre shows Hüon and Reza to him. At the same time these two behold each other in a vision, so that when they awake both are deeply in love.

Oberon wakes Hüon and his faithful shieldbearer, Scherasmin, and promises his help in every time of need. He presents Hüon with a magic horn, which will summon him at any time; Scherasmin receives a cup which fills with wine of itself. Then he immediately transports them to Bagdad.

There we find Rezia with her Arabian maid, Fatima. The Calif's daughter is to wed Babekan, a Persian Prince, but she has hated him ever since she saw Hüon in her vision. Fatima has discovered the arrival of Hüon. It is high time, for in the beginning of the second act we see the Calif with Babekan, who wants to celebrate the nuptials at once. Rezia enters, but at the same time Hüon advances, recognizing in Rezia the fair one of his dream. He fights, and stabs Babekan. The Turks attack him, but Scherasmin blows the magic horn, and compels them to dance and laugh until the fugitives have escaped.

In the forest they are overtaken, but Hüon and Scherasmin, who has come after his master with Fatima, put the pursuers to flight.

Oberon now appears to the lovers, and makes them promise upon oath that they will remain faithful to each other under every temptation. He immediately after transports them to the port of Ascalon, from which they are to sail homeward. Oberon now puts their constancy to the proof. Puck conjures up the nymphs and the spirits of the air, who raise an awful tempest. Hüon's ship sinks; the lovers are shipwrecked. While Hüon seeks for help, Rezia is captured by the pirates, and Hüon, returning to save her, is wounded and left senseless on the beach. Oberon now causes him to fall into a magic sleep, which is to last seven days.

In the third act we find Scherasmin and his bride, Fatima, in Tunis, dressed as poor gardeners.

A corsair has saved the shipwrecked lovers and sold them as slaves to the Emir of Tunis. Though poor and in captivity they do not lose courage, and are happy that they are permitted to bear their hard lot together.

Meanwhile the seven days of Hüon's sleep have passed. Awakening, he finds himself, to his astonishment, in Tunis, in the Emir's garden, with his servant beside him, who is not less astonished at finding his master.

Fatima, coming back, relates that she has discovered Rezia in the Emir's harem. Hüon, who finds a nosegay with a message which bids him come to the myrtle bower during the night, believes that it comes from Rezia, and is full of joy at the idea of meeting his bride. Great is his terror when the lady puts aside her veil and he sees Roschina, the Emir's wife. She has fallen in love with the noble knight, whom she saw in the garden, but all her desires are in vain; he loathes her, and is about to escape, when the Emir enters, captures and sentences him to be consumed by fire. Roschina is to be drowned. Rezia, hearing of her lover's fate, implores the Emir to pardon him. But she has already offended him by her unwillingness to listen to his protestations of love, and when he hears that Hüon is her husband he condemns them to be burned together. Their trials, however, are nearing their end. Scherasmin has regained the long-lost horn, by means of which he casts a spell on everybody, until, blowing it with all his might, he calls Oberon to their aid. The Elfin King appears, accompanied by Queen Titania, who is now happily reconciled to him, and, thanking the lovers for their constancy, he brings them safely back to Paris, where Charlemagne holds his court. The Emperor's wrath is now gone, and he warmly welcomes Sir Hüon and his lovely bride, promising them honor and glory for their future days.

L'OISEAU BLEU

Symbolic Opera in four acts by ALBERT WOLFF

The libretto is based on MAURICE MAETERLINCK'S drama of the same name

This opera was first produced in New York in 1919. The scenes are not localized in any particular country or time.

The opera follows the action of the play. Tyltyl and Mytyl, the woodcutter's children, are watching from their window the preparations being made in a wealthy neighbor's home for the celebration of Christmas. They know that there will be no tree nor Christmas stocking for them. As they are gazing longingly at their neighbor's sweetmeats and gifts, the Fairy Berylune enters. She tells Mytyl and Tyltyl that they must bring her the grass that sings and the blue bird of happiness so that her little girl who is ill may be restored to health. Upon their agreeing to go on the quest, the fairy gives Tyltyl a magic cap with a diamond which has the power to disclose the past and the future and to turn inanimate objects and dumb animals into speaking creatures. Everything around the children begins to take voice and life—bread, sugar, water, fire, light, the cat and the dog. The window opens and invites the children to begin their search.

They visit first the Land of Memory and find their grandparents and their little dead brothers and sisters—but the bird there is black. In the Palace of Night, Tyltyl discovers a garden of beautiful birds but, alas, they die when the children touch them. They next journey to the Palace of Happiness where they meet the sensual luxuries and the true happinesses and joys. The radiance of Tyltyl's jewel transforms the Cemetery which they next visit into a place of serene peace. Then in the Kingdom of the Future, they see old Father Time send down myriads of unborn babes to earth, and as Light calls out that she has caught the blue bird, the scene changes.

The children are back before their own door. They have not found the blue bird. When Christmas morning dawns, the parents wake the sleeping children and listen in bewilderment to the story of their adventures in search of the bird of happiness. And now Neighbor Beringot, who resembles very much the Fairy Berylune, enters to ask if Tyltyl will give her little sick daughter his turtle dove to cheer her through her illness. Looking around, the children are amazed to see that their pet bird has turned blue. They gladly send it to the sick child who recovers. When she comes in later with the bird, Tyltyl asks it back and as she is hesitating about returning it, the blue bird escapes from both and disappears.

L'ORACOLO

Tragic Grand Opera in Italian by FRANCO LEONI

Text based upon an American melodrama, "The Child and the Cherub," by C. B. FERNALD. Libretto by CAMILLO ZANONI

The first production took place in 1905, in London. The scene is Chinatown, San Francisco, before the great fire of 1906. There is only one act, but a number of scenes, with change of location.

In Hatchet Row, Chinatown, the early dawn of the Chinese New Year sees the keeper of an opium den, Chim Fen, eject an obstreperous client, and having done so, he shakes his fist at the gleaming windows of his neighbor, the wealthy Hoo Tsin. He is enraged at the contrast between his own misery and the wealth of his neighbor. Meeting the nurse employed in Hoo Tsin's home, he demands from her the return of a handsome fan, a gift from San Luy to the merchant's beautiful daughter, Ah Yoe. The nurse is greatly frightened and promises to obey him. A Chinese sage, Win Shee, deeply learned and of great influence among his countrymen, in passing Chim Fen's place, answers Chim Fen's wishes of the season by stopping and warning the other of the sinfulness of his calling. When a policeman passes, Win Shee, although such a sage, nevertheless is particular to caution Chim Fen not to pay attention to this "American dog." Afterwards San Luy, the sage's son, under the window of Ah Yoe sings a serenade in her praise, and the two exchange holiday greetings. Chim Fen amid all the rejoicing of the day plucks up courage enough to ask Hoo Tsin for the hand of his daughter. Hoo Tsin, instead of declining outright, merely hopes that all the opium in Chinatown may pass through his neighbor's hands. Chim Fen, however, understands the reply to be a negative one, and flies into a rage, all the more because the rabble in the street mocks at him.

On this same New Year's day Hoo Tsin, in conformity with ancient home tradition, has the oracle consulted relative to the fortune of his infant son and heir. The oracle plays on the safe side: part of it is favorable, part unfavorable. But before the little child can be taken home again, Chim Fen, out of a feeling of revenge, kidnaps him, and hides him in the depths of his cellar. Then he visits the inconsolable father, to whom he makes a proposition. He pledges himself to make a thorough search for the missing baby, and asks, in case he should find him and restore the child unharmed to the father, for the hand of Ah Yoe. San Luy, not to be behindhand, makes the same bargain. By him the baby is traced to Chim Fen's cellar, but when he attempts to penetrate there, Chim Fen discovers him, and the two rivals during a struggle fall down the steps of the cellar, and San Luy is killed. The news spreads. Ah Yoe mourns for her lover, and Win Shee, the sage and father of the victim, resolves to exact retribution. He finds the missing child, and when Chim Fen tries to prevent him from carrying off the baby, they grapple, and Chim Fen is slain. Just after the deed, one of those vigilant American policemen draws near and is on the point of discovering the murder. Win Shee adopts a singular stratagem to deceive him. He props up the corpse on the sidewalk, and as the officer comes nearer he apparently carries on a spirited conversation with the dead man. The officer is deceived and goes on. Justice according to the Chinese notion, has been done.

ORFEO AND EURYDICE

Opera in three acts by GLUCK

Text by RANIÉRO DI CALZABIGI

This opera is the oldest of all we possess in our répertoire. Gluck had already written more than forty operas, of which we do not even know the names now, when he composed his Orfeo, breaking with the old Italian traditions and showing a new and more natural taste. All the charm of Italian melody is still to be found in this composition, but it is blent with real feeling united to great strength of expression, and its value is enhanced by a total absence of all those superfluous warbles and artificial ornaments which filled the Italian operas of that time. The libretto, taken from the old and beautiful Greek tragedy, is as effective as the music.

Orpheus, the celebrated Greek musician and singer, has lost his wife, Eurydice. His mournful songs fill the groves where he laments, and with them he touches the hearts not only of his friends but of the gods. On his wife's grave Amor appears to him, and bids him descend into Hades, where he is to move the Furies and the Elysian shadows with his sweet melodies, and win back from them his lost wife.

He is to recover her on a condition, which is, that he never cast a look on her during their return to earth, for if he fail in this, Eurydice will be forever lost to him.

Taking his lyre and casque, Orpheus promises obedience, and with renewed hope sallies forth on his mission. The second act represents the gates of Erebus, from which flames arise. Orpheus is surrounded by furies and demons, who try to frighten him; but he, nothing daunted, mollifies them by his sweet strains, and they set free the passage to Elysium, where Orpheus has to win the happy shadows. He beholds Eurydice among them, veiled; the happy shadows readily surrender her to him, escorting the pair to the gates of their happy vale.

The third act beholds the spouses on their way back to earth. Orpheus holds Eurydice by the hand, drawing the reluctant wife on, but without raising his eyes to her face—on and on through the winding and obscure paths which lead out of the infernal regions. Notwithstanding his protestations of love and his urgent demands to her to follow him, Eurydice never ceases to implore him to cast a single look on her, threatening him with her death should he not fulfil her wish. Orpheus, forbidden to tell her the reason of his strange behavior, long remains deaf to her cruel complaints, but at last he yields, and looks back, only to see her expire under his gaze. Overwhelmed by grief and despair, Orpheus draws his sword to destroy himself, when Amor appears, and stays the fatal stroke.

In pity for Orpheus's love and constancy he reanimates Eurydice (contrary, however, to the letter of the Greek tragedy), and the act closes with a beautiful chorus sung in Amor's praise.

OTHELLO

Opera in four acts by GIUSEPPE VERDI

Text by ARRIGO BOITO

In his seventy-third year the maestro gave to his time an opera which surpasses his former compositions in many respects. It proved that Verdi's genius remained admirably fresh, and that the new views and revelations which Wagner opened to the musical world were fully understood by the Italian. He broke with the unnatural traditions of the Italian opera, and in Othello gave us a work which secures to him a place among the great dramatic composers.

It must not be forgotten that Verdi had a splendid second in the person of Boito, the high-minded and capable composer of Mefistofele. He omits in his action all that is incidental, and as a consequence the force of thought and expression is the more powerful. It is written clearly after Shakespeare's original.

The first scene represents the people following excitedly the course of Othello's ship, which battles with the waves. After he has landed and informed the assembly of his victory over the Turks, shouts of joy and exultation rend the air.

Then follows a convivial chat between Cassio, Rodirigo, and Iago, in the course of which the latter makes Cassio drunk. Iago's demoniacal nature is masterfully depicted here, where he soon succeeds in ruining Cassio, who loses his rank as captain.

In the third scene we see Desdemona with her husband, both rejoicing in the felicity of their mutual love.

In the second act Iago proceeds to carry out his evil intents, by sending Cassio to Desdemona, who is to intercede for him with Othello. Iago then calls Othello's attention to the retiring Cassio and, by making vile insinuations, inflames his deadly jealousy. Desdemona appears, surrounded by women and children, who offer her flowers and presents. She comes forward to plead for Cassio, and Othello suspiciously refuses. She takes out her handkerchief to cool her husband's aching forehead with it, but he throws it down, and Emilia, Iago's wife, picks it up. Iago wrenches it from her and hides it.

In the next scene Iago's villainous insinuations work upon Othello, who becomes wildly suspicious. Iago relates a dream of Cassio's, in which he reveals his love for Desdemona, then he hints that he has seen Othello's first love-token, her lace handkerchief, in Cassio's hands, and both swear to avenge Desdemona's infidelity.

In the third act Othello, pretending to have a headache, asks for Desdemona's lace handkerchief. She has lost it, she tells him, but he is incredulous and charges her with infidelity. All her protests are useless, and at length he forces her to retire. Meanwhile Iago has brought Cassio and urges Othello to hide himself. Cassio has a lady-love named Bianca, and of her they speak, but Iago dextercusly turns the dialogue so as to make Othello believe that they are speaking of his wife. His jealousy reaches its climax when Cassio draws forth Desdemona's handkerchief, which Iago has deposited in Cassio's house. All his doubts now seem to be confirmed. A cannon shot announcing the arrival of a galley interrupts the conversation and Cassio quickly leaves.

In the following scene Iago advises Othello to strangle his wife. Othello consents and gives Iago a captaincy.

Lodovico, an Ambassador of Venice, arrives with other nobles to greet their liberator, Othello. Desdemona once more asks pardon for Cassio, but is roughly rebuked by her husband. The latter reads the order which has been brought to him, and tells Cassio that he is to be General in his stead by will of the Doge of Venice, but while Cassio is confounded by this sudden change of fortune, Iago secretly vows his death, instigating his rival Rodirigo to kill him. At last Othello faints, overcome by conflicting emotions.

In the fourth act Desdemona, filled with sad forebodings, takes a touching farewell of Emilia. When she has ended her fervent prayer (one of the most beautiful things in the opera) she falls into a peaceful slumber. Othello awakes her with a kiss, and tells her immediately thereafter that she must die. She protests her innocence, but in vain, for Othello, telling her that Cassio can speak no more, smothers her. Hardly has he completed his ghastly work than Emilia comes up, announcing that Rodirigo has been killed by Cassio. Desdemona with her dying breath once more asserts her innocence, while Emilia loudly screams for help. When the others appear, Emilia discovers her husband's villainy, Iago flies, and Othello stabs himself at the feet of his innocent spouse.

PAGLIACCI

Musical Drama in two acts and a Prologue

Music and text by R. LEONCAVALLO

In the summer of the year 1892 a rumor was going through the musical world that Mascagni had found his equal, nay, his superior, in the person of another young Italian composer. When the Pagliacci, by Leoncavallo, was executed in Italy, it excited a transport of enthusiasm almost surpassing that of Cavalleria, so that Berlin and Leipsic brought the opera on the stage as quickly as possible, and Dresden followed their examples on January 22, 1893, with the same great success.

The opera is indeed eminently qualified to produce impression. Though less condensed in its tragic depths than Cavalleria, the music is nobler without being less realistic. In Leoncavallo the feeling of artistic form is more developed. Though of southern temper, he never lets passion get the better of the beautiful and true harmony; also he is Mascagni's senior by eight years.

Leoncavallo's excellent musical education is as unmistakable as the influence of Wagner's music on his genius. He, too, introduces the "leading motives," but he is far from imitating his great predecessor. Like Wagner, he did his text himself, and it must be owned that it is very good. The idea was suggested to him by an event which he witnessed at Montalto in Calabria during the summer of 1865, and which impressed him deeply.

In the Prologue, a wonderful piece of music, Tonio the Fool announces to the public the deep tragic sense which often is hidden behind a farce, and prepares them for the sad end of the lovers in this comedy.

The introduction, with its wonderful largo, is like a mournful lamentation; then the curtain opens, showing the entry of a troop of wandering actors, so common in southern Italy. They are received with high glee by the peasants, and Canio, the owner of the troop, invites them all to the evening's play. Canio looks somewhat gloomy, and he very much resents the taunts of the peasants, who court his beautiful wife Nedda, and make remarks about the Fool's attentions to her. Nevertheless Canio gives way to his friends' invitation for a glass of Chianti wine, and he takes leave of his wife with a kiss, which, however, does not quite restore her peace of mind, Nedda's conscience being somewhat disturbed. But soon she casts aside all evil forebodings, and vies with the birds in warbling pretty songs, which, though reminding the hearer of Wagner's "Siegfried," are of surpassing harmony and sweetness.

Tonio the Fool, spying the moment to find Nedda alone, approaches her with a declaration of love, but she haughtily turns from him, and as he only grows more obtrusive and even tries to embrace her, she seizes a whip and slaps him in the face. Provoked to fury, he swears to avenge himself. Hardly has he turned away when the peasant Silvio appears on the wall. He is Nedda's lover, and, having seen Canio sitting in the tavern, he entreats her to separate herself from the husband she never loved and take flight with him. Nedda hesitates between duty and passion, and at last the latter prevails, and she sinks into his arms. This love duet is wonderful in style and harmony. Tonio unfortunately has spied out the lovers and returns with Canio. But on perceiving the latter's approach Silvio has leaped over the wall, his sweetheart's body covering his own person, so that Canio is unable to recognize his rival; he once more reminds Nedda to be ready that night and then takes flight. With an inarticulate cry Canio rushes after him and Nedda falls on her knees to pray for her lover's escape, while Tonio the Fool triumphs over her misery. The husband, however, returns defeated; panting, he claims the lover's name, and, Nedda's lips remaining sealed, he is about to stab his wife, when Beppo the Harlequin intervenes, and, wrenching the dagger from his unfortunate master's hands, intimates that it is time to prepare for the play. While Nedda retires, Canio breaks out into a bitter wail of his hard lot, which compels him to take part in the farce, which for him is bitter reality. With this air the tragic height of the opera is reached.

In the second act the spectators throng before the small stage, each of them eager to get the best seat. Nedda appears, dressed as Columbine, and while she is collecting the money she finds time to warn Silvio of her husband's wrath. The curtain opens, and Nedda is seen alone on the stage, listening to the sentimental songs of Arlequin, her lover in the play. Before she has given him the sign to enter, Tonio, in the play called Taddeo the Fool, enters, bringing the food which his mistress has ordered for herself and Arlequin. Just as it really happened in the morning, the poor Fool now makes love to her in play; but when scornfully repulsed he humbly retires, swearing to the goodness and pureness of his lady-love. Arlequin entering through the window, the two begin to dine merrily, but Taddeo reenters in mocking fright, to announce the arrival of the husband Bajazzo (Canio). The latter, however, is terribly in earnest, and when he hoarsely exacts the lover's name, the lookers-on, who hitherto have heartily applauded every scene, begin to feel the awful tragedy hidden behind the comedy. Nedda remains outwardly calm, and mockingly she names innocent Arlequin as the one who had dined with her. Then Bajazzo begins by reminding her how he found her in the street, a poor waif and stray, whom he nursed, petted, and loved, and, Nedda remaining cold, his wrath rises to fury and he wildly curses her, shrieking "The name! I will know his name!" But Nedda, though false, is no traitress. "Should it cost my life, I will never betray him," she cries, at the same time trying to save her life by hurrying from the stage amongst the spectators. Too late, alas! Canio already has reached and stabbed her, and Silvio, who rushes forward, also receives his death-stroke from the hands of the deceived husband, who has heard his name slip from the dying lips of his wife. All around stand petrified; nobody dares to touch the avenger of his honor, who stands by his wife's corpse limp and broken-hearted: "Go," says he, "go, the farce is ended."

PARSIFAL

A festival Drama by RICHARD WAGNER

In Parsifal the heavenly greatness of the Christian idea of God, which is at the foundation of the legend of the holy Grail, finds grand expression. There scarcely exists another composition of such lofty and religious spirit as finds expression in the communion scene. It is not possible to imagine a more vivid contrast than that between the saintly melodies and those of the fascinating fairies, which latter, glowing with poetry and ravishing music, captivate all senses.

The contents are those of the ancient German legend. The first scene is laid in a forest on the grounds of the keepers of the Grail, near Castle Monsalvat. Old Gurnemanz awakes two young Squires for their morning prayer, and bids two Knights prepare a bath for the sick King Amfortas, who suffers cruelly from a wound dealt him by the sorcerer Klingsor, the deadly foe of the holy Grail. The Grail is a sacred cup, from which Christ drank at the last Passover, and which also received his holy blood. Titurel, Amfortas's father, has built the castle to shield it, and appointed holy men for its service. While Gurnemanz speaks with the Knights about their poor master's sufferings, in rushes Kundry, a sorceress in Klingsor's service, condemned to laugh eternally as a punishment for having derided Christ while He was suffering on the cross. She it was who with her beauty seduced Amfortas, and deprived him of his holy strength, so that Klingsor was enabled to wring from the King his holy spear Longinus, with which he afterward wounded him. Kundry is in the garb of a servant of the Grail; she brings balm for the King, who is carried on to the stage in a litter, but it avails him not: "a guileless fool" with a child's pure heart who will bring back the holy spear and touch him with it, can alone heal his wound.

Suddenly a dying swan sinks to the ground, and Parsifal, a young Knight, appears. Gurnemanz reproaches him severely for having shot the bird, but he appears to be quite ignorant of the fact that it was wrong, and, when questioned, proves to know nothing about his own origin. He only knows his mother's name "Herzeleid" (heart's affliction), and Kundry, who recognizes him, relates that his father, Gamuret, perished in battle, and that his mother reared him, a guileless fool, in the desert. When Kundry mentions that his mother is dead, and has sent her last blessing to her son, Parsifal is almost stunned by this, his first grief. Gurnemanz conducts him to the castle, where the Knights of the Grail are assembled in a lofty hall. Amfortas is laid on a raised couch, and, from behind, Titurel's voice is heard, imploring his son to efface his guilt in godly works. Amfortas, writhing with pain, is comforted by the prophecy:

By pity lightened, the guileless fool—
Wait for him,—my chosen tool.

The Grail is uncovered, the blessing given, and the repast of love begins. Amfortas's hope revives, but toward the end his wound bursts out afresh. Parsifal, on hearing Amfortas's cry of agony, clutches at his heart, without, however, understanding his own feelings.

The second act reveals Klingsor's magic castle. Kundry, not as a demon now, but as a woman of imperious beauty, is awakened by Klingsor to seduce Parsifal. She yearns for pardon, for sleep and death, but she struggles in vain against the fiendish Klingsor.

The tower gradually sinks; a beautiful garden rises, into which Parsifal gazes with rapture and astonishment. Lovely maidens rush toward him, accusing him of having destroyed their lovers. Parsifal, surprised, answers that he slew them because they checked his approach to their charms. But when their tenderness waxes hotter, he gently repulses the damsels and at last tries to escape. He is detained, however, by Kundry, who tells him again of his beloved mother; and when Parsifal is sorrowstricken at having forgotten her in his thoughtless rambles, she consoles him, pressing his lips with a fervent kiss. This rouses the dreamy youth: he awakes to his duty, he feels the King's spear-wound burning; the unconscious fool is a fool no longer, but conscious of his mission and distinguishing right from wrong. He calls to the Saviour to save him from a guilty passion, and at last he starts up, spurning Kundry. She tells him of her own crime, of Amfortas's fall, and curses all paths and ways which would lead him from her. Klingsor, appearing at her cry, flings the holy spear at Parsifal, but it remains floating over his head, and the youth, grasping it, destroys the magic by the sign of the cross.

In the third act Gurnemanz awakes Kundry from a death-like sleep, and is astonished to find her changed. She is penitent and serves the Grail. Parsifal enters from the woods. Gurnemanz recognizes and greets him, after his wanderings in search of the Grail, which have extended over long years. Kundry washes his feet and dries them with her own hair. Parsifal, seeing her so humble, baptizes her with some water from the spring, and the dreadful laugh is taken from her; then she weeps bitterly. Parsifal, conducted to the King, touches his side with the holy spear, and the wound is closed. Old Titurel, brought on the stage in his coffin, revives once more a moment, raising his hands in benediction. The Grail is revealed, pouring a halo of glory over all. Kundry, with her eyes fixed on Parsifal, sinks dead to the ground, while Amfortas and Gurnemanz render homage to their new King.

LES PÊCHEURS DE PERLES

Tragic Grand Opera in three acts by GEORGES BIZET

Text by M. CARRÉ and P. E. PIESTRE

The first production was in Paris, 1863. The action takes place in Ceylon, in the remote past. The cast comprises but four persons.

In the first act pearl fishers of Ceylon are seen celebrating an annual festival on the shore of the sea, near their native village. Seizing this opportunity one of them, Zurga, proposes the selection of a chief to bear authority, and he himself is chosen. Nadir enters, being welcomed by Zurga as a friend of former days. Subsequently the two converse, and Nadir says that he has overcome his early love, although he has not forgotten it. They recall how, during their joint travels, they had once seen a vision of loveliness. The apparition, in the shape of a woman of exquisite beauty, had been seen by them in a Brahman temple, and had been adored by the people as a goddess. This woman had spread out her arms to them both, as if in longing, and hence had sprung jealousy and rivalry. Finally, they remind each other, they had agreed to shun this woman altogether, so as to preserve their own friendship. After the recital they pledge each other anew to a mutual regard that nothing shall destroy.

Then a small vessel is seen approaching the shore. Zurga relates how according to immemorial custom, a fair stranger, charming and wise, is being brought to the village from afar, to dwell in the ancient temple on the summit of a steep rock close by, and how she is to drive away demons and obtain an increase in the catch of the fishermen by her prayers and incantations. When the boat lands, Nourabad, the priest of Brahma, and Leila, closely veiled, leave it and are greeted with shouts of joy by the fisher-folk. Zurga as chief makes her take the oath: never to remove her veil, never to betray her vows of chastity, and never to cease praying both night and day to the all-powerful gods. The maiden makes a solemn pledge to this effect, and Zurga promises that she shall be rewarded for such faithful service by receiving the most flawless and costly pearl of the season, but if she prove fickle she shall die. Upon hearing this terrible alternative, Nadir trembles with foreboding, and the virgin herself—for she is none other than the divine apparition of Zurga's tale—also shivers and her voice breaks. Zurga notes this and points out to the fair unknown that she has her choice. Leila's pride is touched and she elects to stay. The priest and the virgin withdraw to the interior of the temple. Nadir is left alone, but he has recognized Leila, and felt again the violence of his love for her. Although he deplores his insincerity towards his generous friend Zurga, love proves the stronger, and slowly draws him nearer and nearer to her. When the priest at last emerges from the rock-bound temple, Nadir ventures to approach Leila, murmuring to her that he will watch over her, that he still loves her dearly, and that in case of need he will defend her. Leila, rejoicing, confesses her own passion for Nadir and thanks him for his promises of protection.

In the second act Nourabad warns Leila to be careful in keeping her vow, assuring her that in that case she need have no fear. Leila in token of her intended obedience, tells the priest that once when still a child, she was threatened with death for not revealing the hiding place of a fugitive who had implored her aid, but that she did not betray her trust, and that the fugitive out of gratitude gave her a costly necklace as a gift. Later Leila is unable to sleep and suspects that Nadir is near. He reveals his presence by a love song, after which she in her joy tells him about the hidden path that leads to her retreat. He ascends it, and she then out of fear bids him leave her. But Nadir soothes her and then swears he is unable to restrain his passion for her. Since Leila shares his feelings they vow to be true to each other, although fear again becomes uppermost with the maiden, and the risks they both run make her despondent. However, she promises to meet him on the morrow. Nourabad, the priest, suspicious of Leila's faith, enters with a throng of people, and a great thunderstorm breaks, this being interpreted by the superstitious laymen as indicative of the wrath of the gods. Nadir has escaped, but is apprehended and brought back. The people condemn the two lovers to death. But Zurga enters, and drives the people away, saying that it is his own prerogative to punish or forgive. Out of pity for his old friend, he wants to show him leniency and bids them both be gone. But the priest, in a rage, tears off the veil from Leila's face. Zurga then for the first time becomes aware that Leila is the unknown beauty of the temple and that Nadir has been guilty of double treason, wherefore he, too, pronounces the death sentence over him. Leila's pleading for mercy is unavailing. Since the fury of the storm is increasing, the people want to appease the gods by offering the two guilty ones as a sacrifice.

The last act shows Zurga mourning because Nadir, whom he, after all, treasures as his friend from childhood up, is to die ignominiously and by his own doing. Leila seeks an interview with him, exonerates Nadir, and assumes all guilt herself, begging him to save her lover. But Zurga's own passion for Leila is roused by her charms, and he avows his love for her. She scorns him and taunts him for being false to his friend and cruel to them both. Nourabad interrupts, announcing that the hour for expiation has struck. Leila submits and hands to Zurga a necklace, to give to her mother when she is dead. Zurga recognizes the necklace as the one with which he rewarded Leila for having saved his life many years ago, for he was the fugitive whom the child had saved. Meanwhile the people are dancing with joy at the expected death of the two victims. The sacrificial pile is erected, and Leila and Nadir mount it and encourage each other. Zurga suddenly enters, shouting that their village is on fire, and that the rabble had better save what they can. They hastily disperse and run home. Then Zurga owns that he himself has been the incendiary and commands the lovers to flee together. They do so. But Nourabad has overheard Zurga's words, denounces him to the people and forces him to ascend the funeral pyre.

PELLÉAS AND MÉLISANDE

Opera in four acts by CLAUDE DEBUSSY

The libretto of Pelléas and Mélisande, for which Claude Debussy wrote the music, is taken from the play of that name, by Maurice Maeterlinck, the famous Belgian dramatist and mystic.

The first scene of the first act discovers Mélisande sitting on the edge of a fountain, weeping. Prince Golaud, the eldest grandson of old King Arkel, of Allemond, enters and sees her. He has been hunting in the forest and has lost his way. Seeing Mélisande, he asks her why she is there alone and weeping. She tells him not to touch her. He questions her as to who she is and where she comes from. She tells him that her name is Mélisande, and that she has been cruelly treated. She will not tell him anything now. The bright thing shining at the bottom of the water is the crown some one gave her, which she let fall when crying; but she does not wish Golaud to recover it for her. If he does she says she will throw herself in its place. She asks him why he came there, and he tells her he lost his way following a boar. He asks her to go with him, and when she wants to know where he is going, he replies he does not know; he has lost his way. They depart together.

The second scene of the same act is a room in the castle, in which are discovered Geneviève, mother of Golaud and Pelléas, and Arkel, the King of Allemond. Geneviève reads to Arkel a letter from Golaud to Pelléas, in which Golaud tells his brother that he has wedded

Mélisande. He is afraid that the step he has taken might not be pleasing to his grandfather, and asks Pelléas to prepare his return for him. If the king consents to receive Mélisande, then Pelléas shall place a lighted lamp in the tower that looks on the sea, so that he may see it from his ship. If there is no light, he will know his grandfather disapproves, and will sail on, never to return. Arkel will say nothing, but he feels that Golaud, since the death of his wife, has been sad in being alone. It is destiny, therefore, and he will not interfere. Let it, then, be as Golaud wishes. Pelléas enters and tells Arkel that he has just received a letter from his friend Marcellus, who is about to die, and who has written calling on him to see him. Arkel asks Pelléas to wait awhile, and leaves. Geneviève warns Pelléas to be careful to light the lamp in the tower.

The third scene shows the front of the castle. Geneviève and Mélisande enter. Mélisande complains of the gloom of the gardens and the forests about the castle. She hears a noise, and Geneviève tells her it is Pelléas. Pelléas enters to show Mélisande the way. He offers his support, for the way is steep and dark.

The first scene of the second act shows Pelléas and Mélisande standing by a fountain in the park of the castle. Mélisande tries to reach the water and fails to do so; her hair, however, falls down and gets wet, for it it very long. She plays with her wedding ring, tossing it in the air and catching it again. Pelléas warns her to take care, begging her not to throw it so high. An exclamation from Mélisande follows, and the ring falls, sinking out of sight into the water. She is greatly distressed at the mishap, and asks: "What shall we say to Golaud if he asks where it is?" "The truth, the truth, the truth!" cries Pelléas.

The second scene is an apartment in the castle, in which Golaud is seen lying sick on his bed, with Mélisande waiting on him at the head. At the very moment when Mélisande's wedding ring had fallen into the water Golaud's horse had run away with him and Golaud was dashed against a tree. Tenderly Mélisande nurses him, but he begs her not to tire herself. She bursts into tears, and Golaud asking her the reason for her weeping, she tells him that she is sick here, that she is not happy. Golaud questions Mélisande as to a reason for her unhappiness. "Is it Pelléas, perhaps?" he asks. She thinks Pelléas does not like her; but Golaud advises her not to mind him. Caressing her hand, he notices that she no longer wears her wedding ring. He asks her where it is. She says it slipped off her finger while she was looking for shells for little Yniold (Golaud's son) and fell into the sea. The tide coming in, she had to go before she could find it again.

Golaud tells her he would sooner have lost all he has than lose this ring. She must go that night and find it; she must take Pelléas with her. She leaves, weeping.

In the third scene of this second act Pelléas and Mélisande are seen before the entrance to the grotto. Pelléas begs Mélisande to wait until the moon appears to light the place. She must be able, he says, to describe the place if Golaud questions her. The moon, coming out from behind a bank of clouds, lights up the entrance and they see three old blind men with white hair, seated side by side, supporting each other and asleep against a boulder. Mélisande is greatly afraid and cries out, begging Pelléas to come away. Pelléas fears that the old blind men presage a famine in the land. The two leave.

The first scene of the third act discovers Mélisande at a window of one of the towers of the castle combing her hair, preparatory to arranging it for the night. A watchman passes under a window of the tower. She is singing, "My long hair hangs to the base of the tower." Pelléas comes in and, seeing her, calls out to her. He asks her to lean forward that he may see her loosened hair and to kiss her hand before he departs. She will not give him her hand unless he promises to stay. In her endeavors to give him her hand she leans so far forward that her hair falls down and covers him. An ecstasy of love seizes Pelléas, and Mélisande herself is filled with the same emotion. Pelléas, in spite of her remonstrances, will not release her. While they are thus bound to each other two doves come out of the tower and fly about them. Mélisande begs Pelléas to let her lift her head, for she hears footsteps approaching. Just then Golaud enters. He tells Mélisande not to lean that way out of the window. It is late, he says, and they must not play thus in the dark. "You are two children," he says, laughing nervously. And Golaud goes out with Pelléas.

The second scene shows the vaults of the castle. Golaud enters, leading Pelléas to the edge of a rock overlooking a stagnant lake. This is the water of which Golaud had spoken to his brother. "Do you see the abyss?" he asks Pelléas. Pelléas begs that they go away. They leave in silence.

The third scene is the outside of the vaults. Pelléas is delighted to find himself once more breathing the pure air. He espies Mélisande and Geneviève at a window of the tower. Golaud is dispirited, and tells Pelléas that he heard of what took place between him and Mélisande last night. He knows it was only a child's game they were playing, but he says it must not be repeated. Mélisande is delicate of health, and the least emotion might bring about a misfortune. He has noticed before that there was something between them, and he asks Pelléas to avoid her as much as possible.

The fourth scene shows the castle tower and the window of Mélisande's room. Golaud enters, leading his little child Yniold. He questions him as to the doings of Pelléas and Mélisande, and the child tries to shield them. He lifts him to Mélisande's window, which is lighted up, so that he might find out what is going on in the room. The child tells him he sees Mélisande and Pelléas in the room. When he asks him what they are doing he tells him they are standing motionless, looking at the light. Yniold begs his father to let him down, as he is afraid he is going to cry out. They leave together.

The first scene in the fourth act is a passageway in the castle. Pelléas is begging Mélisande to meet him at the fountain in the park, for this last time before he goes away. They separate and go out on hearing voices talking behind the door. Arkel comes in, accompanied by Mélisande. He sympathizes with her on her joyless life in the castle, telling her how he has pitied her these past months. Golaud enters, enraged. Arkel notices some blood on his forehead, but Golaud explains it away. Mélisande offers to wipe it off, but he pushes her away, demanding his sword. He is not going to kill her, he says, but hints darkly at danger for her. In a fit of maddened rage, he seizes her by the hair, dragging her hither and thither. Arkel runs forward to interfere, when Golaud suddenly ceases his rage, and saying "I shall await chance," goes out.

The second scene is the terrace shrouded in gloom. Yniold is trying to lift a rock in order to find his golden ball. Bleating of sheep is heard in the distance, and the boy asks a shepherd, who is not seen, why the sheep no longer speak. The voice of the shepherd answers: "Because it is not the way to the stable." The child becomes afraid of the dark, and goes out.

In the third scene Pelléas is waiting in the park at the fountain for the arrival of Mélisande. She comes late, but explains that Golaud had a bad dream and that her gown was torn by being caught on the nails of the gate. Pelléas, embracing her, confesses his love, and she tells him that she loves him, too. The mutual confession causes both of them to be overcome alternately with joy and fear. Mélisande hears a noise, the crackling of dead leaves, she says. Pelléas only hears the beating of her heart in the darkness. By the light of the moon, however, they see Golaud. Realizing that they are lost, they throw themselves into each other's arms as Golaud rushes forward with drawn sword and strikes his brother with it on the head. Mélisande flies, terror-stricken, with Golaud pursuing her through the wood in silence.

The fifth act consists of but one scene. It is an apartment in the castle, in which Mélisande is lying extended on her bed. Arkel, Golaud, and the physician are in the room also. The physician is assuring them that Mélisande cannot die from the little wound she has received, and begs them not to grieve. Mélisande has been ill for weeks, but she now partly recovers consciousness. Golaud, dragging himself toward the bed, calls on her by name. She answers him that she barely recognizes him. Golaud begs Arkel and the physician to leave him alone with his wife. When they have gone he begs Mélisande for forgiveness; but he must know the truth. Did she love Pelléas? "Yes," she answers. Has she been guilty with him? He will have the truth. She seems not to understand him. Seeing Arkel and the physician at the door he tells them they can come in, for she is already far from them. He believes he has killed her. Mélisande becomes conscious again, but has not the strength to do what Arkel asks of her. The room is then filled, one by one, with the maid servants of the castle, who range themselves in silence by the walls and wait. All realize that Mélisande is dying, and on Arkel's request that all speak low, the servants fall suddenly on their knees. Arkel asks what is the matter; the physician approaches the bed and feels the body. "They are right," he says. Mélisande was dead.

PETER IBBETSON

Lyric Drama in three acts from the novel of GEORGE DU MAURIER, by DEEMS TAYLOR

Libretto by CONSTANCE COLLIER and DEEMS TAYLOR

This opera, first produced at the Metropolitan Opera House, New York, on February 7, 1931, is the only American grand opera which has shown sufficient vitality to remain in the regular repertory for more than two seasons. While this is partly due no doubt to the fact that the story is magnificently suited to the stage, Deems Taylor has none the less written music which is dramatically suitable, and has proved himself in it the first American composer who both knows the requirements of the lyric stage, and who has been able to project them in his score.

Peter Ibbetson incurs the enmity of his uncle, Colonel Ibbetson, by inadvertently revealing the fact that a supposedly original poem of the Colonel's is a plagiarism. After the quarrel, which occurs at Mrs. Deane's ball, Mrs. Deane tries to put Peter at his ease and to her he reveals the story of his early life in Paris with his French father, Pasquier, his English mother, and Mimsie Seraskier, his playmate, whom he has always loved, but whom he thinks is dead. Mrs. Deane's best friend, Mary, Duchess of Towers, arrives and sees Peter. She says he reminds her of a little French boy, Gogo Pasquier, whom she once knew, and she is disappointed when Mrs. Deane tells her his name is Ibbetson. Peter watches her, fascinated, but is too shy to meet her.

In Paris Peter again sees the Duchess of Towers driving by the window of his inn, and thinking of her he falls asleep. In his dream he returns to his childhood, sees his parents, his friends, and Mimsie. The Duchess stands beside him and warns him that he mustn't speak to the dream people, or his dream will vanish. Peter wakes just as the Duchess enters the inn, having taken refuge from a storm. She discovers that he is Gogo Pasquier. He tells her his dream, and to his astonishment she completes it. They then realize that their spirits have really met in the dream. She tells him that as she is not free they must never meet again, not even in a dream.

Peter arrives back in London and finds a letter in which Colonel Ibbetson has written that Peter is his natural son. Peter confronts the Colonel, and when the latter says the letter is true, Peter hits him with a cane and kills him. Peter is condemned to death, but his sentence is commuted to life imprisonment through Mrs. Deane's efforts. When he says he would rather die than pass his days in prison, Mrs. Deane tells him she has a message to him from Mary to "sleep and dream true." Peter falls asleep and dreams. In his dream he goes back to his youth again. All those he has loved are with him, including Mary, who tells him that every night when he is asleep she will come to him, and that they will live as one.

Thirty years later Peter lies dying in his cell in Newgate Prison. Mrs. Deane comes to him to tell him that Mary is dead, but he already knows it, as in his dream of the night before for the first time in thirty years she wasn't there. Peter dies. The back wall of the cell vanishes and in its place is his childhood home in France.

Mary appears and stretches out her arms to him. From the dead body on the cot rises young Peter Ibbetson. He goes to Mary and they stand enfolded in each other's arms.

By permission of Deems Taylor.

PETROUCHKA

A Ballet-burlesque by IGOR STRAVINSKY

First production, Petrograd, 1912.

In a public square of Petrograd, a magician is giving his puppet show before a motley crowd. He sets his little ballerina with her two companions a-dancing. These companions are the romantic Petrouchka and the sensual Moor. A fierce quarrel breaks out between these two suitors to her favor. Petrouchka is overpowered by the gigantic Moor and is thrust into a dark dungeon, there to bemoan his ill-luck in failing to captivate the ballerina and in missing even his opportunity to effect an escape. He is unable to win sympathy for his hard fate until finally the Moor kills him outright. This violent episode causes consternation among the spectators, until the magician shows the audience that what lies stark and stiff on the ground is not a man but merely a rag-doll.

PHILÉMON AND BAUCIS

Opera in two acts by CHARLES GOUNOD

Text by JULES BARBIER and MICHEL CARRÉ

This is a truly delightful musical composition, and though unpretending and not on the level with Gounod's Margaretha, it does not deserve to be forgotten.

The libretto is founded on the well-known legend. In the first act Jupiter comes to Philémon's hut, accompanied by Vulcan, to seek refuge from a storm which the god himself has caused. He has come to earth to verify Mercury's tale of the people's badness, and finding the news only too true, besides being uncourteously received by the people around, he is glad to meet with a kindly welcome at Philémon's door.

This worthy old man lives in poverty, but in perfect content with his wife Baucis, to whom he has been united in bonds of love for sixty long years. Jupiter, seeing at once that the old couple form an exception to the evil rule, resolves to spare them, and to punish only the bad folks. The gods partake of the kind people's simple meal, and, Jupiter, changing the milk into wine, is recognized by Baucis, who is much awed by the discovery. But Jupiter reassures her and promises to grant her only wish, which is to be young again with her husband, and to live the same life. The god sends them to sleep, and then begins the intermezzo.

Phrygians are seen reposing after a festival, bacchants rush in and the wild orgies begin afresh. The divine is mocked and pleasure praised as the only god. Vulcan comes, sent by Jupiter to warn them, but as they only laugh at him, mocking Olympus and the gods, Jupiter himself appears to punish the sinners. An awful tempest arises, sending everything to rack and ruin.

In the second act Philémon's hut is changed into a palace; he awakes to find himself and his wife young again. Jupiter, seeing Baucis's beauty, orders Vulcan to keep Philémon apart while he courts her. Baucis, though determined to remain faithful to her Philémon, feels nevertheless flattered at the god's condescension, and dares not refuse him a kiss. Philémon, appearing on the threshold, sees it, and violently reproaches her and his guest, and though Baucis suggests who the latter is, the husband does not feel in the least inclined to share his wife's love even with a god. The first quarrel takes place between the couple, and Vulcan, hearing it, consoles himself with the reflection that he is not the only one to whom a fickle wife causes sorrow. Philémon bitterly curses Jupiter's gift; he wishes his wrinkles back, and with them his peace of mind. Throwing down Jupiter's statue, he leaves his wife to the god. Baucis, replacing the image, which happily is made of bronze, sorely repents her behavior toward her beloved husband. Jupiter finds her weeping, and praying that the gods may turn their wrath upon herself alone. The god promises to pardon both if she is willing to listen to his love. She agrees to the bargain on one condition, namely, that Jupiter shall grant her a favor. He consents, and she entreats him to make her old again. Philémon, listening behind the door, rushes forward to embrace the true wife and joins his entreaties to hers. Jupiter, seeing himself caught, would fain be angry, but their love conquers his wrath. He does not recall his gift, but, giving them his benediction, he promises never more to cross their happiness.

THE PIPE OF DESIRE

Opera in one act by FREDERICK S. CONVERSE

The music, by Frederick S. Converse, to George Edward Barton's dramatic poem, was first played in New York during the opera season of 1909-10, at the Metropolitan Opera House. It is, perhaps, a misnomer to call the work an opera. It is not an opera, in the usual meaning of that word. It is rather a dramatic cantata for the stage. But, whether an opera or cantata, the work is the production of a musical poet, and its analysis deserves a place in this volume, if only for the fact that it is the first opera by an American produced for the first time in America.

The entire opera consists of but one act, the scene of which is laid in an imaginary sylvan place during the first day of Spring. When the curtain rises a level grass-covered place is discovered, backed by a boulder and the trees of an old forest. A dozen elves are busily and merrily engaged in their work. One of them is scattering seeds to the wind, others are removing dead leaves from flowers and breathing on them to melt the frost which has covered them. As they work they sing of the awakening of Nature from her winter's sleep, of the sap rising in the stems of growing things, and of the sun's coming to free them from the prison of frost. In the midst of their singing the voice of Iolan, a peasant, is heard carolling in the distance, and growing more and more distinct as he approaches. The elves know him, and plan to play a trick upon him and tease him. The sylphs suggest that they cheer him on his way or dance to him. The gnomes and undines are surprised that it should be suggested they should show themselves to a man, but the others can see no harm in it. So they call to him. As they call the Old One enters and upbraids the elves for their madness in desiring to show themselves to a man. Iolan demands to know now who is calling, and as he enters the elves hide behind the boulder. Iolan imagines himself to be dreaming, he feels so full of joy. He catches sight of the elves as they emerge from behind the trees, and knows they are the wood-folk.

The elves dance round him and promise to protect his vine and roof and grant joy to all who trust in their good-will. Iolan shows them money he has earned, and tells them he is to wed Naoia to-morrow. He bids them come to the feast. The Old One tells him it is forbidden to show themselves to man. No good can come of it. When Iolan asks to know who this gloomy person is, he is informed, with great reverence, that he is the mightiest of them all—the Old One. Iolan asks to see his crown and sceptre and purse of gold. The Old One tells him the ten thousand years of life is his crown, the earth itself his purse of gold, and his sceptre is the Pipe which hangs round his neck. Iolan jests at the Pipe; his goat-horn could be heard ten times as far. He is warned not to mock at the Pipe. A dance is called for by the third elf, and the cry is taken up by the rest in a semi-chorus.

The Old One is asked to play for them, but he refuses. It is madness. They press him to play, and finally he consents, though he tells them it is an evil hour in which he plays. He plays a weird tune. Gnomes, sylphs, undines, and salamanders come out as he plays. The sky becomes overcast, but in a soft green light which suffuses the place the undines dance their mad dance, Iolan watching the while, sitting on a log, highly amused. As the elves dance, they sing their Spring Song, which ends in a burst of victorious joy. When dance and song are ended most of the elves disappear in the woods, leaving behind the Old One and a few of his companions.

The fourth elf asks Iolan if he now believes in the power of the Pipe, but Iolan thinks any other would have done just as well for those who wished to dance. The elf retorts by saying that it would make him, also, dance. Iolan answers that no power on earth could make him dance, except with his bride. The elves feel their Pipe to be insulted, and ask the Old One to make him dance. The Old One would prefer not to do this, but, being urged by the elves, he sadly accedes, Iolan protesting that he will not dance.

The Old One plays, and Iolan, unable to resist dancing, begs him to stop playing. The elves laugh and shout at him to dance. Iolan is compelled to dance, and in dancing curses the Pipe. He snatches the Pipe from the hands of the Old One and breaks the cord which holds it. A cry of terror from the elves, and all are silent. When Iolan now tells the Old One that his feet must now win back the sceptre, because he is going to play on it and make him dance, the Old One begs him not to blow on the Pipe. They will give him anything he may want—power, gold, or wine; but let him not play on the Pipe. Iolan jeers at him to think that he is afraid. The Old One tells him then that it is the Pipe God gave to Lilith, who played it to Adam in Eden, but since woman broke its charm, it is now played by the elves that its music may be heard by those who walk in solitude and are restlessly searching. Iolan calls this a tale to tell to children. The elves warn him not to play, and the Old One now pronounces the curse and tells Iolan that the mortal who plays the Pipe without knowledge of its secret will die when he has understood it.

Iolan now puts the Pipe to his mouth and blows a harsh, discordant note. As the sound issues from the Pipe the Sun becomes clouded over, the elves vanish with a startled cry. The Old One also is about to run away, but Iolan catches him and prevents him going off by placing a stone on his cloak so that he cannot free himself. Iolan blows again on the Pipe, but seems unable to master it. If only he could play the music that is now rising up in his soul, he cries. He begins once again, and this time beautiful music issues from it, which he repeats. He drops the Pipe, and his eyes become fixed, as if looking at a vision before him. He speaks to himself, and says the music was the music he heard within his soul. The vision that he is seeing, he says, pictures the utmost of his desires. He is wealthy, has horses, goats, and wine. His harvesters are singing at their work. He sees his house and his children playing at the door. His wife, Naoia, is coming to him through the roses. He calls on her passionately to leave everything and come to him. With the last note of his call the sun shines again, and the Old One recovers his Pipe and frees himself from the stone.

As Iolan turns to go the Old One bids him stay and listen to what he has to say. The Pipe, the Old One tells him, when he played it sounded but what he, Iolan, desired; but if he will listen again he will see the ill he had wrought. The Old One plays, and at the first note the vision he before saw comes again to Iolan. Naoia now enters, her clothing in rags and her face bleeding.

She tells him she has come to his call. Iolan, seeing her thus, bemoans his folly. He who loved her so had, through his own heedlessness, brought her misfortune. Had he but known, he would have spared her all the agony she tells him she has endured. He will never leave her more. She becomes delirious and talks of being together with him and their son, little Iolan. They exchange beautifully expressed wishes to each other, and Naoia, begging him to hold her closer, closer, dies.

Iolan is broken from grief, and almost bereft of his reason. He curses and invokes God, who has given him gold, only to turn it into lead. The Old One tells him God's laws are eternal and may not be disobeyed with impunity. If man has his will, man must pay the penalty.

The elves now come out and wail because, intending to give Iolan joy, they brought only grief on him. The Old One now takes the Pipe and plays on it the Song of Autumn. Iolan listens, and the notes send his soul back to his loved one. The Pipe soothes him to sleep, and he sinks down by the body of Naoia and dies in a burst of glad music. The elves come out and say that they who die for love have accomplished their life. Nothing is wasted.

THE PIPER OF HAMELN

Opera in five acts by VICTOR NESSLER

Text by FR. HOFMANN from JULIUS WOLFF'S legend of the same name

Without any preliminary introduction to the musical world, Nessler wrote this opera and at once became not only known, but a universal favorite; so much so that there is scarcely a theatre in Germany in which this work of his is not now given.

The subject of the libretto is a most favorable one, like that of Nessler's later composition, The Trumpeter of Saekkingen, the principal personage, Singuf, being particularly well suited for a first-rate stage hero.

Then Wolff's poetical songs are music in themselves, and it was therefore not difficult to work out interesting melodies, of which, as a matter of fact, we find many in this opera.

The scene of the following events is the old town of Hameln on the Weser in the year 1284. The citizens are assembled in council as to how the rat-plague of the town is to be got rid of. No one is able to suggest a remedy, when suddenly the clerk of the senate, Ethelerus, announces a stranger, who offers to destroy all the rats and mice in the place, solely by the might of his pipe. Hunold Singuf, a wandering Bohemian, enters and repeats his offer, asking one hundred marks in silver as his reward, and forbidding anybody to listen or to be present while he works his charm.

The senators comply with his request, promising him in addition a drink from the town-cellar when the last rat shall have disappeared, which is to be when the moon is full.

In the following scene the Burgomaster's daughter, Regina, is with her old cousin, Dorothea. She expects her bridegroom, the architect of the town and the son of the chief magistrate, Heribert Sunneborn, who has just returned home from a long stay abroad. While the lovers greet each other, Ethelerus, who has wooed Regina in vain, stands aside greatly mortified.

The second act opens in an inn, where Hunold makes the people dance and sing to his wonderful melodies. There he first sees the maid who has appeared to him in his dreams. She is Gertrud, a fishermaiden, and "to look is to love"—they are attracted to each other as by a magic spell. Wulf, the smith, who loves Gertrud, sees it with distrust, but Hunold begins to sing his finest songs. In the evening the lovers meet before Gertrud's hut, and, full of anxious forebodings, she tries to turn him from his designs, and is only half quieted when he assures her that no fiendish craft is at work, and that he will do it for the last time.

In the third act Ethelerus holds council with magister Rhynperg as to the means by which they can best succeed in teasing and provoking the proud Sunneborn. Hunold enters and, agreeable to an invitation of theirs, sits down to drink a bottle of wine. They make him drink and sing a good deal, and he boasts of being able to make the maidens all fall in love with him, if he chooses. Rhynperg suggests that he must omit the Burgomaster's daughter, Regina, and he succeeds in making Hunold accept a wager that he will obtain a kiss from her before his departure.

The following night Hunold accomplishes the exorcism of the rats, which may be seen running toward him from every part of the town and precipitating themselves into the river. Unhappily, Wulf, standing in a recess, has seen and heard all and, coming forward to threaten Hunold, the latter hurls his dagger after him, upon which Wulf takes flight.

In the fourth act the whole town is assembled to rejoice in its deliverance from the awful plague, but when Hunold asks for his reward the Burgomaster tells him that a so-called rat-king, a beast with five heads, has been seen in his (the Burgomaster's) cellar, to which complaint Hunold replies that it is the smith's fault, who listened against his express prohibition. He promises to destroy the rat-king on the same day, and once more claims his due, together with the promised parting gift, which he begs to be, not a drink of wine, but a kiss from Regina's lips. Of course everybody is astounded at his insolence, and the angry Burgomaster bids him leave the town at once, without his money. But Hunold, nothing daunted, begins to sing so beautifully that the hearts of all the women yearn toward him; he continues still more passionately, addressing himself directly to Regina, and never stops till the maiden, carried away by a passion unconquerable, offers her lips for a kiss, swearing to be his own forever. A great tumult arises and Hunold is taken to prison, notwithstanding the remonstrances of Ethelerus, who bitterly repents having had anything to do with Rhynperg's bad joke.

The fifth act takes us to the banks of the Weser, where Gertrud sits in despair. She deems herself betrayed by Hunold, but resolves, nevertheless, to save his life.

Hunold is brought before the judges and condemned to be burnt alive as a sorcerer, when Gertrud steps forth, claiming his life. In pursuance of an old privilege,

Hunold is free when a maid of the town claims him, but he is banished from the country and Gertrud with him.

Hunold promises never to return, but Gertrud throws herself into the river.

Then Hunold swears to avenge the death of his bride. While the citizens are in church he lures away their children by playing on his pipe; all follow him, both great and small. When he has led them safely over the bridge, he calls the people from church. All gather on the banks of the stream, but they are only just in time to see the bridge fall into the river, while the mountain opposite opens, swallowing up Hunold and the children for ever.

PIQUE-DAME

Opera in three acts by PETER TSCHAIKOWSKY

Libretto by MODESTE TSCHAIKOWSKY after PUSHKIN'S story

The first performance took place at St. Petersburg in 1890. The action takes place in eighteenth century Petrograd.

Act I. Herman, a penniless lieutenant in the Hussars and an inveterate gambler, loves Lisa, granddaughter of an old Countess who was once the belle of St. Petersburg and is famous in her old age as the luckiest of card players. It is rumored that the Countess, nicknamed the Queen of Spades, owes her success at the gaming tables to a secret combination of three cards. This secret she gained from her lover who warned her that she would die when a third lover demanded the combination.

Although Lisa returns the love of the young lieutenant, she becomes engaged to Prince Yeletsky. Herman's only hope is to win enough gold at cards to obtain Lisa's hand in marriage.

Act II. There is a gorgeous masked ball in progress. The Prince is alarmed at Lisa's melancholy which cannot be dispelled by the gaiety around her. She sends Herman a note, asking him to meet her in the gardens. There she gives him the key to her rooms and tells him to come the next day. He declares that he will not be able to wait and gains her consent to visit her that evening after the masquerade. He has determined to wrest the old Countess' secret from her in order to win Lisa.

Therefore, he hides in the grandmother's room and when she enters, tired from the ball, and falls asleep, he rushes out and demands the secret. She is too frightened to speak, so he draws his revolver. She dies of fear. Lisa, entering then, realizes that Herman came to get the secret and not for love of her, and she indignantly sends him away.

Act III. Herman is brooding over the death of the Countess when a note arrives from Lisa, asking him to meet her on the Winter Canal. At the same moment the ghost of the old Countess appears and whispers the secret combination to him. Wild with joy he hastens to Lisa but she is dismayed at the thought of using the knowledge gained in so ghastly a fashion. She realizes that he is insane and when he leaves her to go to the gaming tables, she drowns herself in the Neva.

Herman plays against Prince Yeletsky and wins twice by the secret combination. He stakes everything on the third trial—but he turns up, not the expected card, but the queen of spades! At the same instance the spectre of the Countess, smiling in malicious triumph, appears across the table from him. Mad with disappointment and terror, Herman stabs himself.

THE POACHER

or

"THE VOICE OF NATURE"

by LORTZING

Text after a comedy by KOTZEBUE

The music of this opera is so fresh, so full of gayety and of charming melodies, that it might be compared with Lortzing's Czar and Zimmermann, if only the text were as well done. Unhappily, it lacks all the advantages which characterize the opera just named, as it is frivolous, without possessing the grace and "esprit" which distinguished French composition of a similar kind.

Nevertheless the good music prevails over the bad text, and the opera holds its own with success in every German theatre.

The contents of the libretto are as follows:

A schoolmaster, Baculus by name, has had the misfortune unintentionally to shoot a roe-buck belonging to the forest of his master, Count of Eberbach. Baculus, who is on the eve of his wedding with a young girl named Gretchen, is much afraid when the consequences of his unlucky shot show themselves in the shape of a summons to the castle, where he is looked on as a poacher, and is in danger of losing his position. His bride offers to entreat the Count to pardon him, but the jealous old schoolmaster will not allow it. In this embarrassing position the Baroness Freimann, a young widow, appears, disguised in the suit of a student, and accompanied by her chambermaid Nanette, who is dressed as her famulus or valet. Hearing of the schoolmaster's misfortune, she proposes to put on Gretchen's clothes and to crave the Count's pardon under the bride's name. Baculus gladly accepts the student's proposal and accompanies him to the castle. Everybody is charmed by the graces and naïveté of the country girl. The Count tries to make love to her, while Baron Kronthal, who is present, is so much enamored that he thinks of marrying her despite her low birth. Kronthal is the Countess of Eberbach's brother, but she does not know him as such, though she feels herself greatly attracted by him. In order to save the girl from persecution the Countess takes her with her into her room. Meanwhile the Count offers the sum of 5,000 thalers to Baculus for the renunciation of his bride. The silly schoolmaster accepts the offer, thinking that the Count wishes to win the real Gretchen. By waking the latter's vanity he succeeds in turning her affection to the Count, but great is his perplexity when the Count rejects his bride and scornfully asks for the other Gretchen. Baculus avows at last that the latter is a disguised student. Baron Kronthal, full of wrath, asks for satisfaction, the student having passed the night in his sister's room. On this occasion the others for the first time hear that the Countess is the Baron's sister. He demands an explanation, and then it is discovered that the student is the Baroness Freimann, sister of the Count of Eberbach. Everybody is content, for the Count, who was detected in the act of kissing the country girl, declares that with him it was the voice of nature that spoke, and the Countess, to whom he now presents Kronthal as her brother, makes a like statement. The unhappy Baculus receives full pardon from the Count, on condition that he will henceforth teach the children of the village instead of shooting game.

THE POSTILION OF LONGJUMEAU

Comic Opera in three acts by ADOLPHE ADAM

Text by LEUVEN and BRUNSWICK

This charming little opera is well worthy of being named among the best of its kind, both on account of its delightful music and because the text is so entertaining and funny as entirely to captivate the hearer's interest.

The whole opera is essentially French in the best sense of the word, and we scarce can find a more graceful and witty composition. Its subject, written originally in good French verse, is as follows:

Chapelou, stage-driver at Longjumeau, is about to celebrate his marriage with the young hostess of the post-house, Madeleine. The wedding has taken place, and the young bride is led away by her friends, according to an old custom, while her bridegroom is held back by his comrades, who compel him to sing. He begins the romance of a young postilion who had the luck to be carried away by a Princess, having touched her heart by his beautiful playing on the cornet. Chapelou has such a fine voice that the Superintendent of the Grand Opera at Paris, the Marquis de Corcy, who hears him, is enchanted, and, being in search of a good tenor, succeeds in winning over Chapelou, who consents to leave his young wife in order to follow the Marquis's call to glory and fortune. He begs his friend Bijou, a smith, to console Madeleine, by telling her that he will soon return to her. While Madeleine calls for him in tenderest accents, he drives away with his protectors, and

Bijou delivers his message, determined to try his fortune in a similar way. The desperate Madeleine resolves to fly from the unhappy spot where everything recalls to her her faithless husband.

In the second act we find Madeleine under the assumed name of Madame de Latour. She has inherited a fortune from an old aunt, and makes her appearance in Paris as a rich and noble lady, with the intention of punishing her husband, whom she, however, still loves. During the six years that have passed since their wedding day Chapelou has won his laurels under the name of St. Phar, and is now the first tenor of the Grand Opera and everybody's spoiled favorite. Bijou is with him as leader of the chorus, and is called Alcindor. We presently witness a comical rehearsal in which the principal singers are determined to do as badly as possible. They all seem hoarse, and, instead of singing, produce the most lamentable sounds. The Marquis de Corcy is desperate, having promised this representation to Mme. Latour, at whose country seat near Fontainebleau he is at present staying. As soon as St. Phar hears the name of his lady, his hoarseness is gone, and all sing their best. We gather from this scene that Mme. Latour has succeeded in enthralling St. Phar; he has an interview with her, and, won by his protestations of love, she consents to marry him.

St. Phar, not wishing to commit bigamy, begs his friend Bijou to perform the marriage ceremony in a priest's garb; but Mme. Latour locks him in her room, along with Bourdon, the second leader of the chorus, while a real priest unites the pair for the second time.

St. Phar enters the room in high spirits, when his companions, beside themselves with fear, tell him that he has committed bigamy. While they are in mortal terror of being hanged, Mme. Latour enters in her former shape as Madeleine, and, blowing out the candle, torments St. Phar, assuming now the voice of Mme. Latour, now that of Madeleine. After having sent her fickle husband into an abyss of unhappiness and fear, the Marquis de Corcy, who had himself hoped to wed the charming widow, appears with the police to imprison the luckless St. Phar, who already considers himself as good as hanged, and in imagination sees his first wife, Madeleine, rejoicing over his punishment. But he has been made to suffer enough, and at the last moment Madeleine explains everything, and Chapelou obtains her pardon.

PRECIOSA

Music by CARL MARIA VON WEBER, **libretto by** ALEXANDER WOLF

Francesco's son, Alonzo, loves Preciosa a Gypsy girl, and to win her joins the gypsies. Eugenio, the son of Francesco's friend, Azevado, wants to get Preciosa to dance for his father's silver wedding, and rouses Alonzo's jealousy. Alonzo is thrown into prison. Azevedo's wife, Clara, tells Preciosa she will try to gain Alfonso's liberty. Francesco arrives and pardons his son, Preciosa giving him up. Clara entreats her husband to buy Preciosa as she is sure she is a stolen child. The chief of the gypsies confesses that Preciosa is Clara's own daughter, who was stolen many years before and was believed drowned. Because of Preciosa's plea the gypsies are pardoned and Preciosa marries Alonzo.

PRINCE IGOR

Opera in a prologue and four acts by A. P. BORODIN

First produced in Petrograd in 1890.

The text is based on an ancient Russian national epic, called "The Epic of the Army of Igor," and the scene is laid in Southern Russia, in the twelfth century. The text is alive with Russian sentiment, and the plot is colorful and characteristic.

The prologue shows a public square of Poutivle, where the populace are assembled to bid God-speed to the departing troops. Prince Igor is going to war against an invading Mongolian foe, the Polovtsi and enters the square with great pomp, followed by his warriors and nobles, all streaming out of the cathedral. But of a sudden the sky darkens and the sun is eclipsed. The people are dismayed, while the nobles, especially Galitsky, his brother-in-law, and Vladimir, his son, regard it as an evil omen. They try to hold Prince Igor back from the expedition, but he is unafraid and orders a review of his army before starting. Two gamblers, Eroshka and Scoula, do their best to stir up a mutiny. Igor sends for the women to bid them farewell, and his wife, Jaroslavna, wants him to stay, but he gently reminds her that it is his duty as a ruler to go. He commends her to the care of Galitsky, who accepts the charge.

Prince Galitsky is seen at work in the first act trying to wean away the people from their loyalty to Igor by lavish hospitality and gifts. In return Galitsky is flattered by the whole court. To the people he often points out the difference between himself and his brother-in-law, the latter merely carrying on bloody and unprofitable war and he himself cherishing the delights of peace. A young girl has been abducted for Galitsky by the scoundrel Eroshka, and a petition is presented by a delegation of maidens to restore her to her family, but Galitsky laughs them to scorn. The fickle people offer him the crown in place of the absent Igor, and proclaim him ruler. Meanwhile Jaroslava mourns her husband's absence. She hears from a deputation of Galitsky's vile deeds, and when the latter enters she threatens him with a complaint on Igor's return, but her brother mocks her, saying that Igor is dead and he himself, master. After Galitsky leaves, news comes to Jaroslavna that her husband has lost a battle and been taken captive by the enemy. A delegation of nobles offer to defend the city against the pagan assaults of the Polovtsi, but while they are boasting flames proclaim that the city has been surprised and taken.

In the second act Prince Igor and his son Vladimir are in the camp of the Polovtsi as prisoners of war, and the son has fallen in love with Khan Kontchak's handsome daughter. A chorus of young girls sing of the joys of love, and the chief's daughter joins them. As the imprisoned Russians pass by, the girls offer them food and drink. Vladimir serenades the maiden who converses with him. Finally they confess their mutual love. Ovlour, a Polovtsian convert to Christianity, favors Vladimir and offers him the means of flight from camp. But Igor scouts the idea. Kontchak himself tries to reconcile his vanquished foe, being willing to liberate him, merely on condition of abandoning any revengeful war and becoming his friend and ally. Igor refuses. There is dancing and singing, both by men and maidens.

The third act opens with the return of the other khan, Gzak, who has taken Poutivle and now brings with him many prisoners. Tales are told by the victors which grieve the souls of the Russian prisoners at the camp, by showing the destruction of their old home. Igor and his son Vladimir lament the misfortunes of their country, and the former becomes convinced that his duty lies in escaping from prison and rallying all for the defense of home. In fleeing Igor reaches Poutivle, but Vladimir, his son, is caught and owes his life only to the intervention of Kontchak's daughter.

Act four opens with Igor's return to Poutivle, and the reunion of husband and wife. A grand reception is given him by the populace who have wearied of Galitsky's rule.

LA PRINCESSE D'AUBERGE

Tragic Opera in three acts by JEAN BLOCKX

Text by PIERRE VANEGHEM

The first production of this work took place in Brussels, in 1902.

Act I. The scene is at Brussels, in 1750, during Austrian rule, and Rita, the handsome daughter of Bluts, the innkeeper, has made his tavern very popular by reason of her beauty, recklessness and gay humor, so that it is the resort of the young "sports" of the town. Rabo, a blacksmith, is awaking at dawn on the steps of the inn, having been ejected from there. Peasants are coming to market. A blustering scene follows. Merlyn, a composer and man of great talent, is inveigled by Rita to join in a debauch. Reinilde, in love with Merlyn, is unable to restrain him from following Rita's invitation. Marcus, enamored of Reinilde, is jilted by her. Rabo is witnessing a love scene between Merlyn and Rita, and threatens both.

Act II. Katelyne, mother of Reinilde, deplores Merlyn's downfall. Since Rita has taken hold of him he has sadly deteriorated, drinking all day long, and Merlyn promises to change his ways. Reinilde sings one of the songs composed by him, and declares she loves him still. He denounces Rita as the source of all his woes. Marcus enters, and tempts him to come to the inn. When Merlyn refuses, he excites his jealousy, telling him that Rita, weary of being left alone, shows favor to others. He sets out for the inn, and Rita induces him to go with her to the carnival. In the next scene Rita and Merlyn are the centre of the gay mummers. Rabo threatens violence.

Act III. At the inn. Rita watches Merlyn recovering from his last debauch. Rabo comes, and declares his passion for Rita, but she rejects him and shows him the door. He threatens those present with death. Rita's sisters enter and upbraid her for imagining herself to be a "tavern princess," and next Katelyne and Reinilde come, seeking Merlyn. They are turned away, but at that moment Merlyn drops in, and he is followed by Rabo, Marcus, and others. Rabo and Merlyn, both enamored of Rita, fight to the death. As Merlyn falls the news is brought in that he has been victorious in the great national music contest for which he competed. Merlyn dies in the arms of his mother, and Reinilde curses Rita as the cause of his murder.

LE PROPHÊTE

Opera in five acts by GIACOMO MEYERBEER

Text by SCRIBE

Though Meyerbeer never again attained the high standard of his Huguenots, the Prophet is not without both striking and powerful passages; it is even said that motherly love never spoke in accents more touching than in this opera. The text is again historical, but though done by Scribe it is astonishingly weak and uninteresting.

The scene is laid in Holland at the time of the wars with the Anabaptists.

Fides, mother of the hero, John von Leyden, keeps an inn near Dordtrecht. She has just betrothed a young peasant girl to her son, but Bertha is a vassal of the Count of Oberthal and dares not marry without his permission.

As they set about getting his consent to the marriage, three Anabaptists, Jonas, Mathisen, and Zacharias, appear, exciting the people with their speeches and false promises. While they are preaching, Oberthal enters; but, smitten with Bertha's charms, he refuses his consent to her marriage and carries her off, with Fides as companion.

In the second act we find John waiting for his bride; as she delays, the Anabaptists try to win him for their cause; they prophesy him a crown, but as yet he is not ambitious, and life with Bertha looks sweeter to him than the greatest honors. As night comes on, Bertha rushes in to seek refuge from her pursuer, from whom she has fled. Hardly has she hidden herself, when Oberthal enters to claim her. John refuses his assistance; but when Oberthal threatens to kill his mother, he gives up Bertha to the Count, while his mother, whose life he has saved at such a price, asks God's benediction on his head. Then she retires for the night, and the Anabaptists appear once more, again trying to win John over. This time they succeed. Without a farewell to his sleeping mother, John follows the Anabaptists, to be henceforth their leader, their Prophet, their Messiah.

In the third act we see the Anabaptists' camp. Their soldiers have captured a party of noblemen, who are to pay ransom. They all make merry, and the famous ballet on the ice forms part of the amusement. In the background we see Münster, which town is in the hands of Count Oberthal's father, who refuses to surrender it to the enemy. They resolve to storm it, a resolution which is heard by young Oberthal, who has come disguised to the Anabaptists' camp in order to save his father and the town.

But as a light is struck he is recognized and is about to be killed, when John hears from him that Bertha has escaped. She sprang out of the window to save her honor, and, falling into the stream, was saved. When John learns this he bids the soldiers spare Oberthal's life, that he may be judged by Bertha herself.

John has already endured great pangs of conscience at seeing his party so wild and bloodthirsty. He refuses to go further, but hearing that an army of soldiers has broken out of Münster to destroy the Anabaptists, he rallies. Praying feverently to God for help and victory, inspiration comes over him and is communicated to all his adherents, so that they resolve to storm Münster. They succeed; and in the fourth act we are in the midst of this town, where we find Fides, who, knowing that her son has turned Anabaptist, though not aware of his being their Prophet, is receiving alms to save his soul by masses. She meets Bertha, disguised in a pilgrim's garb. Both vehemently curse the Prophet, when this latter appears, to be crowned in state.

His mother recognizes him, but he disowns her, declaring her mad, and by strength of will he compels the poor mother to renounce him. Fides, in order to save his life, avows that she was mistaken, and she is led to prison.

In the last act we find the three Anabaptists, Mathisen, Jonas, and Zacharias, together. The Emperor is near the gates of Münster, and they resolve to deliver their Prophet into his hands in order to save their lives.

Fides has been brought into a dungeon, where John visits her to ask her pardon and to save her. She curses him, but his repentance moves her so that she pardons him when he promises to leave his party. At this moment Bertha enters. She has sworn to kill the false Prophet, and she comes to the dungeon to set fire to the gunpowder hidden beneath it. Fides detains her, but when she recognizes that her bridegroom and the Prophet are one and the same person she wildly denounces him for his bloody deeds, and stabs herself in his presence. Then John decides to die also, and after the soldiers have led his mother away he himself sets fire to the vault.

Then he appears at the coronation banquet, where he knows that he is to be taken prisoner. When Oberthal, the Bishop and all his treacherous friends are assembled, he bids two of his faithful soldiers close the gates and fly. This done, the castle is blown into the air, with all its inhabitants. At the last moment Fides rushes in to share her son's fate, and all are thus buried under the ruins.

I PURITANI

Grand Opera in three acts by VINCENZO BELLINI

Text by COUNT PEPOLI

The libretto of this, the last work of Bellini, is the poorest of all his operas, yet the score contains some of his most finished and fascinating melodies. It was first presented at the Theatre Italian, Paris, in 1835.

The scene is laid in England during the reign of Charles II, and the principal incidents take place in a fortress near Plymouth, held by the parliamentary forces, under command of Lord Walton, a Puritan general.

Elvira, daughter of Lord Walton, is in love with Lord Arthur Talbot, a partisan knight of the Stuarts, but her hand has been promised to Sir Richard Forth, a Puritan colonel. Her uncle, Sir George Walton, at last gains the consent of her father to her marriage with Lord Arthur, who therefore is admitted to the fortress in order to celebrate the nuptials.

Henrietta of France, widow of Charles I, is a prisoner in the fortress, and has been condemned to death by Cromwell. She discloses her identity to Arthur who, in order to assist his Queen to escape, conceals her in Elvira's wedding veil. Just as they are making their escape they are met by Arthur's rival, Sir Richard, but on discovering that the lady is Henrietta and not Elvira, he allows them to pass. Elvira and the soldiers discover the fleeing couple as they are passing the drawbridge, and she, thinking that her lover has eloped with

Henrietta, loses her reason. Arthur is condemned to death by the Parliament, and a large reward is offered for his capture. Sir George and Sir Richard realize that if Elvira is to be restored to reason Arthur must be saved, so they agree to use their influence in his behalf, providing that he is captured without arms.

In spite of the vigilant watch, Arthur succeeds in getting access to his beloved, and the sudden joy of seeing him, and hearing that he still loves her, restores her to reason. Their interview is interrupted by the entrance of soldiers, who arrest him in the name of the Parliament, and are about to condemn him to death when the order comes from Cromwell to pardon all captives and political offenders, as the King has been defeated and the peace of England reëstablished. Thus the lovers are happily united.

THE QUEEN OF SHEBA

(DIE KÖNIGIN VON SABA)

Grand Opera in four acts by CHARLES GOLDMARK

Text by MOSENTHAL

Charles Goldmark was born in Hungary in 1852. He received his musical education in Vienna.

The well-known name of Mosenthal is in itself a warrant that the libretto is excellently suited to the music. The opera is considered one of the best and finest of our modern compositions.

It is noble, original, and full of brilliant orchestral effects, which, united to a grand, not to say gorgeous, mise en scène, captivate our senses.

The incidents are these:

A magnificent wedding is to be celebrated in King Solomon's palace at Jerusalem. The High-priest's daughter, Sulamith, is to marry Assad, King Solomon's favorite. But the lover, who has, in a foreign country, seen a most beautiful and haughty woman bathing in a forest well, is now in love with the stranger and has forgotten his destined bride.

Returning home, Assad confesses his error to the wise King, and Solomon bids him wed Sulamith and forget the heathen. Assad gives his promise, praying to God to restore peace to his breast.

Then enters the Queen of Sheba in all her glory, followed by a procession of slaves and suitors. Next to her litter walks her principal slave, Astaroth.

The Queen comes to offer her homage to the great Solomon, with all the gifts of her rich kingdom.

She is veiled, and nobody has seen her yet, as only before the King will she unveil herself.

When she draws back the veil, shining in all her perfect beauty, Assad starts forward; he recognizes her; she is his nymph of the forest. But the proud Queen seems to know him not; she ignores him altogether. Solomon and Sulamith try to reassure themselves to console Assad, and the Queen hears Solomon's words: "To-morrow shall find you united to your bride!" She starts and casts a passionate look on the unfortunate Assad.

The Queen is full of raging jealousy of the young bride. But though she claims Assad's love for herself, she is yet too proud to resign her crown, and so, hesitating between love and pride, she swears vengeance on her rival. Under the shade of night her slave-woman, Astaroth, allures Assad to the fountain, where he finds the Queen, who employs all her arts again to captivate him, succeeding, alas! only too well.

Morning dawns, and with it the day of Assad's marriage with Sulamith. Solomon and the High-priest conduct the youth to the altar; but just as he is taking the ring, offered to him by the bride's father, the Queen of Sheba appears, bringing as a wedding gift a golden cup filled with pearls.

Assad, again overcome by the Queen's dazzling beauty, throws the ring away and precipitates himself at her feet. The Levites detain him, but Solomon, guessing at the truth, implores the Queen to speak. Assad invokes all the sweet memories of their past; the Queen hesitates, but her pride conquers. For the second time she disowns him. Now everybody believes Assad possessed by an evil spirit, and the priests at once begin to exorcise it; it is all but done, when one word of the Queen's, who sweetly calls him "Assad," spoils everything. He is in her power: falling on his knees before her, he prays to her as to his goddess. Wrathful at this blasphemy in the temple, the priests demand his death.

Assad asks no better, Sulamith despairs, and the Queen repents having gone so far. In the great tumult Solomon alone is unmoved. He detains the priests with dignity, for he alone will judge Assad.

There now follows a charming ballet, given in honor of the Queen of Sheba. At the end of the meal, the Queen demands Assad's pardon from Solomon. He refuses her request. She now tries to ensnare the King with her charms as she did Assad, but in vain. Solomon sees her in her true light and treats her with cold politeness. Almost beside herself with rage, the Queen threatens to take vengeance on the King and to free Assad at any risk.

Solomon, well understanding the vile tricks of the Eastern Queen, has changed the verdict of death into that of exile. Sulamith, faithful and gentle, entreats for her lover, and has only one wish: to sweeten life to her Assad, or to die with him.

We find Assad in the desert. He is broken down and deeply repents his folly, when, lo! the Queen appears once more, hoping to lure him with soft words and tears. But this time her beauty is lost upon him; he has at last recognized her false soul; with noble pride he scorns her, preferring to expiate his follies by dying in the desert. He curses her, praying to God to save him from the temptress. Henceforth he thinks only of Sulamith, and invokes Heaven's benediction on her. He is dying in the dreadful heat of the desert, when Sulamith appears, the faithful one who, without resting, has sought her bridegroom till now. But alas! in vain she kneels beside him, couching his head on her bosom; his life is fast ebbing away. Heaven has granted his last wish; he sees Sulamith before his death, and with the sigh "Liberation!" he sinks back and expires.

QUO VADIS

Religious Opera in five acts by J. NOUGUES

Text based on SIENKIEVICZ' famous novel of the same name

The initial performance of this work was given at Nice, 1909. The scene is laid in Rome, about 50 A.D.

Act I. At the gardens of Petronius. Eunice and Iras, slaves, decorate statues. Petronius enters with Vinicius, the latter telling of his infatuation for Lygia. Eunice tells Vinicius of a soothsayer who can predict the future. He is summoned and says Lygia is daughter of a king, and is now a Roman hostage. Chilon, the fortune-teller, is sent out to ascertain the meaning of a symbol—a fish—which Lygia had once traced in the sand.

Act II. Nero, the emperor, gives a great festival. At Nero's side is a beautiful stranger, Lygia, and this arouses the jealousy of Nero's favorite mistress, Poppaea, but Petronius soothes her. Vinicius and Lygia are left alone together, and he pleads for her love. Lygia answers that she cannot be his because she is a Christian and he a pagan. Suddenly a ruddy glare overspreads the sky. It is Rome burning, but Nero goes on singing and playing the lyre untroubled by the danger. The populace suddenly rise, accusing Nero of having caused the great fire. Poppaea begs Petronius to allay the roused passion of the multitude.

Act III. The scene is a wineshop on the banks of the Tiber, filled with soldiers, gladiators, and sailors. Chilon traces the sign of a fish. Demas, a Christian, tells him that the apostle will be among them that night. Chilon has ascertained that the fish is a symbol of Christianity. He also learns that Lygia is with Demas's wife, Myriam, and that these two will go forth that evening. Chilon bids Croton, the giant gladiator, come with him. The Christians assemble at a house on the river, and Lygia and St. Peter, entering this house, are observed, and many of the Christians taken prisoner.

Act IV. First scene is at the arena of the Colosseum. Christian martyrs are seen, among them Demas and Myriam. Peter comforts them. Vinicius enters, telling Lygia to be hopeful, as he has contrived for her escape. But Petronius shuts off the means of escape, and Vinicius declares his intention of following Lygia to death. The next scene shows the imperial box, with Nero and Poppaea. Ursus, a slave of Lygia's down in the arena, by his enormous strength saves Lygia from being killed by a fierce aurochs, and Nero grants her life. Chilon creates a mob scene in the circus, and Nero is charged with being the incendiary that set Rome afire, and has to flee from the popular fury.

Act V. Petronius at his rural estate is urged by Lygia and Vinicius to go with them to Sicily, but he declines, and issues a letter of parting to Nero. Being convinced that this will mean his death, he has his arteries opened by Theocles, the physician, and dies with Eunice, who confesses her love for him toward the last. The news of Nero's death and of the safety of Petronius arrives too late to prevent Petronius' end.

LA REGINETTA DELLE ROSE

Opera in three acts by RUGGIERO LEONCAVALLO

Text by ZANDONAI

This opera was first produced in Rome, 1912. The scene changes several times.

Act I. At a charity fair in London, Max, the heir-apparent of Portowa, is among the visitors. He there sees an extremely pretty flower girl, Lillian, and falls desperately in love with her. The tutor of Max, Gin, prevails upon her to follow the prince of Portowa, as without her he will not return there. Max is on his way to his own coronation, his father having just died, but Lillian is ignorant of this and of his royal rank, acting in the matter just out of mere good-nature.

Act II. This is at the palace of Portowa. Lillian is at once arrested after her arrival as a dangerous person. She sees her lover in royal robes, but thinks she is the victim of a plot. Max reassures her. The dowager queen, Max's mother, schemes to make him marry his royal cousin, Anita, but Anita is in love with Max's cousin, Pedro, and is not inclined to further this plan. The populace of Portowa, being of a free-and-easy disposition, in the meantime have heard of Lillian's incarceration, and threaten to upset the throne if she is not liberated immediately. The dowager stops interfering and leaves for parts unknown.

Act III. Max, after freeing Lillian, invites her to share the throne with him. He proclaims her not alone his consort, but dubs her his "reginetta delle rose" (little queen of roses), and signs the act of succession with a rose stem instead of a penholder.

LA REINE FIAMETTA

Tragic Opera by XAVIER H. N. LEROUX

Book based on Italian chronicles

The initial performance of this work took place at Paris, 1903. The scene is Bologna, and the time the fifteenth century.

A military adventurer, Giorgio d'Asti, meets the Cardinal Cesare Sforza, who offers him the throne if he will rid the country of Queen Orlanda. Together they concoct a clever plot for the assassination of the queen. A youth, Danielo, is chosen as the fittest instrument. At first Danielo refuses to listen, as he is unwilling to kill a woman. But Sforza prevails upon him by telling him a mendacious story to the effect that his brother had been murdered at the instigation of the queen. Then he is given a dagger and speeded on his mission of death.

The queen, ignorant of the plot, is meanwhile greatly enjoying herself in a Clarissian convent, where she has been admitted under the pseudonym of Helena. And it is there she meets Danielo. Instantly they fall in love with each other, neither being aware of the purposes or identity of the other. At last, though, Danielo discovers who it is he has learned to love. The discovery unmans him. He is handed over to a tribunal of Franciscan friars. Queen Orlanda, abdicating in order to save her lover's life, is herself condemned as a heretic. But the two lovers are nevertheless united in death. The same axe strikes both.

DAS RHEINGOLD

Prelude to Der Ring der Nibelungen

This grand dramatic work, which cannot any longer with justice be called an opera, differing as it does so considerably from the ordinary style of operas, is the result of many years of study and hard work.

Wagner took the subject from the German mythology, the oldest representative of which is found in the Edda.

We have first to do with the fore-evening, called the "Rhinegold."

The first scene is laid in the very depths of the Rhine, where we see three nymphs frolicking in the water. They are the guardians of the Rhinegold, which glimmers on a rock.

Alberich, a Nibelung, highly charmed by their grace and beauty, tries to make love to each one of them alternately. As he is an ugly dwarf, they at first allure and then deride him, gliding away as soon as he comes near, and laughing at him. Discovering their mockery at last, he swears vengeance. He sees the Rhinegold shining brightly, and asks the nymphs what it means. They tell him of its wonderful qualities, which would render the owner all-powerful if he should form it into a ring and forswear love.

Alberich, listening attentively, all at once climbs the rock, and, before the frightened nymphs can cry for help, has grasped the treasure and disappeared. Darkness comes on; the scene changes into an open district on mountain heights. In the background we see a grand castle, which the rising sun illumines. Wotan, the father of the gods, and Fricka, his wife, are slumbering on the ground. Awakening, their eyes fall on the castle for the first time. It is the "Walhalla," the palace which the giants have built for them at Wotan's bidding. As a reward for their services they are to obtain Freia, the goddess of youth; but already Wotan repents of his promise and forms plans with his wife to save her lovely sister. The giants Fafner and Fasold enter to claim their reward. While they negotiate, Loge, the god of fire, comes up, relates the history of Alberich's theft of the Rhinegold, and tells Wotan of the gold's power. Wotan decides to rob the dwarf, promising the treasure to the giants, who consent to accept it in Freia's stead. But they distrust the gods and take Freia with them as a pledge. As soon as she disappears, the beautiful gods seem old and gray and wrinkled, for the golden apples to which Freia attends, and of which the gods partake daily to be forever youthful, wither as soon as she is gone. Then Wotan, without any further delay, starts for Nibelheim with Loge, justifying his intention by saying that the gold is stolen property. They disappear in a cleft, and we find ourselves in a subterranean cavern, the abode of the Nibelungs.

Alberich has forced his brother Mime to forge a "Tarnhelm" for him, which renders its wearer invisible. Mime vainly tries to keep it for himself; Alberich, the possessor of the all-powerful ring, which he himself formed, takes it by force and, making himself invisible, strikes Mime with a whip, until the latter is half dead.

Wotan and Loge, hearing his complaints, promise to help him. Alberich, coming forth again, is greatly flattered by Wotan and dexterously led on to show his might. He first changes himself into an enormous snake and then into a toad. Wotan quickly puts his foot on it, while Loge seizes the Tarnhelm. Alberich, becoming suddenly visible in his real shape, is bound and led away captive. The gods return to the mountain heights of the second scene, where Alberich is compelled to part with all his treasures, which are brought by the dwarfs. He is even obliged to leave the ring, which Wotan intends to keep for himself. With a dreadful curse upon the possessor of the ring, Alberich flies.

When the giants reappear with Freia, the treasures are heaped before her; they are to cover her entirely, so it is decided, and not before will she be free. When all the gold has been piled up, and even the Tarnhelm thrown on the hoard, Fasold still sees Freia's eyes shine through it, and at last Wotan, who is most unwilling to part with the ring, is induced to do so by Erda, goddess of the earth, who appears to him and warns him. Now the pledge is kept and Freia is released. The giants quarrel over the possession of the ring, and Fafner kills Fasold, thereby fulfilling Alberich's curse. With lightened hearts the gods cross the rainbow bridge and enter Walhalla, while the songs and wailings of the Rhine nymphs are heard, imploring the restitution of their lost treasure.

RIENZI, THE LAST OF THE TRIBUNES

Tragic Opera in five acts by RICHARD WAGNER

In this first opera of Wagner's one hardly recognizes the great master of later times. Though Wagner himself disowned this early child of his muse, there is a grand energy in it, which preserves it from triviality. The orchestration is brilliant, and here and there one may find traces of the peculiar power which led up to the greatness of after years, and which sometimes make one think of "Tannhäuser."

The libretto, taken by Wagner from Bulwer's novel, is attractive and powerful.

The hero, a pontifical notary, is a man of lofty ambition, dreaming in the midst of the depravity of the fourteenth century of reërecting the old Rome, and making her once more the Sovereign of the world. He receives help and encouragement from the Church; Cardinal Raimondo even bids him try all means in order to attain his end. The clergy as well as the people are oppressed by the mighty and insolent nobles.

In the first scene we witness an act of brutality directed against Rienzi's sister, Irene, who is, however, liberated by Adriano, son of the noble Colonna. A Colonna it was who murdered Rienzi's little brother in sheer wantonness. Rienzi has sworn vengeance, but, seeing Adriano good and brave and in love with his sister, he wins him to his cause.

The nobles having left Rome to fight out a quarrel which had been started among them, are forbidden to reënter the town. Rienzi calls the people to arms and is victorious. The strongholds of the nobles are burned, and they are only admitted into Rome on promising submission to the new laws, made and represented by Rienzi, who has been created Tribune of Rome.

The hostile parties of Colonna and Orsini then join to destroy the hated plebeian. In the midst of the festivity in the Capitol, Orsini makes an attempt to murder Rienzi, but the latter wears a shirt of mail under his garments, and, besides, he is warned by Adriano, who has overheard the conspiracy. The whole plot fails, and the nobles who have taken part in it are unanimously condemned to death. But Adriano, full of remorse on account of his treason against his own father, implores Rienzi to save their lives, and as Irene joins her prayers to those of her lover, the culprits are pardoned and obliged to renew their oath of fidelity. From this time on Rienzi's star begins to pale. The nobles do not adhere to their oath; in the third act they again give battle, and though Rienzi is again victorious, it is only at the cost of severe sacrifices. The nobles are slain, and now Adriano, who had in vain begged for peace, turns against Rienzi.

In the fourth act Adriano denounces him as a traitor; the people, easily misled, begin to mistrust him, and when even the Church, which has assisted him up to this time, anathematizes him on account of his last bloody deed, all desert him. Irene alone clings to her brother, and repulses her lover scornfully when he tries to take her from Rienzi's side. Both brother and sister retire into the Capitol, where Adriano once more vainly implores Irene to fly with him. For the last time Rienzi attempts to reassert his power, but his words are drowned in the general uproar. They are greeted by a hail of stones, the Capital is set on fire, and they perish like heroes in the flames, through which Adriano makes his way at the last moment, and thus finds a common grave with his bride and her brother, the last of the Tribunes.

RIGOLETTO

Opera in three acts by VERDI

Text by PIAVE from VICTOR HUGO'S drama: "Le roi s'amuse"

Rigoletto is one of the world's most popular operas. The Duke of Mantua, a wild and debauched youth, covets every girl or woman he sees, and is assisted in his vile purpose by his jester, Rigoletto, an ugly, humpbacked man. We meet him first helping the Duke to seduce the wife of Count Ceprano, and afterward the wife of Count Monterone. Both husbands curse the vile Rigoletto and swear to be avenged. Monterone especially, appearing like a ghost in the midst of a festival, hurls such a fearful curse at them that Rigoletto shudders.

This bad man has one tender point: it is his blind love for his beautiful daughter Gilda, whom he brings up carefully, keeping her hidden from the world, and shielding her from all wickedness.

But the cunning Duke discovers her, and gains her love under the assumed name of a student, called Gualtier Maldé.

Gilda is finally carried off by Ceprano and two other courtiers, aided by her own father, who holds the ladder, believing that Count Ceprano's wife is to be the victim. A mask blinds Rigoletto, and he discovers, too late, by Gilda's cries that he has been duped. Gilda is brought to the Duke's palace. Rigoletto appears in the midst of the courtiers to claim Gilda, and then they hear that she, whom they believed to be his mistress, is his daughter, for whose honor he is willing to sacrifice everything. Gilda enters and, though she sees that she has been deceived, she implores her father to pardon the Duke, whom she still loves. But Rigoletto vows vengeance, and engages Sparafucile to stab the Duke. Sparafucile decoys him into his inn, where his sister Maddalena awaits him. She, too, is enamored of the Duke, who makes love to her, as to all young females, and she entreats her brother to have mercy on him. Sparafucile declares that he will wait until midnight, and will spare him if another victim should turn up before then. Meanwhile Rigoletto persuades his daughter to fly from the Duke's pursuit, but before he takes her away he wants to show her lover's fickleness, in order to cure her of her love.

She comes to the inn in masculine attire, and, hearing the discourse between Sparafucile and his sister, resolves to save her lover. She enters the inn and is instantly put to death, placed in a sack and given to Rigoletto, who proceeds to the river to dispose of the corpse. At this instant he hears the voice of the Duke, who passes by, singing a frivolous tune. Terrified, Rigoletto opens the sack, and recognizes his daughter, who is yet able to tell him that she gave her life for that of her seducer, and then expires. With an awful cry, the unhappy father sinks upon the corpse. Count Monterone's curse has been fulfilled.

RIP VAN WINKLE

Opera in three acts and seven scenes by REGINALD DE KOVEN
Text by PERCY MACKAYE

This opera was produced for the first time at Chicago in 1920. The scenes are laid in a Dutch community in the Catskills during the middle of the eighteenth century.

Act I. Nicholas Vedder, landlord of the village inn, has two daughters, Katrina and Peterkee. Katrina, a shrewish girl, is betrothed to Rip Van Winkle, a happy-go-lucky vagabond of the village, while Peterkee, still in her early teens, attends the school of Derrick Van Bummel whose son, Jan, desires Katrina's hand for himself and is favored by Nicholas because of his prosperity. The wedding settlement between Katrina and Rip is ready to be signed but Rip cannot be found. At last he comes in with a group of school children with whom he has been playing, having forgotten his wedding engagement with Katrina. She berates him soundly and leaves him crestfallen.

A goose girl now persuades Rip to join her and the children in a dance which is ended by a thunder shower. Peterkee arrives just in time to hear Rip's story of Hendrick Hudson who returns every twenty years in the ghostly *Half Moon* to hold a bowling party in the mountains. At the climax of the tale, there is a clap of thunder and Hendrick Hudson himself appears. All flee in terror save Rip and Peterkee whom the navigator invites to his party at midnight when he promises to give Rip a magic flask as a wedding gift. As Hudson vanishes upon the reappearance of Katrina, she mocks Rip's account of what has happened and tells him to return with the magic flask by tomorrow's sunset or she will marry Jan. Peterkee and Rip start out to the mountains to keep their rendezvous with Hudson.

Act II. After stopping at Rip's hut to prepare for their journey, they continue on their way and encounter Dirck Spuytenduyvil, mate of the *Half Moon,* with two kegs of liquor which Rip helps carry to the mountain peak. There they are welcomed by Hendrick Hudson and his ghostly crew to the party of ninepins, during which Hendrick and Dirck plot to have Rip marry Peterkee. To this end, she is allowed to win the magic flask and is sent back to the village while Rip is given a sleeping potion which will detain him on the mountain peak until the next appearance of the *Half Moon.*

Act III. The score of years has passed. Rip awakens and is amazed to find that he is an old man. He makes his way to his hut which is in ruins. Here Peterkee, in bridal clothes, comes to search for the magic flask, and, seeing the white-bearded and weather-beaten Rip, she thinks him a fairy goblin.

On the village green, Hans Van Bummel, younger brother of Jan who married Katrina, is about to be wedded to Peterkee. Barking dogs and mocking children announce the entrance of Rip who has come to claim his bride at sundown. In swift compassion, Peterkee hands the old man the magic flask. As he raises it to his lips, there is a great burst of thunder and lightning and Hendrick Hudson and his crew troop forth from the church. The draught from the flask has miraculously restored Rip's youth and he and Peterkee celebrate their wedding.

ROBERT LE DIABLE

Opera in five acts by MEYERBEER

Text by SCRIBE and DELAVIGNE

Though the text which embodies the well-known story of Robert the Devil, Duke of Normandy, is often weak and involved, Meyerbeer has understood in masterly fashion how to adapt his music to it, infusing into it dramatic strength and taking his hearer captive from beginning to end. The instrumentation is brilliant, and the splendid parts for the human voice deserve like praise. The famous cavatina, "Air of Grace," as it is called, where the bugle has such a fine part, and the duet in the fourth act between Robert and the Princess Isabella, in which the harp fairly rouses us to wonder whether we are not listening to celestial music, are but two of the enchanting features of an opera in which such passages abound.

The following are the contents of the libretto:

Robert, Duke of Normandy, has a friend of gloomy exterior, named Bertram, with whom he travels, but to whose evil influence he owes much trouble and sorrow. Without knowing it himself, Robert is the son of this erring knight, who is an inhabitant of hell. During his wanderings on earth he seduced Bertha, daughter of the Duke of Normandy, whose offspring Robert is. This youth is very wild, and has therefore been banished from his country.

Arriving in Sicily, Isabella, the King's daughter, and he fall mutually in love.

In the first act we find Robert in Palermo, surrounded by other knights, to whom a young countryman of his, Raimbaut, tells the story of "Robert le Diable" and his fiendish father, warning everybody against them. Robert, giving his name, is about to deliver the unhappy Raimbaut to the hangman, when the peasant is saved by his bride Alice, Robert's foster sister. She has come to Palermo by order of Robert's deceased mother, who sends her last will to her son, in case he should change his bad habits and prove himself worthy. Robert, feeling that he is not likely to do this, begs Alice to keep it for him. He confides in the innocent maiden, and she promises to reason with Isabella, whom Robert has irritated by his jealousy, and who has banished him from her presence.

As a recompense for her service Alice asks Robert's permission to marry Raimbaut. Seeing Robert's friend, Bertram, she recognizes the latter's likeness to Satan, whom she saw in a picture, and instinctively shrinks from him. When she leaves her master, Bertram induces his friend to try his fortune with the dice, and he loses all.

In the second act we are introduced into the palace of Isabella, who laments Robert's inconstancy. Alice enters, bringing Robert's letter, and the latter instantly follows to crave his mistress's pardon. She presents him with a new suit of armor, and he consents to meet the Prince of Granada in mortal combat. But Bertram lures him away by deceiving him with a phantom. Robert vainly seeks the Prince in the forest, and the Prince of Granada is in his absence victorious in the tournament and obtains Isabella's hand.

The third act opens with a view of the rocks of St. Irene, where Alice hopes to be united with Raimbaut. The peasant expects his bride, but meets Bertram instead, who makes him forget Alice, by giving him gold and dangerous advice. Raimbaut goes away to spend the money, while Bertram descends to the evil spirits in the deep. When Alice comes, Raimbaut is gone, and she hears the demons calling for Bertram. Bertram extracts a promise from her not to betray the dreadful secret of the cavern. She clings to the Saviour's cross for protection, and is about to be destroyed by Bertram, when Robert approaches, to whom she decides to reveal all. But Bertram's renewed threats at last oblige her to leave them.

Bertram now profits by Robert's rage and despair at the loss of his bride, his wealth and his honor, to draw him on to entire destruction. He tells Robert that his rival used magic arts, and suggests that he should try the same expedient. Then he leads him to a ruined cloister, where he resuscitates the guilty nuns. They try to seduce Robert first by drink, then by gambling, and last of all by love. In the last, Helena, the most beautiful of the nuns, succeeds and makes him remove the cypress branch, a talisman by which in the fourth act he enters Isabella's apartment unseen. He awakes his bride out of her magic sleep, to carry her off, but overcome by her tears and her appeal to his honor, he breaks the talisman, and is seized by the now awakened soldiers; but Bertram appears, and takes him under his protection.

The fifth act opens with a chorus sung by monks, which is followed by a prayer for mercy. Robert, concealed in the vestibule of the cathedral, hears it full of contrition. But Bertram is with him, and, his term on earth being short, he confides to Robert the secret of his birth and appeals to him as his father.

He almost succeeds, when Alice comes up, bringing the news that the Prince of Granada renounces Isabella's hand, being unable to pass the threshold of the Church. Bertram urges Robert all the more vehemently to become one with him, suggesting that Isabella is likewise lost to him, who has transgressed the laws of the Church, when in the last extremity Alice produces his mother's will, in which she warns him against Bertram, entreating him to save his soul. Then at last his good angel is victorious, his demon-father vanishes into the earth, and Robert, united by prayer to the others, is restored to a life of peace and goodness.

LE ROI L'A DIT

(THE KING HAS SAID IT)

Comic Opera in three acts by LÉON DÉLIBES

Text by EDMOND GONDINET

It is impossible to imagine music more charming or more full of grace and piquancy than that which we find in this delightful opera. Every part abounds in exquisite harmonies, which no words can give any idea of. On hearing them one is compelled to the conclusion that all the graces have stood godmother to this lovely child of their muse.

The libretto, though on the whole somewhat insipid, is flavored with naïve and good-natured coquetry, which lends a certain charm to it.

The Marquis de Moncontour has long wished to be presented to King Louis XIV., and as he has been fortunate enough to catch the escaped paroquet of Mme. de Maintenon, he is at last to have his wish accomplished. By way of preparation for his audience he tries to learn the latest mode of bowing, his own being somewhat antiquated, and the Marquise and her four lovely daughters, and even Javotte, the nice little ladies' maid, assist him. After many failures the old gentleman succeeds in making his bow to his own satisfaction, and he is put into a litter, and borne off, followed by his people's benedictions. When they are gone, Benoit, a young peasant, comes to see Javotte, who is his sweetheart. He wishes to enter the Marquis's service. Javotte thinks him too awkward, but she promises to intercede in his favor with Miton, a dancing master, who enters just as Benoit disappears. He has instructed the graceful Javotte in all the arts and graces of the noble world, and when he rehearses the steps and all the nice little tricks of his art with her, he is so delighted with his pupil that he pronounces her manners worthy of a Princess; but when Javotte tells him that she loves a peasant, he is filled with disgust, and orders her away. His real pupils, the four lovely daughters of the Marquis, now enter, and while the lesson goes on Milton hands a billet-doux from some lover to each of them. The two elder, Agathe and Chimene, are just in the act of reading theirs, when they hear a serenade outside, and shortly afterward the two lovers are standing in the room, having made their way through the window. The Marquis Flarembel and his friend, the Marquis de la Bluette, are just making a most ardent declaration of love, when Mme. la Marquise enters to present to her elder daughters the two bridegrooms she has chosen for them. The young men hide behind the ample dresses of the young ladies, and all begin to sing with great zeal, Miton beating the measure, so that some time elapses before the Marquise is able to state her errand. Of course her words excite great terror, the girls flying to the other side of the room with their lovers and receiving the two elderly suitors, Baron de Merlussac, and Gautru, a rich old financier, with great coolness and a refusal of their costly gifts. When the suitors are gone the two young strangers are detected, and the angry mother decides at once to send her daughters to a convent, from which they shall only issue on their wedding day.

When they have departed in a most crestfallen condition, the old Marquis returns from his audience with the King and relates its astounding results. His

Majesty had been so peremptory in his questioning about the Marquis's son and heir, that the Marquis, losing his presence of mind, promised to present his son at Court on the King's demand. The only question now is where to find a son to adopt, as the Marquis has only four daughters. Miton, the ever-useful, at once presents Benoit to the parents, engaging himself to drill the peasant into a nice cavalier in ten lessons. Benoit takes readily to his new position; he is fitted out at once, and when the merchants come, offering their best in cloth and finery, he treats them with an insolence worthy of the proudest seigneur. He even turns from his sweetheart, Javotte.

In the second act Benoit, dressed like the finest cavalier, gives a masked ball in his father's gardens. Half Versailles is invited, but, having taken the Court Almanac to his aid, he has made the mistake of inviting many people who have long been dead. Those who do appear seem to him to be very insipid, and, wanting some friends with whom he can enjoy himself, the useful Miton presents the Marquises de la Bluette and de Flarembel, who are delighted to make the acquaintance of their sweethearts' brother.

Benoit hears from them that he has four charming sisters who have been sent to a convent, and he at once promises to assist his new friends. Meanwhile Javotte appears in the mask of an Oriental Queen and Benoit makes love to her, but he is very much stupefied when she takes off her mask, and he recognizes Javotte. She laughingly turns away from him, when the good-for-nothing youth's new parents appear, to reproach him with his levity. But Benoit, nothing daunted, rushes away, telling the Marquis that he intends to visit his sisters in the convent. Miton tries in vain to recall him.

Then the two old suitors of Agathe and Chimene appear, to complain that their deceased wife and grandmother were invited, and while the Marquis explains his son's mistake, the four daughters rush in, having been liberated by their lovers and their unknown brother, whom they greet with a fondness very shocking to the old Marchioness. The elderly suitors withdraw, swearing to take vengeance on the inopportune brother.

In the last act Benoit appears in his father's house in a somewhat dilapidated state. He has spent the night amongst gay companions and met Gautru and de Merlussac successively, who have both fought him and believe they have killed him, Benoit having feigned to be dead on the spot.

When the old Marquis enters, he is very much astonished at receiving two letters of condolence from his daughters' suitors. Miton appears in mourning, explaining that, Mme. de Maintenon's visit being expected, they must all wear dark colors, as she prefers these. Meanwhile Benoit has an interview with Javotte, in which he declares his love to be undiminished, and he at once asks his father to give him Javotte as his wife, threatening to reveal the Marquis's deceit to the King if his request is not granted. In this dilemma help comes in the persons of the two young Marquises, who present their King's condolences to old Moncontour. This gentleman hears to his great relief that his son is supposed to have fallen in a duel, and so he is disposed of. Nobody is happier than Javotte, who now claims Benoit for her own, while the Marquis, who receives a Duke's title from the King in compensation for his loss, gladly gives his two elder daughters to their young and noble lovers.

The girls, well aware that they owe their happiness to their adopted brother, are glad to provide him with ample means for his marriage with Javotte, and the affair ends to everybody's satisfaction.

LE ROI D' YS

Opera in three acts by EDOUARD LALO

Libretto by BLAU after a Breton legend

The first production was given in Paris in 1898. The scenes are laid in legendary Brittany.

Act I. Margared and Rozenn, daughters of the King of Ys, a city on the Breton sea, both love the warrior Mylio who cares only for Rozenn. Margared, the Pearl of Brittany, has been betrothed by her father for political reasons to Prince Karnac. Shortly after she is led away to be robed for her marriage, she learns that Mylio has returned to Ys and refuses to wed Karnac. The Prince challenges the Breton king to mortal combat and Mylio picks up Karnac's gauntlet.

Act II. Margared is torn by conflicting emotions. Seeing her sister Rozenn's tender parting with Mylio, she cries that she hopes he will never return from battle. Rozenn, believing her sister mad, tries in vain to calm her. Margared curses her and St. Corentin, patron saint of Brittany. When Mylio comes back victorious, Margared, her love turned to hatred, steals to the defeated Karnac and offers to help him conquer Ys by opening the dykes which hold back the waters of the sea.

Act III. Rozenn is wedded to Mylio according to the charming customs of ancient Brittany. As the nuptial procession returns from the chapel, Margared warns them that the flood gates are down and the waters are already filling the streets of the city. On a hill near the sea, the people of Ys kneel in prayer as the waves roll higher. Margared admits her guilt and suddenly, eager to atone for the evil she has done, she casts herself from a great rock into the raging flood. A vision of St. Corentin appears in a golden glory to accept her sacrifice and the floods retire. The city is saved.

ROMEO ET JULIETTE

Grand Opera in five acts by CH. GOUNOD

Text by BARBIER and CARRÉ

This highly favored opera by Gounod presents much that is worthy of admiration, though it does not rise to the high level of his Faust. The libretto follows Shakespeare's version pretty accurately.

The first act opens with the masked ball in Capulet's palace, where the first meeting between the lovers takes place, Romeo being disguised as a pilgrim. They fall in love with each other, and Tybalt, Capulet's nephew, recognizing Romeo, reveals, but too late, their true names and swears to take revenge on his foe, who has thus entered the Capulet's house uninvited.

The second act represents the famous scene of the balcony between Juliet and her lover.

In the third act Romeo visits Friar Lorenzo's cell, to get advice from him. There he meets Juliet. Lorenzo unites the lovers, hoping thereby to reconcile the hostile houses of the Montagues and the Capulets.

The following scene represents the street before Capulet's palace, where the rivals meet; there ensues the double duel, first between Tybalt and Romeo's friend Mercutio, who falls, and then between Romeo, who burns to avenge his comrade, and Tybalt. Tybalt is killed, and Romeo is obliged to fly, all the Capulets being after him.

In the fourth act Romeo sees Juliet in her room, but when the morning dawns he is obliged to leave, while

Juliet's father comes to remind her of his last promise to the dying Tybalt, which was to marry Juliet to Count Paris.

Juliet in great perplexity turns to Friar Lorenzo for help. He gives her a draught which will cause her to fall into a deep swoon, and after being laid in her ancestors' tomb she is to be awakened by Romeo and carried away into security.

In the fifth act Romeo, after having taken poison, enters the tomb to bid farewell to Juliet, whom he, by a fatal misunderstanding, believes to be dead. She awakes, and seeing her bridegroom die before her eyes, she stabs herself, to be united with her lover in death, if not in life.

LA RONDINE

Opera in three acts by GIACOMO PUCCINI

Libretto by ADAMI

The first performance was given at Monte Carlo in 1917. The scenes are laid in France during the Second Empire.

Magda, a beautiful demi-mondaine living under the protection of the rich banker, Rambaldo, is unable to forget her first love who was a poor young student. At a *Bal Bullier* she meets Ruggero who is also young and poor and a student. He falls in love with her at first sight and she responds to his impetuous wooing.

They leave Paris for Nice where they plan to lead an idyllic existence. Ruggero writes to his parents for their consent to his marriage. He describes Magda with a lover's glowing ardor but his parents reply that if the girl he loves be virtuous, she will be received with open arms. Since remorse cannot undo the past, Magda now believes that she is unworthy of Ruggero's love and like Violetta in La Traviata, she renounces her happiness and dismisses Ruggero lest she should bring dishonor upon him.

LE ROSSIGNOL

Lyric opera in three acts by IGOR STRAVINSKY

Libretto by the composer after HANS ANDERSEN'S fairy tale

The initial performance was given in Paris in 1914. The scenes are laid in China during legendary times.

The Emperor of China hears a little brown bird singing and the beauty of its song so delights him that he coaxes it to come to live in the palace. All the court is happy, listening to the modest little bird. Then envoys of the Emperor of Japan bring an artificial nightingale, decked with pearls and gleaming precious stones, to the Chinese ruler. There is a contest between the two small singers and the thrills of the jeweled bird so enchant the Son of Heaven and his courtiers that the little brown nightingale is forgotten. One day the Emperor happens to ask about the bird and learns that it has flown away. He is so angry that he banishes the nightingale from his realm.

Then Death comes to court. He seats himself on the Emperor's bed and steals his sceptre and crown. Just as he is about to place his icy hand upon the royal brow, the little nightingale flies in and Death, listening to the exquisite melody of his song, is charmed and foregoes his prey. The next morning the courtiers enter the royal bedchamber, expecting to find the Son of Heaven a corpse, but he is alive and well. Then all pay honor to the little brown nightingale.

RUSSALKA

Opera in three acts by ALEXANDER DARGOMIJSKY

Libretto by the composer from a poem by PUSHKIN

This opera was first produced in Petrograd in 1856. Russia in its legendary youth furnishes the setting.

Act I. A young Prince betrays Natasha, daughter of an old Miller. When the Prince is forced to abandon Natasha and marry in his own rank, he seeks to console the girl with gifts of jewels and gold. Left alone to face the consequences of their secret union, Natasha throws herself into the mill-stream and becomes a Russalka whose duty it is to lure mortals to a watery doom.

Act II. The Prince celebrates his nuptials. The happiness of the occasion is marred by the eerie, wailing cry of the Russalka each time the Prince attempts to embrace his bride.

Act III. Several years have passed. The mill has fallen into ruins and Natasha's father has become crazed through his misfortunes. The unhappy Prince, wandering one day about the scene of his early love, encounters a Russalka child who tells him that she is his daughter and that her mother bids him join them at the bottom of the stream. While he is hesitating, the Mad Miller, with a hideously meaningless laugh, flings him into the pond. A final tableau shows the Prince happily reunited with the Russalka and their child.

RUSSLAN AND LUDMILLA

Fairy Opera in five acts by MICHAEL IVANOVITCH GLINKA

Text after a poem of the same name by PUSHKIN

This highly tuneful opera has been the forerunner of fanciful works of a similar scope by later Russian composers like Rimsky-Korsakoff, Stravinsky, and others. It uses for the first time in Russian opera a deal of Oriental color, and is in this as in other respects a pioneer work.

It was first produced in Petrograd, where it shocked many by its lack of conventionality, and delighted others, and has since been performed with great approval at Berlin and other capitals.

The first act takes us to the festivities held by Prince Svetozar of Kiev in honor of his daughter's suitors, these being Russlan, the Russian knight-errant; Ratmir, the ardent Tartar prince; and a rather faint-hearted Varangian chief, Farlaf. The daughter, fair Ludmilla, smiles on Russlan, and her father orders thereupon the nuptials to be solemnized immediately. But mortals must reckon with the favor or disfavor of supernatural beings. And scarcely is finished the jubilant invocation to Lel, the god of Love, when a terrific storm approaches. Flashes of lightning and terrific claps of thunder are heard, and darkness descends upon the scene. When light returns it is seen that the princess is missing. Then Svetozar, distracted at the loss of his child, makes a solemn vow to bestow her upon him who will discover Ludmilla and restore her to him. The three suitors at once take up this challenge and set out for unknown parts to find the missing princess.

The second act deals with the supernatural beings who are concerned in the fate of Ludmilla. Russlan finds Finn, a mighty sorcerer and the good genius of Russlan, in his cave, and discloses to him that Ludmilla has been carried off by Chernomor, the wonder-working dwarf, who is enamored of the princess. Finn warns Russlan against the magical schemes of Naina, tells him how to avoid her counter-plots, and speeds him on the way. Farlaf meanwhile has already despaired of winning the maiden by legitimate means. He meets Naina, who advises him to steal Ludmilla from whoever is going to rescue her. She promises to frustrate the efforts of both Russlan and Ratmir to overcome him.

Russlan arrives upon a deserted battle-field shrouded in mist and strewn with the bodies of the fallen. He picks up there a wondrous spear and shield and perceives simultaneously the severed gigantic head of Chernomor's brother. The lifeless head nevertheless blows in self-protection a devastating gale through its nostrils, a breath sufficient in its power to kill Russlan. However, our hero by a mighty spear-thrust renders the head impotent, and underneath this head Russlan unearths the magical sword by which he will free his sweetheart.

In the third act the scene shifts to the enchanted abode of Naina. A chorus of seductive Persian virgins is wheedling Ratmir, the Tartar suitor, and Gorislava pleads with Ratmir to come back to her whom he has basely deserted. Her appeal is heard, but Ratmir soon forgets her again to follow the fascinations of the other maidens. Russlan enters the place, and likewise is threatened by a similar fate. Finn, his powerful protector, saves him, and by the incantations of Finn the splendid palace of Naina crumbles into dust, whereupon Russlan is at liberty to continue his search for Ludmilla.

The fourth act at last discovers Russlan on the right track, in the enchanted domain of Chernomor. Ludmilla is there, having succumbed from weariness to sleep. The powerful ogre, Chernomor, suddenly makes his appearance, seats himself near Ludmilla, and orders the festivities in her honor continued. It is at this moment that Russlan intrudes, and the wonder-working dwarf plunges her immediately into a trance, and then issues forth to encounter his bold foe, Russlan. But Russlan by the aid of the magic sword conquers. However, he is unable to break the spell which holds Ludmilla in the bonds of unconsciousness. Ratmir and his reconciled sweetheart, Gorislava, now join him, and on their advice he takes his way back to Kiev.

The fifth act opens with the display of Naina's power, since Russlan's bride has, by the connivance of this female demon, been taken away from Russlan by Farlaf. Chernomor's spell, though, still holds good. Farlaf is unable to awaken Ludmilla to life, although he brings her back to her father's home in Kiev. But at last Russlan comes on the scene ready and able to rescue her, for Russlan brings with him the magic ring of Finn, and delivers her. The opera concludes with general rejoicing.

THE SACRIFICE

A Dramatic Opera in three acts by FREDERIC S. CONVERSE

The text likewise by him

It was first produced in Boston, 1911. The scene is laid in California, in 1846.

The first act takes place in the house of Señora Anaya, a lady of distinction and entirely of Mexican lineage. Her niece, the beautiful Señorita Chonita, is visiting her, in order to be near her lover, Bernal, an officer in the Mexican army, then at war with the United States. The latter have been defeating the Mexicans, and California is passing out of Mexican control. Bernal is compelled by these novel circumstances to pay clandestine visits to his sweetheart. She has another wooer, Captain Burton, who is fighting in the American army, and who is calling on the handsome Mexican lady to push his own suit. Bernal, hiding in a clump of bushes, jealously watches the American officer, grinding his teeth in impotent rage. Meanwhile Señorita Chonita is pretending to return Burton's affection so as to enjoy his favor during the dangerous war times. But Bernal, unmindful of these facts, is merely roused more and more to anger by the rivalry existing between himself and the American protector of the family.

The second act passes in the interior of a church structure. American invaders have converted a mission church into their barracks, demolishing shrines and altars in the process. There is a typical camp scene. American troopers are relating their adventures during the last battle with the Mexicans. Suddenly a company of gay girls, dancers and singers enter and then go with the American soldiers into the large gardens of the mission. Chonita and her maid Tomasa enter unobserved, their purpose being to inform themselves of the events previous to the recent fighting. Burton, being appealed to for information, tells about Bernal's death. He then learns for the first time that Bernal was betrothed to Chonita. However, it turns out that Bernal, instead of having been killed in the engagement, has only been wounded, and a while after he seeks shelter in the church, where Chonita conceals him in one of the confessionals. The American soldiers become aware of the presence of a supposed spy, and suddenly Bernal betrays himself by creeping out of his hiding and springing on his rival, Burton, who has joined Chonita in order to renew his wooing. When Bernal makes his attack on Burton, Chonita throws herself between the two men, and accidentally is wounded· by Burton, while Bernal is taken captive by the American troops.

The last act is in the bedchamber of Chonita, where she lies seriously injured and in a delirium of fever. In that state she imagines that Bernal is being executed by the Americans as a spy. A Mexican priest has been sent for. He obeys the call, and a band of Mexicans follow in his wake. The padre conveys a message to Burton, requesting his permission to Bernal's paying a call on the sick girl. Burton not only allows this, but comes in person with Bernal. He witnesses the meeting of the two Mexican lovers, and the latter forget everything else in the transports of their reunion. Burton makes up his mind not to stand in their way any longer, but to yield the way to his rival. His regard for the girl is great and unselfish enough to wish for her happiness above all. Suddenly the band of Mexicans creep up and make an attack upon the house. Burton recklessly exposes himself to their bullets, is hit, and dies soon after. Chonita only then understands the great sacrifice her American suitor made in her behalf. She rises with difficulty from her couch, is helped to where the body of her generous wooer lies, and kneels down and says a prayer for the soul of him who was slain for her sake.

SADKO

Opera in seven tableaux by NICOLAI RIMSKY-KORSAKOFF

The libretto is based on Russian folk tales

The first production was given at Moscow in 1897. The scenes are laid in Russia and in a mythical kingdom of the sea.

Sadko, skilled both as a singer and a gusli-player, lives in the city of Novgorod on Lake Ilmen near the Baltic Sea. One day while wandering despondent beside the seashore, depressed by the mockery of his townsmen, his song captivates the Princess Volkhova, daughter of the sea king Morskoi. She tells him that there are golden fish in Lake Ilmen which will make him the wealthiest man in the world. When he asks his townsmen to help him catch the golden fish, they think him insane. He wagers his head that the fish are in the lake and when he wins the bet, the people hail him as the reincarnation of their legendary hero.

Sadko becomes rich and powerful as Princess Volkhova had predicted. Eager to gain even greater wealth, he determines to set sail for distant shores. After hearing a Viking, an Indian and a Venetian sing of the charms of their native lands, he decides to sail for Venice.

Twelve years later, his ship laden with fabulous treasures, Sadko starts for home. One day they are becalmed, for the sea king Morskoi is angry with Sadko for not paying him tribute during the past twelve years. A human sacrifice is demanded and Sadko is placed adrift upon a raft while the ship sails homeward. Sadko is carried to the depths of the sea where Morskoi dwells in a strange and beautiful palace. Sadko strikes up a dance whose rhythm the sea king and his court cannot resist. The swaying dancers call in vain on the minstrel to stop while the upper waters of the sea, stirred by the mad whirl of the lower depths, tear down cities along the shore and strew the waves with wreckage. At last as Morskoi sinks exhausted, the Princess Volkhova snatches the gusli from Sadko's hand and the waters grow calm as the two rise to the surface and are borne along toward Novgorod. They reach the coast of Sadko's home at last but the sea princess cannot live out of the water and so she is transformed into a mighty river, the Volkhova. Sadko's wife and friends discover him on the shore the next morning. He believes that the past twelve years is a dream until, at the shouts of his townsmen, he looks up to see his treasure-laden fleet sailing up the new river of Volkhova. A chorus of rejoicing ends the opera.

SALAMMBO

Opera in five acts by ERNEST REYER

Libretto by DU LOCLE after FLAUBERT'S novel

The first production was given in Brussels in 1890. The scenes are laid in Carthage during the third century.

Act I. In the gardens of Hamilcar at Megara, the mercenaries are feasting in honor of their victories. While they are toasting their protecting deities, Salammbo, Hamilcar's daughter, enters to reprove them for their license. She accepts the goblet of wine offered by Matho, one of the barbarian chiefs, while Narr'Havas, a Numidian king, looks on jealously. After Salammbo leaves, Spendius convinces Matho that he can win Salammbo by leading a revolt of the mercenaries.

Act II. Spendius bring Matho into the temple of Tanit, tutelary deity of Carthage, while the high priest Shahabarin is holding worship. Matho is to steal the Zaimph, the sacred veil of Tanit, and symbol of the city's safety and greatness. Salammbo enters and seeks to persuade the high priest to let her hold the sacred veil and thus ease the fears she has for the welfare of Carthage. Shahabarin, horrified by her sacrilegious desire to touch the Zaimph, leaves her. Matho steps from the shadows where he has been hiding with Spendius and gives her the veil. Salammbo believes him to be a god and is ready to worship him. When his protestations of love prove his mortality, she is outraged and her cries bring the priests, whom Matho defies as he escapes wrapped in the sacred veil of Tanit.

Act III. The ancients are holding council when Hamilcar enters and is told of the revolt of the mercenaries, the loss of the veil and the love of his daughter for Matho. He denies the possibility of Salammbo's loving the leader of the mercenaries.

Meantime, Salammbo is suffering from bitter self-reproach for the theft of the Zaimph and is readily persuaded by Shahabarin that she should go to the barbarian camp to reclaim the veil. She is robed in the rich garments prepared for her wedding.

Act IV. Narr'Havas is treacherously offering to aid the mercenaries when Salammbo enters veiled. Matho refuses to give her the Zaimph until they both succumb to a true and passionate love when he wraps the veil about her. Their exchange of vows is interrupted by the entrance of Hamilcar and his generals shouting their triumphs. Salammbo exhibits the sacred veil, and Matho, whose defeat is due to the traitor Narr'Havas, is sentenced by Hamilcar to be sacrificed on the altar of Tanit.

Act V. A joyous crowd swarms about the forum of Carthage for it is the wedding day of Salammbo and Narr'Havas. Matho is brought forth and Salammbo, as the rescuer of the sacred veil, is given the honor of killing him. To the horror of all she stabs herself instead, and the Libyan, taking her in his arms, kills himself with the same sword.

SALOMÉ

Opera in one act by RICHARD STRAUSS

The production of this now famous opera, by Richard Strauss, at Dresden, on December 9, 1905, created a tremendous excitement at the time. Its success was immense and its performance became the subject of much discussion, both in England and America. In England it was forbidden by the censor. In America, however, it was produced with great magnificence, and obtained an enormous vogue.

Strauss took for his text the play as written by Oscar Wilde. In this play Salomé is given an individuality totally different from that which the Biblical tale presents. In the Bible story, Salomé is simply the tool of her mother, Herodias, who urges her to ask for the head of Jokanaan. In Wilde's play she is a passionate woman, in revolt against the life of the court of Herod the Tetrarch, and in love with Jokanaan, whom she admires for his courage and daring. Jokanaan, however, repulses her and declines to accept her love. It is because of this that her love turns into hatred and makes her determined to avenge herself on him.

Jokanaan had aroused Herod's anger for preaching against his marriage with his brother's wife. He has Jokanaan imprisoned in a cistern in the palace and guarded by Roman soldiers. Salomé, passing by the cistern, hears the voice of the prisoner prophesying the ruin of Jerusalem. Attracted by his beautiful voice, she asks the guard to let her see the prisoner.

The scene of the play is the great terrace of Herod's palace, set above the banqueting hall, where some soldiers are seen hanging over the balcony. It is a moonlight night, and a young Syrian soldier is telling of Salomé's beauty, as he saw her that night. Salomé enters and hears Jokanaan crying from the cistern. She begs the young Syrian for a sight of the prisoner, and fascinates him into an obedience, though he knows he is acting against orders. When Jokanaan comes out of the cistern, he begins a prophetic anathema against him "who in a robe of silver shall one day die in the face of all the people," and against her "who hath given herself to the young men of the Egyptians." He will not have Salomé look at him. He does not desire to know who she is. It is not to her that he would speak. Salomé begs him to go on speaking. "Thy voice is as music to mine ear," she tells him. He tells her to get away from him, but she answers that she is amorous of his body. When he spurns her she scorns him and derides him. The young Syrian soldier, unable to endure her words to Jokanaan, kills himself and falls between Salomé and Jokanaan. Salomé continues to beg Jokanaan to let her kiss his mouth, but he curses her and goes down into the cistern again.

Herod, Herodias, and the court now enter and see the dead body of the soldier. The body is removed and the Tetrarch calls for wine, asking Salomé to drink. She declines to drink or to eat. The voice of Jokanaan is now heard from the cistern, prophesying that the day of which he spoke is at hand. Herodias bids that he be silenced, but Herod tells the Jews that the prophet is a holy man and must be kept from harm. Five Jews declare him to be an impostor, and ask for his death, but Herod agrees with the Nazarenes that he is the prophet

Scene from Richard Strauss's "Salome"

Elias. Jokanaan's voice is again heard telling of the coming of the Savior. Herod asks who the Savior is, and the Nazarenes tell him that he is the Messiah who is already come and who has performed many miracles, even to raising the dead. Herod is incredulous, declaring that the dead should not be raised.

The voice of Jokanaan is again heard, declaring that the coming Messiah will ascend Herod's throne. Herod, trembling with fear, asks Salomé to dance for him, hoping that by this means his mind will be diverted from thinking on the prophet's warnings and words. She declines to dance, but Herod promises her anything she asks of him, even to the half of his kingdom, if she will but dance for him. Herodias does not wish Salomé to dance, but Herod insists that he will have her dance. He gives a solemn oath that he will keep his promise to grant her any wish.

In spite of Herodias's repeated command that she should not dance, Salomé declares herself ready. The musicians then begin to play a furious dance music. Salomé, at first motionless, straightens herself and makes a sign to the musicians, who suddenly change the impetuous music to a sweet, lulling melody. Salomé then executes the "Dance of the Seven Veils." At one time, in the dance, she appears to weaken, but, beginning again with renewed passion, she dances so that she approaches the cistern in which Jokanaan is imprisoned. She remains for an instant, as if in an ecstasy, at the edge of the cistern. Then, rushing forward, she falls in a sweep at Herod's feet.

Herod praises her dancing and asks what he shall give her. Salomé requests that she shall have brought to her, on a silver charger, the head of Jokanaan. Herod cries, "No, no"; but Herodias says that Salomé has done well to ask for Jokanaan's head. Herod begs Salomé to listen to him. He has ever been kind to her, let her therefore not ask this thing of him. Salomé simply repeats her demand for the head of the prophet. "Give me the head of Jokanaan," is her repeated answer to all Herod's pleadings. Finally he consents, and the executioner is sent into the cistern to bring the head. Salomé leans over the cistern and listens eagerly. She wonders why there is no sound; but when the executioner comes out of the cistern bearing the head on a silver shield, Salomé seizes it, while Herod hides his face in his cloak, and Herodias smilingly fans herself. The Nazarenes fall on their knees in prayer. The head of the prophet in her possession, Salomé, in an amorous ecstasy, makes love to it, kissing its lips and caressing it passionately. Herod looks on in horror. "She is monstrous, thy daughter," he says to Herodias, in a low voice, but Herodias replies: "I am well pleased with my daughter. She has done well." Herod, rising, says: "Ah, there speaks my brother's wife." He will stay no longer in this place, but, rising, commands that the torches be extinguished. "Hide the moon," he cries; "hide the stars! Let us hide ourselves, Herodias! I begin to be afraid." Salomé is on the ground, exhausted, but still caressing the head and toying with its hair. "I have kissed thy mouth, Jokanaan," she keeps repeating, exultingly. As Herod is about to leave, he turns and sees Salomé in this position, illumined in a ray of the moonlight. A great disgust overcomes him. "Kill that woman!" he cries. The soldiers rush forward and crush Salomé beneath their shields.

SAMSON ET DALILA

Opera in three acts by C. SAINT-SAËNS

Text by FERDINAND LEMAIRE

This is probably the masterpiece of the composer, the music being rich and varied, and eminently dramatic in its composition. The score contains some perfect melodies, the duet between Samson and Dalila ranking among the finest love scenes ever written.

The opera opens in the city of Gaza, in Palestine, where Samson is discovered trying to revive the courage of the disheartened Hebrew soldiers.

Abimelech, Satrap of Gaza, appears on the scene with a throng of Philistines, but they are quickly dispersed, and the Satrap himself is slain by Samson. The High Priest of Dagon, on discovering the dead body of Abimelech, calls on his followers to avenge the murder, but all in vain. Finding that Samson is not to be captured by force, the wily priest devises a more cunning mode of attack. He seeks the assistance of the beautiful Dalila, and persuades her to exert her charms upon his enemy. Her graces prove so seductive that Samson half succumbs, in spite of the warnings of the Hebrews.

The scene of the second act is in the valley of Soreck, where Dalila and the High Priest are found conspiring to deliver Samson to the Philistines, by means of the blandishments of the enchantress. Samson, yielding to her continued entreaties, tells her that his strength lies in his hair. Soothing him to sleep, she shaves off his locks and puts out his eyes. He is then easily captured and put in prison, where we find him in the third act, shorn and blind, meekly turning a hand-mill, and sorrowfully listening to the rebukes of his fellow Hebrew captives, for his weakness in yielding to the love of a woman.

The last scene is the temple of Dagon, where the Philistines are celebrating their victory and praising Dalila for her cleverness. Samson is led in by a youth, and is hailed with shouts of derision by his enemies, who scoff him for being enticed by a woman's wiles. Samson, overwhelmed with grief, remains silent, his lips moving in prayer. The High Priest, determined upon his death, pours a deadly poison into a cup of wine, and commands Dalila to serve it to the blind hero, who, while pretending to approach the shrine, whispers to the youth to guide him to the pillars of the temple. This being done, he prays aloud to the God of Israel to renew his strength for just one instant. The prayer is granted, and seizing the pillars he overturns them, the temple collapsing amid the shrieks and cries of the terrified Philistines.

SAPPHO

Grand Opera in five acts by JULES MASSENET

The opera of "Sappho," by Jules Massenet, has for its plot the love-story of modern Parisian life, as told in Alphonse Daudet's novel of the same name. The libretto was written in French by Henri Cain and Bernède.

The first act takes place in the drawing-room of the house of the sculptor Caoudal, in which a masquerade ball is in progress. As the curtain rises the music of a make-believe Gypsy orchestra is heard playing loudly from the studio leading off the drawing-room. Caoudal and his friend, La Borderie, now enter, accompanied by the guests, and all in a merry humor. La Borderie complains of being tired and tries to get away. He is, however, brought back in triumph by the girls, who will not let him go. Jean Gaussin, the hero of the play and a simple young man from the country, is also a guest. He comes in from the studio in his desire to get away from the hubbub and merry-making. Caoudal jeers him for his mood and points out the pretty ladies to him. He will not be presented to them for fear of their ridicule; nor will he go back with them into the studio. He is left alone and is about to depart, when he hears the voice of Fanny, the model, singing the old studio song in company with the rest of the merrymakers. Jean's spirit is at variance with his surroundings; he sighs for his home where the Rhone bounds along, the land of promise that nursed him. Fanny enters suddenly, followed by a crowd of artists, among whom are Caoudal and La Borderie. They clamor for her kisses, but she repels them laughingly. They surround her, but as she tries to free herself she sees Jean. Turning aside to Caoudal, she asks him who the handsome boy is, but he answers absently. In the meantime Jean has been gazing at her as if spellbound. He falls in love with her at first sight, so to speak, while she, on her part, is inexplicably drawn towards him. She manages to get him aside, and on questioning him discovers, to her joy, that he is not an artist, knows nothing of the life of the Latin Quarter, but is just arrived fresh from the country of Provence. She is afraid he will find out who she is and what the life is that she is leading. Anxious to retain his good will, she persuades him to slip away with her quietly, as Caoudal comes out from the studio and summons all to supper. From the studio comes cries of "Sappho! Sappho!" The great curtain at the back is drawn aside and the guests are all disclosed sitting at small tables at supper. Caoudal, who has noticed Fanny leaving with Jean, calls some friends to him, and they laughingly exchange gestures of pity for the young fellow. As the curtain falls some gypsies at the back execute a dance.

The action of the second act takes place in Jean Gaussin's lodgings in the Rue d'Amsterdam, Paris. Jean is discovered at his work in company with his father, Césaire. Jean is singing while working. Passing from singing to talk, we learn that Césaire and Divonne, his wife, have come to Paris to place Jean in some position, and to take home with them, on their return to Provence, Jean's cousin, Irene, the companion of his childhood days. Divonne and Irene then come in, the former in a great state of excitement from seeing Paris. Césaire and Divonne go off to make ready for their departure, and Jean and Irene indulge in sentimental recollections of the happy days they spent together in the past. The parents come in and catch the young people in a lover's embrace, and laugh good-naturedly at their embarrassment. A touching scene follows, in which the parents take leave of Jean and finally depart with Irene. Jean is left meditating sadly on his loneliness. He is not alone long. Fanny enters without knocking and approaches him quietly. She has waited until he should be alone, and finds him in the very mood for her companionship. She examines the room and admires its pretty arrangement. Noticing a statuette of Sappho by Caoudal for which she herself had been the model, she becomes confused and almost betrays herself. Recovering herself, she turns the conversation and hums him a tune which reminds Jean of his old country life. Jean, transported with passion, declares his love for her and they plight their troth to each other.

When the curtain goes up on the third act, a year is supposed to have elapsed. Jean is now living with Fanny as husband and wife. He is, if anything, more in love with her now than he was when she came to his lodgings. Fanny, on her part, is really in love with him. She is overjoyed in the belief that her new life may continue, and that she has left for ever the old life of the Latin Quarter. The first scene of this act is a passionate love duet, in which each expresses to the other the depth of their mutual affection. They walk off together, happy in their love. As they disappear Caoudal, La Borderie, and some young people enter. They see an inn near the cottage, and, attracted by its appearance, call to the rest of their companions to join them, and ask loudly for the landlord. A lively scene ensues, followed by a supper. Strolling musicians passing by, the company follow them, with the exception of Caoudal and

La Borderie, who remain behind. Jean returns alone to meet his Bohemian friends. In a casual way Caoudal asks Jean if he is still living with "Sappho," the name by which Fanny has been known among the artists of the Latin Quarter. Jean does not understand to whom his friend refers. The truth, however, is soon made evident to him, and he realizes for the first time that the model of the statuette Caoudal gave him is the girl to whom he has given his whole heart. The realization fills him with disgust, and he denies to Caoudal that Fanny is still with him. Caoudal then tells him of some of Fanny's adventures as a model, and that she has a child living with her father got by a former lover. Jean, overcome with rage and anger, voices his feelings in terms of hatred against her. Fanny enters at this instant radiant with happiness. Seeing Caoudal and La Borderie with Jean and noticing Jean's disfigured countenance, she realizes that she has been betrayed. Jean reviles her for her deception. "All my love has been changed to gall," he cries. Fanny curses her past friends as a pack of cowards. She believes they have purposely told on her to deprive her of the joy of the one pure love of her life, and the curtain falls on the agony of her despair.

In the fourth act we are taken to Jean Gaussin's parental home in Provence. A house to the right and a garden with a well to the left are backed by the Rhone and the landscape of the country round Villeneuve. Césaire, Divonne, and Irene are present with Jean, who is distressed and sad because he finds himself unable to endure his old life in the country. The parents try to comfort him, and his cousin reminds him of the days of their childhood when they were Joseph and Mary to each other. But all is of no avail. Césaire suddenly comes in and bids his wife and Irene to go away. While they are there he will not explain his reason for the request, but when they leave he tells Jean that "Sappho" is come. He begs his son to be brave, and Jean promises his father that he will never give way. Césaire goes out and Fanny comes in, walking slowly and looking about her. Seeing Jean, she rushes toward him as if to throw her arms about his neck, but Jean's aspect holds her back. "Blame me not that I have sought you," she cries; she cannot bear his absence from her. Her seductive beauty and simple pleading so touch him that his resolves melt away, and he is about to become reconciled to her when his father and mother come in. They are just in time, as they see, and Césaire orders his son into the house. Fanny steps forward to go to Jean, but finds herself face to face with his mother. Fanny asks her who she is and Divonne tells her she is Jean's mother. Fanny, in confusion, begs her pardon, and then, seeing Jean going away, she stretches out her arms to him and leaves, sobbing.

It is winter when the curtain rises on the fifth act. The scene is the dismantled room of the little house at Ville d'Avray, where Jean and Fanny had lived their year's happiness. The snow-covered country can be seen through a glass door at the back. Fanny is alone, sad, but resigned. She tears up some letters of Jean's she has been reading, and resolves to devote herself to the upbringing of her child. Jean enters suddenly and surprises her in the midst of her meditations. He could not stay away any longer. He has come back to live with her. He has left his parents, given up his home, resigned his career, only that he might be with her again. He is tired and worn out by the conflict of emotions he has endured since she left him. In this reconciliation Fanny calls him by the endearing "my love," which sends Jean back again into a fit of doubt and jealousy. He is reminded by it of Caoudal's vivid description of an earlier love adventure Fanny had played with another lover, and the recollection maddens him. Tired out, however, he falls wearily into a chair and goes off to sleep. Fanny has now realized that she can never again live with Jean in the happy state she had dreamed of, and of which she had had so intoxicating a draught. She writes him a letter of farewell, while he is restlessly sleeping, and, bidding him good-by, she goes out slowly, leaving him still sleeping.

LE SAUTERIOT

Opera in two acts by SYLVIO LAZZARI

Libretto by ROCHE and PERRIER, based on KEYSERLING'S drama, "Sacre de Printemps"

This opera was first produced in Chicago in 1918. Lithuania of the past century provides the setting.

Orti, a Lithuanian Cinderella, nicknamed the Grasshopper, is the natural daughter of Mikkel whose wife Anna lies dying as the curtain rises. The doctor gives Orti medicine for Anna in case she grows worse, warning the girl that more than ten drops of the drug would be fatal. Anna's old mother, Trine, tells Orti the legend of the woman who prayed that she might die instead of her baby—and her prayer was granted. Knowing that she is despised and a drudge, Orti prays that death will take her in Anna's place.

Orti is secretly in love with Indrik who has eyes for no one save Madda, Mikkel's young sister. At the village festival, Indrik, who has been cast off by Madda after a quarrel, fights with Josef, his successor in her affections. As knives flash, Orti rushes forward in time to prevent Josef's fatal thrust. She is the heroine of the festival. Indrik makes love to her and for the first time the little Grasshopper tastes happiness. A few days later however she discovers that he has gone back to Madda, and, believing that she no longer has anything to live for, Orti takes a fatal overdose of Anna's medicine.

SCHWANDA

Folk Opera in two acts by JAROMIR WEINBERGER

Libretto by MILOS KARES

This work was first given in Prague on April 27, 1927.

Schwanda is one of the most charming works which has appeared on the operatic stage for the last decade. Its music has melodic invention, and the action is well developed and characterized, yet despite this fact it has not had any real success in America. Perhaps if it had been given more often the public might have responded.

Schwanda, the Bagpiper of Strakonitz, lives on a farm with his wife Dorota. Babinsky, a bandit, hides in a tree from pursuing soldiers, and when they are gone conceives a plan to win Dorota from her husband. He tells Schwanda of the glories of the great world, and persuades him to accompany him to Queen Ice-Hearts court. Dorota, finding Schwanda gone, decides to follow him. To the court of the Queen, who has sold her living heart to the Sorcerer, Schwanda's merry bagpipe brings happiness and laughter. The Sorcerer leaves in anger and the Queen has just told Schwanda that she will marry him when Dorota appears. The furious Queen then orders Schwanda to be condemned to death.

Schwanda is about to be executed before the city gate. He asks one last request—to be permitted to play his bagpipes, but these have been hidden by the Sorcerer and cannot be found. The Headsman raises his axe, but only strikes Schwanda with a broom which Babinsky has substituted for it. Babinsky then hands Schwanda his pipes, and the power of his music sends the Queen, Sorcerer, soldiers, and judges dancing back to the city, leaving Schwanda, Babinsky, and Dorota alone. Schwanda tells Dorota that if he has ever kissed the Queen, "may the Devil take him to Hell on the spot," and the Bagpiper sinks at once into the earth amid thunder and lightning. Dorota then rejects Babinsky's advances and Babinsky, moved by her love for her husband, agrees to restore him to her.

In Hell Schwanda refuses to play for the Devil, who orders him tortured. Babinsky appears and offers to play cards with the Devil, staking his own and Schwanda's souls against half Satan's kingdom. The Devil wins, but Babinsky proving that he has cheated, is declared the winner. Babinsky restores the Devil half the kingdom he has forfeited, and then sets off with Schwanda for the upper world, where he is restored to his faithful wife.

THE SECRET OF SUSANNE

Interlude in one act by E. WOLF-FERRARI

Text by E. GOLISCIANI

The first production was at Berlin, 1910. The scene is Piedmont, and the time the present.

Count Gil and his bride Susanne are spending their honeymoon at the young husband's estates in Piedmont, and here, in the pleasant drawing-room of the old château, the count coming in suddenly, notices the unmistakable odor of tobacco smoke. It is really the bride, Susanne, who is passionately fond of her cigarette, and who is mortally afraid this may displease her husband. She has therefore bribed the butler, Sante, to connive at the deception and to give her an opportunity every little while to indulge her foible. But Count Gil has, of course, no notion of this simple truth. Instead, the young husband, when he kisses his bride on her hair and discovers the traces of smoke, jumps at once to the conclusion that he has a rival even thus early, and grows desperately jealous. He begins to heap reproaches on his young wife, and she, thinking he refers only to her habit of smoking, tries to pacify him, but in a rather light vein. The count deems this quite intolerable, and takes exception to her tone of levity, without, however, speaking out plainly as to his suspicions. Thus the couple talk and upbraid each other at cross-purposes, until a full-sized quarrel ensues, in the course of which furniture is overturned and glassware is smashed. A sort of reconciliation is patched up, and Susanne reminds Gil that he has an engagement at that hour. He says nothing, goes off, but has his suspicions newly aroused by the above circumstance. Therefore he returns without warning to Susanne's boudoir, and detects anew the odor of cigarette smoke. In his uncontrollable fury he seizes the supposed culprit's hand, and in doing so burns his fingers with the glowing cigarette she had attempted to hide. Gil, instantly sizing up the situation, sees that he has made a fool of himself, bursts out in hearty laughter, and Susanne confesses the whole awful truth to him. As a token that he has forgiven her he even hands his wife a new cigarette, and daintily helps her light it.

SEMIRAMIDE

Lyric Tragedy in two acts by GIOACHINI ROSSINI
Text by GAETANO ROSSI

This is one of the best of the fifty operas written by Rossini. The subject is taken from Voltaire's "Semiramis." It was first presented in Venice in 1823. The music is stirring in its passion, and has throughout the smoothness and richness of melody which characterize the work of its versatile composer.

The scene is laid in Babylon. In the first act, Ninus, the King, is murdered by his Queen, Semiramis, who is assisted in her evil design by her lover Assur, an aspirant to the throne. Semiramis had given over her son, Ninia, at an early age, to the priest Oroe, who had brought him up to believe that he was of Scythian origin. Nina enters the service of the Queen under the name of Arsaces, and soon becomes a renowned warrior.

On returning victorious from the wars, he is loaded with honors by Semiramis, who, totally ignorant of his parentage, falls in love with him and openly avowing her passion, asks him to marry her. Arsaces refuses, as he is already in love with the royal princess Azema.

During a gathering of the Babylonians in the temple, while Semiramis is announcing to her people her choice for their future King, the gates of Ninus' tomb suddenly open, and his ghost appears in their midst, predicting that Arsaces will be his successor to the throne, and commanding him to avenge his death upon the enemy who shall visit the tomb that night. In the meantime the

Priest Oroe has revealed to Arsaces the true circumstances of his birth, whereupon he informs his mother of his parentage. The repentant Queen declares that he shall be the successor to the crown, and warns him against the aspiring and evil Assur.

At midnight Arsaces descends to the tomb of his father, and is followed by Assur, who has deliberately planned to murder him. Semiramis, fearful for the life of her son, follows Assur into the tomb, and Arsaces, who is lying in wait for him, hears the footsteps of his mother approaching, and, thinking her to be Assur, stabs her. She dies in his arms, and Assur, being imprisoned, all obstacles are removed, and Arsaces, after marrying Azema, is proclaimed King of Babylon.

IL SERAGLIO

Opera in three acts by MOZART

Text after BRETZNER by G. STEPHANIE

Mozart modestly called this opera a vaudeville (in German, Singspiel). They were the fashion toward the end of the last century, but Il Seraglio ranks much higher, and may be justly called a comic opera of the most pleasing kind. The music is really charming, both fresh and original.

The libretto is equally happy. It particularly inspired Mozart, because given him by the Emperor Joseph at the time when he, Mozart, a happy bridegroom, was about to conduct into his home his beloved Constanze. The story is as follows:

Constanza, the betrothed bride of Belmonte, is with her maid Bionda (Blondchen) and Pedrillo, Belmonte's servant, captured by pirates. All three are sold as slaves to Selim Pasha, who keeps the ladies in his harem, taking Constanza for himself and giving Bionda to his overseer Osmin. Pedrillo has found means to inform his master of their misfortune, and Belmonte comes seeking entrance to the Pasha's villa in the guise of an artist. Osmin, who is much in love with Bionda, though she treats him haughtily, distrusts the artist and tries to interfere. But Pedrillo, who is gardener in the Pasha's service, frustrates Osmin's purpose and Belmonte is engaged. The worthy Pasha is quite infatuated with Constanza, and tries hard to gain her affections. But Constanza has sworn to be faithful till death to Belmonte, and great is her rapture when Bionda brings the news that her lover is near.

With the help of Pedrillo, who manages to intoxicate Osmin, they try to escape, but Osmin overtakes them and brings them back to the Pasha, who at once orders that they be brought before him. Constanza, advancing with noble courage, explains that the pretended artist is her lover, and that she will rather die with him than leave him. Selim Pasha, overwhelmed by this discovery, retires to think about what he shall do, and his prisoners prepare for death, Belmonte and Constanza with renewed tender protestations of love, Pedrillo and Bionda without either fear or trembling.

Great is their happiness and Osmin's wrath when the noble Pasha, touched by their constancy, sets them free, and asks for their friendship, bidding them remember him kindly after their return into their own country.

SHANEWIS

Opera in two parts by CHARLES WAKEFIELD CADMAN

Book by EBERHART

This opera was produced for the first time in 1918 in New York. The action takes place in a modern American city and on an Oklahoma Indian reservation.

Act I. Shanewis, an Indian girl whose voice has been cultivated through the generous aid of Mrs. Everton, a wealthy society woman, sings at a fashionable soirée given to celebrate the return of Amy Everton from Europe. At the entertainment Lionel Rhodes, Amy's fiancé, falls in love with Shanewis at first sight and proposes to her. She tells him that her acceptance depends upon the consent of her people on the Oklahoma reservation. She is unaware that Lionel is already engaged to Amy, who does not suspect her fiancé's unfaithfulness.

Act II. During the ceremonial dances on the Indian reservation, Lionel tries to persuade the dark-eyed Shanewis to marry him. Her Indian suitor, Philip, gives her a bow and poisoned arrow which another Indian maiden has used to slay a false white lover. Suddenly Mrs. Everton and Amy appear, and poor Shanewis learns of Lionel's duplicity. She curses the white race but does not use the poisoned arrow. Philip, however, has no such compunctions and shoots the gay deceiver through the heart while Shanewis cries: "He is mine in death!"

SIBERIA

Tragic Opera in three acts by UMBERTO GIORDANO

Text by F. CIVININI

This opera was first produced in 1903, at Milan.

The first act takes place in a palace at Petrograd, which was given by Prince Alexis to his mistress, Stephana. Ivan, a trusted servant of the prince, and Nikona are watching for the homecoming of their mistress. Ivan drops off to sleep. Day breaks at last. Gleby, a spy in the pay of the prince, enters and inquires for Stephana. He is told that she is still abed, but he opens the door to her chamber, and finds the room empty and the bed undisturbed. Prince Alexis suddenly appears, having friends with him, whom he wishes to entertain. He asks for Stephana, and this time Gleby, in order to shield himself for neglect of duty, pushes Nikona into the vacant room, and pretends that Stephana has not yet risen and must not be disturbed. Alexis remains for some little while, awaiting Stephana, but when she does not appear, departs with his friends. Hardly, however, has he done so, when Stephana is seen at the garden gate. Gleby, the spy, stops her, asking her who her new lover may be. But Stephana ignores his questions, and is about to enter her own room, when Prince Alexis, who has Captain Walitzin with him, returns. The latter has come to bid farewell to Stephana, having been summoned to join his regiment which is stationed in a Siberian town. The prince leaves with Walitzin. Vassili, a young officer, enters. He tells

Nikona about a young girl he has met and with whom he is smitten. Stephana enters, and Vassili recognizes in her his unknown fair one. But Stephana is not aware of his adoration, and takes him to be a spy of the prince, sent by him to watch her, and upbraids him. Nikona gives Stephana the key to the situation, and Vassili declares his love for Stephana, who accepts it. Then she and Nikona both press Vassili to leave before the prince should discover him. Suddenly Alexis returns, and finding Vassili present under suspicious circumstances, he wants to know who he is. Stephana replies: "It is he whom I love." Alexis is stung by jealousy, and makes an insulting remark to Vassili. Both draw, and Vassili wounds the prince, his superior in the army. With this he realizes his dangerous position, and cries out: "Farewell to glory!"

The second act shows a convict station at the borders of Siberia. A captain is awaiting with impatience a body of political offenders banished to Siberia. Incidental scenes in which pedlars and peasants figure. The train of convicts halts at the station. Stephana comes in and shows a written permit to speak to Convict No. 107, who is brought in. It is Vassili, and the two have a tender meeting, Vassili speaking pathetically of the tortures he has suffered lately. Stephana implores him to allow her to join the band of convicts and share his fate, but he demurs, saying that the sacrifice would be too great. Stephana persists, and both enter the ranks of the banished and march into exile.

The scene of the third act is at the prison town in Siberia. It is Eastertime. Walitzin, who is in command, orders that work cease and the holidays be observed. The rude blockhouse of Vassili and Stephana is visible in the rear. A fugitive comes and outlines plans of escape to the two lovers, who decline. Walitzin expresses his sympathy for the fate of Stephana, but she repels his advances, and tells him she is happy to share the lot of her beloved. Gleby enters and details a plan to ameliorate the harsh conditions under which Stephana is living. She, however, refuses to listen to him. Gleby, who had acted under instructions from Prince Alexis, grows angry at being spurned and falsely informs Vassili that Stephana has been unfaithful to him. Vassili is heartbroken at the news, but is soon furnished proof that the charge is false. The two then prepare for flight, but Gleby betrays their intentions to the guards, who shoot at the fugitives. The report of a gun is heard. Stephana has been mortally wounded and Vassili is apprehended. Stephana appeals to Walitzin to set her lover free, and Walitzin, touched at her devotion, complies with her request. Stephana is overjoyed, rallies, and sinks into the arms of her lover, where she finally breathes her last.

SIEGFRIED

Second day of the Nibelungen Ring by WAGNER

Musical Drama in three acts

The first act represents a part of the forest where Fafner guards the Rhinegold and where Sieglinda has found refuge. We find her son Siegfried—to whom when she was dying she gave birth—in the rocky cave of Mime the Nibelung, brother of Alberich, who has brought up the child as his own, knowing that he is destined to slay Fafner and to gain the ring, which he covets for himself. Seigfried, the brave and innocent boy, instinctively shrinks from this father, who is so ugly, so mean and vulgar, while he has a deep longing for his dead mother, whom he never knew. He gives vent to these feelings in impatient questions about her. The dwarf answers unwillingly and gives him the broken pieces of the old sword Nothung (needful), which his mother left as the only precious remembrance of Siegfried's father.

Siegfried asks Mime to forge the fragments afresh, while he rushes away into the woods.

During his absence Wotan comes to Mime in the guise of a wanderer. Mime, though he knows him not, fears him, and would fain drive him away. Finally he puts three questions to his guest. The first is the name of the race which lives in earth's deepest depths, the second the name of those who live on earth's back, and the third that of those who live above the clouds. Of course Wotan answers them all, redeeming his head and shelter thereby; but now it is his turn to put three questions. He first asks what race it is that Wotan loves most, though he dealt hardly with them, and Mime answers rightly that they are the Waelsungs, whose son Siegfried is; then Wotan asks after the sword which is to make Siegfried victorious. Mime joyously names "Nothung," but when Wotan asks him who is to unite the pieces he is in great embarrassment, for he remembers his task and perceives too late what question he ought to have asked. Wotan leaves him, telling him that only that man can forge it who never knew fear. Siegfried, finding the sword still in fragments when he returns, melts these in fire, and easily forges them together, to Mime's great awe, for he sees now that this boy is the one whom the stranger has meant.

In the second scene we see the opening of Fafner's cavern, where Alberich keeps watch for the dragon's slayer, so long predicted.

Wotan, approaching, warns him that Alberich's brother Mime has brought up the boy who is to slay Fafner, in the hope of gaining Alberich's ring, the wondrous qualities of which are unknown to Siegfried.

Wotan awakes Fafner, the dragon, telling him that his slayer is coming.

Mime, who has led Siegfried to this part of the forest under the pretext of teaching him fear, approaches now, and Siegfried, eager for combat, kills the dreadful worm. Accidentally tasting the blood, he all at once understands the language of the birds. They tell him to seek for the Tarnhelm and for the ring, which he finds in the cavern. Meanwhile the brothers, Alberich and Mime, quarrel over the treasure, which they hope to gain. When Siegfried returns with ring and helmet he is again warned by the voice of a wood-bird not to trust in Mime.

Having tasted the dragon's blood, Siegfried is enabled to probe Mime's innermost thoughts, and so learns that Mime means to poison him, in order to obtain the treasure. He then kills the traitor with a single stroke. Stretching himself under the linden-tree to repose after that day's hard work, he again hears the voice of the wood-bird, which tells him of a glorious bride, sleeping on a rock surrounded by fire; and flying before him, the bird shows Siegfried the way to the spot.

In the third scene we find Wotan once more awakening Erda, to seek her counsel as to how best to avert the doom which he sees coming, but she is less wise than he and so he decides to let fate have its course. When he sees Siegfried coming, he for the last time tries to oppose him by barring the way to Brünnhilde, but the sword Nothung splits the god's spear. Seeing that his power avails him nothing he retires to Walhalla, there to await the "Dusk of the Gods."

Siegfried plunges through the fire, awakes the Walkyrie, and after a long resistance wins the proud virgin.

SILVANA

Romantic Opera in four acts by WEBER

Text by ERNST PASQUÉ

This opera was left unfinished by Weber. It has, however, recently been completed, the text by Ernst Pasqué, and the music by Ferdinand Langer, who re-arranged the manuscript with loving care, interweaving different compositions from Weber, as, for instance, his "Invitation à la valse" and his "Polonaise," which are dexterously introduced into the ballet of the second act.

The action is taken from an old German legend which comes to us from the land of the Rhine. There we may still find the ruins of the two castles Sternberg and Liebenstein.

Of these our legend says that they belonged to two brothers, who hated each other, for the one, Boland, loved his brother's bride and was refused by her. By way of revenge he slew his brother and burned down his castle. But in the fray the wife he coveted disappeared with her child, and both were supposed to have perished in the flames.

Since then Boland has fallen into deep melancholy, and the consequences of his dreadful deed have never ceased to torment him. His only son, who lost his mother in early childhood, has grown up solitary, knowing nothing of woman's sweetness, of peace and happiness. His only passion is the hunt. He has grown into manhood, and his father and his vassals wish him to marry, but never yet has he found a woman who has touched his heart with love.

In the beginning of the first act we see him hunting in the forest. He has lost his way and his companions, and finds himself in a spot which he has never before seen. A beautiful maiden comes out of a small cottage, and both fall in love at first sight. The returning collier would fain keep his only child, who has not yet seen anything of the world; but the nymph of the forest, Silvana's protectrice, beckons him away. When at length the Count's fellow-hunters find him, he presents Silvana to them as his bride. The unfortunate collier is made drunk with wine, and during his sleep they take his daughter away to the castle of the old Rhinegrave.

But Silvana is protected in the new world into which she enters by the nymph, who follows her in the guise of a young minstrel. The old Count, hearing of his son's resolution, is quite willing to receive the bride, and even consents to go to the peasants' festival and look at the dancing and frolicking given in honor of his son's bridal.

There we find Ratto, the collier, who seeks his daughter Silvana, telling everybody that robbers took her away from him, and beseeching help to discover her. Meanwhile Silvana arrives in rich and costly attire between Gerold, the young Count, and the old Rhinegrave. The latter, attracted by her fairness and innocence, has welcomed her as his daughter without asking for antecedents. When the dances of the villagers have ended, the nymph enters in the guise of a minstrel, asking to be allowed to sing to the hearers, as was the custom on the banks of the Rhine.

She begins her ballad, the contents of which terrify the Rhinegrave, for it is his own awful deed which he hears. Springing up, he draws his sword against the minstrel, but Silvana rises, protecting him with outstretched arms. All are stupefied; Gerold looks with suspicion on his bride, hanging on the breast of the stranger. He asks for an explanation, but Silvana is silent. It is part of her trial, not to betray the nymph. At the same moment Ratto, the collier, recognizes and claims Silvana as his daughter. Everybody now looks with contempt on the low-born maiden, and the Rhinegrave commands them to be put into prison; but Gerold, believing in his bride's innocence, though appearances are against her, entreats her once more to defend herself. Silvana only asserts her innocence and her love for Gerold, but will give no proofs. So the collier and his daughter and the minstrel are taken to prison. But when the keeper opens the door in the morning the minstrel has disappeared.

The old Count, disgusted at the idea of his son's union with a collier's daughter, accuses her of being a sorceress. He compels her to confess that she seduced his son by magic arts, and Silvana consents to say anything rather than injure her lover. She is conducted before a court and condemned to the funeral pile. Gerold, not once doubting her, is resolved to share her death, when in the last critical moment the minstrel once more raises his voice and finishes the ballad which the Rhinegrave had interrupted so violently. He tells the astonished hearers that the wife and daughter of the Count, who was slain by his brother, were not burned in the castle, but escaped to the forest, finding kindly refuge in a poor collier's hut, where the mother died, leaving her child, Silvana, under his protection.

The Rhinegrave, full of remorse, embraces Silvana, beseeching her forgiveness, and the lovers are united.

SIMON BOCCANEGRA

Opera in a Prologue and three acts by GIUSEPPE VERDI

Libretto by F. M. PIAVE and A. BOITO

Simon Boccanegra was first given in its revised version, which Verdi worked over late in life, in Milan in 1880 with Victor Maurel, Tamagno, and Edouard de Reszke. Originally written in one of Verdi's early periods, the music of the revised version in the first acts shows the great Italian composer at his best, the opening scene in particular reminding one of the style which he revealed in his "Othello." Until it was sung at the Metropolitan Opera House on Jan. 28, 1932, it had never been heard in America. It's success was immediate and profound.

Simon Boccanegra, a Genonese corsair loves Maria, the daughter of Fiesco, a great noble of Genoa, who opposes the suit, despite the fate that Maria has had a daughter by Simon. When the opera begins Paolo and Pietro, two ambitious plebians, are plotting to make Simon Doge of Genoa, Simon knowing that if he becomes Doge Fiesco will be powerless to forbid his union with his daughter, who is being held a prisoner in her father's palace. Simon enters the palace and Fiesca confronts him, haughtily refusing consent to the marriage unless Simon can bring to him the daughter who was born to him and Maria. Simon, despite all his efforts, has been unable to find her, as she had disappeared when her old nurse died. Thus the reconciliation is impossible, and Simon entering the palace finds Maria dead.

Twenty-five years pass. Simon's lost daughter has been living near Genoa under the name of Amelia Grimaldi under the care of Fiesco, who after Simon's accession to the dogeship, has changed his name to Andrea. Fiesco does not know Amelia's real identity, believing her to be an orphan found in a convent on the day the real Amelia died. Fiesco has been hatching a plot to overthrow Simon, and his chief confederate is Gabriele Adorno with whom Amelia is in love. Simon on visiting the Grimaldi house to ask Amelia in marriage with his courtier Paolo, discovers her identity, and reveals himself as her father. When Amelia tells she is already in love, Simon refuses to give her to Paolo, and thereby incurs Paolo's hatred, who then has Amelia abducted.

Gabriele is brought to the Doge accused of having killed Lorenzin, in whose house Amelia has been hidden, and as Amelia has been rescued, Paolo, fearing discovery, starts to leave the council chamber, but is prevented by Simon. Gabriele thinks it is the Doge himself who has abducted Amelia, and he attempts to kill Simon, but is prevented by Amelia, who throws herself between them. Simon suspects the real villain is Paolo, and demands that Paolo join him in cursing the abductor. This Paolo has to do, and Gabrielle and Fiesca are kept prisoners in the Palace.

Paolo, terrified by the curse he has pronounced against himself, puts poison into Simon's cup, and also asks Fiesco to stab Simon while he sleeps. When Fiesco refuses Paolo tells Gabriele that the Doge has evil intentions toward Amelia, whereupon Gabriele accuses Amelia of loving Simon. She acknowledges it, but says that her love is pure. She hides Gabriele just as her father enters. She pleads with Simon for Gabriele's life, and Simon agrees to grant it. Simon then drinks the poisoned cup, and when he begins to feel drowsy, Gabriele comes out of his hiding place to kill him. Amelia, however, prevents it, telling him that Simon is her father. When the conspirators break in to dethrone Simon, Gabriele fights by his side.

The revolt is quelled, and Paolo, who is captured, is condemned to death, but mockingly tells Fiesco that the Doge will die first. The poison now begins to take effect, and Fiesco declares their enmity at an end—too late. Simon gives Amelia and Gabriele his blessing, and bestows the Doge's crown upon Gabriele just before he dies.

John Charles Thomas as Athanael in "Thais"

SNEGOUROCHKA

Opera in four acts with a prologue by
NICOLAI RIMSKY-KORSAKOFF

Book by OSTRAVSKY based upon a national epic

The first performance took place at Petrograd in 1882. The setting is legendary Russia.

In the prologue, Snegourochka, daughter of Winter and Spring, begs her parents to permit her to lead the existence of a mortal. She has heard the song of the Shepherd Lel, and longs to leave the forest where she has been carefully sheltered since Summer has decreed her death with the first ray of sunshine and love that touches her. Unwillingly her parents entrust her to the care of a peasant couple, Bobyl and Bobylika, and Spring bids her daughter seek her by the lakeside should she encounter trouble.

Act I. Snegourochka is seen outside the cottage of the peasants. She is attracted to Lel, darling of the villiage girls, who will have none of her. Mizgyr, a wild young Tartar merchant, loves the Snow Maiden at first sight and abandons Kupava, his betrothed bride, for her sake. Lel comforts the unhappy Kupava.

Act II. At the court of the mythical king of Benderei, Kupava demands justice. Mizgyr pleads the beauty of Snegourochka in his defense. When the Snow Maiden appears, she wins the Tsar's favor and he promises her hand to any of his courtiers who can win her love before sunrise the next morning.

Act III. The people of Benderei hold arcadian revels.

Lel and Kupava wander with them through the forests while Mizgyr continues his vain wooing of Snegourochka who is protected by the wood sprites that force him to lose his way. The Snow Maiden goes in search of her mother.

Act IV. Spring comes to her daughter and grants her wish to love as a mortal. Mizgyr appears and she responds to his renewed pleading. But at the same moment a ray of sunlight strikes her and she vanishes, leaving her lover to kill himself as the people's chant to the midnight sun rises on the air.

LA SONNAMBULA

Opera in two acts by VINCENZO BELLINI

Text by FELICE ROMANI

This opera is decidedly of the best of Bellini's muse. Though it does not reach the standard of Norma, its songs are so rich and melodious that they seem to woo the ear and cannot be heard without pleasure.

Add to these advantages a really fine as well as touching libretto, and it may be easily understood why the opera has not yet disappeared from the stage repertory, though composed more than fifty years ago.

It is a simple village-peasant story which we have to relate. The scene of action is a village in Switzerland, where the rich farmer Elvino has married a poor orphan, Amina. The ceremony has taken place at the magistrate's, and Elvino is about to obtain the sanction of the church to his union, when the owner of the castle, Count Rudolph, who fled from home in his boyhood, returns most unexpectedly and, at once making love to Amina, excites the bridegroom's jealousy. Lisa, the young owner of a little inn, who wants Elvino for herself and disdains the devotion of Alexis, a simple peasant, tries to avenge herself on her happy rival. Lisa is a coquette and flirts with the Count, whom the judge recognizes. While she yet prates with him, the door opens, and Amina enters, walking in her sleep and calling for Elvino. Lisa conceals herself, but forgets her handkerchief. The Count, seeing Amina's condition and awed by her purity, quits the room, where Amina lies down, always in deep sleep. Just then the people, having heard of the Count's arrival, come to greet him and find Amina instead. At the same moment Elvino, summoned by Lisa, rushes in, and finding his bride in the Count's room turns away from her in disdain, snatching his wedding ring from her finger in his wrath, and utterly disbelieving Amina's protestations of innocence and the Count's assurances. Lisa succeeds in attracting Elvino's notice and he promises to marry her.

The Count once more tries to persuade the angry bridegroom of his bride's innocence, but without result, when Teresa, Amina's foster-mother, shows Lisa's handkerchief, which was found in the Count's room. Lisa reddens, and Elvino knows not whom he shall believe, when all of a sudden Amina is seen, emerging from a window of the mill, walking in a trance, and calling for her bridegroom in most touching accents.

All are convinced of her innocence when they see her in this state of somnambulism, in which she crosses a very narrow bridge without falling. Elvino himself replaces the wedding ring on her finger, and she awakens from her trance in his arms. Everybody is happy at the turn which things have taken; Elvino asks Amina's forgiveness and leaves Lisa to her own bitter reflections.

SUOR ANGELICA

Romantic Opera in three acts by GIACOMO PUCCINI

Text by ILLICA and GIACOSA

First performance in Rome, 1914. The scene is Italy, end of the fifteenth century.

Act I. Sister Angelica, a daughter of a noble family of Florence, has been compelled by her proud relatives to take the veil because of a youthful error. For seven long years she has been vainly waiting to hear from all those dear to her. Her soul has been torn by repentance and longing. The abbess of the convent of which she is an inmate enters and makes announcement that Angelica's aunt, the princess, has come to call on her. The abbess warns the sister that she must be full of submission and humility in conversation with her visitor.

Act II. The princess coldly tells Angelica that she has come to ask her to sign a certain act of release, a document made legally necessary by the approaching nuptials of Angelica's younger sister. She adds that only one course is open to Angelica, namely, strict and life-long expiation. Finally, in answer to urgent questions by Sister Angelica, the princess informs her that her child, "the babe she had seen and kissed only once since its birth," had died two years previously.

Act III. Angelica, in a sudden frenzy of despair, after hearing this news, concocts a poison and attempts suicide. But remorse seizes her. She implores the Virgin not to let her die in mortal sin, and then the miracle takes place. The Mother of Comfort suddenly appears on the threshold of the little church, enveloped in heavenly radiance; a blond child walks in front of the Virgin who, with a gesture of ineffable benevolence, gently pushes the boy into the arms of his dying mother, whilst a choir of nuns and angels sings: "Thou art saved!"

IL TABARRO

One-act opera by GIACOMO PUCCINI

Book by ADAMI after GOLD'S "La Hauppelande"

The first production was given in New York in 1918. The setting is a barge on the Seine during modern times.

The longshoremen are leaving Michele's barge after the day's work. One of them, Luigi, who is in love with Michele's young wife, Giogetta, lingers to whisper that she is to strike a match to let him know when he may safely return to her arms. Michele comes on deck. He suspects his wife and in an effort to awaken her early love for him, he reminds her of the times when he used to shelter her under his great cloak. But these reminiscences only bore Giogetta who feigns weariness and goes down into the cabin.

It has grown dark. Michele, sitting alone on the barge, lights his pipe. Thinking that the flaring match is Giogetta's signal, Luigi climbs aboard and is seized and choked to death by Michele who covers the body with his cloak. He re-lights his pipe. Giogetta, who has heard muffled noises, comes on deck and is reassured when she sees her husband quietly smoking. To atone for her earlier frigidity, she now begins to talk of the days when Michele first loved her. She wishes that she could again find shelter in the folds of his big coat. For reply, Michele raises the cloak—and Giogetta sees her lover's body.

THE TAMING OF THE SHREW

Comic Opera in four acts by HERMANN GOETZ

Text done after Shakespeare's comedy by J. V. WIDMANN

This beautiful opera is the only one which the gifted young composer left complete, for he died of consumption in his early manhood. His death is all the more to be lamented, as this composition shows a talent capable of performances far above the average. Its melodies are very fresh and winning, and above all original.

As the subject of the libretto is so generally known, it is not necessary to do more than shortly epitomize here. Of the libretto itself, however, it may be remarked, in passing, that it is uncommonly well done; it is in rhymes which are harmonious and well turned. The translation is quite free and independent, but the sense and the course of action are the same, though somewhat shortened and modified, so that we only find the chief of the persons we so well know.

Kate is the same headstrong young lady, though she does not appear in a very bad light, her wilfulness being the result of maidenly pride, which is ashamed to appear weak before the stronger sex. She finds her master in Petruchio, however, and after a hard and bitter fight with her feelings she at last avows herself conquered, less by her husband's indomitable will than by her love for him, which acknowledges him as her best friend and protector.

Then her trials are at an end, and when her sister Bianca, and her young husband, Lucentio, and her father, Baptista, visit her, they are witnesses of the perfect harmony and peace which reign in Kate's home.

THE TALES OF HOFFMANN

A fantastic Opera in three acts by JACQUES OFFENBACH

Of the many operas by the brilliant Jacques Offenbach this of Hoffmann's Tales is acknowledged to be the masterpiece. Offenbach composed it during the summer of 1880, and became seriously ill before he had finally revised and orchestrated it. He himself felt it was the finest work he had done, and was most anxious to be present at its performance. But he was destined not to have his wish fulfilled. In October of 1880 Offenbach was dead, and the opera could not be got ready before the February of 1881, when it was given for the first time at the Opera Comique in Paris. The best judges of music consider this posthumous opera the work of a genius.

It is charming in its grace and is filled with true poetic feeling. It is remarkable in its realization of the fantastic imagination of the tales themselves.

The libretto, written in French by Jules Barbier, is founded on three tales by that poetically gifted and highly imaginative writer, E. Th. A. Hoffmann, whose "Tales" are classics in Germany.

The first act is really a prologue to the opera. Its scene is laid in Luther's famous wine cellar in Nuremberg. When the curtain rises on the interior of the German inn a chorus of students praises the master of the tavern. Hoffmann, the hero of the opera, is also there drinking and carousing with the rest, but seemingly despondent and morose. He is asked by the students to sing them a song, and he begins to sing the weird ballad of "Klein-Zach," but instead of finishing the ballad he wanders off into a chant of praise for a beautiful woman. His comrades chaff him and tell him he is in love. He assures them that he has left love and such matters behind him. He is depressed because of his past unfortunate experiences and promises to tell them of his three love adventures which brought him to his present state of mind. The rest of the opera, with the exception of the Epilogue, is devoted to the enactment of the three adventures, and the first act begins with that of the first, the one relating to Olympia.

In the first act the curtain rises and reveals the house of Spalanzani, the famous scientist. Hoffmann is in the house ostensibly as a pupil of the physiologist, but in reality to become acquainted with his beautiful daughter Olympia, whom he had only seen at a distance through a window. Olympia is not Spalanzani's daughter, but an automaton made by the scientist and his friend Coppelias. She is a doll that can sing, dance, and talk like a human being. It does this so successfully that the professor buys it from Coppelias in order to enrich himself by means of it. He pays his friend for it with a draft on a Jew, Elias by name, who, Spalanzani knows, will not meet the draft because he is a bankrupt. Coppelias has persuaded Hoffmann to buy a pair of spectacles through which to look at Olympia, and seeing her thus Hoffmann takes her for a beautiful living woman, and falls passionately in love with her. When left alone with her Hoffmann tells her of his passion, and in his ardor believes she returns his love, though she only answers him with "Ja, Ja." He tries to embrace her, but she trips away immediately he touches her. His friend Nickias, who knows of the truth of Olympia, tries to enlighten him, but Hoffmann is too exalted by love to understand or even to listen to him. At the entertainment which Spalanzani gives, Hoffmann engages Olympia in a dance, and the two dance on, faster and faster, until Hoffmann sinks to the floor in a swoon. In his fall the spectacles he is wearing are broken. Olympia, however, still keeps on dancing by herself, faster and faster, until she dances out of the room in spite of an attempt of Cochenille to stop her. Dr. Coppelias now enters in a rage with Spalanzani, having found that his draft had been dishonored and was worthless. He rushes into the room into which Olympia has disappeared. When Hoffmann recovers from his swoon he hears a tremendous noise as of breaking and smashing, and is amazed at Spalanzani bursting upon him with cries that Coppelias had destroyed his priceless automaton. It is then that Hoffmann learns that he has been in love with a mere doll. The guests, entering, confuse the poor fellow with shouts of laughter, the while Spalanzani and Coppelias are quarreling and abusing each other. Thus ends Hoffmann's first love adventure.

The second deals with Giulietta, and the second act shows us her palace in Venice. She is in love with Schlemihl, but she nevertheless receives Hoffmann graciously, much to the disgust of Schlemihl. Nickias, Hoffmann's friend, who is also courting the beautiful lady, warns him against her and thinks she is no better than she ought to be. Hoffmann laughs at Nickias and ridicules the suggestion that he would be likely to make love to a courtesan. Giulietta is really a creature of the magician Dapertutto, who is in truth the evil spirit maleficent towards Hoffmann in all the three adventures. Giulietta it is who for him has stolen Schlemihl's shadow, and he now bribes her with a magic diamond to enslave Hoffmann so that she might get from him his reflection in a looking glass, as she got Schlemihl's shadow. Dapertutto plays on her wounded vanity by telling her that Hoffmann has spoken disdainfully of her. Hoffmann is soon brought to her feet, and in a beautiful love-duet in which she succeeds by her wiles, they are surprised by the jealous Schlemihl. Giulietta promises Hoffmann the key of her room if he can get it from Schlemihl, her former lover. Hoffmann is then left alone with Schlemihl and Dapuertutto, and demands the key of the former. When his demand is refused a duel follows, for which Dapertutto supplies Hoffmann with his own sword. Schlemihl is killed after a few passes, and Dapertutto disappears. A moment later Giulietta's gondola is seen by him passing before the balcony, and he finds her leaning on Dapertutto's arm, singing a mocking farewell to him. Thus ends Hoffmann's second love adventure.

The third adventure deals with Antonia. The curtain of the third act rises on a room in Rath Krespel's house in Munich. Krespel's daughter Antonia is gifted, like her mother, with a remarkably beautiful voice, but, like her mother, also, she is afflicted with the deadly disease of consumption. Although singing gives her the greatest happiness, her father had forbidden her tasking her strength in this way because he knows it will be fatal for her. She is engaged to be married to Hoffmann, but Krespel does not encourage the alliance. He fears for his daughter's life, because he knows Hoffmann to be very fond of music and would delight in hearing Antonia sing. He keeps his daughter confined in the house and has given his servant, Franz, strict injunctions not to permit anybody to see Antonia when he is away from home. Franz, however, is quite deaf, and, misunderstanding Krespel's orders, eagerly welcomes Hoffmann when he comes to visit Antonia. In a charming love scene between Hoffmann and Antonia the girl proves to her lover that her voice has in no way lost its beauty. They refrain from further love making when they hear Krespel returning. Antonia, to avoid her father, retires to her own room, and Hoffmann, anxious to know why Krespel keeps his daughter so confined, hides himself in an alcove. Krespel comes in and is followed immediately by Dr. Mirakel. Mirakel is the evil genius of Hoffmann. He is the Coppelias of the first adventure and the Dapertutto of the second. Krespel is terribly afraid of this man, because he believes it was he who killed his wife, and because he fears he has now designs to kill his daughter. As Hoffmann listens to the talk between Krespel and Mirakel he learns the secret of Antonia's affliction and why it is that she is so carefully guarded by her father. When Mirakel has finally been sent out and Krespel has also left, the two lovers meet again. Hoffmann now earnestly begs Antonia never to sing again. After much entreaty, she finally gives him her promise not to sing again. When Hoffmann, however, leaves, Mirakel returns and goads her on to break her promise. He invokes the spirit of her mother to assist him in his arguments, so that she is persuaded to sing. He urges her on to further effort, but the girl sinks back exhausted. Krespel and Hoffmann, returning, find her dying, and with some short words of farewell she dies in her father's arms, Hoffmann a heartbroken witness. Thus ends the third and last adventure.

The Epilogue takes us back to Luther's wine cellar in Nuremberg, the same scene in which the Prologue was enacted. His boon companions cheer him with their thanks for his three tales, and leave him. In their place comes the Muse of Art to offer Hoffmann consolation as a balm for his wounded heart. For a moment he is roused and his soul filled with an ecstatic joy, but his drinking has been too much for him. He falls face forward on the table and goes sound asleep. When Stella asks Nicklausse if Hoffmann is asleep, he answers, "No, dead drunk." As Stella takes Lindorf's arm to leave, she turns to look at Hoffmann and throws a flower from her bouquet at his feet.

TANNHÄUSER

Romantic Opera in three acts by RICHARD WAGNER

With this opera begins a new era in the history of the German theatre. Tannhäuser is more a drama than an opera; every expression in it is highly dramatic. The management of the orchestra, too, is quite different from anything hitherto experienced; it dominates everywhere, the voice of the performer being often only an accompaniment to it. Tannhäuser is the first opera, or, as Wagner himself called it, drama, of this kind, and written after this one all Wagner's works bear the same stamp.

Wagner took his subject from an old legend, which tells of a minstrel called Tannhäuser (probably identical with Heinrich von Ofterdingen), who won all prizes by his beautiful songs and all hearts by his noble bearing. So the palm is allotted to him at the yearly "Tournament of Minstrels" on the Wartburg, and his reward is to be the hand of Elizabeth, niece of the Landgrave of Thuringia, whom he loves. But instead of behaving sensibly this erring knight suddenly disappears, nobody knows where, leaving his bride in sorrow and anguish. He falls into the hands of Venus, who holds court in the Hörselberg, near Eisenach, and Tannhäuser, at the opening of the first scene, has already passed a whole year with her. At length he has grown tired of sensual love and pleasure, and notwithstanding Venus' allurements he leaves her, vowing never to return to the goddess, but to expiate his sins by a holy life. He returns to the charming vale behind the Wartburg, he hears again the singing of the birds, the shepherds playing on the flute, the pious songs of the pilgrims on their way to Rome. Full of repentance he kneels down and prays, when suddenly the Landgrave appears with some minstrels, among them Wolfram von Eschinbach, Tannhäuser's best friend. They greet their long-lost companion, who, however, cannot tell where he has been all the time, and as Wolfram reminds him of Elizabeth, Tannhäuser returns with the party to the Wartburg.

It is just the anniversary of the Tournament of Minstrels, and in the second act we find Elizabeth with Tannhäuser, who craves her pardon and is warmly welcomed by her. The high prize for the best song is again to be Elizabeth's hand, and Tannhäuser resolves to win her once more. The Landgrave chooses "love" as the subject whose nature is to be explained by the minstrels. Everyone is called by name, and Wolfram von Eschinbach begins, praising love as a well, deep and pure, a source of the highest and most sacred feeling. Others follow; Walther von der Vogelweide praises the virtue of love, every minstrel celebrates spiritual love alone.

But Tannhäuser, who has been in Venus' fetters, sings of another love, warmer and more passionate, but sensual. And when the others remonstrate, he loudly praises Venus, the goddess of heathen love. All stand aghast; they recognize now where he has been so long. He is about to be put to death, when Elizabeth prays for him. She loves him dearly and hopes to save his soul from eternal perdition. Tannhäuser is to join a party of pilgrims on their way to Rome, there to crave for the Pope's pardon.

In the third act we see the pilgrims return from their journey. Elizabeth anxiously expects her lover, but he is not among them. Fervently she prays to the Holy Virgin; but not that a faithful lover may be given back to her—no, rather that he may be pardoned and his immortal soul saved. Wolfram is beside her, he loves the maiden, but he has no thought for himself; he only feels for her, whose life he sees ebbing swiftly away, and for his unhappy friend.

Presently, when Elizabeth is gone, Tannhäuser comes up in pilgrim's garb. He has passed a hard journey, full of sacrifices and castigation, and all for nought, for the Pope has rejected him. He has been told in hard words that he is for ever damned, and will as little get deliverance from his grievous sin as the stick in his hand will ever bear green leaves afresh.

Full of despair Tannhäuser is returning to seek Venus, whose siren songs already fall alluringly on his ear. Wolfram entreats him to fly, and when Tannhäuser fails to listen, he utters Elizabeth's name. At this moment a procession descends from the Wartburg, chanting a funeral song over an open bier. Elizabeth lies on it, dead, and Tannhäuser sinks on his knee beside her, crying: "Holy Elizabeth, pray for me." Then Venus disappears, and all at once the withered stick begins to bud and blossom, and Tannhäuser, pardoned, expires at the side of his beloved.

Tannhäuser was represented in the Dresden Theatre in June, 1890, according to Wagner's changes of arrangement, done by him in Paris, 1861, for the Grand Opera, by order of Napoleon III. This arrangement the composer acknowledges as the only correct one. These alterations are limited to the first scene in the mysterious abode of Venus, and his motives for the changes become clearly apparent when it is remembered that the simple form of "Tannhäuser" was composed in the years 1843 and '45 in and near Dresden, at a time when there were neither means nor taste in Germany for such high-flown scenes like those which excited Wagner's brain. Afterwards success rendered Wagner bolder and more pretentious, and so he endowed the person of Venus with more dramatic power, and thereby threw a vivid light on the great attraction she exercises on Tannhäuser. The decorations are by far richer and a ballet of sirens and fauns has been added, a concession which Wagner had to make to the Parisian taste. Venus' part, now sung by the first prima donnas, has considerably gained by the alterations, and the first scene is far more interesting than before, but it is to be regretted that the Tournament of Minstrels has been shortened and particularly the fine song of Walther von der Vogelweide omitted by Wagner. All else is as of old, as indeed Elizabeth's part needed nothing to add to her purity and loveliness, which stands out now in even bolder relief against the beautiful but sensual part of Venus.

THAIS

Opera in three acts by JULES MASSENET

The libretto of Thais, by Louis Gallet, for which Jules Massenet wrote the music, is taken from the novel, by Anatole France, which deals with a monk of the sect of Cenobites who, in his enthusiasm for his religion, determines to convert the famous beauty and reigning courtesan of Alexandria, Thais by name. This monk is known as Athanael. In his more youthful days he had been a man about town, who had lived the gay, dissipating life of the rich aristocrat of the city. He had, however, turned away from this life of pleasure, and sought to repent for the error of his ways by turning monk. The opera was first produced in Paris, in 1894.

The first scene of the first act is laid in the Thebaid, the desert of Thebes in Egypt. Here are the huts of the Cenobites. It is the evening of the day, and twelve monks and old Palemon are sitting at a long table partaking of the frugal repast. Athanael's seat is vacant. The monks discuss Athanael and wonder at his long absence. Palemon tells them the hour of his return is near, because a dream showed him to him. Athanael appears, advancing slowly, as if exhausted with fatigue and sorrow. The brothers greet him respectfully, and Athanael sits down wearily, gently declining the food they offer him. His heart is filled with bitterness. He has been to the city given over to sin, and he returns now in mourning and affliction. A woman, Thais, fills Alexandria with scandal, and, through her, hell reigns there.

Palemon prays him not to meddle with the people of the time, and the monks, with mysterious fear, pray that the black demons of the abyss may move off from their way.

Athanael stretches himself before his hut and lays his head on a wooden pallet. Then, praying a short prayer, he falls asleep. The evening becomes darker until black night is over all. After a short space of quiet, a light appears in the midst of the darkness, and in a mist which rises appears the interior of the theater at Alexandria. The place is crowded with people, and on the the stage is Thais, half clothed, but with face veiled, performing the dance of Aphrodite. As if from a great distance is heard the applause of the audience, calling on Thais by name. The vision disappears, and suddenly the day breaks, and it is dawn.

Athanael gradually awakes. He has been dreaming. When he realizes what it was he had seen in his vision, he prays to God for help. He vows he will deliver this woman from the thralldom of the flesh. The more guilty she is the more compassionate does he feel. His mission is now revealed to him, he prays, and he must return to the accursed city. God forbid, he cries, lest Thais sink deeper in the pit of wickedness. Palemon comes in just then and repeats what he had said at the table the night before, that they should not meddle with the people of the time. But Athanael is already preparing to leave. The Cenobites surround him and accompany him on the road; then, kneeling in groups, they answer to him as his voice is lost to them in the desert, praying that his spirit be armed for the combat, and that he be stronger than the archangel against the charms of the demon.

The second scene represents the terrace in the house of Nicias at Alexandria, which overlooks the town and the sea. Athanael slowly appears and stops at the back.

A servant, seeing him, rises and bids the beggar, as he thinks he is, to go and find alms elsewhere. Athanael gently begs the servant to tell his master that a friend desires to speak with him. The servant is about to strike Athanael, but it restrained by the calm dignity of Athanael's attitude, and goes to inform his master. Voices and laughter are heard, and shortly afterwards Nicias appears, leaning on the shoulders of two beautiful and smiling slaves, Crobyle and Myrtale. At the sight of Athanael he stops; then, recognizing him as his old friend of the earlier and gay days, he welcomes him with open arms. When he is told of Athanael's mission, he laughs and warns him not to offend Venus, whose priestess Thais is. Athanael, however, is determined, and Nicias listens to his request for some decent clothes in which he may meet Thais. Athanael is dressed and perfumed by Crobyle and Myrtale, who admire him for his handsome appearance. As they finish dressing him in his fine clothes, acclamations are heard from a distance, and Nicias, mounting the terrace, announces the coming of Thais.

Thais now enters, preceded by actors and actresses and some friends of Nicias. Nicias receives her gallantly, and leads them all to the banqueting-room behind the draperies. When Athanael leaves the banqueting-room later with Nicias's philosopher friends, Thais, who has been attracted by the stranger with the fierce eyes, asks Nicias as to who he is. Nicias tells her he is a philosopher of a rude soul, and bids her take heed, since he has come for her. Athanael, coming in, advances towards her, but she tells him to begone, because she believes in love only. He tells her straight that he is come to take her to the only true God, and shall vanquish Hell in triumphing over her. As he is about to leave, he says to her: "I shall go to thy palace and bring thee salvation." Thais, as she makes ready to enact the Aphrodite love scene, dares him to brave Venus. Athanael, seeing her preparing to unrobe herself, rushes away in horror.

The first scene of the second act takes us into Thais's house. A statue of Venus is in the foreground, before which is a censer. Thais enters with her train, but immediately dismisses them. She is tired to death of men, their brutality, and their indifference. Her life of gay love is become a weariness to her. She prays to Venus for eternal beauty. Athanael appears, and she turns to him, bidding him beware lest he love her. He does love her, he tells her, but not as she understands love. He loves her in spirit, and in truth. She asks to be shown that love. He tells her that the love she knows begets only shame; but the love he brings her is glorious love. He would not offend her, he would but try to make her yield to the truth. Thais looks at him with a vague fear. She cannot understand him when he speaks to her of the life everlasting. She takes a spatula of gold and throws some incense in the censer. The aroma excites Athanael, and a light mist envelopes Thais and the statue as she prays to Venus. Athanael, tearing his borrowed robe from him, cries to her to arise. Thais, in fear, begs him not to harm her. He, on his part, conjures her to become the bride of Christ. A new strength comes to her at his words. The voice of Nicias, approaching, is then heard calling on Thais. She cries out that he has never loved anyone; that he has only loved love. She bids Athanael to go and tell Nicias that she despises all rich men; that Nicias must forget her. Athanael says sternly that he will be at her doorstep until dawn, and await her coming; but she, with a last effort at resistance, cries out that she will remain Thais, Thais the courtezan. She believes in nothing and wants nothing more. She breaks off into a nervous laugh, and then throws herself face down on the pillows, sobbing, as Athanael departs. As the curtains slowly come together, hiding her from the audience, the orchestra plays a symphonic religious music.

The second scene is the square facing Thais's house. It is not yet daylight. On the last steps of the portico, under which is seen a small statue of Eros, lies Athanael, asleep. In the rear is a house in which Nicias and his friends are still making merry. The windows are lighted up. The door of Thais's house opens, and she appears, carrying a lamp over her head. Seeing Athanael lying there, she puts the lamp down and approaches him mysteriously. She is come as Athanael commanded. She will follow if he will lead. She begs but for one thing to take with her, the statuette of Eros. She explains that it was Nicias who had given it to her. Athanael, in great anger, curses the poisoned source of the gift, and smashes the statuette on the pavement, and tells her to put a lighted torch to all her possessions. When Thais and Athanael have gone into the house, Nicias and his friends appear. Singing and dancing are in progress, when Athanael comes quickly from the house, carrying a lighted torch in his hand. Nicias recognizes him, and his friends jeer him. Athanael bids them be silent. Thais is the spouse of God, he says. The infernal Thais is dead, dead for ever. Thais now appears, meanly clad, with her hair in disorder. The house takes fire and a crowd, attracted by the noise and the laughter, fills the stage. Athanael is begging Thais to come away with him, while Nicias is incredulous at the idea that she is willing to go. Athanael is wounded by a stone thrown from a man in the crowd. Great confusion and uproar ensue. Athanael and Thais are ready to die. The crowd roars "Death," and Nicias tries to appease them by throwing gold to them. As the mob scrambles for the gold, Nicias bids farewell to Athanael and Thais, who escape. The palace continues to burn, and the curtain falls.

Athanael and Thais have travelled a long journey and are now, as the curtain rises on the first scene of the third act, arriving at an oasis in the desert. Thais is overcome by fatigue and can scarcely move. She is faint from the journey and the heat, and when she complains, begging to stay awhile, Athanael will have her walk on. She must purify the body she gave to pagans and infidels by breaking it, by destroying the flesh. Thais can go no further. She sways and is about to fall, when he holds her in his arms and seats her in the shade. As he contemplates her, he notices the blood flowing from the bruised feet, and compassion for her fills him. He falls before her and kisses her feet, calling her a saint. Thais, recovering, would go on; but now Athanael would have her rest, and he gives her food. As she is eating the fruit he has brought her, the music of psalmody is heard in the distance, and voices chanting the Paternoster. Albine and the White Ladies now appear, and Athanael places Thais in their care. Thais bids him a touching farewell, as she moves away with the White Ladies, and Athanael is left alone, leaning on his stick and looking longingly down the road taken by Thais. The curtain falls.

The second scene takes us back to the Thebaid and the huts of the Cenobites, by the river Nile. The monks are looking towards the sky with a vague terror. Sounds of a windstorm are heard in the distance. Palemon suggests that the food be placed within the huts to save it from the storm. One monk asks where Athanael is. Palemon says he has been back for twenty days, and has not eaten or drunk in all that time. Athanael comes out of his hut and passes through without noticing his brother monks. When he is left alone with Palemon, he turns to him in humility and begs him to remain. He confesses he cannot keep the image of Thais's face out of his thoughts. Palemon simply and gently repeats his old advice: "Let us not meddle, my son, with the people of the time." Athanael rises from the ground by the feet of Palemon, where he has fallen in shame of his confession, and kneels on the mat. Palemon leaves him, and Athanael stretches himself and goes to sleep.

Thais appears to him in a vision in the same guise in which he first saw her. She tempts him to the love of Venus, and Athanael cries out in his sleep: "I die, Thais! Come!" Thais disappears, laughing loudly, and a new vision appears, revealing Thais stretched motionless in the garden of the convent of the White Ladies. Around her are kneeling the nuns. Voices mourn that Thais is about to die. Athanael, in his dream, becomes wildly excited and cries aloud that Thais must not die. He will come to take her. She must be his. He rises from his sleep and rushes out into the night. The curtain closes to music.

The last scene is the garden of the convent of Albine. Thais is stretched out beneath a fig tree as if dead. She is surrounded by Albine and the nuns. All pray. Athanael appears at the entrance of the garden, and Albine, seeing him, goes toward him, while the White Ladies surround the prostrate form of Thais so that he may not see it. Albine bids Athanael welcome. He asks eagerly for Thais. She tells him that she is about to see the eternal light. He sees Thais, and, calling her by name, he falls, broken with grief, kneeling, by her side. Opening her eyes to answer his call, she reminds him of his words to her and tells him that she sees heaven opening for her. As she dies, he gives a terrible cry and falls prostrate by her side.

TIEFLAND

A Dramatic Opera in prologue and three acts by
EUGENE D'ALBERT

The book is by RUDOLPH LOTHAR, after a story

This work was first seen at Prague, 1903. The scene is laid in the Pyrenees and a valley in Catalonia; time, the present.

The prologue shows a mountain pass in the Pyrenees. Pedro, the shepherd, has hitherto passed his days in these mountains and has seldom seen any other human face save that of Nando, his comrade. Scarcely ever has he met women, but he longs for the day when the Virgin will send him some nice woman for a wife. One day Pedro's employer comes to see him, leading by the hand a handsome girl from the plains below. He tells him that this shall be his wife if he will come forth from his rocks and go to live with her near the mill. Pedro does not know when this offer is made to him that Martha, the girl thus offered to him, has been the mistress of Sebastiano, and that the latter is simply using this means with unsophisticated Pedro to restore before the world Martha's respectable name.

The interior of the mill is shown in Act I. The servants of Sebastiano are all aware of Martha's intimate relations, with the exception of Pedro himself, and in consequence they amuse themselves highly with his ignorance. Sebastiano at this time is engaged to a well-to-do farmer's daughter, and plans that the marriage with Pedro should furnish a convenient cloak for his illicit relations with Martha. The latter, however, is not at bottom of a deceitful nature, and as she has found much in Pedro she likes and esteems, she hates deluding him constantly as Sebastiano expects her to do. She is unable to discover a way out of the difficulty, and at last the wedding of Pedro and Martha is celebrated with much noise. Pedro in his ignorance of the real state of affairs accepts delightedly the mock congratulations of the other servants. Sebastiano's purpose is to continue his relations with Martha immediately after the wedding ceremony, but Martha foils him by a ruse and knows also how to baffle her nominal husband.

In the second act Nuri, a young peasant girl who is secretly in love with Pedro, accidentally finds him alone and begins to chat with him. Martha surprises these two, and straightway grows jealous. She orders Nuri out of the house, and Pedro goes with her. Martha is wretched and goes to old Tomaso for advice, but when he says the best way would be to make a clean breast of it to Pedro she is unwilling to do that, because she fears to lose Pedro altogether thereby. Then Pedro comes back to her, saying that he has been considering matters and finds his proper place is the highland, not the plains. Martha then pleads: "Ah, take me along!" But Pedro, now enlightened, suddenly flares up and advances with a dagger, but is prevented from harming her. Then the two patch up a sort of peace and resolve to flee. This for the moment is rendered impossible by the entrance of Sebastiano, who is followed by a group of villagers eager to reap all the amusement possible from the situation. Sebastiano thrums a guitar and bids Martha to dance for the crowd. But Pedro in a rage flies at Sebastiano's throat, and the puzzled villagers have to separate these two.

The last act shows the rupture of Sebastiano's engagement because his betrothed has discovered his duplicity and immoral conduct. When he next approaches Martha and wishes to resume their former relations, she spurns him to his utter amazement. He flies into a fury and tries to overpower the girl. But Martha screams for help, and Pedro comes to the rescue, his trusty dagger in his hand. Seeing that Sebastiano is unarmed, he throws the weapon aside, and attacks his opponent with his bare fists. After a terrific struggle he is victorious and throws Sebastiano into a corner, powerless. The crowd of villagers, who came to jeer at him, are now dumb with fear. Pedro hurls defiance at them all. "Why don't you laugh now?" he demands. Then he shoulders his handsome young bride and strides off into the freedom of his mountains.

LA TOSCA

Melodrama in three acts by GIACOMO PUCCINI

Text by SARDOU, ILLICA and GIACOSA

La Tosca was first presented at Covent Garden, London, in 1900, and though it was a gorgeous production it was not as well received as La Bohême. The libretto, which is taken from Sardou's tragedy, is not one adapted to operatic treatment. It is cleverly orchestrated, however, and the intensely dramatic action is handled with considerable skill. The music is strong in effect, and original and vivacious in style.

The scene is laid in Rome in the year 1800, and the first act presents the interior of the Church of Sant' Andrea. Angelotti, an imprisoned consul of the Roman Republic, makes his escape with the assistance of his sister, and appears in the church in prison garb, hunting for the key which she has hidden there for him. Just as he is about to make his escape, he hears footsteps approaching, and hastily conceals himself as Cavaradossi, an artist, enters the church and proceeds to paint a portrait of the Madonna. Cavaradossi, hearing a noise behind him, investigates, and discovers Angelotti, who proves to be an old friend of his. He promises to help him escape, but is interrupted by the entrance of Tosca, a celebrated songstress, who is madly in love with him. Hearing whispers she becomes suspicious, believing that Cavaradossi has played her false, but, after much persuasion, is finally induced to withdraw. Cavaradossi is then about to conduct his friend to his own villa, when the booming of cannon is heard, announcing the escape of the prisoner. They hurry out just as Scarpia, the chief of police, enters the church in search of Angelotti. Tosca returns hoping to see her artist lover, and the wily Scarpia, who is jealous of Cavaradossi and himself in love with Tosca, makes her believe that her lover has fled with another woman, by showing her a fan which has been left behind by the sister of Angelotti.

The second act presents the apartments of Scarpia in Farnese Palace. Cavaradossi, who has been captured in his villa, is brought before the Chief of Police, and, on being commanded to reveal the hiding place of Angelotti, denies all knowledge of the whereabouts of the fugitive. Scarpia, therefore, devises a fiendish plan to discover his secret. He orders Tosca to be brought before him, and she, having learned that it was the prisoner and not a rival that Cavaradossi had fled with, throws herself into his arms at finding him safe and unharmed. Scarpia, enraged and jealous, orders Cavaradossi to be taken to the torture chamber, and the distracted Tosca, hearing his groans of pain, is at last persuaded to reveal the hiding place of Angelotti. Cavaradossi is then brought in, bleeding and unconscious, and Scarpia gives the order for his execution.

Tosca beseeches him not to fulfil the order, and he promises to save her lover if she will grant him her favor. After vain prayer, she consents to his wish, under the condition that he will write out a passport to enable Cavaradossi and herself to leave the country in safety. Scarpia consents to her plan, but gives a secret order for Cavaradossi to be hung at sundown. He then proceeds to write out the passport, and while doing so Tosca steals up from the rear and stabs him in the back, making good her escape.

"Tristan and Isolde," Act I, as given by the Philadelphia Opera Company

The third act presents a cell in the Castle Sant' Angelo, where Cavaradossi is imprisoned, awaiting his sentence. Tosca rushes in with the passport, and, after explaining how she killed Scarpia, tells him that the soldiers are to pretend to shoot him, and that he must fall as if really shot, after which she will take him secretly away in her carriage. He is placed against the wall, and after a volley of shots from the soldiers, falls as directed by Tosca. After the guard has disappeared she hurries to his side, only to find his body riddled with bullets. In an agony of grief she throws herself on his dead body. The soldiers entering at this moment accuse her of the murder of Scarpia, but she, eluding their efforts to seize her, leaps upon the parapet of the terrace, and throws herself into space, before the horror-stricken soldiers are aware of her intention.

DIE TOTE STADT

Opera in three acts by ERICK WOLFGANG KORNGOLD

Book by SCHOTT after RODENBACH'S novel, "Bruges la Morte"

The first production was given at Vienna in 1920. The setting is Bruges of the early twentieth century.

Act I. Paul, living in Bruges, the city of the past, preserves the room in which his wife Marie died as a shrine sacred to her memory. One day while out walking he meets Marietta, a dancer and the image of his beloved wife. At his request she visits him but leaves shortly when she foresees no likelihood of an intrigue. Paul sinks into a chair: Marie appears to him in a vision, stepping out of her picture frame, and the dream pictures born of his love and longing take shape on the stage.

Act II. Paul is walking before Marietta's house on a moonlit street when suddenly a merry party comes along the canal in boats, led by Count Albert of Brussels. They improvise a serenade and champagne party in the street and Marietta gives a ghostly performance of the scene of the dead nuns in Meyerbeer's "Robert le Diable." Paul rushes forward and tears the winding sheet from her body. When the others intervene, Marietta sends them away and induces Paul to take her to his home.

Act III. In the shrine to Marie's memory, Marietta triumphs over her dead rival. When Paul begs her to leave the room, the dancer's hatred of the wife breaks out in curses. Seeing the golden lock of Marie's hair, she winds it about her neck and dances shamelessly before the horrified Paul who finally throws her to the ground and strangles her with the shining strand of his dead wife's hair. . . .

Waking from his terrible dream, Paul finds himself alone in the room. At that moment the real Marietta returns, pretending to have forgotten some trifle. Paul ignores her inviting smile and lets her go in silence. His friend, Frank, then persuades him to leave Bruges with its tragic memories and begin a new life elsewhere.

LA TRAVIATA

Opera in three acts by VERDI

Text taken from the French by PIAVE

The original of the libretto is Dumas' celebrated novel "La dame aux camélias."

The opera is, like all of Verdi's works, full of melody, and there are numberless special beauties in it. The prelude which opens the opera, instead of an overture, is in particular an elegy of a noble and interesting kind. But as the text is frivolous and sensual, of course the music cannot be expected to be wholly free from these characteristics.

The scene is laid in and near Paris. Alfred Germont is passionately in love with Violetta Valery, one of the most frivolous beauties in Paris. She is pleased with his sincere passion, anything like which she has never hitherto known, and openly telling him who she is, she warns him herself; but he loves her all the more, and, as she returns his passion, she abandons her gay life and follows him into the country, where they live very happily for some months.

Annina, Violetta's maid, dropping a hint to Alfred that her mistress is about to sell her house and carriage in town in order to avoid expenses, he departs for the capital to prevent this.

During his absence Violetta receives a visit from Alfred's father, who tries to show her that she has destroyed not only his family's but his son's happiness by suffering Alfred to unite himself to one so dishonored as herself. He succeeds in convincing her, and, broken-hearted, she determines to sacrifice herself and leave Alfred secretly. Ignoring the possible reason for this inexplicable action, Alfred is full of wrath and resolves to take vengeance. He finds Violetta in the house of a former friend, Flora Bervoix, who is in a position similar to that of Violetta. The latter, having no other resources and feeling herself at death's door (a state of health suggested in the first act by an attack of suffocation), has returned to her former life.

Alfred insults her publicly. The result is a duel between her present adorer, Baron Dauphal, and Alfred.

From this time on Violetta declines rapidly, and in the last act, which takes place in her sleeping room, we find her dying. Hearing that Alfred has been victorious in the duel, and receiving a letter from his father, who is now willing to pardon and to accept her as his daughter-in-law, she revives to some extent and Alfred, who at last hears of her sacrifice, returns to her, but only to afford a last glimpse of happiness to the unfortunate woman, who expires, a modern Magdalen, full of repentance, and striving tenderly to console her lover and his now equally desolate father.

TRISTAN UND ISOLDE

Lyric Drama in three acts by RICHARD WAGNER

The music to this drama is deemed by connoisseurs the most perfect ever written by Wagner, but it needs a fine and highly cultivated understanding of music to take in all its beauty and greatness. There is little action in it, and very often the orchestra has the principal part, so that the voice seems little more than an accompaniment; it has musical measures, too, which cannot be digested by an uneducated hearer, but, nevertheless, many parts of it will interest everyone.

Isolde's love song, for instance, is the noblest hymn ever sung in praise of this passion.

The first act represents the deck of a ship, where we find the two principal persons, Tristan and Isolde, together. Tristan, a Cornish hero, has gone over to Ireland, to woo the Princess for his old uncle, King Marke. Isolde, however, loves Tristan, and has loved him from the time when he was cast sick and dying on the coast of Ireland and was rescued and nursed by her, though he was her enemy. But Tristan, having sworn faith to his uncle, never looks at her, and she, full of wrath that he woos her for another instead of for himself, attempts to poison herself and him by a potion. But Brangäna, her faithful attendant, secretly changes the poisoned draught for a love potion, so that they are inevitably joined in passionate love. Only when the ship lands, its deck already covered with knights and sailors, who come to greet their King's bride, does Brangäna confess her fraud, and Isolde, hearing that she is to live, faints in her attendant's arms.

In the second act Isolde has been wedded to Marke, but the love potion has worked well, and she has secret interviews at night with Tristan, whose sense of honor is deadened by the fatal draught. Brangäna keeps watch for the lovers, but King Marke's jealous friend Melot betrays them, and they are found out by the good old King, who returns earlier than he had intended from a hunt.

Tristan is profoundly touched by the grief of the King, whose sadness at losing faith in his most noble warrior is greater than his wrath against the betrayer of honor. Tristan, unable to defend himself, turns to Isolde, asking her to follow him into the desert, but Melot opposes him, and they fight, Tristan falling back deadly wounded into his faithful servant Kurvenal's arms.

The third act represents Tristan's home in Brittany, whither Kurvenal has carried his wounded master in order to nurse him. Isolde, so skilled in the art of healing wounds, has been sent for, but they look in vain for the ship which is to bring her.

When at last it comes into sight, Tristan, who awakens from a long swoon, sends Kurvenal away, to receive his mistress, and as they both delay their coming his impatient longing gets the better of him. Forgetting his wound, he rises from his couch, tearing away the bandages, and so Isolde is only just in time to catch him in her arms, where he expires with her name on his lips. While she bewails her loss, another ship is announced by the shepherd's horn. King Marke arrives, prepared to pardon all and to unite the lovers. Kurvenal, seeing Melot advance, mistakes them for foes, and running his sword through Melot's breast, sinks, himself deadly wounded, at his master's feet. King Marke, to whom Brangäna has confessed her part in the whole matter, vainly laments his friend Tristan, while Isolde, waking from her swoon and seeing her lover dead, pours forth rapturous words of greeting, and, broken-hearted, sinks down dead at his side.

IL TROVATORE

Opera in four acts by GIUSEPPE VERDI

Text by SALVATORE COMMERANO

Two men of entirely different station and character woo Leonore, Countess of Sergaste. The one is Count Luna, the other a minstrel, named Manrico, who is believed to be the son of Azucena, a gypsy.

Azucena has, in accordance with gypsy law, vowed bloody revenge on Count Luna, because his father, believing her mother to be a sorceress and to have bewitched one of his children, had the old woman burned. To punish the father for this cruelty Azucena took away his other child, which was vainly sought for. This story is told in the first scene, where we find the Count's servants waiting for him, while he stands sighing beneath his sweetheart's window. But Leonore's heart is already captivated by Manrico's sweet songs and his valor in tournament. She suddenly hears his voice, and in the darkness mistakes the Count for her lover, who, however, comes up just in time to claim her. The Count is full of rage, and there follows a duel in which Manrico is wounded, but though it is in his power to kill his enemy, he spares his life, without, however, being able to account for the impulse.

In the second act, Azucena, nursing Monrico, tells him of her mother's dreadful fate and her last cry for revenge, and confesses to having stolen the old Count's son with the intention of burning him. But in her despair and confusion, she says, she threw her own child into the flames, and the Count's son lived. Manrico is terrified, but Azucena retracts her words and regains his confidence, so that he believes her tale to have been but an outburst of remorse and folly.

Meanwhile he hears that Leonore, to whom he was reported as dead, is about to take the veil, and he rushes away to save her. Count Luna arrives before the convent with the same purpose. But just as he seizes his prey, Manrico comes up, and liberates her with the aid of his companions, while the Count curses them.

Leonore becomes Manrico's wife, but her happiness is short-lived.

In the third act the Count's soldiers succeed in capturing Azucena, in whom they recognize the burned gipsy's daughter. She denies all knowledge of the Count's lost brother, and as the Count hears that his successful rival is her son, she is sentenced to be burned. Ruiz, Manrico's friend, brings the news to him. Manrico tries to rescue her, but is seized too, and condemned to die by the axe.

In the fourth act Leonore offers herself to the Count as the price of freedom for the captives, but, determined to be true to her lover, she takes poison. She hastens to him, announcing his deliverance. Too late he sees how dearly she has paid for it, when, after sweet assurance of love and fidelity, she sinks dead at his feet.

The Count, coming up and seeing himself deceived, orders Manrico to be put to death instantly.

He is laid away, and only after the execution does Azucena inform the Count that his murdered rival was Luna's own long-sought brother.

LES TROYENS

(THE TROJANS)

Musical Drama in two parts and eight acts by
HECTOR BERLIOZ

The text by MERIMEE

This work was first shown in Paris, 1863. The action is partly based on the Aeneid.

Part I. Act I. The Trojans are robbing the deserted camp of the Greeks before Troy and gazing upon the great wooden horse left behind; Cassandra prophesies that evil will befall them.

Act II. News of the dreadful death of the priest, Laocoon, is brought to the Trojans, and to appease the goddess, Pallas, whom the priest had slighted, they drag inside the city walls the gigantic horse. Again Cassandra presages terrible consequences.

Act III. The spirit of Hector tells Aeneas of the sad fate of Troy and urges him to land on Ansonian shores and found a new nation. The Greeks meanwhile are burning Troy. In the next scene, at the palace of Priam, Cassandra relates the facts about the death of Choroebus and the retreat of Aeneas. She herself, rather than be taken prisoner, commits suicide.

Part II. Act I. Dido's palace. Jarbas endeavors to coerce Dido to marry him. She receives Aeneas kindly.

Act II. Aeneas and his companions defeat Jarbas and rescue Dido, who falls in love with the hero. Mercury, the messenger of the gods, advises Aeneas not to loiter, but to speed on to Italy.

Act III. Narbal warns Dido that Aeneas will not neglect his mission because of her love. In another scene Dido and Aeneas, while out on the chase, are overtaken by a storm and seek shelter in a cave.

Act IV. Aeneas now makes up his mind to return to Italy. He sees the vessels of the Trojans in the harbor. Although Dido attempts to hold him back from departure, he succeeds in boarding his ship.

Act V. First scene, Dido's palace. The queen is still bent on delaying Aeneas' going, but in vain. When she realizes that he has sailed away she issues orders that her own funeral pyre be erected. In the next scene she is seen mounting the pyre, whence she predicts that an avenger will rise from her ashes.

DER TROMPETER VON SÄKKINGEN

(THE TRUMPETER OF SAEKKINGEN)

Opera in three acts, with a prelude, by VICTOR NESSLER

Text by RUDOLF BUNGE after SCHEFFEL'S poem

Seldom in our days is an opera such a complete success in all German theatres as this composition of Nessler's has proved to be. To tell the truth, it owes its popularity in great degree to the libretto, which has taken so many fine songs and ideas from its universally known and adored original. Nessler's Trompeter is, however, in every way inferior to Scheffel's celebrated poem.

Nevertheless, the music, though not very profound, is pleasing, and there are several airs in it which have already become popular.

The prelude opens at Heidelberg, where a chorus of students make a great noise after one of their drinking bouts. They presently serenade the Princess-Electress, and a law-student, named Werner, a foundling and the adopted son of a professor, distinguishes himself by a solo on the trumpet. He is heard by the trumpeter of the Imperial recruiting officers, who tries to win him, but without success, when suddenly the Rector Magnificus appears to assist the major-domo, and announces to the astounded disturbers of peace that they are dismissed from the university.

Werner, taking a sudden resolution, accepts the press-money from Konradin the trumpeter, marches away with the soldiers, and the prelude is closed.

The first act represents a scene at Säkkingen on the Rhine. There is a festival in honor of St. Fridolin, at which young Baroness Maria assists. She is insulted by the peasants and Werner protects her from them. She is much pleased by the noble bearing of the trumpeter, and so is her aunt, the Countess of Wildenstein, who detects a great resemblance between him and her son, who was stolen by gypsies in his childhood. The second scene takes us into the Baron's room, where we find the gouty old gentleman in rather a bad humor. He is restored to good temper by a letter from his friend the Count of Wildenstein, who lives separated from his first wife, the above-mentioned Countess, and who proposes his son, born in second wedlock, as Maria's husband.

The Baron receives Maria kindly, when she relates her adventure and begs him to engage Werner as trumpeter in the castle. At this moment the latter is heard blowing his instrument, and the Baron, who has a great predilection for it, bids Werner present himself, and at once engages him.

In the second act Werner gives lessons on the trumpet to the lovely Maria; of course the young people fall in love with each other, but the Countess watches them, until friend Konradin for once succeeds in drawing her aside, when there follows a glowing declaration of love on both sides. Unhappily it is interrupted by the Countess, who announces her discovery to the Baron. Meanwhile the destined bridegroom has arrived with his father. Damian, that is the young man's name, is a simpleton, and Maria declares at once that she never will be his. But in the presence of the whole company, assembled for a festival, the Baron proclaims Maria Count Damian's bride; to the over-bold Werner he forbids the castle.

The last act opens with a siege of the castle by the rebellious peasants. Damian shows himself a coward. In the last extremity they are relieved by Werner, who drives the peasants back with his soldiers. He is wounded in the fray, and while the wound is being dressed a mole detected on his arm proclaims him the stolen child of Countess Wildenstein. All now ends in joy and happiness; the Baron is willing enough to give his daughter to the brave young nobleman and very glad to be rid of the cowardly Damian.

TURANDOT

Opera in three acts by GIACOMO PUCCINI

Book by SIMON and ADAMI

The first performance was given in Milan in 1926. The scenes are laid in ancient Pekin, the capital of China.

Act I. A crowd has gathered in the palace courtyard to listen to the reading of a royal decree: The Princess Turandot, fair and chaste, will become the bride of the suitor who unravels three enigmas which she shall propose. All who fail to answer the riddles will lose their heads. A rumor flies through the crowd—the Prince of Persia is coming to try his fortune. Amid the confusion an old man makes his way across the courtyard. He is supported by a young girl, Liú. A youth sees them and hurries forward—it is Calaf, the Unknown Prince, and the old man is his father, Timur, the dethroned king of the Tartars. The cortège of the Persian Prince arrives, followed by the executioner, for the Prince has failed to solve cruel Turandot's enigmas. Touched by the youth of the Persian, the crowd demands clemency of Turandot who, when she appears on the balcony, awes them into silence by her matchless beauty. There is the sound of the executioner's axe—and the Prince's head is suspended on an iron spike over the Pekin gates.

The Unknown Prince, at sight of Turandot's beauty, forgets her cruelty and determines to try to win her. Ping, Pong and Pang, court dignitaries, seek in vain to dissuade him while the ghosts of Turandot's dead lovers and the pleas of old Timur and gentle Liú alike fail to shake his resolution.

Act II. Again a multitude has assembled for the approaching trial of the Unknown Prince. Turandot tells them of her grandmother, the pure and chaste Princess Lo-u-ling, who was ravished by the invading Tartars. It is to avenge her ancestress that Turandot has proposed such cruel terms for her suitors. She turns to the Unknown Prince and asks: "What twin doves bring man tidings from the Land of Heart's desire?" He replies: "Hope and faith!" "Which twin pillars uphold Paradise?" asks the Princess. "Knowledge and power!" he answers. "Which twin flower hides the riddle of the world?" demands Turandot and the Unknown Prince gives the answer: "Love!" The crowd rejoices but poor Turandot entreats her father to save her from the arms of the foreigner. The Emperor reminds her that her vow is sacred—the Unknown Prince has won her according to her own conditions. She turns to the Prince who agrees to release her if she can tell him his name before the next dawn.

Act III. It is night. Heralds move through the city, warning the people on pain of death not to sleep until they have discovered the name of the Unknown Prince. They seek him out and try to bribe, then to frighten him into disclosing his identity—but to no avail. Some one remembers seeing old Timur and Liú in the company of the stranger. Guards drag the two before Turandot who orders them tortured until they tell the Prince's name. Liú cries that she alone knows it. The excutioner is summoned but Liú, in terror lest she reveal the identity of the Prince, stabs herself with a knife snatched from one of the soldiers. All are moved to pity. Turandot is troubled—what prompted the little slave girl to such heroism? The Unknown Prince reproaches Turandot and, to punish her, clasps her in his arms and kisses her. Then is Turandot vanquished. She confesses that she has loved the Prince all the while and when he says that he is Calaf, son of the Tartar king, she declares that it is not so—for his name is Love.

UNDINE

Romantic Opera in four acts by ALBERT LORTZING

Text after FOUQUE'S tale

With this opera Lortzing for the first time tried his genius in another field. Until then he had only composed comic operas, which had met with a very fair measure of success, but in this opera he left the comic for the romantic, and was peculiarly happy both in his ideas and choice of subject, which, as it happened, had previously had the honor of being taken up by Weber. The first representation of Undine at Hamburg in the year 1845 was one of the few luminous moments in Lortzing's dark life.

His melodies are wonderfully captivating and lovely, and the whole charm of German romance lies in them.

The contents of the libretto are:

The gallant knight, Hugo von Ringstetten, has been ordered by the Duke's daughter, Berthalda, to go in search of adventures, accompanied by his attendant Veit. Being detained for three months in a little village cut off from communication with the outer world by an inundation, he sees Undine, the adopted daughter of an old fisherman, named Tobias, and falling in love with her he asks for her hand. In the first act we see the priest uniting the young couple. The knight recognizes in the old man a traveller whom he once saved from robbers, and is glad to see him. Undine behaves most childishly, and finally says that she has no soul. She is herself grieved, and the others do not believe her. Hugo now tells them of the proud and beautiful Berthalda, whose scarf he received in a tournament, and who sent him away on this adventure. He then returns to the capital with his young wife, in order to present her at the ducal court. Meanwhile Veit has met Kühleborn, the mighty King of the water-fairies, and is asked by him whether his master has quite forgotten Berthalda. The valet gives as his opinion that the poor fisher-maiden is deceived, and will soon be abandoned by her husband. This excites Kühleborn's writh, for Undine is his daughter, and he forthwith resolves to protect her.

In the second act Undine confesses to her husband that she is a water-fairy, one of those whom men call "Undinas." They have no soul, but if they are loved faithfully by man they are able to gain a soul, and through it immortality. Though he shudders inwardly, Undine's purity and liveliness conquer Hugo's fright, and he once more swears to be eternally true to her.

The proud Berthalda, who loves Hugo, has heard with feelings of mingled anger and despair of the knight's marriage. She determines to honor the King of Naples with her hand; but before her wedding takes place a sealed document has to be opened, which says that Berthalda, instead of being a Duke's daughter, is a poor foundling. Kühleborn, who is present, declares that she is the real child of Undine's foster parents. Berthalda is now obliged to leave the palace. She loathes her fate and curses her low-born parents. Then Kühleborn derides her, and the attendants are about to seize him in order to turn him out of doors, when the statue of the water-god breaks into fragments, while Kühleborn stands in its place, the waters pouring down upon him. All take flight, but Undine raises the prostrate Berthalda, promising her protection in her husband's castle.

In the third act Berthalda succeeds in again drawing Hugo into her toils. Though warned by the water-fairies not to perjure himself, he neglects their advice, and Undine finds him in the arms of her rival. He repels his wife, and Kühleborn takes her back into his watery kingdom. But Undine has lost her peace of mind forever; she cannot forget her husband.

In the fourth act Hugo has given orders to close the well with stones, to prevent all possible communication with the water-fairies. Undine's pale face pursues him everywhere, he continually fancies he hears her soft voice and touching entreaties, and to stifle his remorse he appoints the day of his wedding with Berthalda.

His attendant, Veit, however, unable to forget his sweet mistress, removes the stones which cover the well. Undine rises from it and appears at midnight at the wedding. Hugo, forgetting Berthalda, and drawn toward his lovely wife against his will, falls into her arms and dies at her feet. The castle comes crashing down, floods penetrate everywhere and carry Hugo and Undine into Kühleborn's crystal palace.

Undine obtains pardon for Hugo, and his only punishment is that he must forever stay with his wife in her fairy domains.

VERSIEGELT

Comic Opera in one act by LEO BLECH

Text by BATKA and PORDES-MILO

This was first produced in Hamburg, 1908. The scene is a small town in Germany; time, 1830.

Braun, the burgomaster, is in love with a pretty widow, Frau Schram, but she has thus far avoided a definite answer to his suit. Braun's daughter, Else, is in love with Bertel, the town clerk. This, however, does not please the mayor, who desires a more exalted match for his child. In attempting to visit his wrath upon Bertel's mother, Frau Willmer, he is about to seize her furniture for unpaid taxes. A huge wardrobe, the most cherished piece of her household goods, she begs Frau Schramm, who is friendly to her, to keep at her house till the trouble is over. Lampe, the bailiff, accidentally sees this bulky piece of furniture being deposited at Frau Schramm's, whereupon that petty official hies him to the burgomaster and reports the case. Braun does call, but when he confronts Frau Schramm he is much more concerned with herself than with the wardrobe. The widow has pity upon the love-lorn burgomaster at least to the extent of permitting him to implant a chaste kiss. But at that moment there is a knock at the door, and Braun conceals himself in the huge piece of furniture. Lampe enters and places the official seal upon the wardrobe, but immediately thereafter hears a queer noise issuing from the locked and sealed wardrobe. He calls for help, and Else and Bertel enter. The arch widow now makes these two play a bit of wilful comedy for the benefit of the hidden burgomaster. In a bantering conversation the two young lovers say they would not elope —oh, no—but that they will not unlock that wardrobe and let out its "contents" until Braun has indicated his consent to their union. So Braun at last gives his approval, and when Lampe, who all this time has been away to summon aid, now returns, Bertel pretends that he was locked up accidentally in the wardrobe. The doughty burgomaster is accepted as her second husband by the blooming widow, and everything is once again in order.

LA VESTALE

Opera in three acts by GASPARO SPONTINI

Book by DE JOUEY

The first production was given in Paris in 1807 at the command of Napoleon. The action takes place in Rome during the days of the Republic.

Licinius, the Roman Consul, returning victorious from a campaign against the Gauls, finds upon his arrival in Rome that Julia, his bethrothed, has become a Vestal priestess. He succeeds at length in obtaining the promise of a meeting with her.

It is night. Julia is tending the holy flame of Vesta which must never be allowed to go out. After the departure of the other priestesses, Julia unbars the temple gate for Licinius. As they lament the cruelty of fate, Julia in her lover's arms forgets the sacred fire. Suddenly the flame dies and Julia falls fainting at the foot of the altar. Before Licinius can carry her away, the other vestals enter. News of the sacrilege spreads and the Romans, clamouring for the death of the recreant priestess, surround the temple. The Pontiff Maximus arrives and condemns Julia to be buried alive, the penalty for neglecting her duties. Her white veil, which she is no longer worthy to wear, is placed upon the altar while the Pontiff Maximus covers her with a black one.

On the brink of the tomb in which she is to be buried alive, Julia addresses her last prayer to the gods. Licinius, arriving with his legionnaires, declares that he alone is guilty and demands death in Julia's stead. The priests deny his request. At that moment a bolt of lightning strikes Julia's veil setting it a-fire. The people rejoice, for the goddess Vesta, in thus rekindling her holy flame, shows that she has forgiven her young priestess. As Licinius takes the fainting Julia in his arms, the Pontiff Maximus admonishes them to worship Venus, goddess of love. Their marriage vows are exchanged while games and dances begin in their honor.

LA VIDA BREVE

Lyric-drama in two acts and four tableaux by
MANUEL DE FALLA
Book by FERNANDEZ-SHAW

The initial performance was given at Nice in 1913. The setting is present-day Granada.

Act I. The cries of street vendors, the merry laughter of girls and the chime of church bells mingle with the clank of steel from a nearby forge as Salud, a gypsy girl, enters her home in the Albaicin, gypsy quarter of Granada. Salud tells her grandmother that her love for Paco is so great that it makes her sad, and to the rhythm of clanging forge hammers, she sings the song of the flower born at dawn to die at eve. Then Paco comes and protests his undying devotion to the gypsy girl. Her uncle, Sarvaor, who has discovered that Paco is about to marry Carmela, a wealthy girl of his own class, enters and would kill the youth but for the intervention of Salud's grandmother. The fierce old gypsy cannot bear to tell Salud of Paco's unfaithfulness and goes to his forge, leaving the lovers locked in each other's arms.

Act II. Guitar playing, singing and dancing brighten the home of Carmela and Manuel, her brother, for her betrothal to Paco is being celebrated. While the merrymakers whirl through the Andalusian folk dances, Salud, watching from the street outside with her uncle and grandmother, sings of her unhappy love. Paco, hearing the song through the window, trembles with sudden fear. The gypsies approach Carmela's door.

As they enter Manuel comes forward to inquire what they want. His guests, thinking the gypsies have come to dance for their amusement, greet them with applause. But to the amazement of all, Salud tells how Paco has betrayed her. When he cries out that she is lying, she turns toward him and with infinite tenderness calls his name—then falls dead. Her grandmother and Sarvaor curse the faithless Paco while a murmur of horror sweeps through the assembly.

LA VIVANDIÈRE

Romantic Opera in three acts by J. GODARD

Text after an historical novel

This work saw its initial performance in Paris, 1875. The scene is in France, during the great revolution.

The first act happens in Lorraine, 1794. Republican soldiers are quartered near the mansion of the Marquis de Rieul, a royalist, and the latter's son, Georges, who favors the cause of the republic, is in love with Jeanne, a peasant maid who has been reared at the mansion. Marion, the vivandière, arriving with her donkey cart, serves wines to the soldiers who sing a merry song. Georges comes upon this scene by accident, and being asked by Marion to join the defenders of his country, declares himself ready for it at once. Before enlisting he bids farewell to Jeanne, but is discovered by his father, who disowns his son and drives Jeanne from his estate. Georges follows the Republican ranks, in order to enlist. Jeanne faints on the spot, and is dumped by the vivandière into her famous donkey cart.

The second act occurs a year after, in the vendée, where Republican troops are waiting for reënforcements in order to attack a royalist stronghold. Unknown to Georges it is his father who commands the royalist forces in the town. Marion, aware of this, induces Georges to go off on a special military mission. Some pretty by-play between the vivandière and Jeanne occurs. Sergeant La Balafré tells of stirring battle feats.

Act III. The Republicans have won the long and bloody campaign, and the civil war is over. The victory is being celebrated. The marquis, father of Georges, is taken prisoner and held in Marion's hut, but she permits him to escape at the risk of her own life. Marion is tried by a court martial, despite the efforts of Captain Bernard to shield her. Sentence of death is on the point of being pronounced against her, when Sergt. Le Balafré brings news of pardon, granted to all concerned.

THE WALKYRIE

First day of the Nibelungen Ring by WAGNER

In the first scene we are introduced into the dwelling of a mighty warrior, Hunding, in whose house Siegmond, a son of Wotan and of a mortal woman, has sought refuge, without knowing that it is the abode of an enemy. Sieglinda, Hunding's wife, who, standing alone and abandoned in the world, was forced into this union against her will, attracts the guest's interest and wins his love.

When Hunding comes home from the fight he learns to his disgust that his guest is the same warrior who killed his kinsmen, and whom they vainly pursued. The laws of hospitality forbid him to attack Siegmund under his own roof, but he warns him that he shall only await the morrow to fight him.

Sieglinda, having fallen in love with her guest, mixes a powder with her husband's potion, which sends him into profound sleep. Then she returns to Siegmund, to whom she shows the hilt of the sword, thrust deep into the mighty ash-tree's stem, which fills the middle space of the hut. It has been put there by an unknown one-eyed wanderer (Wotan, who once sacrificed one of his eyes to Erda, wishing to gain more knowledge for the sake of mankind). No hero has succeeded until now in loosening the wondrous steel. Siegmund reveals to Sieglinda that he is a son of the 'Waelsung," and they recognize that they are twin brother and sister. Then Sieglinda knows that the sword is destined for Siegmund by his father, and Siegmund, with one mighty effort, draws it out of the ash-tree. Sieglinda elopes with him and the early morning finds them in a rocky pass, evading Hunding's wrath.

In the second scene we see Wotan giving directions to the Walkyrie Brünnhilde, who is to shield Siegmund in his battle with Hunding. Brünnhilde is Wotan's and Erda's child and her father's favorite. But Fricka comes up, remonstrating violently against this breach of all moral and matrimonial laws; she is the protector of marriages and most jealous of her somewhat fickle husband, and she forces Wotan to withdraw his protection from Siegmund, and to remove the power of Siegmund's sword.

Wotan recalls Brünnhilde, changing his orders with heavy heart and sending her forth to tell Siegmund his doom. She obeys, but Siegmund scorns all her fine promises of Walhalla. Though he is to find his father there and everything besides that he could wish, he prefers foregoing all this happiness when he hears that Sieglinda, who has been rendered inanimate by grief and terror, cannot follow him, but must go down to Hel after her death, where the shadows lead a sad and gloomy existence. He wins Brünnhilde by his love and noble courage, and she for the first time resolves to disobey Wotan's orders given so unwillingly, and to help Seigmund against his foe.

Now ensues the combat with Hunding, Brünnhilde standing on Siegmund's side. But Wotan interferes, breaking Siegmund's sword; he falls, and Wotan kills Hunding, too, by one wrathful glance.

Then he turns his anger against the Walkyrie who dared to disobey his commands, and Brünnhilde flies before him, taking Sieglinda on her swift horse Grane, which bears both through the clouds.

In the third scene we find the Walkyries arriving through the clouds on horseback one after the other. Every one has a hero lying before her in the saddle. It is their office to carry these into Walhalla, while the faint-hearted, or those of mankind, not happy enough to fall in battle are doomed to go to Hel after their death.

There are eight Walkyries without Brünnhilde, who comes last with Sieglinda in her saddle, instead of a hero. She implores her sisters to assist her and the unhappy woman. But they refuse, fearing Wotan's wrath. Then she resolves to save Sieglinda and to brave the results of her rash deed alone. She first summons back to the despairing woman courage and desire to live, by telling her that she bears the token of Siegmund's love, then sends her eastward to the great forest with Grane, where Fafner the giant, changed into a dragon, guards the Rhinegold and the ill-fated ring, a spot which Wotan avoids.

She gives to Sieglinda the broken pieces of Siegmund's sword, telling her to keep them for her son, whom she is to call Siegfried and who will be the greatest hero in the world.

Wotan arrives in thunder and lightning. Great is his wrath, and in spite of the intercession of the other Walkyries he deprives Brünnhilde of her immortality, changing her into a common mortal. He dooms her to a long magic sleep, out of which any man who happens to pass that way may awaken her and claim her as his property.

Brünnhilde's entreaties, her beauty and noble bearing at last prevail upon him, so that he encircles her

Frederick Schorr and Kirsten Flagstad in the last act of "Die Walkure"

with a fiery wall, through which none but a hero may penetrate.

After a touching farewell the god, leading her to a rocky bed, closes her eyes with a kiss, and covers her with shield, spear and helmet. The he call up Loge, who at once surrounds with glowing flames the rock on which Brünnhilde sleeps.

WERTHER

Opera in four acts by JULES MASSENET

The book follows rather closely GOETHE'S famous story

In Act I Werther, a young man of hypersensitive disposition, is secretly in love with Charlotte, although the latter is already betrothed to Albert, an old and intimate friend of his. Charlotte on her part has a preference for Werther and returns his feelings, but considers herself by honor bound to Albert. The latter is not aware of the true state of affairs, and Charlotte implores her despondent lover to leave her forever.

When the second act opens Albert and Charlotte have been married for three months, while Werther is still unable to hide his sentiments. He departs finally, in conformity with a promise exacted from him by Charlotte.

At the opening of Act III Werther, finding his exile unbearable, returns and at a chance meeting with Charlotte cannot withhold a renewed confession of his passion. He contemplates suicide, as that seems to him the only way out of the dilemma. Pretending to set out on a lonely journey, he writes a note to Albert, requesting the loan of his pistol. After receiving the weapon Werther shoots himself.

The last act shows Charlotte who has suspected Werther's intentions, and now finds him in a dying condition. This last scene is perhaps the most effective, as there is a strongly dramatic clash between this last melancholy meeting of the lovers, the merry Christmas carols of the children, and the pealing of the bells.

WILLIAM TELL

Grand Opera in three acts by ROSSINI

This last opera of Rossini's is one of his most perfect works and it is deeply to be regretted that when it appeared he left the dramatic world, to live in comfortable retirement for thirty-nine years. How much he could still have done if he had chosen! In "Tell" his genius attains its full depth. Here alone we find the highly dramatic element united to the infinite richness of melody which we have learned to associate with his name and work.

The text is founded on the well-known story of Tell, who delivered his Fatherland from one of its most cruel despots, the Austrian governor Gessler.

The first act opens with a charming introductory chorus by peasants, who are celebrating a nuptial fête.

Tell joins in their pleasure, though he cannot help giving utterance to the pain which the Austrian tyranny causes him. Arnold von Melchthal, son of an old Swiss, has conceived an unhappy passion for Mathilda, Princess of Hapsburg, whose life he once saved; but he is Swiss and resolved to be true to his country. He promises Tell to join in his efforts to liberate it. Meanwhile Leuthold, a Swiss peasant, comes up. He is a fugitive, having killed an Austrian soldier, to revenge an intended abduction of his daughter. His only safety lies in crossing the lake, but no fisherman dares to row out in the face of the coming storm. Tell steps forth and, seizing the oars, brings Leuthold safely to the opposite shore.

When Rudolf von Harras appears with his soldiers, his prey has escaped and, nobody being willing to betray the deliverer, old father Melchthal is imprisoned.

In the second act we find Princess Mathilda returning from a hunt. She meets Arnold, and they betray their mutual passion. Arnold does not yet know his father's fate, but presently Tell enters with Walter Fürst, who informs Arnold that his father has fallen a victim to the Austrian tyranny. Arnold, cruelly roused from his love-dream, awakes to duty, and the three men vow bloody vengeance. This is the famous oath taken on the Rütli. The deputies of the three cantons arrive, one after the other, and Tell makes them swear solemnly to establish Switzerland's independence. Excited by Arnold's dreadful account of his father's murder, they all unite in the fierce cry: "To arms!" which is to be their signal of combat.

In the third act Gessler arrives at the marketplace of Altdorf, where he has placed his hat on a pole, to be greeted instead of himself by the Swiss who pass by.

They grumble at this new proof of arrogance, but dare not disobey the order, till Tell, passing by with his son Gemmy, disregards it. Refusing to salute the hat, he is instantly taken and commanded by Gessler to shoot an apple off his little boy's head. After a dreadful inward struggle Tell submits. Fervently praying to God, and embracing his fearless son, he shoots with steady hand, hitting the apple right in the centre. But Gessler has seen a second arrow, which Tell has hidden in his breast, and he asks its purpose. Tell freely confesses that he would have shot the tyrant had he missed his aim. Tell is fettered, Mathilda vainly appealing for mercy. But Gessler's time has come. The Swiss begin to revolt. Mathilda herself begs to be admitted into their alliance of free citizens and offers her hand to Arnold. The fortresses of the oppressors fall. Tell enters free and victorious, having himself killed Gessler, and in a chorus at once majestic and grand the Swiss celebrate the day of their liberation.

ZAMPA

Opera in three acts by HEROLD

Text by MELLESVILLE

This opera has met with great success both in France and elsewhere; it is a favorite of the public, though not free from imitating other musicians, particularly Auber and Rossini. The style of the text is somewhat bombastic, and only calculated for effect. Notwithstanding these defects the opera pleases; it has a brilliant introduction, as well as nice chorus pieces and cavatinas.

In the first act Camilla, daughter of Count Lugano, expects her bridegroom, Alfonso di Monza, a Sicilian officer, for the wedding ceremony. Dandolo, her servant, who was to fetch the priest, comes back in a fright and with him the notorious pirate captain, Zampa, who has taken her father and her bridegroom captive. He tells Camilla who he is, and forces her to renounce Alfonso and consent to a marriage with himself, threatening to kill the prisoners if she refuses compliance. Then the pirates hold a drinking bout in the Count's house, and Zampa goes so far in his insolence as to put his bridal ring on the finger of a marble statue standing in the room. It represents Alice, formerly Zampa's bride, whose heart was broken by her lover's faithlessness; then the fingers of the statue close over the ring, while the left hand is upraised threateningly. Nevertheless Zampa is resolved to wed Camilla, though Alice appears once more, and even Alfonso, who interferes by revealing Zampa's real name and by imploring his bride to return to him, cannot change the brigand's plans. Zampa and his comrades have received the Viceroy's pardon, purposing to fight against the Turks, and so Camilla dares not provoke the pirate's wrath by retracting her promise. Vainly she implores Zampa to give her father his freedom and to let her enter a convent. Zampa, hoping that she only fears the pirate in him, tells her that he is Count of Monza, and Alfonso, who had already drawn his sword, throws it away, terrified to recognize in the dreaded pirate his own brother, who has by his extravagances once already impoverished him.

Zampa sends Alfonso to prison and orders the statue thrown into the sea. Camilla once more begs for mercy, but, seeing that it is likely to avail her nothing, she flies to the Madonna's altar, charging him loudly with Alice's death. With scorn and laughter he seizes Camilla, to tear her from the altar, but instead of the living hand of Camilla he feels the icy hand of Alice, who draws him with her into the waves.

Camilla is saved and united to Alfonso, while her delivered father arrives in a boat, and the statue rises again from the waves, to bless the union.

ZINGARI

Tragic Opera in two acts by R. LEONCAVALLO

Text by the composer

The first performance of this work occurred in London, 1912.

The first act is supposed to happen at a gypsy camp. Fleana, queen of the band, has been watched, and the fact has been noticed that every night she steals away to meet her lover outside. On one occasion several members of the band follow her, and take the two lovers captive. The stranger is not a gypsy, but he makes a solemn declaration that he will become one and join the band if Fleana is wedded to him. The stranger, Radir by name, is pardoned and takes oath not to have any more dealings with his own people. The band is satisfied with this arrangement, but Tamar, the gypsy poet, takes exception to this. He protests vehemently, avows his passion for Fleana, and is by her rebuked for his presumption. Radir wants to fight Tamar, but the latter ignores him and vanishes. The wedding of Radir and Fleana is celebrated with great pomp and the observation of quaint rites, while in the distance may be heard the mourning song of Tamar.

In the second act Fleana's love for Radir has grown cold, although she sings an exuberant love song in her tent. At this Radir is troubled for he realizes that her affections have swerved elsewhere. She confesses that her love for him is dead, while her song waxes wilder and wilder. He attempts to prevent her flight, but she eludes him and goes to meet Tamar, who has returned and whose jubilant voice is heard from afar. Together they disappear in the latter's tent. Radir is left without in despair, brooding upon revenge and sure that Fleana has merely played with him. In a gust of fury he steals up to the tent which houses the two and sets it on fire. Both Fleana and Tamar perish in the flames.

INDEX OF THE OPERAS

INDEX OF THE COMPOSERS